Rights and Riches

European University Studies
Europäische Hochschulschriften
Publications Universitaires Européennes

Series XXIII
Theology

Reihe XXIII Série XXIII
Theologie
Théologie

Vol./Band 867

PETER LANG
Bern · Berlin · Bruxelles · Frankfurt am Main · New York · Oxford · Wien

Kjetil Fretheim

Rights and Riches

Exploring the Moral Discourse of Norwegian Development Aid

PETER LANG
Bern · Berlin · Bruxelles · Frankfurt am Main · New York · Oxford · Wien

Bibliographic information published by Die Deutsche Bibliothek
Die Deutsche Bibliothek lists this publication in the Deutsche Nationalbibliografie;
detailed bibliographic data is available on the Internet at
‹http://dnb.ddb.de›.

British Library Cataloguing-in-Publication Data:
A catalogue record for this book is available from *The British Library*, Great Britain

Library of Congress Cataloging-in-Publication Data

Fretheim, Kjetil.
Rights and riches : exploring the moral discourse of Norwegian development aid /
Kjetil Fretheim.
p. cm. -- (European university studies. Series XXIII, Theologie, 0721-3409 ; v. 867)
Includes bibliographical references.
ISBN 978-3-03911-662-1 (alk. paper)
1. Economic assistance, Norwegian--Moral and ethical aspects.
2. Nongovernmental organizations--Moral and ethical aspects--Norway.
I. Title.
HC60.F759 2008
174--dc22
2008020771

Published with the support of MF Norwegian School of Theology.

ISSN 0721-3409
ISBN 978-3-03911-662-1

Preface

Why did I embark on this project? My own motives are probably as mixed as the motives donors have for providing development aid. At the personal level curiosity and commitment have been important factors. Noticing how the Norwegian development aid discourse in the media and aid agencies' publications is often morally loaded, made me curious about how moral terms and related moral arguments are understood, as well as what function they play in the wider context of this discourse. Further, I have been involved in development work both as a volunteer in the YMCA movement and as a staff member of Norwegian Church Aid. I have visited several so-called developing countries, and the poverty and suffering of my fellow human beings have made a strong impression on me. Accordingly, this study is also motivated by a commitment to the poor and to making a constructive contribution to the discussion on what development is or should be, and how it can be brought about.

This commitment has both influenced and been influenced by my academic interests. Studies in history, social anthropology, and Christian theology have, in different ways, directed my attention to the changing relationship between North and South, to images of the Other, and the struggle for human dignity, for example as articulated by various liberation theologians. Of course, this constitutes an important part of the presumptions and perspectives I brought with me when formulating the research question and approaching the material of this study.

Although I have worked on it in the context of the PhD programme at MF Norwegian School of Theology, this thesis is multi-disciplinary. It can also be labelled a qualitative, empirical-ethical study. However, I see the following primarily as a contribution to the field of development ethics. Most development ethicists not only have an academic interest in development issues, they also seek to promote what they see as positive changes in global society, improving the living conditions of the world's poor. I too subscribe to this agenda. Thus, although I set out to examine the moral discourse of Norwegian development aid, my agenda is ultimately to be critically constructive, hopefully contributing to a continued and empirically informed debate on development issues in general and Norwegian development aid in particular.

Acknowledgements

This thesis has come into being with the help of a large number of people. First of all I would like to thank all the interviewees who took time to be part of this project. I would also like to thank my supervisor Jan-Olav Henriksen who has followed this project from its beginning and given valuable and appreciated advice along the way. Several colleagues at MF Norwegian School of Theology (MF) have commented on draft manuscripts at the bi-annual seminars for doctoral students, including Svein Olaf Thorbjørnsen, Lars Østnor, and Peder Gravem. Thanks to all of them. Thanks also to Aud V. Tønnesen and Ivar B. Neumann for valuable comments at these seminars. Fellow doctoral students at MF have contributed with encouraging support and constructive criticisms in both formal and informal ways, and I am indebted to all of them.

A number of colleagues at other institutions should also be mentioned. Ulla Schmidt at Centre for Church Research (KIFO) has commented on several of my early drafts and done so in an especially fruitful way. Inger Furseth, also at KIFO, shared at an early stage her experience of doing interviews and working with interview material, and has also read and commented on a first full draft of the thesis. From Agder University College Ralph H. Vaags, Pål Repstad, and Paul Leer-Salvesen have all commented on shorter texts, as have Svein Aage Christoffersen (University of Oslo) and Knut Alvsvåg (School of Mission and Theology, Stavanger). In addition, both Kurt Christensen (Lutheran School of Theology in Aarhus, Denmark) and Tage Kurten (University of Åbo, Finland) have given helpful feedback at the Nordic Conferences for Systematic Theology in Oslo and Copenhagen. Thank you all.

Fellow students at the Ethics Programme at the University of Oslo should also be thanked for their inputs and comments. At various workshops and seminars organised by the Ethics Programme Thomas Pogge, Jens Erik Paulsen, Tove Pettersen, Henrik Syse, Andreas Føllesdal, Kai Dramer, and Beate Elvebakk have commented on various drafts and they are all thanked.

In the initial phase of working on this thesis I was affiliated to the Centre for Development and the Environment (also at the University of Oslo). Desmond McNeill was my supervisor at that time and gave motivating and inspiring feedback. In addition Benedicte Bull and Dan Banik have given useful comments. In this early stage Denis Goulet, Des Gasper, and Asun St. Claire also offered helpful advice and recommendations. I thank all of them.

I also want to thank the Nordic Africa Institute in Uppsala for a stimulating visit in May 2004 and for travel grants to do interviews. Similarly, I want to thank the Norwegian Research Council for financial support to do further interviews and for proofreading of the manuscript. And thanks to John W. Kaufman for doing the proofreading.

Finally, I thank <www.klemfm.no> for providing the right atmosphere for research through their never ending broadcasting of popular hits and ballads. I also want to thank Ivar Holm, who has read and commented on several chapters, and also thanks to other friends and members of my family for encouraging comments and interested questions. My father Kristen Fretheim has been a special support and discussion partner, while my mother Brita Fretheim should be particularly thanked for helpful guidance with the translation of the interviews. Not least I want to thank my wife Jenny for her most unique support and excellent help with the English language.

Of course, I bear the sole responsibility for factual errors, misinterpretations, broken English, spelling mistakes, and other shortcomings of the following.

Oslo/Annemasse, April 2008

Contents

List of abbreviations

ACT	Action by Churches Together
AP	Fighting Poverty. Norway's Action Plan 2015 for Combating Poverty in the South. Executive Summary
CDI	Commitment to Development Index
DAC	Development Assistance Committee of the OECD
EAA	Ecumenical Advocacy Alliance
EU	European Union
FPT	Report No. 35 to the Storting (2003–2004) Fighting Poverty Together. A Comprehensive Development Policy
GNI	Gross National Income
HDI	Human Development Index
IMF	International Monetary Fund
LO	Norwegian Trade Union
LWF	Lutheran World Federation
MDG	Millennium Development Goals
MF	MF Norwegian School of Theology
MFA	Norwegian Ministry of Foreign Affairs
MSF	Médecins Sans Frontières
NATO	North Atlantic Treaty Organisation
NCA	Norwegian Church Aid
NDA	Norwegian Development Aid
NGO	Non-governmental organisation
NIEO	New International Economic Order
NLM	Norwegian Lutheran Mission
NMS	Norwegian Mission Society
NORAD	Norwegian Agency for Development Cooperation
NPA	Norwegian People's Aid
ODA	Official Development Aid
OECD	Organisation for Economic Cooperation and Development
PD	Norwegian Church Aid's Policy Document
PS	Policy and Strategy for NPA's International Humanitarian and Development Work 2003–2007

SCN	Save the Children Norway
UDHR	United Nations Declaration on Human Rights
UN	United Nations
UNICEF	United Nations Children's Fund
WCC	World Council of Churches
WTO	World Trade Organisation

Introduction

'Men are born and remain free and equal in rights.' This statement, boldly put forward in the French Declaration of the Rights of Man and of the Citizen in 1789 (National Assembly of France 2001), proclaims a notion now widely shared across borders, cultures, faiths, etc. Still, the world of equal men remains a world of inequality. Parallel to prosperity there is enslaving poverty, and equal rights stand in stark contrast to differences in living conditions. While all are said to have rights, riches remain the prerogative of the few.

Since the French declaration Western societies have seen an accumulation of wealth unprecedented in history. Not only the elite but also a large middle class now enjoy a life of welfare, security, and comfort. The contrast to the poor of these societies is striking, although welfare states or non-governmental groups in many countries assume the responsibility to provide for these groups. The contrast to the poverty in non-Western societies is equally striking, and in this case too the inequality is recognised. One response is rich countries' development aid to poorer countries.

Norway is a telling example of this situation. From being one of the poorest countries in Europe at the beginning of the last century, Norway moved to become one of the richest countries in the world. Norway has never before had the kind of resources it now possesses, and Norwegians generally enjoy living conditions that surpass most other countries. Since 2001 Norway has topped the United Nations' human development index (HDI).[1] And further, Norway has become a significant development aid donor. While the net amount of Norwegian development aid remains small, it is one of the largest when measured as a percentage of gross national income (GNI). In 2005 Norway allocated 0,94% of its GNI to official development aid, making it, together with Sweden, the most

1 HDI is a composite measure based on the indicators life expectancy, adult literacy, school enrolment, and purchasing power parity (income). See United Nations Development Programme 2006 or <www.undp.org>.

generous donor among OECD countries. The average country effort that year was 0,47%.[2]

Development aid concerns both rights and riches. This study explores how it is discursively perceived in a Norwegian context.

2 See OECD 2006 (available at <www.oecd.org/dataoecd/52/18/37790990.pdf>, accessed 14.01.07). On the Commitment to Development Index (CDI) for 2006, however, Norway ranks fourth, surpassed by the Netherlands, Denmark, and Sweden. CDI considers seven policy areas: aid (quantity and quality), trade, investment, migration, environment, security, and technology. See Center for Global Development 2006 or <www.cgdev.org/cdi>.

Part I

Research design

1 Speaking of development aid

Take up the White Man's burden
Send forth the best ye breed
Go, bind your sons to exile
To serve your captives' need;
To wait, in heavy harness,
On fluttered folk and wild
Your new-caught sullen peoples,
Half devil and half child.

Rudyard Kipling, *White Man's Burden*, February 1899

Actors in the field of development aid express different motives for the work they do and they do development work in different ways. Discussions on both the why and the how of development work can at times be quite heated, and may concern not only questions of what is right or wrong in development aid policies, but also what it implies to be a good development worker. My intention in the following is to explore, analyse, and discuss the conceptualisation of such issues in the context of Norwegian development aid. In other words, the research question I want to address is this: What characterises the moral discourse of Norwegian development aid as it is articulated in key development agencies' policy documents and in interviews with development workers? The development agencies studied are the Norwegian Ministry of Foreign Affairs, Norwegian Church Aid, Save the Children Norway, and Norwegian People's Aid, and 23 staff members and representatives of these organisations have been interviewed. The documents studied are from the period 2002–2005, and the interviews were done in 2004 and 2005. The emphasis will be put on the study and analysis of the interviews.

By addressing the different components of the research question, I will in this introductory chapter explain in more detail the task ahead. Firstly, I will clarify the two key terms, 'moral discourse' and 'Norwegian development aid', and then address the delimitation of the study implied in the research question. This concerns both the focus on development agencies and development workers as the key actors of this study, as well as the choice of documents and interviews. Finally, I will discuss aim and relevance, and give an outline of the study as a whole.

1.1 Moral discourse

The term discourse, as it is used in the research question, refers to 'a particular way of talking about and understanding the world (or an aspect of the world)' (Jørgensen and Phillips 2002:1). This 'way of talking' constitutes a system or structure that shapes our language use. The concept of discourse thus directs the attention to the ways in which language frames our thoughts, beliefs, and ideas, and also how it defines the way we understand who we are, reality at large, specific phenomena, etc.[3]

Often a discourse will be dominated by a given representation, or what Ernesto Laclau and Chantal Mouffe call nodal points (Laclau and Mouffe 1985:112). These are privileged signs that organise discourses. Other signs are ordered around them and acquire their meaning from these nodal points. Thus, these are concepts that play a more central role than others in the given discourse, although the nodal points too are defined in and by their use, as well as in their relation to other terms. To the extent that a given representation has been dominant over a longer period of time, the discourse can be said to be stable. And as it appears as stable, the discourse also appears as normal, as do the understandings that follow from it. Further, a discourse excludes other discourses. What is excluded Laclau and Mouffe call 'the field of discursivity' (Laclau and Mouffe 1985:111). This discursive field is everything that is irrelevant to the discourse in question, as well as competing discourses. Thus, a discourse, although its boundaries might be unclear, stands in contrast to other discourses. Still, a particular discourse can very well be a part of a wide range of different discourses, just as it may comprise several sub-discourses.

3 For an overview of different definitions of 'discourse', see Mills 2004:1–7.

The structural aspect of the discourse implies that discourses shape language use. However, although discourses have a shaping power on our thoughts and ways of speaking, they are not top-down dictates. Individuals are not only products of discourse; they are also producers of it. Instead of seeing discourses only as systems determining how people speak, they should therefore rather be regarded as resources people draw from in their own shaping and understanding of the world. They are interpretative repertoires, 'clusters of terms, descriptions and figures of speech' (Wetherell and Potter 1992:90), that provide ways of speaking, enabling meaning and understanding (see section 2.2.1).[4] And due to creative language use, discourses will be in a constant flux, as for example individuals combine interpretative repertoires and move between different discourses. Thus, at this level the pragmatic use of discourses that might seem to exclude each other is possible. As the constant use of language will always imply a creative element that produces new ways of speaking of and thus understanding the world, total discursive hegemony is only a theoretical possibility.

In other words, it is always possible for some voices, even if only a few peripheral ones, to articulate resistance to the dominant discourse and thus engage in a fight to define reality. Consequently, a given discourse may not only be challenged, but also replaced by another. This is, however, a slow process, and discourses will usually stand out as relatively stable. This relative stability indicates how power is a key aspect of discourse. That they can be and are challenged, however, is important to note, as this implies that change is possible and allows for an analysis of discursive processes (see section 2.2).

As this study concerns development aid, the discourse to be discussed can be seen as a political discourse. Terence Ball notes how political discourse is characterised by how it 'borrows from and draws upon more specialized discourses' and 'consists of concepts whose meanings are not always agreed upon but are often heatedly contested' (Ball 1988:12). By drawing on a number of discourses ('lesser languages') the political discourse frames and gives meaning to the issue it concerns in an inclusive manner. Regarding the contested concepts of political discourse, this also points to how key concepts can have a

4 In this I am inspired by the rhetorically oriented discursive psychology of Wetherell and Potter (Potter and Wetherell 1987 and Wetherell and Potter 1992).

number of meanings ascribed to them. Such concepts are floating signifiers (Jørgensen and Phillips 2002:28). If, however, the multiple meanings ascribed are too many, they might end up as unclear or meaningless, and they are therefore empty signifiers. This 'emptiness' might, however, strengthen their mobilising power. Further, a political discourse will often be structured by a limited number of opposing positions (left vs. right, liberal vs. conservative, democratic vs. despotic, etc.).

The ability to make some concepts key concepts and others not, and to define the meaning of these concepts, involves having power. The potential impact of such conceptual power becomes clear if one considers that concepts and discourses shape not only the understanding of a given social phenomenon, but also influence the perception of related actions (social practice). To illustrate with an example: Giving the starving mother and child food is not simply a fact or an action, because what giving is is inseparable from the meaning ascribed to the term. And further, the meaning ascribed to giving will not only be shaped by our former experiences of the use of the word, but also by the context in which it is used, in this case 'the starving mother and child'. Action and language together create meaning. Studying language and language use is for this reason also a study of meaning and conditions for actions.

Note, however, that it is not the Norwegian development aid discourse as a whole that is to be explored in the following[5], nor is the emphasis on this discourse as a political discourse. My interest here is in the moral discourse of Norwegian development aid (NDA). With this qualification I want to indicate an interest in a discourse that refers to matters concerning 'what is right or ought to be done' (Frankena 1973:5). To this, however, it is necessary to add two comments. Firstly, I understand ethics to concern matters that imply considerations for the Other. Duties one might have toward oneself are accordingly moral duties only to the extent that they influence the ability to act morally towards others. Secondly, doing a given task the right way is not necessarily a moral matter, but can be rather a practical matter or a question of doing this task in a suitable or expedient manner. But again, if practical matters come to have implications, they can also become moral matters (Schmidt 2006:83–84). Thus, by moral discourse I mean a

5 By 'the Norwegian development aid discourse as a whole' I mean quite broadly the ongoing exchange in debates and discussions (formal or informal) regarding Norwegian development aid.

particular way of talking about and understanding a given social practice with respect to how this practice, or aspects of this practice, is regarded as morally right or something that ought to be done.[6] Focussing on moral discourse implies then enquiring about articulations of motivations for, and reasons why, development aid is provided, as well as the values and normative principles that are seen as important in its implementation. Thus, this discourse becomes articulated in different contexts and is related to different aspects of development work. This happens when development workers explain their individual motivations for being involved in this kind of work, when the Norwegian government justifies its involvement, or when aid agencies appeal to the Norwegian public to donate more money.

The word 'characterises' in the research question above indicates that it is the 'character' of the discourse I am interested in. This implies that the task ahead will be to describe its dominant sub-discourses and implicit interpretations, and thus give an empirically informed account of the main features of this discourse. Accordingly, although the research question is phrased as a 'what'-question, there are also 'how'-questions hidden in this term: how the moral discourse is structured, how key terms are used, how concepts are understood, etc.

Being interested in moral discourse implies that it is a given aspect of a larger discourse that is to be addressed. This raises the issue of how a moral discourse can be delimitated from other discourses. The definition given above provides certain criteria, but gives no clear-cut definition. For example, the distinction between relief discourse and development aid discourse remains undefined at this point, as does the distinction between the moral discourse of development aid and the moral discourse of Norwegian foreign policy. To state these criteria would, however, be an impossible task ahead of the study itself, and must rather be understood as part of the research task itself. However, it can already now be noted that in the present study I am interested in contemporary discourse, not in tracing how the moral discourse of NDA has evolved over the years. The documents studied have all been published in the last seven years, and if several versions have been published during these years (for example in the case of strategic plans) I

6 Relying on the definition of discourse quoted above (Jørgensen and Phillips 2002:1).

have chosen the most recent publication. The interviews were done in 2004 and 2005 (see sections 1.3.3 and 2.1). When I make historical references, this is to contextualise the contemporary discourse.

1.2 Norwegian development aid

To get a firmer grip on what is meant by development aid, an often referred to definition of official development aid (ODA) can be useful. OECD's Development Assistance Committee (DAC) defines ODA as:

> Grants or loans [...] which are: (a) undertaken by the official sector; (b) with promotion of economic development and welfare as the main objective; (c) at concessional financial terms [if a loan, having a grant element (q.v.) of at least 25 per cent]. (OECD/DAC Glossary)[7]

This definition is not uncontroversial and both more restrictive and wider definitions have been suggested. For our purposes, however, it is sufficient to note that ODA is recognised by its main objective, the promotion of economic development and welfare, as well as its concessional character. Development aid aims at helping others improve their lives and living conditions, and is (at least to some extent) given as a grant. Accordingly, private investments, commercial loans, and military support will normally not belong to development aid. The transfer of funds, know-how, and other resources from the North to the South as a response to poverty and degrading living conditions will normally fulfil these criteria. This can come in the form of technical assistance, project or programme assistance, etc. However, when I use the term development aid in the following, this refers not only to development aid provided by government agencies, but also aid provided by non-government organisations (NGOs). Further, I understand development aid as long-

7 See <www.oecd.org/glossary/> (accessed 15.01.07). The OECD/DAC glossary includes technical support in this definition, while support for military purposes is excluded.

term oriented, as opposed to relief or humanitarian aid which deals with short-term responses in acute crisis situations.[8]

Development aid then amounts to transfers that often go from the North to the South, or from the Western, industrialised world to the Third World, meaning non-Western, developing countries. Put in more general terms, development aid takes place between (at least) two parties, from the donor to the recipient, the latter being the one the aid is intended to assist or benefit.[9] However, all these terms are value-laden and ideologically loaded, and categorising one society as more (or less) developed than another, has a number of problems attached to it. By which criteria should such an assessment be made? What is meant by 'North' and 'South'? Is it reasonable to talk about the Third World when the Second is gone – and what about the Fourth World? Still, these terms remain in use not least because they do function as markers of real differences – the divide between wealth and poverty that does not correspond with, but can still be expressed through, this distinction. In the following I will primarily speak of North and South, as well as donors and recipients as my main categories. For the sake of terminological variation, however, I also refer to the Western world and the Third World, and developed and developing countries. No pejorative meaning is implied in any of these terms.

Further, the research question limits the scope of this study to the Norwegian subsystem of international aid. This is motivated not purely by pragmatic considerations (financial constraints, language, etc.), but by the fact that Norway is a country that is relatively generous in terms of official development aid allocations (see Introduction). Accordingly, Norway is an example of a wealthy developed country, and development aid from this country can therefore be regarded as a typical expression of aid transfers from the North to the South.

8 I use the terms development aid, development assistance, and development co-operation interchangeably. Similarly, I use official development aid and foreign aid as synonyms, both referring to governments' development aid (and thus a sub-category of development aid). Further, I use international aid as a generic term encompassing both relief (humanitarian aid) and development aid.

9 Other commonly used terms for the latter are beneficiary, client, and partner, but some prefer terms like oppressed, victim, or survivor (of conflict, hunger, poverty, etc.).

Despite its continuously changing character, I claim that there is a sufficient degree of diachronic and synchronic continuity that gives reason to speak of a specific discourse of NDA characterised by a number of regularities that define and reproduce it. Key words and expressions in the discourse are repeated again and again by institutions (e.g. aid agencies) and individuals (e.g. development workers), and this gives the discourse a certain permanence and stability. Thus, the NDA discourse produces not only an understanding of NDA but this understanding is also 'consumed' as it is reproduced, reinterpreted, and occasionally also rejected.

1.3 Actors and articulations

One way of studying discourses, the method which is applied here, is to approach language use and thus analyse concrete articulations of discourses. However, this raises the question of where articulations of the discourse can be found. In other words: what would constitute relevant material for this study? To identify this material it is necessary to single out the relevant actors that uphold the discourse in question, and in the case of development aid there is a wide range of different actors involved. I have chosen to turn to two key categories of actors in NDA: development aid agencies (organisations) and development workers (individuals). Before I return to the issue of material, I will first explain this choice of focus.

1.3.1 Development agencies

In Norway, as in many other countries, there is a wide range of institutions involved in development aid. I have chosen four development aid agencies for closer study, one governmental and three non-governmental: The Ministry of Foreign Affairs (MFA, *Utenriksdepartementet*), Norwegian Church Aid (NCA, *Kirkens Nødhjelp*), Save the Children Norway (SCN, *Redd Barna*) and Norwegian People's Aid (NPA, *Norsk Folkehjelp*).

This selection is based on four considerations. Firstly, as I want to discuss what characterises the dominant moral discourse of NDA, it seems reasonable to choose from among the larger aid agencies. The Norwegian government is, as already mentioned, a major actor in this field and the three others constitute, together with the Norwegian Red Cross and the Norwegian Refugee Council, the so-called group of 'the big five' among Norwegian development aid NGOs. Norwegian Red Cross and the Norwegian Refugee Council have, however, more specific mandates than the other three NGOs (see below). Secondly, this selection allows for a study of both governmental and non-governmental aid. Over the last twenty years this distinction has become blurred as NGOs in many countries, Norway included, receive substantial government funding and there are several points of contacts between them. In the Norwegian context this is often referred to as 'the Norwegian model' (see section 3.3.2). Given their integrated nature it seems reasonable to study the two together and within the same framework.[10] Thirdly, these agencies have different historical and sociological roots, and one can assume this might have consequences for how they justify, understand, and implement their efforts for poverty alleviation. While MFA is a government ministry, NCA is a Christian, ecumenical organisation owned by the Protestant churches of Norway. NPA belongs to the labour movement, whilst SCN regards itself as a religiously neutral and human rights based membership organisation.[11] Despite their shared features they can therefore still be considered distinct and different. Fourthly and finally, the four agencies are all involved both in relief and development work, and in this sense are multi-mandate agencies. Accordingly, as organisations they must prioritise between short-term humanitarian aid and long-term rehabilitation or development efforts. Still, their emphasis can be said to be on development aid, and it is this aspect of their work that will be discussed here.[12]

10 Terje Tvedt describes this as a 'South political regime' (*sørpolitisk system*) consisting of not only government institutions, NGOs and their representatives, but also academics, journalists, etc. (Tvedt 2003:26–31).

11 These organisations will be presented more thoroughly in chapter 4.

12 Several commentators criticise the dichotomy often made between relief and development aid. Hugo Slim sees 'signs, however, of a growing recognition that all development and relief work is essentially rights-based, and of efforts to integrate thinking and practice under one common set of principles' (Slim 2000:491).

By selecting these organisations the discourse to be studied is also delimited, and a number of other organisations that are involved in Norwegian development work are excluded. Corresponding to the four considerations above, these can be identified firstly as the smaller organisations (for example the Development Fund of Norway, the Afghanistan Committee and the Atlas Alliance), and secondly as international NGOs or multilateral organisations financed by Norwegian funds (for example the World Bank and United Nations agencies). Thirdly, organisations with other kinds of value basis for their work are not included. One group among these consists of the many, and in some cases relatively large, mission societies (e.g. Norwegian Mission Society (NMS), Norwegian Lutheran Mission (NLM), Normisjon). These represent an important historical background for NDA and together they are one of the major recipients of funds from the Norwegian government.[13] However, these organisations see themselves as mission organisations and understand their development work as part of their missionary activities (although the relationship between development aid, mission, diaconal service, and evangelisation is discursively construed in different ways by these organisations). Including NCA in this study makes the issue of the relationship between aid, mission, diaconate, etc. relevant to the present discussion, but from the perspective of an organisation not regarded as a mission organisation but rather as an aid agency. Fourthly and finally, organisations with more specific mandates are not included. For instance Médecins Sans Frontières (MSF) has become an increasingly visible actor on the Norwegian international aid scene, but sees itself as a 'medical relief organisation'. The Norwegian Refugee Council focuses on refugees and internally displaced people, and similarly the Norwegian Red Cross is primarily involved in relief work.

13 Sixteen Norwegian missionary organisations unite in the umbrella organisation Norwegian Missions in Development (*Bistandsnemnda* – see <www.bistandsnemnda.no>). For 2007 The Norwegian Agency for Development Cooperation (NORAD), a directorate under the Norwegian Ministry of Foreign Affairs (MFA), allocated 140 million NOK to these organisations. In comparison Norwegian Church Aid got 151 million NOK, Norwegian People's Aid 109 million NOK and Save the Children Norway 104 million NOK. These were the top four recipients of government funding.

1.3.2 Development workers

NDA consists not only of development agencies, but also of the people who transform ideas into actions and financial funding into projects. The professional development workers are an important category among these individuals, and whether it is by emphatically defending the work they do or through (self-) critical reflection, they interpret the work they do and their role in NDA. In this they create and maintain the NDA discourse, and as part of this the moral discourse of NDA.

The term development worker as used here might not correspond to popular perceptions of aid workers. Just as the various aid agencies can be categorised in different ways, this is also the case when it comes to different groups of aid workers. One group of aid workers is the relief workers involved in humanitarian aid. They are the ones at the forefront of the aid agencies' intervention in times of war and natural disasters (floods, drought, famine, etc.). Another category of aid workers has development work as its primary task. Preventive intervention, sustainable development, and capacity building are often key issues here. A third group could be those who have an overall responsibility for both emergency relief and long-term development efforts. This means the aid worker is employed by and responsible for the activities of a multi-mandate agency.

When I use the term development worker in the following, I refer to aid workers who belong to the second and third of these categories and who work for MFA, NCA, SCN, or NPA. Further, these development workers work and live in developing countries. Accordingly they should also be distinguished from those working with aid management in the donor countries, e.g. in the head offices of the aid agencies studied here. Further, development workers are understood here as paid staff, and can thus be distinguished from both volunteers and consultants (hired for shorter periods of time). They are professional development workers. Still, although they are professionals, they constitute a profession only in a relatively loose understanding of the term.[14] There is no formal training, no institutionalised union or professional organisation, and no commonly accepted code of conduct for professional development

14 For a general discussion of professions and professionalism, see Burrage and Torstendahl 1990. Issues regarding professional ethics are discussed in Bayles 1981 and Chadwick 1994.

workers. Being teachers, engineers, medical doctors, etc. by training, development workers can rather be considered representatives of different professions. However, the fact that they work with development aid and live in development countries connects them. They implement the policies and projects approved and funded through the agencies they work for, and, as they live in developing countries, they also live in relative close contact with the projects or programmes they run and the beneficiaries of their work, the poor or their representatives. As such they represent the donor and the wealthy North while living in the South. If they work as field workers, this contact is more direct than that of those working in an urban, office environment, but even the latter meet the poor and see their suffering as part of their work (during formal and informal meetings, fieldtrips, etc.). The development workers studied here belong to this latter category.

1.3.3 Documents and interviews

The phrase '…as it is articulated in…' in the research question refers to the understanding mentioned above regarding how discourse can be made an object for systematic analysis. However, it is also a qualification that limits the scope of this study, as it will rely on an analysis of empirical material: documents and interviews.

Regarding the development agencies, possible sources of material could be policy documents, information bulletins, statements made by either a secretary general or chairman of the board, etc. I have, however, chosen to turn to written sources, key policy documents (from the period 2002–2005). Such policy papers are easily available for research and can be assumed to express the value basis of these agencies. As such they can be said to play a key role in the NDA discourse. They are 'monuments' in the discourse, as they are texts that constitute a nodal point in the discourse of these agencies (Andersen 1994:33). I will only draw on documents that are publicly available. In addition, the organisations' respective internet sites will be referred to.

In the case of the individual development workers' articulations of moral discourse, I have chosen to use individual, semi-structured interviews. Of course, here too other sources could have been used: diaries, informal conversations, (focus) group interviews, etc. The latter of these, focus groups, provides a relaxed setting corresponding more closely to how opinions and beliefs are constructed in everyday life. One problem with this approach, however, is the power dynamics that inevitably will be in play in such groups, easily suppressing minority views. The semi-structured interview establishes an arena for open, non-binding reflection not possible in the group interview. As it has been important to establish an arena less influenced by perceived constraints due to organisational affiliation, individual interviews have been chosen.[15]

In the context of this study, the role of the interviews is to explore the interviewee's own reflections, and how he or she interprets the various experiences as a development worker.[16] In contrast to, for example, survey questionnaires or more structured interviews, the semi-structured interviews provide a suitable arena for the individuals' own expressions, terminology, emphasis, etc. to be articulated. And as Steinar Kvale remarks:

> interviews are particularly suited for studying people's understanding of the meanings in their lived world, describing their experiences and self-understanding, and clarifying and elaborating their own perspective on their lived world (Kvale 1996:105)

15 Thus the research strategy adopted is different from the approach chosen by Terje Tvedt in his study *Utviklingshjelp, utenrikspolitikk og makt. Den norske modellen* [Norwegian Development Aid, Foreign Policy and Power. The Norwegian Model] (Tvedt 2003). Tvedt relies on written sources and a comprehensive questionnaire, and argues explicitly against extensive use of interviews when studying NDA, which he calls a 'South political regime' or the 'Norwegian goodness regime'. One of the reasons he gives is that: 'the description by the Norwegian goodness regime of itself has been so dominating that the actors will only be able to liberate themselves to a limited extent from the historicity of its language (former actors' and their own) when asked to reflect on their experiences' (Tvedt 2003:323). However, in contrast to Tvedt's aims, this study seeks to probe more deeply into precisely the language these actors use when asked to reflect on their own experiences. The issue here is therefore not whether or not the actors are able to liberate themselves from the historicity of the language of 'the Norwegian goodness regime', but rather to analyse the language used. Further, it is my assumption that the 'Norwegian goodness regime' is not totally determined and rigid, but rather that it is open for criticism and change by the actors involved in it.

16 I use the term interviewee where others prefer informant, respondent, or conversational partner.

This indicates also the most obvious argument for doing interviews – they give access to information that cannot be found anywhere else.

It is worth noting how the documents and interviews constitute two different sources of material. The documents have been 'recorded without the intervention of a researcher' (Silverman 2000:825), and are fixed texts and can be studied in a non-obtrusive and non-reactive way. The interviews, however, must be understood as products of constructive processes. In the interview the researcher is not simply reading and analysing the material in question, but is actively involved in the very construction of the material (see section 2.1). Further, both the institutions' normative understanding of development aid and the reflections of the development workers will necessarily be shaped in and by a given context. However, to a large extent they have been shaped in different contexts. While the documents are discussed and developed in the Norwegian domestic debate, the development workers' normative reflections on development aid take place in relatively close contact with the recipients. Therefore, the contexts for policy formulation and aid implementation might influence the two categories differently.

Still, one should be aware of how the documents and the interviews are not entirely unrelated. As the documents are results of organisational processes, some of the interviewees may actually have been actively involved in the making of these documents. Conversely, the interviewees are development workers and employed staff and representatives of these organisations in the settings where they work. One may therefore reasonably assume that the responses from the interviewees are influenced by the official statements given by the aid agencies in these documents.

The fact that both kinds of material are included in this study is due to their complementary character. While the official discourse of the aid agencies can be studied by focussing on their official statements, the interviews provide both examples of how development workers might interpret such official statements and rhetoric, as well as their own conceptualisation of the work they do and the lives they lead. Further, while the official documents express abstract principles and values, the development workers' reflections might express their interpretations of such abstract principles in the context of being faced with concrete decisions. The moral reasoning of development workers will thus have a dialectical character, mediating between principles (and theories) on the one hand and cases (and their individual judgements) on the other

(Beauchamp 2001:490). Thus, together these sources of material make possible a rich description of the moral discourse of NDA within these agencies.

Still, in the following the main emphasis is on interviews with individuals, not on the analysis of the documents. The moral discourse of NDA will be explored by addressing issues such as how the interviewees present themselves as individual development workers (part III), their understanding of the development industry in general (part IV) and the dominant ideas and approaches in contemporary aid policies (part V), as well as the various donor-recipient encounters they experience (part VI). Key questions will be: how do development workers reflect ethically upon their own professional practice, how do they explain their motivation for being involved in aid, and how do they interpret the stated value basis for development aid? Further, how do development workers conceptualise their professional challenges, and what do they consider to be good professional conduct on the part of development workers in these situations? The analysis of the documents sets the stage for approaching these questions, while the interviews provide the main material for exploring them.

1.4 Aim and relevance

Development workers face difficult challenges in their work, as they must make decisions that potentially have wide ranging consequences. In some cases their decision could, directly or indirectly, be a matter of life or death. One response to this could be to develop a code of conduct for aid practitioners. This could resolve the issue of how one should behave towards local staff, the recipients of aid, and poor people in general, and could list the expected skills and attitudes of the professional development worker. Such an approach would, however, suffer from significant weaknesses. Firstly, it would only provide limited guidance in complex real life situations where the exercise of informed judgement is necessary. Secondly, and related to the first point, it would not be too helpful to the development workers in their interpretation of the situations they will find themselves in. Rather, the scope of professional ethics should be to encourage and contribute to a continued debate on the experiences of, judgements, and reflections on professional work.

For the ethical reflection on the professional work of development workers to fulfil this function, it must relate its generalised and normative discussions to the practitioners' experiences. It is from this premise that this study begins. Accordingly, this study is meant as a contribution to the ongoing debate on development aid, and more specifically to the moral discourse of NDA. My aim is to provide insight into the aid agencies' and the aid workers' perspectives on development aid, making their experiences more visible and explicit, and through the analysis contribute to an improved, empirically informed development aid debate.

To clarify further the aim of this study it might be helpful to point out what is not the aim. The aim is neither to evaluate the practice of NDA or the work of NDA workers nor to discuss the discourse of NDA in comparison with similar discourses in other countries or at other times. The purpose is not to prescribe a normative understanding of what the value basis for development aid should be – nor how it should be perceived. Further, the aim is not to assess the claims made in the policy documents, for example that the work of SCN is based on and governed by children's rights. I am, as David Silverman has put it: 'more concerned with the processes through which texts depict "reality" than with whether such texts contain true or false statements' (Silverman 2000:826). Regarding the individual development workers, the aim is neither to arrive at any representative conclusions about the ethical reasoning or moral conduct of development workers in general, nor to measure in any statistical sense their support for or opposition to contemporary aid policy. Accordingly, the aim is not to expose the hypocrisy or deception that might appear if the aid workers' moral conduct is compared with their ethical reasoning, but rather to grasp the ethical reflection in question on its own terms, characteristics, and structure. My interest and focus is on the positions that are represented in the material, the different arguments used, and how these are articulated.

The aim of this project is to let the empirical investigation identify the main characteristics of the moral discourse of NDA as articulated by these agencies and individual development workers. However, it is not the typical features alone that are of interest, but also the dissenting voices that constitute the parts of the moral discourse of NDA. In other words, the aim is to explore and interpret the moral discourse of contemporary NDA. In doing this I begin with the assumption that human rights constitutes a key concept in this discourse, based on an intuitive impression of ongoing development debates, aid agencies' advertisements, etc. However, human rights is presumably not the only term available to the aid agencies or the development workers when they assign meaning to the work they do, and for this reason a key aim of this study is to investigate the assumed complexity of the moral discourse of NDA. This implies exploring, looking for variance, detail, and ambiguity.

Development aid is only one of many forms that the relationship between the North and South takes. In many respects, it is not even the most important one. One might argue that the structure and rules of international trade are as important, or even more so, or that the unilateral power of the USA or the influence of trans-national corporations are much more significant. Still, international aid amounts to a considerable proportion of the GNI of a number of countries and is often considered a necessary factor, together with other measures, for alleviating poverty and promoting development. This makes development aid an interesting and relevant field of study. And while the material for this study is exclusively drawn from Norwegian sources, the Norwegian discourse is part of a wider international discourse and thus the topic of this study is an international one.

The role development aid takes, for good or for bad, in both international politics and domestic debates in Norway, indicates also the potential social relevance of this study. As a study exploring actual moral reasoning and language use, this study should, however, also have an academic interest (Potter and Wetherell 1987:35). Qualitative studies like the present prepare the ground for both quantitative and comparative studies on related topics and in related fields. Similarly, the findings of this project might through theoretical generalisation (Seale 1999:109–113) prove useful in analysing and understanding other discourses in other fields.

1.5 Outline of the study

The first part (chapters 1 and 2) of this study explains the research design, and part two (chapters 3 and 4) the wider context for NDA and the organisational context in which the interviewees are situated. In this first chapter the research question has been presented and discussed. The following chapter 2 will address the methodological considerations guiding the constitution of the material as well as the analysis. Chapter 3 deals with the international and national context in which the articulations of the moral discourse to be studied here are made. This implies addressing both the historical and contemporary institutional context. Thus I will situate the following discussion both in the international context and the Norwegian history of development aid, as well as in the contemporary institutional landscape of NDA. Chapter 4 will give a closer presentation of the selected aid agencies based on a reading of their key policy documents. This will identify some of the main topics to be addressed in the following interview analysis. Part three (chapters 5, 6, and 7) is dedicated to how the interviewed development workers present themselves. Chapter 5 focuses on how the interviewees present and understand themselves in the role as professional development workers, while chapter 6 discusses their motivation. Chapter 7 addresses how they view the agencies they are working for.

How the interviewees perceive the development industry[17] as a whole is the topic for part four (chapters 8 and 9), and various ideas and approaches in development aid are discussed in part five (chapters 10, 11, and 12). In chapter 8 the interviewees' reflections on characteristics of governmental and non-governmental aid are addressed, while the general understanding of development aid is the topic of chapter 9. The following chapter draws attention to the understanding of development aid as rights based and human rights as its value basis. This will include a discussion of the conceptual relationship between rights and needs, as well as the notions of responsibilities and duties with regard to development aid. Chapter 11 is closely related to the previous chapter, as it

17 Over the last 60 years development aid has grown into a large field of work, with many institutions, organisations and individuals involved. When I in the following refer to this field as 'the development industry' there is no derogatory meaning implied.

discusses what in the material is often construed as the contrast to rights based aid, namely charity, as well as the concepts of compassion and solidarity. The following chapter, chapter 12, addresses the discourse of justice in terms of distributive and rectificatory justice respectively.

Part six (chapters 13, 14 and 15) illuminates different aspects of donor-recipient encounters. Chapter 13 discusses the concept of partnership, and thus focuses more explicitly on the implementation of development aid. In chapters 14 and 15, however, attention is again drawn to the individual development worker. Chapter 14 follows up on the topic of the previous chapter by discussing how professionalism in aid implementation is perceived, and addresses perceptions of 'the good development worker'. In chapter 15 the more private aspects of being a professional development worker, or in other words, being rich in a poor country, are addressed. In the seventh and last part of the study, chapter 16, the findings from the preceding chapters are summarised and conclusions for the study as a whole drawn.

1.6 Summary

In summary, this study discusses the moral discourse of NDA based on an analysis of two different kinds of material: organisational documents and individual interviews. Of these the interviews constitute the primary material for the study. The interviewees are development workers based in developing countries and working for four different Norwegian aid agencies. The research question is descriptive, as it asks about the character of the moral discourse of NDA. However, it can also be characterised as interpretative as it invites a presentation of discourse that seeks to understand its main characteristics. Further, by the emphasis put on documents and interviews, closeness to the actors in the field is called for.

Focussing on moral discourse and how this is articulated by professional development workers, this study explores new territory in development studies as well as empirical-ethical research. The aim of the study is to describe and interpret, and in that way enable to a deeper and more comprehensive understanding of the moral discourse of NDA. This might subsequently provide insights, concepts or perspectives useful in other fields of research. A welcomed effect might be an increased awareness of how discourses shape our understandings of social reality, also in the field of development aid.

2 Studying moral discourse

Indeed, it is easier for a camel to go through the eye of a needle than for a rich man to enter the kingdom of God.

Luke 18:25 *(The Bible*, New International Version)

An interview study like the present one relies on the one hand on interviewing as a process of constructing the primary material of the study, and on the other hand on the process of analysing the interviews made. In this chapter I will discuss first some methodological considerations related to the process of interviewing, and then discuss the analytical approach adopted. Thus the distinction between interviewing and analysing defines the structure of the presentation. It should be noted, however, that the two are closely related. In fact analysis is an integral part of the process of interviewing. The chapter ends with a section considering assumptions implied when doing this kind of qualitative research, as well as an account of research done in fields and on topics related to those addressed here.

2.1 Doing the interviews

In total I have conducted twenty-three interviews.[18] This number was not set when the project was initiated, but is a result of considerations regarding the composition of interviewees with respect to age, gender, and organisational affiliation, as well as considerations regarding the similarities and variation found in the interviews. However, after twenty-three interviews theoretical saturation (Glaser and Strauss 1999:61–62) seemed achieved, as new interviews added little new to the material.

18 I also did one initial test interview that is not included in the material for this study.

Five interviews were done in September/October 2004, twelve in September/October 2005 and another six in November/December the same year, but the interviewees will remain anonymous throughout this presentation.[19] However, as they have been strategically selected, the criteria used in this process will shed light on who they are. Key selection criteria have been that they can be regarded as development workers as defined above, that they work for one of the selected aid agencies,[20] and that they vary with respect to age, gender, sociological background, work experience, etc. The interviewees were in most cases contacted directly, based on contact details publicly available on the agencies' internet sites.[21] In a few cases they were suggested by colleagues (snowball sampling).

Out of the twenty-three persons interviewed ten are women and thirteen men. Their average age at the time of the interview was approximately forty-eight. In terms of formal training they have backgrounds in a wide range of fields, e.g. business administration, social sciences, the humanities, etc. Eight work at Norwegian embassies, six for Norwegian Church Aid, five for Save the Children Norway and four for Norwegian People's Aid. At the time of the interview all of them worked in Eastern or Southern Africa. This is a region where there are significant development challenges and also an area where famines and crises are recurrent phenomena. The interviews were done in 8 different countries. Accordingly, although they work in the same field of development work, the context (political, cultural, etc.) varies. Further, most of the interviewees are expatriates, meaning Norwegians living abroad, but some hold other citizenships. The majority of them have senior positions. They are either resident representatives of one of the NGOs or ambassadors at Norwegian embassies in countries receiving Norwegian development aid. Four of the interviewees are ambassadors, eleven regional or resi-

19 As the total number of development workers as defined here and working for Norwegian agencies in Eastern and Southern Africa is very limited, the individual interviewees can only be presented in very general terms.

20 This of course does not preclude that some of the interviewees earlier have worked for one of the other agencies. Some of them have in their careers worked either for two or more NGOs, or for both NGOs and MFA. Such circulation of persons within the development field, though with emphasis on elite circulation, has been discussed by Tvedt (Tvedt 2003:181–187).

21 Pragmatic considerations also played a role in the selection of the interviewees. To limit travel costs, countries with several potential interviewees were prioritised.

dent representatives. Those who hold such positions carry the overall responsibility for the work of these agencies in these countries. The remaining eight interviewees hold different intermediate positions, such as counsellor, advisor, coordinator, etc. None of the interviewees hold junior positions.

Although they work abroad, and in this sense in the field, all of the interviewees have their daily work in offices in capital cities. Accordingly, they are not 'in the field' in the sense that they live and work in remote areas, under primitive conditions and enduring exceptional hardship. Rather, they have houses they live in, and they drive their cars to work Monday to Friday, not unlike many of us.

Initially the interviewees were contacted by e-mail with a letter outlining the project and asking them for an interview. Most development workers that were contacted answered positively and gave time to be interviewed. One did not reply, and two declined due to leave of absence or heavy workload. One agreed to be interviewed, but withdrew later because of illness.

In the introductory letter I presented myself as a PhD-student at MF Norwegian School of Theology (MF). MF will be known to most of the interviewees as the institution training the majority of ministers in the Norwegian state Lutheran church, and also for its pietistic and theologically conservative past, and partly also present. One can also assume that NCA staff know MF better than the other interviewees do as NCA has its roots in Norwegian churches and Christian organisations. If these assumptions are valid, it would be reasonable to think that the interviewees might accommodate their answers and reflections during the interview accordingly, for instance by emphasising and addressing religious or moral aspects more often or in more depth than they otherwise would have done. For instance when one interviewee after a thorough line of reasoning adds '[...] and you don't have to be a Christian to share this' I find it reasonable to see this as at least in part prompted by my affiliation to MF.

One piece of information I did not actively convey in my self-presentation was my former employment in Norwegian Church Aid.[22]

22 I have worked as information officer/head of the Information Unit at the head office of NCA in Oslo for about 3 years (2000–2003). In this period I visited several of the projects and field offices of the organisation (but none of those visited as part of this study), and I did not work abroad. Some of the NCA interviewees worked for

Conveying this information could have made the interviewees in the other agencies include in their responses more comparison with NCA than they otherwise would have done, and the NCA interviewees might not have been as detailed in their reflections and explanations had they taken for granted a shared understanding between us. Of course, omitting this information also implied that some interviewees knew something about me that others did not know. One must presume that certain research effects might follow from this fact. However, actively informing the interviewees about my former employment would, I assumed, put unnecessary focus on this affiliation and accordingly create similar (though opposite) effects. In other words, my background from NCA was omitted to mark my position as an outsider to the field, a researcher, not a fellow practitioner. Still, during the interviews, I indicated my knowledge of the field by using of common abbreviations, referring to other agencies, etc. In this way, I tried to position myself also as an insider (Crocker 1991).

Almost all interviews were conducted at the office of the development worker. One was, for practical reasons, done in a private home. Doing the interviews in the interviewees' office was not only practical, but also meant meeting the interviewees in their work setting. On the other hand, being in the office meant there were occasional interruptions. This did not, however, constitute a big problem, although one interview had to be ended after approximately one hour and continued the following day. Doing the interviews in Norway might have increased the perception of the interviews as being a kind of controlling interview, which might have provided more standardised answers in line with official rhetoric.

On average the interviews lasted one and a half hours, the shortest one hour and the longest two and a half hours. Most were conducted in Norwegian, though two were in English, according to the preference of the interviewee. All interviews were digitally recorded, but I also took

---

NCA at the same time as I did, but none of them were close colleagues of mine. This background can be seen both as an advantage and a disadvantage. It has provided me with insight into the institutional context of international aid and the professional work of development workers, although I have never myself been a development worker as defined here. This enables me to identify issues and raise questions of interest to this study, although it might make it more difficult to detect nuances.

summary notes. Before the interview started, after introductory 'small-talk', all interviewees signed a declaration of consent. I stressed that their participation was voluntary, and that they at any point could withdraw. Doing exploratory research and only semi-structured interviews, this is especially important. As the topics that might be addressed cannot be known in advance, the interviewees can also not be fully aware of what they consent to. For the same reason a declaration of consent does not give the researcher a carte blanch to ask any questions he or she wishes, with 'the risk of trespassing on the person' (Fog 1992:212).[23]

Before closing the interview all interviewees were invited to make additional comments. Several of them did, clarifying potential misunderstandings and raising issues on their own initiative. They were also encouraged to contact me after the interview with additional comments or questions. None of them did. It is, however, my impression that the interviewees appreciated the opportunity the interviews represented to reflect on the issues raised. This corresponds with many researchers' experience, that people value being taken seriously and listened to. At the end of the interview one of the SCN development workers said: 'I think it's very important to raise these questions and think through these things, and to question what we are doing, and how we live and work'. Similarly, one of the NCA interviewees said:

> I am happy you have asked me those questions. It's very useful to have to think through these things. Because they are in the back of your mind all the time, but you don't always have the energy to address them. No. So I think this was great fun.

2.1.1 Responsive interviewing

I understand research interviews such as the ones I have conducted here as an extension of ordinary conversations (Kvale 1996:5). The interviews are constituted as the researcher and the interviewee have a conversation, and thus the interviewees are not regarded as subjects to be tested and examined. Although there certainly is asymmetry between re-

23 The present project has been reported to Norwegian Social Science Data Services (NSD) and approved in a letter from NSD dated June 9 2004.

searcher and interviewee, I understand both of them as partners in the research enterprise where the researcher's aim is to explore (rather than control).[24] Thus, I have sought to conduct the interviews as responsive interviewing, in a manner that makes the interviewees participants in the hermeneutical process (Rubin and Rubin 2005:30–37).

As the aim is to explore, the interviews were only semi-structured. Again I draw on Kvale's understanding of such interviews: 'An *exploratory* interview is open and has little structure. The interviewer in this case introduces an issue, an area to be charted, or a problem complex to be uncovered' (Kvale 1996:97, his italics). I have relied on an interview guide, but as implied, this has had a guiding function, only indicating issues to be covered and their order (Lofland and Lofland 1995:85). Accordingly, although I directed the interviews, I did not do so rigidly. Emphasis was on the interviewees' reflections and agendas, and the issues and questions to be addressed were open for revision depending on the information given and assessments made in the course of the interview (Patton 2002:341–347).

Due to the exploratory ambitions of this study, my strategy has been to ask relatively open questions, giving room for different responses and the emphasis and voice of the interviewees. I have sought throughout to encourage and allow for accounts of the interviewees' experiences and their reflections on these. I have also sought to pose only one question at a time, and not ask too leading questions, and I have probed for clarifications, examples and narratives (Gillham 2000:46–50). In the course of the interview I have also tried to vary the questions posed, asking both factual and descriptive questions, as well as more evaluative ones. Some of the questions might have been perceived as sensitive, though the majority of them were probably not. Michael Q. Patton calls for caution with regard to asking 'why'-questions, as they seem to 'presume cause-effect relationships, an ordered world, and rationality' (Patton 2002:363). It can also be difficult for the interviewee to understand what kind of ex-

24 The issue of symmetry or asymmetry in the research interview situation is a complex matter. On the one hand the researcher has initiated the interview, sets the agenda, and guides the conversation. On the other hand, at least in semi-structured interviews, the interviewee is the one with the information and interpretations sought, and is in control of what he or she wants to share. In interviews with professionals, as is the case here, it is the interviewee that possesses the experience and expertise the researcher wants insight into.

planation is expected. However, 'why'-questions can also be door openers, and especially useful when exploring and seeking to understand complexity. For this reason, I have also asked such questions.

Accordingly, the interviews have been interactive processes. Interviewee responses have depended on the questions asked, and the researchers inputs have depended on the answers given. In this the preconceptions of both parties will influence the process. Both the interview guide and the questions posed will inevitably be shaped through my own background and experiences. Similarly, the interviewees will have their biases. For example, by being staff members they are not only individual aid workers but also representatives of their organisations. By conducting individual interviews and granting anonymity, I have tried to create space for individual reflections and criticism of both colleagues and the employing organisation.

2.1.2 Interviewing about ethics

In the invitation to be interviewed certain premises for the following conversation were already set. The interviewees were invited to be interviewed as part of a research project concerning aid and ethics, and they were informed that the 'aim of the project is to discuss normative aspects of Norwegian aid' and that 'interviews with selected aid workers' would constitute part of the material of this study. Accordingly, the stage for the following interview was already discursively set. It was given at the outset that the terms aid and ethics would be related to in the interview, and also that the interviewees had been approached in their capacity as aid workers. However, these terms were not precisely defined. Rather, the interviewees were invited during the interview to comment on these terms, both in regard to the extent they see themselves as 'aid workers' (see chapter 5) and how they understand 'development aid' (see chapter 9). They were not asked about their understanding of 'ethics' or 'normative aspects' in the same way, but rather invited to explain their ethical reasoning on various issues during the interview.

Raising issues related to ethics, morality, moral discourse, etc. poses specific research challenges. On the one hand, in the development aid field words such as human rights, charity, and justice are not uncommon and one can assume they are not entirely new to the interviewees. On the other hand, and in contrast to their organisations, the individual development workers cannot be expected to have a stated set of reasons or values that can be said to be their official declaration of how they regard the value basis for development aid. Further, in one sense interviewing people about ethical reasoning is to address abstract issues, and the interviewees might not be used to talking about ethics or reflecting on ethical terms and language. As Colin Robson points out more generally, beliefs and attitudes 'are relatively difficult to get at. They are often complex and multidimensional, and appear particularly prone to the effects of question wording and sequence' (Robson 2002:272). Accordingly, when one is concerned about moral discourse, there is a risk that the focus on morality or ethical reasoning meets a certain resistance on the part of the interviewees. Some interviewees might perceive issues relating to ethics, critical reflections on their own work and maybe life-projects, and their relationship to their professional superiors as uncomfortable or judgemental.

A few examples from the present material illustrate this point. When asked about the moral responsibility to assist people in need, one of the female SCN development workers says: 'Moral. It's a word I normally don't want to use', and when asked to elaborate, she says: 'I don't like using that word because it has connotations of judgement'. Later the same interviewee explains: 'I think it's because of the way it has been used. Even here when we talk about HIV and AIDS, and people are moralistic, judgemental, and all that. So I am shying away'. One of the male embassy interviewees expresses similar concerns when challenged to express his thoughts on moral motivation. He says:

> That depends on how one understands it, but most people don't accept moralism, but would talk of rights. I think that term is a bit less oppressive. Rights are positively loaded, and moral (*moralsk*) something negative to a lot of people.

Based on such considerations I have tried to establish a sense of trust prior to and during the interviews, and adopted a careful and indirect approach to these issues. On the other hand, when sufficient trust has been established, I have also been confrontational, at times playing the role of the devil's advocate, deliberately challenging the interviewee.

2.1.3 *Transcription and translation*

All interviews have been fully transcribed and I have tried to transcribe them as precisely as possible. Still, I have not deemed it necessary to transcribe all pauses, stuttering, and other aspects of oral language that are normally left out in written language. Longer pauses are indicated with three dots: ... Some repetitions, grammar mistakes, etc. that would make the written text more difficult to read, have been omitted or corrected. My main concern has been to convey the main lines of narration and reasoning, and if too many oral elements are retained, this becomes more difficult. Where parts of the quotes have been left out, this is indicated with brackets: [...], and when specific details have been edited out for reasons of anonymity this is indicated also in brackets, for example: [country]. When the interviewee repeats what others have said, this is marked with quotation marks. I acknowledge that this kind of editing is an interpretative exercise, and constitutes another layer of distance between the interviewees and the readers of this report. Thus, the immediacy of the text is somewhat reduced.

The interviews have been transcribed in the language used of the interview, but are presented here in translations.[25] Of course this constitutes yet another layer between the interviewees and the reader. I have strived to make a translation that reflects the nuances of the original, but avoided a literal word-for-word translation. The aim has been to make the translated transcripts as 'accurate, clear, and sound as natural as possible' (Esposito 2001:571). The same applies also to the translations of citations from the documents referred to.[26] Still, many aspects and nuances are lost in the process, and a presentation of the quotes in their original form would have allowed for a more subtle analysis. For such reasons the analysis will focus on the construction of meaning and argu-

25 Some of the dilemmas when doing such translations in qualitative research are discussed in Temple and Young 2004.

26 All translations of interviews, documents, and literature in Norwegian have been done by the author. Translations of for example book titles and official documents are accordingly not official translations, approved by author or publisher. Translations of the interview quotes have been reviewed by a second reader, but the author takes full responsibility for any short comings.

mentation.[27] Key words and phrases from the original will, however, be included in the presentation.

2.1.4 Assessing interview material

Doing interviews as a research method has advantages and disadvantages. Among the advantages is the already mentioned similarity to ordinary conversations and the everyday situation. This implies that the researcher refrains from controlling the responses and the direction the conversations might take, and rather adopts a flexible approach. This flexibility also allows the researcher to follow up interesting responses and unforeseen perspectives, and ask for clarifications. This makes interviewing a method that can provide rich material, including new perspectives and enabling deeper understanding. On the other hand, this flexibility is also one of the disadvantages of interviewing. With the lack of standardisation, comparison becomes difficult. Further, interviewing is challenging for the researcher as he or she must both listen carefully and continuously interpret what is said, and respond in an appropriate manner. Similarly, interviewing is also challenging for the interviewee, who continuously has to articulate responses to questions and prompts, and reflect on the issues raised. Further, although there are similarities with ordinary conversations, one should be aware that the research interview is a specific kind of conversation, not least because of the asymmetry involved.

In the sense that they are means to an end, for gaining information from the interviewees, the interviews have an instrumental function. They are stimulated conversations, as the interviewees respond to the stimulus of the interviewer (Mishler 1986:14–15). A positivist understanding of interviewing might assume that through this process a given reality is made available to the researcher. Such an understanding, however, does not fit well with the contextual character of these interviews. The interviewees' answers were created in a specific context, and one must assume that had they been conducted at a different time or place, or in a different language, the responses too would have been different.

27 Teun A. van Dijk makes similar considerations in his study on elite discourse and racism in the Netherlands, France, Germany, Great Britain and the United States (van Dijk 1993:71–72).

This contextual character of the interviews is often considered the main difficulty of qualitative interviews. Both interviewer and interviewee shape and colour the interview. The interviewee is interpreting the questions, the interview situation and her general life situation, and might give the answers she thinks the researchers expect. If what the interviewee says is inevitably shaped by her context and the language that this context provides, this raises the question to what extent the interviewee actually has an independent voice. The outcome of the interview is a reflection of the context. This has two aspects. First, the interviewee will identify with a larger group or institution, and will tend to respond in a manner according to what she finds this wider context expects of her. This relates to the second aspect, namely that these institutions uphold a certain discourse and that this is what is articulated in the interviews. The discourse speaks, not the interviewee. As mentioned above, however, although I regard the discourse as influencing the language used, I still see the pragmatic element as important. The individual is not dissolved by the discourses, but can actively and creatively use various discourses as repertoires in her own language use.

2.2 Doing the analysis

The analysis of this kind of interview material must give room for the voice of the interviewees to be heard, and not allow the theoretical or analytical perspectives to influence the presentation and analysis of the material too heavily. In order to grasp nuances, ambiguities, and complexity it is paramount not to force the material into established theoretical categories.

Initially I approached the material by coding the transcribed interviews, identifying and sorting key words, topics, and categories (Patton 2002:462–466). In this, I have benefited from the computer programme Atlas.ti.[28] Of course, this process of coding too is an interpretative exer-

28 While others use such computer programmes more actively to generate theories (grounded theory), my use of Atlas.ti has been limited to the marking and coding of segments in the interviews. By codes I mean 'tags or labels for assigning units of

cise, and a potential problem with this approach is that the material is deconstructed in a way that does not take the inner context of the interviews sufficiently into account. For this reason I have also done the coding process in a flexible manner, looking at smaller sections and the larger context alternately.

2.2.1 Discourse analysis

In line with the definition of discourse given above, discourse analysis can be regarded as a research method that aims at investigating patterns in language use and how a given statement activates and confirms social practices. By delimitating the discourse, identifying its dominant representations and discussing the different layers of meaning ascribed to these representations as well as discourses challenging the present hegemony, a model of a given discourse will appear (Neumann 2001:50–69). Further, in addition to identifying the various elements that constitute a given discourse, doing discourse analysis also implies being interested in the institutions that uphold this discourse. The strength of discourse analysis is precisely that it allows for the language use of individual actors and how they perceive meaning, as well as social practices and institutions as the 'carriers' of discourse to be studied within one and the same approach. This implies further that the issue of power can be an important aspect of the analysis, and highlighting such aspects makes discourse analysis a potentially emancipatory project. The emancipatory ambitions of this study, however, relate primarily to the disclosing of the implicit interpretations in the moral discourse discussed.[29]

One possible starting point when doing a discourse analysis is to emphasise the structural aspect of discourses and then discuss, for example, the subject positions (Jørgensen and Phillips 2002:14–16) they create. However, this approach risks reifying discourse and losing sight of the social practices of discourse use (Wetherell and Potter 1992:90). Alternatively, one can take the subject and its actions or statements as

meaning to the descriptive or inferential information compiled during a study' (Miles and Huberman 1994:56).

29 A more comprehensive analysis of power issues in Norwegian development aid would have required exploring for example how decisions are made, the concrete processes and actual implementation of Norwegian development work.

one's starting point. This is the approach adopted here (see section 1.1). The aim of the research is not then to explain these statements in terms of a common denominator, but rather to identify different interpretative repertoires and how for example interviewees align themselves with different subject positions offered by alternative discourses. Margaret Wetherell and Jonathan Potter explain such repertoires as:

> [...] building blocks speakers use for constructing versions of actions, cognitive processes and other phenomena. Any particular repertoire is constituted out of a restricted range of terms used in a specific stylistic and grammatical fashion. Commonly these terms are derived from one or more key metaphors and the presence of a repertoire will often be signalled by certain tropes or figures of speech. (Wetherell and Potter 1988:172)

The analysis focuses on the way people express themselves, the words they use, the metaphors applied, etc. Understanding discourses as interpretative repertoires implies drawing attention to 'the content of discourse and how that content is organized' (Wetherell and Potter 1992:90, their emphasis). Accordingly, one implication is that disclosing the pluralities and contradictions is just as interesting as continuity. Another implication is that 'social science, and specifically sociological analysis, loses its familiar landscape and demography' (Wetherell and Potter 1992:82). The aim is not to 'try to specify who did what to whom and why' but rather 'how the "what", "whom" and "why" are constituted' (Wetherell and Potter 1992:80). This is not to say that the context in which these statements are made is irrelevant. Rather, from the analysis of the statements one can in turn discuss the social context that they are shaped by, as well as in what way these statements might shape the understanding of a given social context.

Adopting this discourse analytical approach to documents and interviews implies that it is not primarily the authors of these documents nor the biographical background of each of the interviewees that is of interest. For this reason I have not discussed in depth the processes leading up to the final versions of these documents, nor have I given any detailed account of each of the interviewees. The basic unit of analysis will be the statement, either in the documents or made by the interviewees. Accordingly, neither age nor gender will be made the key variable in the analysis. Rather, by focussing the analysis on the statements, the analysis will be thematically oriented, as an 'issue-focused analysis' (Weiss 1994:153). Admittedly, with this approach one risks separating sections of the interviews from their wider context. As the interviewees are not presented individually, their respective lines of thought are not presented, and personal variations and nuances are accordingly lost. For this reason I will provide relatively long quotes in the following. The advantage of the issue-focussed approach is, however, that the anonymity of the interviewees is protected in a better way.

Still, as the discursive variations between the various aid agencies is one of the perspectives adopted, the interviewees' organisational affiliation will be revealed throughout the analysis. To further contextualise the quotes from the interviews age, gender, or the kind of position the interviewee holds in his or her organisation will be stated. For reasons of anonymity, however, only one of these will be stated together with the organisational affiliation at the same time. When the focus is explicitly on the working and living conditions of the development workers, in the chapters concerning the interviewees' self-presentation (part III) or the donor-recipient encounters (part VI), age will be given. In the chapter on the development worker functions (chapter 5), however, the kind of position the interviewee holds in the organisation is stated. Gender will be stated in all the chapters concerning the development industry in general (part IV), and when discussing the ideas and approaches in contemporary aid policies (part V). Note, however, that these variables are given primarily for contextualising the statements quoted. They are not meant to be the variables guiding the analysis. In the chapters where gender is not stated, I will use the feminine pronoun 'she' when referring to a specific interviewee. This is, however, not an indication of the actual gender of the interviewee in question.

2.2.2 Discourse, interviewing, and ethics

In individual qualitative research interviews one of the important matters to address will often be how the interviewee presents herself in the interview situation. As noted above, in responding to the questions given, she might try to give answers that might please the one interviewing or in line with how she thinks others would expect her to respond. In this sense, her identity is relational and situational. By analysing the statements she makes, however, she also provides the researcher with a text – a text which in turn can be made the subject matter of discourse analysis. This might disclose how there are different discourses that force the interviewee into specific subject positions, or alternatively how she uses or seeks to avoid various interpretative repertoires by drawing on competing discourses or innovative language use. The qualitative interviews provide opportunities to address precisely such processes of discursive negotiations. In other words, discourse analysis can point out how language use could have been different, and thus how the meaning assigned to a social phenomenon could have been another and can change. In this lies also a critical aspect of this kind of analysis.

Further, in discourse analysis the concern is not primarily whether what the interviewees say is consistent, or if what they say is a true or false expression of they how they think, feel, or act.[30] Rather, the statements are studied as examples of interpretative practices. Further, the interviews also function as arenas for a discourse on discourses. Asking people to explain how they understand the use of a given term is not only to explore the meaning and use the interviewee in question attributes to it. The answer can also become a reflection on others' use of the term, and thus explicitly becomes a reflection on the more general discourse. In other words, in the interview one is presented with both the interviewee's individual use of terms, ideas, and concepts, and various discourses that become articulated.

How can discourse analysis serve as a tool for ethical analysis? As discourse analysis is a tool for understanding how meaning is constructed, it can also serve as a tool for understanding the use of moral language and meaning assigned to key moral concepts, and thus also moral discourse. In this respect too it will be a matter of understanding what characterises this moral discourse, as well as how it is actively shaped through continuous language use. This implies understanding ethical reasoning as something contextual, and moral discourse as something that draws on the resources and opportunities that this context provides. The analysis can discuss what ethical perceptions occur (and do not occur) in the material, how they are used, and how they are understood. Thus, the concern is to identify the experiences and theories that

30 However, after years of experience Herbert J. Rubin and Irene Rubin conclude: 'In conversational partnerships, most people try to be honest and open; lies are rare and easily discovered in a qualitative project' (Rubin and Rubin 2005:71).

are built into the concepts themselves, and to render a thick description of these.[31]

As the research interest in this study is moral reasoning, my knowledge of contemporary moral-philosophical debates has affected not only the research question posed and the questions asked during the interview, but also the subsequent analysis. Accordingly, there is a risk that I, being the interviewer, pressure the interviewee into a role of being a moral philosopher, making academic ethical discourse the hegemonic discourse. In this, caution must be exercised. However, also 'ordinary people' do think and reflect on moral issues, and they do so using terms and concepts well known in academic ethical discourse. In other words, popular moral discourse is not unrelated to the scholarly moral-philosophical discourse. How then do the interviewees use such concepts, and in what way do they relate them to each other and interpret them? What characterises the moral discourses that shape their moral reasoning? These are issues discourse analysis can address in a fruitful and informative manner.

2.2.3 Ethics and qualitative data

Another question that becomes relevant in a study such as this is how the relationship between empirical data and ethical theory should be understood. One option would be to have one of the ethical theories (deontology, utilitarianism, virtue ethics, etc.) function as the standard that the ethical reflection in Norwegian aid agencies and among development workers is measured against. In this way, ethical theory would operate as a judge, and would determine the justness and adequacy of the material in question. Where the empirical data does not correspond or conform to theory, it can be regarded as misperceived, reductionist, or even false. Alternatively, the relationship could be turned the other way – the empirical data being the sole source for ethical theory. In this case the relationship between empirical data and theory is established by extension, as the latter is determined by the former.

31 My use of the phrase 'thick description' draws on Clifford Geertz's often cited essay *Thick Description: Toward an Interpretative Theory of Culture* (Geertz 1973:6).

As will have become evident, this study relies on neither of these options, but intends rather to establish a fruitful discussion between theory and data. The function of the empirical findings will not only be to provide an understanding of how development workers reflect morally on their professional work, but also to stimulate 'our imaginations in order to renew our traditions' (Dreyer 2004:10). It is in this sense this study aims at contributing constructively to the ongoing development aid debates. Although this is not the main concern here, ethical theories can then function as standards that actual ethical deliberations can be compared to (not normatively measured against), and conversely, the material can challenge standard theory. Herein lays also an understanding of ethical theories as something different from systems of rules. While rules prescribe actions, ethical theories give arguments and rely on the individual to make her own reflective reasoning.[32] It is the discursive praxis of such reasoning that is to be put under critical scrutiny in the following.

Thus, there will be in the following both inductive and deductive elements in the dialectic movement between the empirical findings and theory. This approach can also be described by a term brought into modern philosophy by Charles Sanders Peirce: abduction. This refers to a process of 'moving back and forth between data analysis and the process of explanation and theory construction' (Mason 2002:180).

2.3 Doing qualitative research

The research question of this study could of course have been approached in a number of different ways. One would be a more explicitly normative approach where my ambition would be to develop my own normative perception of how the moral discourse of NDA should be. I could against this background have formulated values, rules, and codes of conduct that I could recommend for the aid community to make its own. Another approach could have been quantitative, where the ambition

32 This distinction between theories and systems of rules is discussed by Martha C. Nussbaum (Nussbaum 2000b:59–64).

would be to reach conclusions about the moral discourse of Norwegian aid that would be representative for the group in question. As already noted, neither of these will be followed here. Further, other interviewees could of course have also been chosen. Relief workers, development workers employed at the aid agencies' head office, volunteers, and various development aid consultants have already been mentioned. In addition, partners and recipients of NDA could have been approached. And of course, a comparative or historical perspective could have been adopted, rather than focussing specifically on contemporary NDA. All these are alternatives well worth exploring, and are reasonable topics for research supplementing the present study. In this study, however, focus is another. My discussion finds its primary starting point in the voices of some of the actors involved on the donor side of the development aid relationship. It begins 'from below', from the statements, reflections, interpretations, and comments of actual people and expressed in factual documents – and proceeds from there in order to identify characteristics of the moral discourse represented in the field.

Focussing on development workers, the individual actors in the development field, this study stands in the tradition of methodological individualism (Elster 1989:13), though the emphasis on context also relates it to methodological situationalism (Knorr-Cetina 1981). Further, these individuals are regarded as acting intentionally, and by interviewing them, focus is placed on how they understand their actions and their social world. In this lies the phenomenological element of the present study.

Another fundamental premise in the present study is the importance of making the voices from the field heard. The development workers are regarded as people who not only do aid work, but who also reflect on what they do. Accordingly, I see them as reflective practitioners (Schön 1983). Such reflection does not take place in isolation from its context. And in this case, the contexts is not only the countries and situations the interviewees work in and live in, but also the organisational context their professional work is part of. In other words, the development workers' ethical reflection on their work is embedded in their professional practice and their experience thereof.

Note also that although this is not a study on development workers' behaviour, their practice is neither irrelevant to nor excluded from the perspective taken here. The development workers' practice is present in the study in a doubly interpreted form – first as narrated by the interviewees, and second through my analysis of these narratives. In this sense this study relies on a double hermeneutics (Giddens 1993:9–10).

This study can further be described as an exploratory empirical-ethical study. It is exploratory as it does not rely on a specific theoretical model or perspective, but rather starts from only some preliminary notions of the subject matter. The aim is to gradually gain new insights and a rich understanding of the field through the analysis. This exploratory intention should, however, not be used as an excuse not to reflect on prejudices and unarticulated hypotheses. The analysis of the documents was in part done ahead of the interviews, and the preliminary findings from this analysis will of course have influenced my approach and interests when doing the interviews. Similarly, as I follow both moral-philosophical and public discussions on NDA in newspapers, television, and elsewhere, I was not a total stranger to either the field or the discourse. However, I did not have any more specific assumptions about how the interviewees would articulate their responses, interpret given concepts or reflect on their professional work. In this sense, they were not approached with a hypothesis to be tested.

Further, this is a constructivist and interpretative study. The main material of the study is the interview material, and this is constructed through the interaction between researcher and interviewee. A key assumption is that meaning is not found, but rather constructed in the conversation between these two. And seeking to understand this construction is regarded as an interpretative exercise. This involves moving into the hermeneutical circle, where the particular is seen in view of the general and vice-versa, and it implies that data is not regarded as brute facts, but rather as laden with understanding.

2.3.1 Understanding the social world

While not denying that there is a reality independent of its articulation in language or otherwise, the interest here lies in how the understanding of this reality is continually shaped and reshaped as people conceptualise their experience of it. In other words, between the ontological world and man there is an unavoidable layer of language. While the ontological world is thus regarded as inaccessible in any immediate way, language is accessible and available for research and inquiry. As a result, also the social world is in constant flux as it is re-conceptualised again and again. This does not prevent the social world from being experienced as relatively stable, but implies that it could be different and that it also could be changed. In this sense, discourse analysis is not concerned with how the world is, but rather with how it is understood and conceptualised.

As a methodological approach discourse analysis combines insights from several disciplines. Just like qualitative interviewing as described above it relies on social constructivism (see Berger and Luckmann 1967 and for a more recent introduction Burr 1995), as it assumes that knowledge and understanding of the world is a product of our categorisation of the world, which in turn is dependent on the historical and cultural context and maintained in social processes. Reality is accordingly neither behind nor blocked by discourse, but rather understood through discourse. Further, discourse analysis belongs to the linguistic turn in social sciences and is a post-positivist research strategy. It finds its roots in both linguistics and social theory inspired by French structuralism (Saussure, Levi-Strauss, Foucault) and the Frankfurt-school (Horkheim, Marcuse, Adorno, Habermas). Discourse analysis, however, also relies on a criticism of structuralism, namely its assumption that all langue can be reduced to an underlying structure. In contrast, discourse analysis as it is adopted here focuses on language as it actually appears and is used (parole) in specific contexts. It is language use that reproduces (and changes) the structure of the language.

Further, discourse analysis shares with critical theory a concern about the social world, how it is shaped, constructed, and reconstructed, as well as the power involved in these processes. The aim to defamiliarise what seems normal and disclose the power involved in taken-for-granted social practices makes it a tool not only to understand but also potentially to change society. This aspect is most emphasised in the more Marxist inspired versions of discourse analysis, for example in Laclau and Mouffe's analysis (Laclau and Mouffe 1985) and in Norman Fairclough's textually oriented critical discourse analysis (Fairclough 1995; Fairclough 2003). Fairclough refrains from describing everything as discourse, and makes a distinction between the discursive and the social, which in turn provides him with a social reality separate from discourse that can (and should) be changed (Fairclough 1992).[33] Wetherell and Potter's version of discourse analysis is, on the other hand, more oriented towards social psychology (Potter and Wetherell 1987; Wetherell and Potter 1992).[34]

This critical element implies asking what remains absent or hidden in these texts, making the implicit explicit, and an interest and focus on relationships of power implied in the texts. Accordingly, my concern in the following is not simply to let the interviewees' voices speak for themselves, but rather to make my own comments and independent analysis of their perceptions. Note then how description and analysis will not be perceived as two separate processes, but rather as two perspectives. They are separate neither temporally nor epistemologically, but are part of the very same process. Thus, there is also a hermeneutical element in discourse analysis.

2.3.2 Generalisation, validity, and reliability[35]

As this study focuses on a limited number of articulations of the moral discourse of NDA, it will of course not be possible to make statistical generalisations. The research question, material, and analytical approach adopted here allow only for identifying tendencies in the material, and an interpretation and discussion of these. Had I studied different organisations involved in NDA and had I interviewed other interviewees, the

33 Mats Alvesson and Kaj Sköldberg describe critical research as a triple hermeneutics comprised of the interpretative double hermeneutics mentioned above as well as a 'critical interpretation of unconscious processes, ideologies, power relations, and other expressions of dominance that entail the privileging of certain interests over others' (Alvesson and Sköldberg 2000:144).

34 For an instructive comparison and discussion of Laclau and Mouffe's discourse theory, Fairclough's critical discourse analysis and Wetherell and Potter's discursive psychology, see Jørgensen and Phillips 2002.

35 Kvale refers to generalisability, validity, and reliability as 'a scientific holy trinity', indicating the status they have achieved in the social sciences (Kvale 1996:229). Several qualitatively oriented researchers have suggested other terms to address this issue of evaluating qualitative studies. Yvonna S. Lincoln and Egon G. Guba, for example, speak of credibility, transferability, dependability, and confirmability (Lincoln and Guba 1985:294–301). The concerns addressed by these various terms are, however, to a large extent the same.

findings would have been different. The interviewees of this study work for Norwegian organisations, and staff members of other organisations would possibly have responded in quite different ways. Similarly, the development workers interviewed work in Africa, and not in Asia or Latin America. This will have had an effect on the interviews done and consequently on the material of this study.

Still, the fundamental issues of inequality, poverty, and wealth, as well as the idea of development aid as a response to this situation would have been similar in all of these situations. And further, as I have chosen to study some key organisations in this field, it is reasonable to assume that the articulations studied here reflect wider discourses. More importantly, if the descriptions and conclusions made here are recognisable and understandable to other development workers, and without being statistically representative, they might still be considered plausible. The discussion and findings of this study might be found useful in order to analyse and understand other discourses in other contexts. This will, however, have to be shown by future research.

As studies such as the present cannot be replicated, the reliability of its findings cannot be tested in this way. Similar studies can, however, be undertaken, and I have tried above to describe the methods and procedures used here comprehensively, as this will make a qualified comparison between studies possible. Similarly, validity will be a matter of degree (Miles and Huberman 1994:262–277). Throughout the process, I have, however, sought to avoid researcher bias by bracketing my own presumptions, not asking leading questions, etc. In addition, drafts of several parts of the analysis have been shared and discussed with research colleagues. The interviewees, however, have not been consulted in this regard. Accordingly, what is presented here is my interpretation of the transcribed interviews. Interviewees might disagree with this interpretation, but also do not have any responsibility for the conclusions drawn here.

2.4 Related research

The discussions on development and ethics have grown both in volume and intensity in recent decades.[36] This study adds to this multitude of studies, but is also located at the crossroads between different academic fields. As it is empirically oriented and relies on a qualitative research method, it draws on insights from the social sciences. The subject matter is moral discourse, however, and as such it can be said to belong to the field of moral, political, or social philosophy. Being a multidisciplinary work, it also relates to previous research in several disciplines.

NDA has been analysed and discussed widely, both by historians and social scientists. In connection with the 50 year anniversary of NDA, a three volume *Norsk utviklingshjelps historie* [History of Norwegian Development Aid] was published in 2003 (Liland and Kjerland 2003; Ruud and Kjerland 2003; Simensen 2003). Further, in *Bilder av "de andre". Om utviklingslandene i bistandsepoken* [Pictures of 'the Others'. On the Developing Countries in the Aid Era] (Tvedt 1990) Terje Tvedt addresses Norwegian understandings of the recipients, while he focuses on the role of civil society and Norwegian NGOs in the comprehensive *Angels of Mercy or Development Diplomats?* (Tvedt 1998). With his *Utviklingshjelp, utenrikspolitikk og makt. Den norske modellen* [Development Aid, Foreign Policy and Power. The Norwegian Model] (Tvedt 2003) Tvedt also gives an analysis of the relationship between Norwegian foreign policy and development aid, which he describes as the Norwegian 'South political system'. As the present study relies on material from both governmental and non-governmental agencies, it can also be regarded as a study of the same 'South political system'. As focus is on the donor side of the development aid relationship it also shares traits with Hilde Beate Selbervik's PhD-thesis *Power of the purse? Norway as a donor in the conditionality epoch 1980–2000* (Selbervik 2003a). The issue of power has also been addressed by Knut

36 Several developments have contributed to this situation. One is the increased attention given to applied ethics in general, and another is the proliferation of development NGOs. This has in turn led to diversity in terms of how the moral basis, aims, and methods of development work are perceived and evaluated. In addition, the doubts about the effects of development aid have further inspired reflection on these issues (Gasper 2004:16–18).

G. Nustad in *Gavens makt. Norsk utviklingshjelp som formynderskap* [The Power of the Gift. Norwegian Development Aid as Trusteeship] (Nustad 2003).[37] Other studies discussing the NDA discourse are easily found, not least in a number of masters thesis (Drag 1995; Groth 1995; Hagelund 1998; Visnes 1999; Melandsør 2002; Ulveseth 2005; Edland 2007).

This study is, however, different from the above mentioned ones as it focuses on development workers' experiences and interpretative perspectives. Other studies on the Norwegian development workers' perceptions of their working situation, contribution to development, etc. include a selection of articles in *Hvor mange hvite elefanter? Kulturdimensjonen i bistandsarbeidet* [How Many White Elephants? The Cultural Dimension in Development Work] (Eriksen 1989), as well as Ellen Linde's master's thesis *Realistiske idealister. Bistandsarbeidere – virkelighetsutforming og hverdagsforståelse* [Realistic Idealists. Development Workers – Sense of Reality and Everyday Understanding] (Linde 1999). In the present study, however, the interviews are analysed with the use of discourse analysis. This approach is similar to the one adopted by Maria Erickson Baaz, who in *The Paternalism of Partnership. A Postcolonial Reading of Identity in Development Aid* (Baaz 2005) also draws on discourse analysis and interviews. However, Baaz focuses on the construction of identity and the understanding of partnership, and does not focus specifically on moral discourse.

Further, moral philosophers, theologians, development researchers (and practitioners) and others have discussed the wealth-poverty divide from a wide range of perspectives (for example Dower 1991; Vikinge 1997; Pogge 2002; Little 2003), and they have discussed the issue of human rights, development, and aid practice (Hamelink 1997; Christoplos 2000; Uvin 2004; Alston and Robinson 2005). There have also been those who have worked and written specifically on the ethical aspects of aid. Examples are *Foreign Aid as a Moral Obligation* by Theodore A. Sumberg (Sumberg 1973), *Foreign Aid Reconsidered* by Roger C. Riddell (Riddell 1987), and *The Moral Foundations of Foreign Aid* by Brian R. Opeskin (Opeskin 1996). These studies are, however, largely theoretical while the present study is an empirical one.

37 For a review article of Simensen 2003, Ruud and Kjerland 2003, Liland and Kjerland 2003, Nustad 2003, and Tvedt 2003 in English, see Borchgrevink 2004.

Thus, this study's choice of material and method, as well as its focus on moral discourse, makes it a novel contribution. As it combines face-to-face interviews, discourse analysis, and a focus on the moral aspects of NDA – moral discourse – this study represents something new.

2.5 Summary

The present study is a qualitative study and relies on the constructivist assumption that interview data are context dependent and a result of the specific situations the interviews were done in, as well as the interaction between researcher and interviewee. Similarly, the analysis focuses on how meaning is constructed through language use. Studying how the interviewees make use of different interpretative repertoires, the aim is to give an empirically informed thick description of the moral discourse of NDA. This implies exploring various aspects of this moral discourse and giving an interpretation of its main characteristics. Although the research design does not allow for making generalisations beyond the material in question, the aim is to provide new insights and perspectives on moral discourse in general and NDA in particular.

Part II

The wider context

3 International and national setting

> Aid has been around for far too long.
> After over 50 years, it is time to bury
> the very idea of 'aid' totally and irrevocably.
> Clearly it is not what its advocates claim it is,
> namely a tool for development.
> It is more likely a tool for underdevelopment.
>
> Yash Tandon, Executive Director of the South Centre[1]

NDA is part of a wider system of resource transfers from the North to the South, and shares traits with the development aid of many other donor countries. However, it also has characteristics of its own, being shaped by the specific social, economic, and political conditions in Norway. In this chapter I will give an account of the international and domestic context for NDA. I begin by discussing key features and normative aspects of poverty and affluence. I then give a brief account of the historical background and international context for contemporary development aid. In the third and final section I outline some of the specific characteristics of the Norwegian context.

3.1 A world of inequality

Ever since its beginnings, the contrast between the affluence of some and the poverty of others has been the context for international development aid. It has been an implicit assumption that the living conditions of the poor can and should be improved, and that aid is one way of doing this.

1 This quote is from a speech Yash Tandon made in December 2006. See <www.southcentre.org/info/EDpage/2006Dec_Basel_Speech_Novartis_Foundation.pdf> (accessed 29.03.07).

In this sense, development aid relies on a normative evaluation of living in such conditions.

3.1.1 Poverty

Among different kinds of poverty one can distinguish absolute and relative poverty.[2] While absolute poverty defines poverty by a given poverty line that is the same in all countries and/or for all human beings, relative poverty defines poverty in terms of the standard of living in a given context.[3]

If poverty is defined by the absolute measure of food and water (over a specified period of time) any human being needs in order to stay alive, living in poverty means living under the imminent threat of death. In such cases it seems reasonable to speak of extreme poverty, and this would be a life threatening poverty. Aid provided to meet these kinds of situations can be said to be life saving (relief or humanitarian aid). However, anyone living just above this absolute poverty line will often also be regarded as poor. Anyone who has the minimum of water and calories covered, but nothing else, will be in need of having supplies provided the next day. And, anyone who has even these future needs covered will also be in need of (basic) medical care, housing, clothes, security, etc. If these other needs are not met, the person is not in any immediate life threatening situation, but might easily end up in one. For these reasons she will by most definitions be regarded as poor. Aid provided to meet such needs is only indirectly life saving, and might rather be called life protecting.

As a life in poverty in some cultural contexts is considered admirable and attractive, and in others is related to shame and disgrace, any generalised answer to the question of how it is to live in poverty will at best be only partly true. This points to the necessity of understanding poverty as a socially constructed and discursive phenomenon (Dean 1992). It seems, however, reasonable to conclude that life in life threatening extreme poverty is universally regarded as something people seek to avoid or escape from. The preservation of life seems to be a uni-

2 For a discussion of the concept of poverty and issues related to defining and measuring it, see Lister 2004:12–50.

3 Combinations of these two definitions are of course also possible.

versally recognised value, although the more specified reasons for holding this value might differ. However, life just above the poverty level (absolute, extreme poverty line) might also be described in the same way as something most people seek to avoid or escape from, and that it is reasonable for them to do so.[4] Life in poverty just above the absolute poverty line is a life in the risk zone of falling below this critical threshold.

Further, such poverty is not only a question of having barely enough to eat and drink, but involves unfreedom in a number of other aspects as well. It involves limited possibilities regarding health and sanitation, education, defining one's own life projects, etc.,[5] and must accordingly be considered degrading and contrary to a life in human dignity. Although it does not entail immediate death, it does involve suffering. Accordingly, it seems fair to regard expectations for such goods and freedoms to be reasonable expectations to have, and the wish to avoid and/or escape this kind of poverty also seems reasonable.

So far I have addressed poverty as it is experienced in the present, and I have emphasised how this is a degrading situation and possibly life threatening. Poverty is bad. However, two more aspects need to be mentioned. It might be argued that both the related past and future have moral significance in regard to our normative evaluation of poverty. If the person in question is living in poverty as a consequence of circumstances in the past, this might have bearing on our present considerations. If this person was unwilling to work although there were job possibilities (he or she has been lazy or maybe done something stupid), her present life in poverty might be given a different evaluation. But also, if her present poverty can be regarded as a consequence of other peoples' actions in the past, that too might indirectly have moral significance in

4 This general argument can also be made regarding the poor (living in relative poverty) in affluent countries. They too can be said to be living in life conditions it seems reasonable that they would want to avoid or escape. However, this should not blur the radical difference between living a life in absolute life threatening poverty (or close to it) and being relatively poor in a Western welfare state. The existence and non-existence of a safety net (or the quality of it) to provide for the poor, constitutes a fundamental difference, though the cases where these safety nets are not effective should be acknowledged.

5 Martha C. Nussbaum proposes in this regard a list of ten normatively central human functional capabilities (Nussbaum 2000a:78–80).

regard to her present situation.[6] Similarly, considerations about the future also have bearing on the evaluation of present poverty. One of the characteristics of life threatening poverty is the non-ability to escape this situation. When, on the other hand, this option is there, it can be argued that the need for assistance is at least not as acute.[7]

Summarising, the poverty that constitutes part of the background for development aid is not only extreme poverty, but also the kind of deep and comprehensive poverty that enslaves people in degrading living conditions and generally limited opportunities. Human suffering and unfreedom characterise both, and consequently, poverty is a state that is normatively negatively charged. Its features can be regarded as reasons for providing development aid, although this can be qualified (strengthened or weakened) if one takes into consideration the reasons why people are living in poverty and their prospects for avoiding poverty in the future.

3.1.2 Affluence

Just as some are living in extreme poverty, others are not only living just above the poverty line, but in extreme affluence. Living in extreme affluence is no guarantee for happiness, but freedom, education, and health services are certainly features of such living conditions. And although the affluent too might become ill, they have the opportunity to obtain the best medical care and attention available. At this end of the scale, all basic needs are not only covered, but widely available and to such a degree that a life in luxury, extravagance, and abundance is made possible. As such, it seems reasonable to describe life in affluence generally as a good life. It is a life of opportunity, security, and wealth.

There are people who actually live their lives in such extreme affluence. However, just as there are many people who live just above the extreme and absolute poverty line, people it will still be reasonable to

6 Wim van Oorschot and Loek Halman discuss four types of popular explanations of poverty: individual blame, individual fate, social blame and social fate (van Oorschot and Halman 2000).

7 Most recognised definitions view poverty as something spanning over a certain period of time. Living on a low income for a limited period of time is often not regarded as living in poverty (for example students in developed countries).

describe as poor, there are also many other than the extremely rich that one may refer to as rich, for example the middle classes of Western countries. No doubt there is a wide difference between the richest man in the world and the ordinary middle class Norwegian. However, compared to the living conditions of the extremely poor, this difference clearly becomes one of degree, not one of fundamental character.

If any rich person's wealth is based on unlawfully and immorally attained goods, this will have consequences regarding our normative evaluation of her wealth. Correspondingly, one might also bring into the discussion the future prospects of the rich. To put aside savings for future expenses such as illness or old age intuitively seems more reasonable than saving for extravagance and luxury. Investing one's assets in industry, trade, or any other business activity might also seem more easily morally defendable than spending on personal consumption. The rich peoples' management of their wealth thus seems to be morally relevant and have bearing on how any give person's affluent way of life is evaluated.

In the perspective of the discussion of poverty above, I find it reasonable to hold that the main divide between people is not between the extremely rich and other rich people (Western middle class), nor between the extremely poor and people living just above the poverty line. The dividing line is between the rich and the poor – between those living in a life situation which is normatively negatively charged on the one hand, and those whose life situation must be regarded as normatively positively charged.

3.2 Development aid discussions

The kind of aid discussed in this study emerged in the aftermath of the Second World War. Although Christian missionaries, colonial powers, and others had made contributions to development and welfare programmes in the South earlier, the development aid of the post-WWII era was something new.

Following President Harry Truman's renowned 'Point Four' speech in 1949, in which he launched the American programme for development aid, several Western countries came together to transfer resources to recipients in other continents. Increased awareness of the plight and suffering of people living in developing countries, as well as the perceived threat of communism, must be considered important contributing factors to this development. In 1961 the United Nations (UN) announced the first Development Decade (1961–1970) and called on all member states to set aside 1 percent of GNI to development aid (later adjusted to 0.7 percent). This first decade was to be followed by the second, third, and fourth development decades, and in 2000 the UN member states agreed on eight Millennium Development Goals (MDGs) to be achieved by 2015.

In its early phase development aid was marked by modernisation theory, paradigmatically expressed by Walt W. Rostow in *The Stages of Economic Growth. A Non-Communist Manifesto* (Rostow 1960). Development aid was perceived in terms of capital that could be invested and thus create economic growth and the goal of development was to reach the level of the industrialised, consumerist, Western society. However, this approach was soon to be heavily criticised. Inspired by Marxist theory Andre Gunder Frank (Frank 1967), Samir Amin (Amin 1974), and others argued that aid was just another tool for the centre capitalists to exploit the poor on the periphery, making development aid increasingly ideologically polarised. These came to be known as dependency theories, as the development in some countries was seen as dependent on the underdevelopment of other countries. According to the modernisation theories, change and development would come about as a consequence of capital input, whereas dependency theorists pointed to the need for the underdeveloped countries to break out of the international economic system and pursue independent, national strategies for development. Dependency theorists thus drew attention to what they saw as the causal relationships between poverty and wealth, rejecting the temporal segregation (Nustad 2003:27) implied in modernisation theory. Poverty is seen as the result of structural exploitation, as growth in industrial countries draws resources out of the periphery. The result is development in the North, and underdevelopment in the South.

Amartya Sen, on the other hand, has voiced a different criticism of modernisation theory, arguing that it does not take social and welfare issues sufficiently into account (Sen 1999). Further, the macroeconomic focus of modernisation theory has been challenged by the basic needs approach (Streeten and Burki 1981). This approach focused on immediate needs, agriculture, and integrated community projects, rather than large scale industrial development, infrastructure, etc.

A more recent criticism of the traditional development theories has been voiced in the so-called post-development discourse (Sachs 1992; Crush 1995; Escobar 1995; Rahnema and Bawtree 1997; Grillo and Stirrat 1997). Here, the critique does not primarily address the question of true or real development, but is rather concerned with analysing the concept of development itself. Michael P. Cowen and Robert W. Shenton have studied the discourse of development over the last two centuries (Cowen and Shenton 1996), and James Ferguson has shown how this discourse upholds itself by making development apolitical and normal – a matter of technicalities rather than of political interests and power (Ferguson 1990). Post-development theorists often criticise the idea that development is something neutral, and are concerned to show how, when a discourse is established, it creates a picture and an understanding of what poverty is and how it should be approached. Cowen and Shenton have pointed to the need to distinguish between immanent and intentional development. Immanent development is a process that unfolds over time, while intentional development is an active intervention in a given situation to create a wanted change (Cowen and Shenton 1996:61). Alberto Arce and Norman Long have brought these discussions further by developing a more actor-oriented approach to the study of development (Arce and Long 2000).[8]

Jean-Philippe Thérien argues that in addition to being shaped by structural changes in the international system, debates on development aid have 'always been framed in terms of an opposition between forces of the Right and forces of the Left' (Thérien 2002:249–250). Thérien bases his argument on two assumptions. Firstly, he assumes that the Left is more egalitarian than the Right, and that this is the main difference between the two. Secondly, he assumes that aid involves a range of policies intended to prompt greater international equality. With these assumptions he argues that it becomes possible to discern how the Left is more favourable than the Right to development assistance, and that while the Left has defended a restrictive understanding of aid, the Right has tended

8 For a updated and informative introduction to development theory, see Nederveen Pieterse 2001. For historically oriented introductions, see Thorbecke 2000 and Hjertholm and White 2000.

to adopt broader definitions (Thérien 2002:451).[9] Though these conclusions might be controversial, Thérien's distinction seems helpful in terms of understanding the evolution of development assistance policies. He summarises:

> Foreign aid came into being in the 1940s under the impetus of a left-wing political culture. However, it was in a predominantly right-wing environment, during the 1950–70 period that development assistance became a major international institution. In the 1970s, the introduction of the concept of basic needs turned the aid regime leftward. Later, during the 1980s, the promotion of structural adjustment coincided with the strong resurgence of the Right. Finally, since the early 1990s, the new emphasis on poverty reduction has signalled the inchoate yet genuine revitalisation of left-wing values. (Thérien 2002:452).[10]

With the end of the Cold War the 1990s saw fundamental changes on the international political arena, and this also impacted on development aid politics. Severine M. Rugumamu argues that

> [...] the end of the Cold War effectively eliminated the main *raison d'etre* for the foreign aid regime as it had existed for the last forty years. The contemporary period, therefore, is defined by the search for a new rationale for continued disbursement of aid. (Rugumamu 1997:9; his italics)

In this situation development aid demands new arguments and some would argue a different value basis. Further, compared to the 1980s, one of the prime features of the 1990s was the increased involvement from politicians, governments, and international organisations in the field of international aid. Through closer involvement in project designs, monitoring and evaluation, greater earmarking, and direct contracting of NGOs, donors and politicians regained the humanitarian initiative. This grows out of and has reinforced a closer integration between aid and political responses. The result is an overarching political approach in international aid and foreign policy. Hans-Otto Sano notes that

9 Marijke Breuning and John T. Ishiyama find that 'the proportion of parliamentary seats held by left parties is the only variable [...] that provides a statistically significant explanation of the dispersion of development aid' (Breuning and Ishiyama 2003:249).

10 Anthony Giddens too refers to this Left – Right distinction and notes how representatives of the Left tend to resist the Right's criticisms regarding the welfare state, but 'present a quite similar argument when discussing the drawbacks of global aid programmes' (Giddens 1996:374).

> [...] the 1990s was not liberalist in the same way as it was in the 1980s. The concept of the state as a body that defines the framework for an enterprising and active environment differs from the concept of a minimalist state for two reasons. First the 1990 agenda implied that state intervention is necessary and desirable to ensure human development and continued improvement of human resources. Second, the goal of good governance places peoples' participation and institutional change on the agenda. The basic thinking about regulation in the 1990s was less market-oriented and more political. Thus, in the 1990s, liberalistic and social agendas were combined and were concerned with both welfare and political participation. Human rights have found a central place in this actor- and social-oriented order. (Sano 2000:740–741)

3.2.1 Realism and idealism

Official development aid can be seen as one of many expressions of the policy a government practices in its encounter with other states in the international arena. Politics in this arena is often debated within the framework of the dichotomy between realism and idealism. Political realists see development aid as a state instrument for pursuing and securing strategic political, military, or economic interests (see for example Morgenthau and Thompson 1993). In other words, donors pursue 'their own narrow national interests rather than those of the recipient' (Cumming 2001:5). A clear example of this position is articulated for example by George Liska, when he claims: 'Foreign aid is an instrument of foreign policy' (Liska 1968:1). President Richard Nixon placed himself in the same strand of thought when he remarked: 'let us remember that the main purpose of American aid is not to help other nations but to help ourselves' (cited by Hayter 1981:83–84). In the realist perspective then, although states may cooperate, the rationale is to pursue national interests, not to live up to some notion of moral obligation towards its non-citizens. Alan Fowler points out the role this perspective has played in the context of development aid:

> From the outset, alongside overt objectives of accelerating economic growth, the covert purpose of aid was to help win the Cold War. [...] This *Realpolitics* undermined the moral grounding that aid could have had in the beginning. Instead, it sent a clear message that northern domestic interests were the issue, not poverty as a moral imperative to act. (Fowler 2000:592; his italics)

In ethical terms, not recognising any moral duties to anyone but oneself means subscribing to ethical egoism. Following this line of reasoning, foreign aid should be funded only when it serves governments' self-interests, the moral premise being that we ought to do whatever helps our group's welfare by helping others to help ourselves. Morality and self-interest are here one and the same, but as most governments draw a distinct line between 'us' and 'them', they in practice subscribe to a combination of altruism (towards their own citizens) and egoism (in relation to other nation-states).

While the importance of self-interest in foreign policy as a descriptive claim is rather uncontroversial, the role that moral values play in the international arena is disputed. Within the idealist paradigm a more optimistic view is taken of the role of moral values and motivation in international politics (see Hertz 1964; Baldwin 1993). Thus, while realists tend to understand ideas in terms of power, idealists are more inclined to 'grant ideas either an ontological or a general explanatory primacy' (Nel 1998:103). Idealism assumes that ideas play an important role in influencing human behaviour, that normative factors shape these ideas, and that normative ideas play an important role in the field of politics (Nel 1998:97–98). Accordingly, idealists argue that states are 'prepared to forego immediate national interests in order to tackle issues such as global poverty' (Cumming 2001:5). For example David Halloran Lumsdaine argues that humanitarian concerns are the driving forces for foreign aid (Lumsdaine 1993:3). When Truman in his speech mapped out a vision of international peace and prosperity, where international aid was seen as a moral action to reach this goal, he was clearly influenced by the tradition of idealism.

The discussion on aid motives is often framed by this realist-liberal divide. Most authors, however, conclude that not only one motivation can be singled out. There is rather a 'confusion of motives' (Rugumamu 1997:50), although some might be more dominant than others. The many different motives can be categorised in different ways. David Sogge distinguishes between three categories: 1) strategic socio-political motives, 2) mercantile motives and 3) humanitarian and ethical motives – all of which he further divides into short-term and long-term motives. However, he also adds two other neglected motives: 'obligations to compensate for suffering and damage, and imperatives to respond to common problems of a region or the globe' (Sogge 2002:44). Paul Hoebink distinguishes between political/strategic motives (reflected in the donor's selection of aid-receiving countries), economic/commercial motives (assessed by analysis of the back-flow of aid), ethical/humanitarian motives (humane internationalism) and environmental motives. However, the latter he claims has so far had very little influence on aid programmes. A fifth motive is the refugee motive (Hoebink 1999:177–179).[11]

Idealist arguments for international aid have regularly been voiced, although with varying intensity and prominence compared to arguments of more political or instrumental character, and they have only to a varying degree been found trustworthy. As motives they have been doubted and found to be 'moral talk' that covers the real underlying determinants of aid. Rugumamu remarks:

> The often-cited aid motives – poverty elimination, disaster relief, solidarity with the poor and oppressed, or moral obligation – are largely secondary to the core national self-interest objectives. Standard debates about the moral imperative for aid are sterile, inconclusive, and mainly irrelevant to the politics of aid. (Rugumamu 1997:52)

In addition to the realist and idealist paradigms, one can also interpret development aid within a neo-Marxist world system theory or from a liberal perspective. In world system theory, foreign aid is considered a tool to disguise economic domination and exploitation, while liberalism sees it as a means of promoting peace and prosperity (Hattori 2003:230). No doubt a dose of scepticism and hermeneutics of suspicion is justified with regard to the so-called humanitarian or idealistic justifications for development aid.

While the above perspectives all regard foreign aid as an active influence, whether reinforcing or mitigating the underlying material inequality, Tomohisa Hattori points to a role of foreign aid that is outside any of these effects. He argues on the one hand that foreign aid is not trade and accordingly should not be categorised as economic exchange. Further, he sees a clear difference between the redistributive system of the welfare state and foreign aid. While the former is considered a right of the citizens, 'foreign aid is a *voluntary* practice of donor states'

11 For a discussion of motives and interests in development aid, see Degnbol-Martinussen and Engberg-Pedersen 2003:7–24.

(Hattori 2001:636; his italics). Against this background and drawing on the works of Marcel Mauss, Marshall Sahlins, and Pierre Bourdieu, Hattori argues development aid should be interpreted as a form of symbolic domination, 'a practice that signals and euphemizes social hierarchies' (Hattori 2001:639). Mauss, who has explored the gift institution in depth, concludes that the purpose of giving is not the allocation of resources, but rather the upholding of social relations (Mauss 2002). However, criticising Mauss for not incorporating power relations sufficiently in his analysis, Sahlins refines his analysis by distinguishing between different forms of reciprocity: generalised (the pure, free gift; sharing; hospitality), balanced (direct exchange; trade) and negative (barter; gambling; theft) reciprocity. While the first is found in societies with a relatively high degree of social cohesion, the second reflects and affirms power symmetries or social relationships between social equals. In the third category reciprocity has become a matter of self-interest (Sahlins 2004:191–196; Hattori 2001:637–639). Hattori then asks which of these foreign aid belongs to, and as it is in part unreciprocated Hattori argues it is a case of negative reciprocity. It arises from conditions of basic material inequality between donor and recipient: one has the resources to give what the other lacks. The goods that are needed or desired by the recipient are provided by the donor as a gift, and thus the status of the latter is transformed from the dominant to the generous. In accepting the gift, the recipient becomes the grateful (Bourdieu 1990:98–111; Hattori 2001:640).

Further, it will be necessary to distinguish between the motives for foreign aid and the stated reasons for the same. The stated reasons are rhetorical arguments addressed either to a domestic audience, the recipients of aid, or other donor countries. Accordingly, the stated moral basis for international aid might be quite different and contrary to the underlying motivations driving it. Hoebink comments that

> [w]hile humanitarian and ethical motives are often highlighted in official documents, White Papers and statements from ministers and aid officials, the underlying political/strategic and economic/commercial motives are downplayed (Hoebink 1999:179)

For such reasons, public statements and documents are often regarded as instrumental and accordingly not reliable sources to identify 'true' motivations. However, stated reasons can also be put forward in different ways, including humanitarian and ethical motives. As pointed out by Nigel Dower: 'Whilst many may share the moral intuition that we have a duty to care for others, there are a variety of ways in which that intuition may be supported or interpreted' (Dower 1991:278). In other words, the references to morality by various donors might actually be appeals to different moral arguments: solidarity, equality, need, etc. (Riddell 1987:7).

Reviewing the literature, Hattori distinguishes between three different ways of morally justifying foreign aid within the liberal tradition. These can be summarised under the headings imperfect obligation, utilitarianism, and humanitarianism. His point is, however, that they all share the same fundamental problem: 'their implicit *idealism*, or the assumption that ideas can have causal force in and of themselves' (Hattori 2003:231; his italics). Accordingly, foreign aid is based on philanthropy, not on redistribution and rights. This leads him to two observations, first that 'the discursive justification for giving as an institutionalised practice is rooted in a specific type of ethical tradition that emphasises the qualities of excellence or virtue in an individual's character' (Hattori 2003:235), and second, that 'although the focus of virtue ethicists is the character of the individual, their larger point of reference is the good society' (Hattori 2003:235). In conclusion, Hattori claims:

> In short, while all of these ethical justifications identify with liberal ideals of rights, humanitarianism, and improvement, the aid practice they justify tends towards the opposite effect, anticipating neither the eventual perfection of donors' obligation into a right, the mitigation of a material hierarchy, nor the remedy of a diseased condition. (Hattori 2003:246)

3.2.2 Donor characteristics

Foreign aid is allocated and justified in different ways in different countries. Marijke Breuning argues that these differences relate to differences in national role conception profiles. She distinguishes between four ideal types: 'the Good Neighbour' (focus on recipients' immediate needs), 'the Activist' (focus on recipients' long-term needs), 'the Merchant' (focus more on needs of the donor country) and 'the Power Broker' (focus on donor country's need to preserve or enhance its own influence) (Breuning 1995:236–240). Studying Dutch, Belgian, and

British politicians' rhetoric when talking about foreign aid in the period 1975–90, she argues that while Dutch rhetoric emphasised social justice, development, and stability (the Activist), the Belgian put more emphasis on how aid should benefit the domestic and international market (the Activist and Merchant). British politicians on the other hand emphasised British power and influence (the Power Broker) (Breuning 1995:250–253).

Peter J. Schraeder, Steven W. Hook, and Bruce Taylor identify six key pieces to the 'foreign aid puzzle' – pieces they see as determinants for foreign aid. These six variables are humanitarian need, strategic importance, economic potential, cultural similarity, ideological stance, and regional identification (Schraeder, Hook and Taylor 1998:303–307). They find that US foreign aid in the 1980s was motivated by strategic and ideological interests, while economic self-interest governed the foreign aid policies of Japan. In the case of France, two other factors are often emphasised: the promotion of French language and culture, and economic interest. Schraeder, Hook, and Taylor conclude that

> [...] the results clearly reject the rhetorical statements of policymakers within the industrialised North who publicly assert that foreign aid is an altruistic tool of foreign policy. Rather than demonstrating a positive relationship between foreign aid and recipient social-welfare factors, our findings discounted the role of humanitarian need in the aid policies of these industrialized democracies. (Schraeder, Hook and Taylor 1998:319–320)

In a similar study Alberto Alesina and David Dollar find

> [...] considerable evidence that the direction of foreign aid is dictated as much by political and strategic considerations, as by the economic needs and policy performance of the recipients. Colonial past and political alliances are major determinants of foreign aid. (Alesina and Dollar 2000:33)

However, Alesina and Dollar also find that there is a substantial degree of similarity in the aid allocations of the Nordic countries, and that these countries target their development aid to the poorest countries (Alesina and Dollar 2000:50). Sogge too finds it reasonable to claim that a sub-regime of the so-called like-minded countries: Norway, Sweden, Denmark, Canada, and the Netherlands has at least existed in the past. 'Much earlier than others, they focused on poverty and on political and civil rights. Since 1975, all except Canada have met the UN spending norm of 0.7 per cent of GNP' (Sogge 2002:41).[12]

3.2.3 States and NGOs

States are important, but not the only, actors in the development field. NGOs have also had a significant, though changing, role over the years. In the 1960s governments viewed development NGOs with scepticism, while the NGOs reacted to the failure of the governments' approach to development and of the private sector philosophies of trickle down (Owens and Shaw 1972). In this sense the scepticism was mutual. In the 1970s the search for new approaches and methods in development work greatly influenced many NGOs. Paulo Freire's ideas of bringing about structural changes in society through education and social mobilisation of the oppressed inspired many (Freire 1970). In effect, as many NGOs became active in the discussions and debates on sustainability and self-sufficiency, the 1980s became the NGO decade in development aid and governments came to see NGOs not only as service providers but also as mechanisms for utilising social and human capital for welfare purposes (Dichter 1999:45). The roles of NGOs were thus complementary to those of governments. From the early 1990s this turned into a close co-operation. Although 'non-governmental' for some NGOs has meant keeping a distance from governments and being different from them, others are now actively seeking close relations.[13]

When governments now express greater interest in NGOs, one must assume that they will make efforts to influence them too. The main mechanism donors use to do this is probably by offering increased financial support. NGOs for their part seek to influence their counterparts through operational collaboration, lobbying, shaming, and blaming. Accordingly, the relationship between NGOs and states can be understood in terms of 'bargaining and negotiation, although at times coercion is a possible strategy' (Hulme and Edwards 1997:11).

12 For an overview of the policies and performances of individual donor countries and the EU, see Hoebink and Stokke 2005.

13 For a discussion of the debates on NGOs and development aid, see Pearce 2000 and Hilhorst 2003.

As noted, one of the criteria for selecting agencies in this study is their organisational and ideological differences. One important dividing line between the agencies studied here is the one between the government agency (MFA), and the non-governmental organisations. Being NGOs, NCA, SCN, and NPA are defined by what they are not. When called non-profit organisations, it is also clear that they are to be understood as different and separate from commercial, profit-seeking actors. As such, and separate from state and market, they are organisations of a third sector – civil society.

In the context of development aid NGOs are often said to 'function as intermediaries to promote sustainable development, social justice and enduring improvement in the circumstances of poor and excluded groups' (Fowler 2000:601, note 1). A more comprehensive definition could be to understand NGOs as organisations that

> [...] provide useful (in some specified legal sense) goods or services, thereby serving a specified public purpose... (2) are not allowed to distribute profits to persons in their individual capacities; (3) are voluntary in the sense that they are created, maintained, and terminated based on voluntary decision and initiative by members or a board; and (4) exhibit value rationality, often based on strong ideological components. (Hudson and Bielefeld, 1997:32, quoted in Lindenberg 1999:150)

The latter element of this definition explains why NGOs can also be labelled value based organisations. However, different values can constitute their value base. Some are 'faith based' (NCA), some are 'solidarity organisations' (NPA), other are 'neutral' (SCN), etc.

The value basis of NGOs is occasionally seen as a positive feature of these organisations. Although their role in international aid and the effects of their work might be doubted, NGOs are commonly recognised for their moral motivation and good intentions. Their staff is considered committed and altruistic, and they are commended for their strengths in terms of being flexible, non-bureaucratic, effective, and cost-efficient. They can adjust quickly to local variations and have close connections with their beneficiaries, and thus have the ability to express people's concerns. However, measuring the effects and achievements of NGOs is difficult, and closer studies have not been able to confirm all of these assumed strengths. While often praised for their independence, efficiency, and moral integrity, they also have their own problems. NGOs do not as a rule reach the poorest of the poor. Their organisations are often hierarchical and bureaucratic, especially the larger ones.[14] Due to the close relations between governments and NGOs, critics argue they are in effect 'becoming more cautious, more bureaucratized, and less nimble and bold, mirroring the very traits of the governments they disdained' (Dichter 1999:47). Many NGOs began as independent relief agencies with a degree of amateurism, and have remained unquestioned and free to do good works wherever and whenever they see fit. They suffer from technical deficiency and lack of accountability.[15] Few of them are self-sufficient, and few of them can cope with the deep structural problems in the societies where they work (Tvedt 1998:128–131; Dichter 1999:43). Thus, they have gained a certain reputation as do-gooders, motivated and guided more by heart than mind. For such reasons it cannot a priori be assumed that NGOs do better or more efficient work compared to their governmental counterparts.[16]

3.2.4 Questioning consequences

Development aid often seems to be implicitly and intuitively understood as something positive, something that should be promoted and applauded. But, there are always questions hiding beneath the surface. Does aid really benefit the recipients? Or is it not rather the reverse, that aid hurts the recipient and benefits the donor? Contrary to the repeated claims of aid agencies, and with support of a wide range of critical evaluations, a number of authors and observers have argued that development aid not only does not help, it even makes matters worse.[17]

14 William Easterly addresses what he considers the 'problem of bureaucracy in foreign aid' (Easterly 2002).

15 For a discussion of accountability in development aid, see Wenar 2006.

16 For a discussion of the comparative advantages of NGOs, see Marcussen 1996.

17 Three recent books that voice such criticisms are *The White Man's Burden. Why the West's Efforts to Aid the Rest Have Done So Much Ill and So Little Good* (Easterly 2006), *The Trouble with Africa. Why Foreign Aid Isn't Working* (Calderisi 2006), and *Foreign Aid. Diplomacy, Development, Domestic Politics* (Lancaster 2007). Related specifically to the Norwegian context Øyvind Østerud recently voiced a similar critique (Østerud 2006). Others, however, conclude positively regarding the effects of development aid (Sachs 2005; Shalendra 2005).

In *Lethal Aid* Rugumamu voices such scepticism. In the introduction he remarks:

> There is growing evidence to suggest that not only has foreign aid failed to mitigate critical problems of underdevelopment but quite often it has helped to debilitate rather than stimulate potential productive energies in Africa. In place of a robust economy and improved standards of living, foreign aid has resulted in unprecedented economic stagnation and waste, a crippling debt crisis, human rights abuse, as well as encouraged extensive foreign interventions in the national economic policy management. (Rugumamu 1997:1)

Graham Hancock, author of *Lords of Poverty*, is another who voices such views. However, his criticism primarily concerns ODA and he reveals a somewhat more positive evaluation of aid channelled through NGOs. He writes: 'They rarely do significant harm; sometimes they do great good' (Hancock 1991:xiii).

Development work is criticised not only with self-interest serving arguments, but also from moral and socio-economic perspectives. It must defend itself against critics who challenge the very concept of development as something that can be intentionally brought about and who point to the (intended or not) negative effects of aid. These adverse effects of development aid might be due to poor institutional capacities, corruption, inefficiency, etc. in the developing countries, or because of the conditions for aid set by the donors (Alesina and Dollar 2000:33).

When reference is made to the harmful effects of aid, it is a consequential argument that is put forward, and one that goes right to the core of development aid, questioning its very right to existence. The implication would be that international aid is morally bad and should therefore be terminated. However, if the negatives effects of international aid could be avoided or sufficiently mitigated, this argument loses its strength. All of the aid agencies studied here, as with most (probably all) aid agencies, dispute the claim that aid (only) hurts. Serious aid agencies do not deny the difficulties and dilemmas involved in relief and development work, and invest both resources and know-how in mitigating the negative effects and in trying to 'do no harm' (Anderson 1999). Most of them will (vehemently) emphasise the overall positive effects, either short or long term. Still, the weighty criticism of the work they do constitutes an important part of the discursive context for NDA (see section 9.6).[18]

3.3 Norway – the donor

The Norwegian government and Norwegian NGOs have been engaged in development aid for more than 50 years. Substantial amounts of money have been granted to combat poverty in different parts of the world, and hundreds of Norwegians have devoted many years of their lives to this work. Seen together, the work of these agencies and individuals constitutes a Norwegian subsystem of the international aid system. This subsystem is shaped by the international economic and political context, but also by the choices and priorities of the Norwegian government and different NGOs involved in international aid.

Formally Norwegian official development aid came about through the allocation of funds from the Norwegian Parliament to the Fund for assistance to underdeveloped countries (The India Fund) in 1952 (Simensen 2003:13). In the early 1950s Norway was still receiving financial assistance through the Marshall Plan, and both domestic reconstruction after WWII and military expenses due to the Korean War put considerable strain on the state budgets. Still, 1952 can be seen as a turning point in the Norwegian post war period (Furre 1992:248). By this year the rebuilding of the country was coming close to completion and the mass unemployment and political and ideological conflicts of the previous decades were no longer there. Further, Norway had been drawn into the Atlantic camp, and with close ties to the USA being established it is of no surprise that the international aid project was seen in light of the Cold War also in Norway.

Norway had had a remarkably large number of missionaries working abroad, and had through its trade and shipping traditions historical and economic ties that stretched all around the world. That Norway

18 For a general discussion of aid effectiveness, see Hansen and Tarp 2000. More specifically, Paul Collier and David Dollar have assessed the effects of Norwegian development aid (Collier and Dollar 2001).

became a donor of international aid can be seen as a continuance of this activity. Further, as the first UN Secretary General was the Norwegian Trygve Lie, a special obligation to follow UN recommendations might have been felt. And finally, the legacy of Fridtjof Nansen[19] and the fact that it is the Norwegian Nobel Committee that awards the Nobel Peace Prize, might have contributed in the same direction.

Ten years later, in 1962, Norwegian ODA was institutionalised in Norsk utviklingshjelp (Norwegian Development Aid), and in 1968 re-organised as the Norwegian Agency for Development Cooperation (NORAD) under the Ministry of Foreign Affairs (MFA).[20] However, as Helge Pharo points out: 'Rhetoric notwithstanding, in 1960 multilateral, bilateral and regional aid amounted to only 0.11 per cent of GNP' (Pharo 2003:537). As late as 1967 Norwegian ODA was among the lowest of the OECD countries. The ambitions, however, gradually increased and have been characterised as an 'expansion with an ever growing altruistic self-understanding' (Lundestad 1999:287). In the 1970s Norwegian foreign policy became radicalised. Pharo mentions three reasons for this radicalisation: the Vietnam War, the egalitarian Norwegian welfare state, and a sense of responsibility that came with economic prosperity, not least due to the oil discoveries in the North Sea in the early 1970s (Pharo 2003:545). Aid came to be seen as an important tool in the fight for human rights and against apartheid and violent militant Latin-American regimes. One expression of this was the explicit support for the New International Economic Order (NIEO).[21]

3.3.1 Small state with moral motives

Several motives for Norwegian ODA can be mentioned. Studying Norwegian parliamentary debates from the early 1950s, Jarle Simensen identifies different groups of arguments (Simensen 2003:41–42). The most

19 Fridtjof Nansen (1861–1930) was a Norwegian explorer, zoologist, and statesman. He was involved in relief work after World War I and awarded the Nobel Peace Prize for this in 1922.

20 In the period 1983 to 1990 NORAD was under the Ministry of Development Aid, and from 1990 it reverted to the Ministry of Foreign Affairs.

21 A comprehensive account of the history of NDA can be found in Simensen 2003, Ruud and Kjerland 2003 and Liland and Kjerland 2003.

prominent is peace, that development assistance would reduce the threat of war. This is in line with other arguments of self-interest, for example that development aid could build future markets.[22] Humanitarian arguments are another large group, reasoning that economic assistance is an expression of common values of the Norwegian society. Arguments that articulate atonement and solidarity with reference to the Western crimes towards peoples of other continents can be included here. A third group of arguments concerns democracy and Cold War. The India Help could be described as a Norwegian initiative and contribution to the fight against communism. Further, as Norway has no colonial past[23] (and accordingly no selfish motives, it was argued), it was also argued in favour of NDA that Norway could be an example to the rest of the world. The assumption that there is a link between poverty and political extremism also had broad support.[24]

Pharo points to other domestic circumstances when he explains Norway's entry into the group of donor countries. He writes:

> The great enthusiasm and the expressions of moral and political obligations were undoubtedly sincere. Yet they cannot wholly account for the remarkable 1952 proposal from a small, non-colonial, recently independent country that still rationed many consumer goods and strained to accomplish its own economic growth and rearmament goals. The key to understanding the timing of the project is to be found in the domestically divisive rearmament programme, in which Norway had to take part as a NATO member. (Pharo 2003:533–534)

A. Maurits van der Veen has also studied the 1952 debate in detail, comparing it with similar data from Belgium, Italy, and the Netherlands (van der Veen 2002). Van der Veen distinguishes between seven categories or 'frames', and seeks to identify the relative importance of each frame in these countries. The categories are 'security, power and influence,

22 However, Helge Pharo notes that 'An articulation of specific Norwegian interests is remarkably absent from the early aid debates' (Pharo 2003:531).

23 As a general claim this is not precise. As pointed out by Knut G. Nustad, the twin-state of Denmark-Norway had colonies (Nustad 2003:16–18).

24 One exemption is the Parliament president Carl Joachim Hambro. He doubted one could buy friendship and peace with other nations through such donations, reacted to the description of India as underdeveloped, and rejected the claim that the colonial era had caused irreparable damage to the countries in question. He distanced himself from the national self-glorification implied in the role others saw Norway play internationally (Simensen 2003:49–51).

economic self-interest (wealth), enlightened self-interest, self-affirmation and reputation, obligation and duty, and humanitarianism' (van der Veen 2002:10). In the case of Norway, van der Veen finds it is the latter categories that get the higher score in his table of relative weighting of different frames for aid. Humanitarianism comes at the top of the list, while enlightened self-interest, self-affirmation, and obligation follow closely. The security, power, and wealth categories receive a far lower score. Compared to the other countries in his study, Norway has the top relative weight in both humanitarianism and enlightened self-interest. He points out how

> Norway, the country with the weakest colonial background, is also the country where legislators are least likely to think of aid in terms of economic self-interest. Conversely, as a country with the most visible missionary tradition, Norway is the country where the enlightened self-interest frame is the strongest. (van der Veen 2002:13)

Van der Veen concludes that in the 1952 debates '[e]nlightened self-interest and humanitarian concerns dominated, coupled with a strong interest in self-affirmation' (van der Veen 2002:22).

The humanitarian concerns could be articulated across the political spectrum, as they fit well with both the social democratic notion of solidarity as well as the Christian and humanist ideals of the centre-right parties (Pharo 2003:531). The role of normative values with respect to NDA is, however, not limited to these initial debates. Pharo remarks:

> The belief in the necessity and possibility of a foreign policy infused by high ethical standards has been a trademark of Norwegian aid policies. So has the belief that the small Nordic powers have a special role to play and an obligation to take on that role. (Pharo 2003:546)

Other scholars also argue along similar lines: the perceived distance between Norway and Europe led to a 'moralising tendency' (Knutsen 1997:25) in Norwegian foreign policy led by a relatively strong 'missionary impulse' (Riste 2001:256). On the other hand, Janne Haaland Matlary finds that Norwegian politicians and civil servants neither think strategically on the utility of value politics, nor do they think very clearly in strategic terms.[25] Further, they do not involve themselves uncritically in all good causes. The value diplomacy that Norway has practiced from the beginning of the 1990s has provided the Norwegian state with a 'capital', although there remains a need to reflect critically and strategically on what this implies (Matlary 2002:75).

There has also been a self-strengthening dynamic, with the involvement of more and more departments, institutions, and individuals in NDA leading to a 'competition in altruism' (Pharo 2003:546). Olav Stokke too argues that a sense of moral obligation has been important in NDA, but also points out that 'instrumental arguments came strongly to the fore in the mid-1990s' (Stokke 2005:450).

The notion that a small country might have a special role to play relies on the premise that small countries differ from large countries. The differences in foreign aid policies between Portugal, Austria, and New Zealand on the one hand, and Norway, Sweden and Denmark on the other, however, 'suggests that one must look beyond the conventional notions of capabilities to explain their behaviour' (Omoruyi 2001:136). In addition to the small state perspective the national role conception must also be considered. Leslie Omoruyi identifies both a humanitarian dimension and an element of commercial interest in Norwegian aid. It is, however, the influence of the national role conception and the effect of the domestic economic culture on Norwegian foreign aid policies that he finds most striking. He remarks that Norway's 'domestic economic culture, straddling welfarism and capitalism as it does, represents two strains that tend to simultaneously propel its aid giving towards humanitarian and parochial interests' (Omoruyi 2001:143). David Gillies arrives, however, at a different conclusion. He writes:

> By showing that Canada, the Netherlands, and Norway are disinclined to adopt assertive policies at the expense of competing national interests, I have demon-

25 Matlary's study is based on interviews with politicians and high level civil servants. She distinguishes between three models for describing this relationship: 1) The activist who is much involved in value diplomacy, but never thinks strategically on what kind of power this potentially gives a small country, 2) the activist who does think strategically, recognising how visibility and reputation have become increasingly important also in international relations, and finally 3) the political realist who is concerned about the significance of value diplomacy to real politic, using the capital derived from value diplomacy in order to pursue foreign policy goals (Matlary 2002:5).

strated that these internationalists are states like any other, driven principally by self-interest and prudence, not altruism. (Gillies 1996:259)

3.3.2 The Norwegian model

In the beginning of the NDA era, there was little discussion of the role of NGOs in this field. In the 1960s, however, government support to Norwegian NGOs was put on the agenda, as it was assumed they could contribute to promoting 'the new development aid project in the Norwegian population and turn it into a national task' (Tvedt 1998:177). In 1978 NORAD established a separate office to deal with the relationship with private organisations. The political breakthrough for the NGOs came, however, in the 1980s. During this decade the NGOs increased both in number and strength, and MFA increased its role as a funding source for these NGOs, supplementing NORAD. In effect, an extensive cooperation has developed between the state and NGOs in Norway. This is often referred to as 'the Norwegian model'.[26]

Terje Tvedt has pointed out that there is both a substantial government funding for NGOs and an extensive exchange of personnel between them. He points to several factors to explain this situation (Tvedt 2003:86–88). Firstly, due to a low population spread out over a large geographical area and an egalitarian society, the organisations have had only limited opportunity to raise sufficient funds from private donors. Secondly, since Norway has no colonial past and relatively few and limited economic and strategic interests in developing countries, NGOs have been less concerned about distancing themselves politically from the state, compared to NGOs in the USA, Great Britain, and France. Thirdly, Tvedt points to the above mentioned national consensus on the legitimacy and political priority given to development aid. Fourth and

26 Jan Egeland gave this model its theoretical expression in his thesis *Impotent Superpower – Potent Small State. Potentials and Limitations of Human Rights Objectives in the Foreign Policies of the United States and Norway* (Egeland 1988; see also Bucher-Johannessen 1999), making close cooperation between the MFA and the NGOs its foundation element. However, such cooperation is not unique to Norway and corresponds to similar patterns internationally.

finally, politicians and bureaucrats have in many cases had close working relationships with people in the civil sector organisations.

The debates on the state-NGO relationship often concern who governs whom, and in particular to what extent the NGOs are governed by the state. Iver B. Neumann points out several reasons for the latter. He argues that Norwegian diplomacy has changed over the last decade, and that the involvement of non-governmental actors in this field is an important element of this change. This has lead to what he calls a 'dual track diplomacy' (Neumann 1999:185). One track is the traditional, governmental state actors (the diplomats), while for example multilateral companies and NGOs make up the new second track. Neumann does not, however, see these changes in diplomatic practice as a weakening of the state as the governing actor of Norwegian policy. With large parts of their budgets funded by the government and related obligations to report to the same government, Neumann argues that the analysis 'can just as well, or even preferably, treat such an organisation as part of the state formation' (Neumann 1999:190).

Finally, it should also be noted that all four agencies studied here rely on individual donors or taxpayers, and thus depend on popular support for NDA in general. However, they must convince the same donors that the work of their own organisations are at least as good as the work of the others, and in the case of NGOs, they must compete for funding from the government. Hence, these agencies can be studied both as competitors and as co-players. With regard to the issue of popular support, some see growing popular frustration and cynicism with regard to development aid (van de Walle 1999:338–341), and others argue that aid is low on the agenda (Thérien and Lloyd 2000:21). This is sometimes taken to indicate donor fatigue. However, surveys indicate that popular support for Norwegian aid remains stable at a relatively high level, although knowledge about development aid might be limited (Bøås 2002:4).[27] This seems to have been reconfirmed in the latest survey done by Statistics Norway, which shows that 9 out of 10 Norwegians have a positive attitude towards NDA.[28]

27 Gorm Rye Olsen notes how 'European public opinion believes that emergency assistance basically is the rationale for development aid' (Olsen 2001:645).

28 This survey is available from Statistics Norway at <www.ssb.no/emner/00/01/30/rapp_200713/rapp_200713.pdf> (accessed 28.03.07). For a discussion of the impact of domestic public support on foreign aid policies, see Otter 2003.

3.4 Summary

NDA must be understood in light of the historical situation in which it emerged and developed, its international context, as well as the specific characteristics of Norwegian society. Further, development aid can be interpreted from a range of different perspectives. Governments' rationale for providing development aid looks different from the perspective of political realism or idealism. The different perspectives have also lead to heated debates on the way development aid is implemented as well as its effects. Various donor countries provide development aid in different ways, as do the many NGOs.

NDA has characteristics often understood in light of Norway's small state status. Several authors consider NDA to be governed by humanitarian or moral motives to a larger extent than many other countries. NDA is further known for a relatively close relationship between the Norwegian government and Norwegian NGOs, and has broad support across the political spectrum and from the population at large.

4 The aid agencies

Angels of Mercy or Development Diplomats?

Book title (Tvedt 1998)

This chapter elaborates on the organisational context the interviewees of this study are working in. I will address the four aid agencies separately, focussing on how they present themselves in key policy documents. Accordingly, this chapter will also introduce the interpretative repertoires these agencies make use of when explaining and justifying their role and mandates. Thus, an initial presentation and analysis of the moral discourse of NDA is made here. I begin with MFA, and turn subsequently to the three NGOs.

The following analysis is based on publicly available policy documents from the selected agencies in the period 2002–2005. They are negotiated texts and, to a certain extent, might reflect the possible disagreements, contradictions, or tensions that may have been part of the negotiations. Accordingly, these documents must be understood as products of internal organisational processes. However, although they are products of negotiation, the focus here will be on the texts as they stand and how they have been formulated at a given point in time. As end products of these processes they are official expressions of the aid agencies' self-presentation.

Being policy documents, and neither reports nor evaluations, these texts are principled and forward looking. Thus, they are prescriptive texts, making claims and contentions about how development aid should be understood. Through the implicit negations in the terms and concepts positively used, they can also be statements about how aid is not perceived by the organisation in question. As such they can be read as expressions of the identity and contemporary self-understanding of the different organisations, and their principled reflection on the values motivating, justifying, and governing their work.

In other words, texts like these are designed to communicate (Hodder 2000:706). The intention of the document is not (only) to draw out the practical implications, but to inspire and gain support for whatever policy is defended. Accordingly, they are written 'in a style chosen mainly to attract, please and persuade you' (Apthorpe 1997:45). For these reasons, such documents provide suitable and relevant material for the type of investigations this study aims at.

4.1 Ministry of Foreign Affairs

The political responsibility for Norwegian ODA is with the Minister of International Development at the MFA. Norway has 7 main partner countries (Malawi, Mozambique, Tanzania, Uganda and Zambia, as well as Bangladesh and Nepal), and 18 other partner countries.[29]

One of the key articulations of the Norwegian government's contemporary development aid policy can be found in *Stortingsmelding nr. 35 (2003–2004). Felles kamp mot fattigdom. En helhetlig utviklingspolitikk.* [Report No. 35 to the Storting (2003–2004). Fighting Poverty Together. A Comprehensive Development Policy] (Ministry of Foreign Affairs 2004a; abb.: FPT).[30] Reporting from its release in April 2004 and quoting then Prime Minister Kjell Magne Bondevik, one of the leading Norwegian newspapers, wrote:

> The Prime Minister says that maybe the most important element in the Report to the Storting [Parliament] is that the rationale for giving development aid has been changed: until now the prevailing opinion has been that aid is given on the basis of charity. The Government wants to change this, and to state the reasons for providing aid in terms of human rights. It is a human right not to live in extreme poverty. Norwegian aid is not about us sacrificing a part of our wealth, but rather

29 For more information on Norwegian ODA, see <www.regjeringen.no> and <www.norad.no>. For an overview over Norwegian ODA statistics, see <www.oecd.org/dataoecd/42/48/1860517.gif> (accessed 29.03.07). Written accounts by former Norwegian ambassadors to Third World countries can be found in Garbo 1993 and Eidhammer 2005.

30 I have discussed this policy paper also in Fretheim 2007.

that those who receive it have a right to receive, says the Prime Minister. (Mathismoen 2004, *Aftenposten*, 30.04.2004).[31]

The claim that the report rejects a charity mode of thinking is easily affirmed. Already in the introductory chapter this issue is addressed: 'Development policy is not charity (*veldedighet*). It is about contributing to having human rights fulfilled for all' (FPT:5). This rejection of charity is actually the only place in the report where the word charity is used. Charity is clearly something the report wants to distance itself from, although what the report means by 'charity' remains unclear.[32]

4.1.1 Dignity and rights

The opening chapter of the report begins with the paragraph Human dignity for all (FPT:5). This paragraph elaborates a rationale for development aid that can be characterised as cosmopolitan and idealistic. It states: 'Human dignity is inviolable. The work for human rights is a natural consequence of this' (FPT:5). Or, as put in the English summary of the report: 'We only have one world. The dignity of every individual is universal and indivisible. This conviction underlies our common strug-

31 Similarly, the Minister of International Development at the time, Hilde Frafjord Johnsen, claimed that 'contrary to earlier attitudes about how development aid is about charity, this report is based on a rights perspective' (cited in Hofsvang: 'Reform-ivrig og utålmodig minister [Reform-Eager and Impatient Minister]' in *Bistandsaktuelt* 4/2004).

32 Reasons for wanting to distance oneself from a charity mode of thinking might be found in the historical roots of the term. Derived from the latin caritas, the term has the etymological meaning love. Evolving from this term, charity could historically refer more specifically to the giving of alms by individuals (Williams 1983). This has a long tradition in the Western world (and elsewhere). Alms giving was encouraged by the Church, maybe primarily as an expression of Christian love between fellow human beings and ultimately as a practical expression of the love of God to mankind. However, although thought of as a duty, alms giving also had a voluntary aspect to it. The when, why, and to whom of alms giving was the prerogative of the donor. Accordingly, alms giving came to be seen not as a duty in any strict sense, but rather as a supererogatory action. It was socially expected, but when done it was praiseworthy. The not-giving of alms, however, was not blameworthy.

gle for human rights' (Ministry of Foreign Affairs 2004b).[33] Thus, the dignity of all human beings and the human rights derived from this dignity become the core of the argument for development aid. The universal scope of these rights is also emphasised. 'Through the UN's Declaration of Human Rights and conventions on civil and political, as well as economic, social, and cultural human rights, it is clear the human rights apply to all and that all have the same rights' (FPT:5).[34]

The role and importance of human rights as the basis for development policy is articulated on several occasions in the document, and most explicitly in a separate section titled A rights based development policy. Here the rights based approach to development is explained. It is seen to be in line with other Norwegian governmental policy papers (FPT:10), the normative framework provided by the United Nations (FPT:11), and the policies of other bilateral donors and non-governmental organisations (FPT:13). Further, the close relationship between human rights and development is stressed, as well as the individual character of human rights. The adoption of individual rights is said to constitute a 'core element in the understanding of what the path out of poverty consists of' (FPT:11). Further, the report makes the point that the human rights way of thinking also constitutes the basis for a more comprehensive understanding of starvation, and can be expressed as freedom to make real choices. Accordingly, 'this perspective implies [...] a challenge to include the human rights way of thinking both in analyses of poverty and in the shaping of development programmes' (FPT:12). The rights based approach is further not regarded as a framework that focuses exclusively on specific target groups. Rather, it 'broadens the question of realising rights to include a range of elements that together contribute to ensuring the rights of the individual' (FPT:12).

Similar statements can be found in the action plan *Kamp mot fattigdom! Regjeringens handlingsplan for bekjempelse av fattigdom i sør mot 2015* [Fighting Poverty. The Norwegian Government's Action Plan for Combating Poverty in the South towards 2015] (Ministry of Foreign

33 The English summary is published as an unpaginated pdf-file on: <www.regjeringen.no/upload/kilde/ud/stp/20032004/0003/ddd/pdts/stp200320040003ud_ddd pdts.pdf> (accessed 21.06.07).

34 These conventions are available at <www.ohchr.org/english/law/pdf/ccpr.pdf> and <www.ohchr.org/english/law/pdf/cescr.pdf> (both accessed 20.03.07).

Affairs 2002a). In its executive English summary it is explicitly stated that: 'Poverty is an attack on human dignity. It is morally and politically intolerable that basic human rights are being violated in such a massive and constant way' (Ministry of Foreign Affairs 2002b:4, abb.: AP), and that 'the war on poverty is about promoting human rights' (AP:8).

Thus, at this stated policy level, the ideas of human dignity and universal human rights constitute the fundamental building blocks of the rationale for Norwegian development policy. It seems that the concept of human rights is used to emphasise a cosmopolitan element in the rationale underlying Norwegian development policy. The rights based approach highlights the equality of all human beings. Human rights are at the core of the policy described in the report, and with a broad conception of the rights based approach, it is, as signalled in the report's subtitle, a comprehensive development policy the government calls for. Accordingly, the challenge 'to integrate the perspective of rights based development better in the development work both multilaterally and bilaterally' (FPT:13) is accentuated.

Further, and as noted above, the report explicitly distances itself from the notion of development policy as charity. However, the report itself actually downplays the discontinuity which the rights language represents. 'A rights based development does not imply a radically new way of understanding development cooperation' (FPT:12). Some commentators have argued that the report actually does not represent a move away from the charity conception of aid. 'The report is marked by development optimism without a sense of history. Thus, development aid becomes characterised by charity, although the government tries to stress the opposite' one commentator says (Halle Jørn Hansen, cited by Hofsvang 2004a in *Bistandsaktuelt* 04/2004).

4.1.2 Norway's responsibility

Along with human rights as a key concept in NDA policy, the report also discusses Norway's responsibility in this regard:

> As one of the world's richest countries, Norway has a special responsibility (*særskilt ansvar*). We are faced with an ethical demand (*etisk krav*) to do something about injustice, and to influence the development in a positive direction, when we have the opportunity to do so. (FPT:6)

Here, the case for NDA is explicitly made a moral concern, as an ethical demand is said to drive this political commitment. In the English summary, this special responsibility is referred to as a 'moral responsibility'. It is, however, worth noting how this ethical demand or moral responsibility is related to the relative wealth of Norway and the corresponding ability to provide aid. As it is put, this implies that those who do not have similar means do not have the same responsibility, although a general obligation might still be valid. It is also worth noting how this acknowledged moral responsibility is not expressed as a moral duty derived from the human rights of the recipients. And further, what kind of 'injustice' the quoted statement refers to is not explained. Thus, although the report is saturated with human rights rhetoric, the role human rights plays in regard to any moral responsibility 'to do something' is not explicitly addressed.

This leaves several questions unanswered. If some people are deprived of their human rights, can others be hold accountable for their misfortune? If so, what is the reasonable and expected measure that should be taken? And further, can some basic core of fundamental human rights be singled out, the non-realisation of which might lead to a strong duty on others, while other rights only have weaker corresponding duties? These questions remain unaddressed in the report. This being the case, the meaning and stringency of 'moral responsibility' remains unspecified. Thus, in *Fighting Poverty Together* the question of the duties of the rich or fortunate is not elaborated on. As noted above, Norway's 'moral responsibility' is acknowledged, but neither duties nor obligations are included in this context. Accordingly, it seems reasonable to ask if one should not expect more from a rights based and justice concerned approach. As one commentator writes: '... such an approach is more challenging than what is put forward in the report' (McNeill 2004:19).

4.1.3 Justice and recipient responsibility

Just as the concept of human rights plays an important role in *Fighting Poverty Together*, justice is also made a key concept in the rationale underlying the development policy presented. Already in the introductory paragraphs the report makes clear: 'The fight against poverty is a matter of justice (*rettferdssak*)' (FPT:5). And later in the report the need for 'just conditions for trade' (FPT:6), 'just resource distribution' (FPT:10), 'just distribution of profit' (FPT:61), and 'just development' (FPT:121) is addressed. As justice in the report is introduced as corollary to viewing development policy as human rights based, the relationship between human rights and justice seems to be regarded as unproblematic. However, despite the introductory, programmatic statement the number of such instances where the terms justice or just is used throughout the report is strikingly small, only 13 cases of justice (*rettferd/-ig/-het*) against 107 instances of human rights (*menneskerett/-er/-igheter*). This suggests that the concept of human rights plays a much more central role in the document than that of justice. Further, the meaning and implicit consequences of seeing poverty as a matter of justice is hardly explained in the report.

On the other hand, the participation of the recipient and recipient responsibility in international aid is repeatedly emphasised, not least in the *Action Plan 2015*. It is put in positive terms on several occasions: 'The international community must listen more carefully to the voice of the developing countries' (AP:6); 'Partner responsibility must be strengthened, governance improved, and corruption combated' (AP:8); 'Developing countries must be given back control over their own development' (AP:9). This emphasis is further explained through a reference to negative previous experiences: 'Developing agencies have for far too long unempowered their cooperation partners by doing their work for them or ignoring their wishes' (AP:9). The same concern is also expressed in *Fighting Poverty Together*, for example when it states: 'It is the countries' own inhabitants and politicians who must decide how their future should be shaped' (FPT:14). In other words, participation and recipient responsibility seem to be important concerns articulated in the Norwegian government's development aid discourse.[35]

35 The recipient responsibility discourse of the Norwegian government is discussed in Hagelund 1999 and Selbervik 2003b.

4.2 Norwegian Church Aid

Norwegian Church Aid was established in 1947 as an emergency response to the plight of people in post-WWII Germany and Austria. However, with a growing awareness of the permanent struggle of poor people around the world, NCA gradually expanded its work into the field of long-term development work. Its first major development project was in Abikaliki in Eastern Nigeria from 1962 onwards. With the Biafran war, relief again became the focus of the organisation, but NCA's efforts during this crisis also represented the organisation's breakthrough as one of the major Norwegian aid agencies. Only a few years later, in 1972, NCA embarked on what was to become the largest Norwegian development programme so far. This comprehensive project in Sudan was part of a general expansion of the organisation's work, both in terms of financial capacity and geographical presence. In the 1980s NCA became especially involved in relief and development projects in Ethiopia and Eritrea, and in the 1990s work in Europe was resumed. In the first decade of the 21st century, NCA is involved in projects in about 70 countries on four continents, often in close cooperation with local, church based partners.[36] In addition to relief and development aid, advocacy has become a third major field of work for NCA.[37]

4.2.1 Ecumenical diaconal service

Norwegian Church Aid has representatives of the Lutheran (state) Church of Norway and a number of free churches and organisations of

36 Increasingly, projects and programmes are planned and implemented in close contact with the international church networks, e.g. Lutheran World Federation (LWF) and World Council of Churches (WCC). In relief operations NCA cooperates with sister organisations through Action by Churches Together (ACT) and on advocacy issues through Ecumenical Advocacy Alliance (EAA).

37 For recent studies on the work of NCA, see Vilberg 2003; Brehm, Tanner, Padrão and Harris-Curtis 2004; Ulveseth 2004; Berge 2005 and Tønnessen 2007. See also <www.nca.no>.

different denominations in its decision making bodies.[38] Compared to the other selected agencies, NCA thus stands out as an organisation with a religious basis for its work. The organisation sees itself as a 'church-based, faith-based and value-based organisation' (Norwegian Church Aid 2005a:12). However, a change in NCA's confessional identity can be traced through the history of the organisation. While emphasis in the early phase of the organisation's history was put on assistance to Christian brothers and sisters (primarily in Europe), this confessional aspect has been moderated and replaced by a much more ecumenical and universal profile. Aud V. Tønnessen notes that 'NCA has developed from being a relief organisation with a distinct denominational identity into a humanitarian aid organisation anchored in Christian values, both concerning fields of work and public image' (Tønnessen 2001:531).

In its policy document *Together for a Just World* (Norwegian Church Aid 2004; abb.: PD)[39] Norwegian Church Aid (NCA) describes itself as 'an ecumenical, voluntary, independent organisation committed to international diaconal service' (PD:5). That NCA is 'ecumenical' means both that NCA's 'constituency is the Christian churches and church-related organisations in Norway' (PD:6) and that its 'diaconal work is carried out within the framework of the worldwide Christian Church' (PD:6). Together with 'ecumenical' the use of the term 'international diaconal service' highlights the Christian identity of the NCA. The term diaconal indicates that NCA can be distinguished from more markedly missional organisations (see section 7.2.1) that also receive government development aid funding and are, just like NCA, Christian and church based NGOs (although most are not ecumenical).[40] NCA understands 'diaconia' as 'serving the Triune God by giving unconditional assistance to the whole human being, catering to spiritual as well

38 In addition to the Norwegian Lutheran State Church, these are: The Evangelical Lutheran Free Church, The Free Evangelical Congregations, The Norwegian Baptist Society, The Norwegian Mission Association, The Salvation Army, The Methodist Church of Norway, the Pentecostal Movement in Norway and representatives of national Christian youth organisations.

39 I refer here to the NCA's English translation of the policy document available at: <english.nca.no/article/view/2362> (accessed 09.02.07).

40 Still, mission organisations and NCA can in some cases have the same partners. In addition, supporting a given church in their development work can also be seen as a support for the totality of the church's work, and thus indirectly also their involvement in evangelisation.

as physical needs' (PD:5). Universality is also a constitutive element of diaconal service: 'This diaconal service shall be given regardless of race, nationality, gender, political persuasion or religious beliefs' (PD:5).[41] Further, NCA understands being international as NCA 'mobilising people in Norway to show concern and take action for people in need outside of Norway's borders' (PD:5). Being voluntary and independent means being 'anchored in the membership base of our constituency in Norway, and in their structures for democratic decision making', and that the organisation also 'seeks to influence our constituency's attitudes and policies related to poverty, injustice and oppression' (PD:6). Further, on its internet site NCA presents itself as a:

> [...] non-governmental and ecumenical organisation that works to ensure the individual's basic rights. Anchored in the Christian faith, NCA supports the poorest of the poor, regardless of gender, political conviction, religious affiliation and ethnicity. (<www.nca.no/article/archive/40>, accessed 26.01.07)

Here, the issue of human rights is put at the forefront of the organisation's self-understanding. Focus is put on the poorest of the poor, but the universal aim of the organisation's aid efforts is clearly emphasised. In other words, being anchored in the Christian faith is not seen as contradictory to providing and offering universal support.

4.2.2 God's love and justice

The guiding values and principles of Norwegian Church Aid are also stated in the NCA's policy document, together with the organisation's vision and mission. The vision, 'Together for a just world', is not given any further explanation. The mission, 'to manifest God's love in the world', however, is explained as:

> [...] promoting basic rights for poor, destitute and oppressed people; participating in strategic alliances which aim to translate God's love and compassion for humanity into practical actions; challenging indifference, greed and cynicism among us who live in societies characterised by affluence and excess consumption; improving the living conditions of the poor and changing the attitudes of the rich. (PD:5)

41 For a discussion of NCA's understanding of 'diakonia' in relation to 'koinonia', 'liturgia' and 'God's oikumene', see Norwegian Church Aid 2005a:10.

Note again the focus on 'basic rights'. The rights language is also widely used in other policy documents, such as the strategic plan *Together for a Just World. Working to Uphold Human Dignity 2005–2009* (Norwegian Church Aid 2005a). This plan describes an analytical framework called the 'Human Dignity Triangle', where human security, human development, and human rights constitute the three corners of the triangle (Norwegian Church Aid 2005a:5). Accordingly, rather than the concept of human rights, human dignity is placed at the centre of this framework. This corresponds to the heading 'Place human dignity first' in *Norwegian Church Aid's 10-Point Political Platform*. Here NCA states: 'Poverty is a violation of human dignity' (Norwegian Church Aid 2005b:4). In the strategic plan human dignity is referred to as the 'heart of the matter' as it is 'at the core of religious values. We are therefore human before we are Christian, Muslim, Jewish, Buddhist or Hindu' (Norwegian Church Aid 2005a:4).

Further, note how 'improving living conditions of the poor' goes hand in hand with 'changing the attitudes of the rich'. Similarly, in the strategic plan the concept of rights-holders is followed by the concept of duty-bearers (Norwegian Church Aid 2005a:8–9), and the plan argues:

> People who are privileged with wealth and power lose their dignity through self-interest, greed, and indifference in the face of global poverty and injustice. NCA, with its constituency in one of the world's richest countries, is therefore also called to a ministry to the privileged. (Norwegian Church Aid 2005a:5)

Further, in the political platform it is argued that: 'It is important [that] these economic, social and cultural rights are regarded as real and binding obligations' (Norwegian Church Aid 2005b:4). Thus, regarding the concept of donor duties NCA comes across as different from MFA, which rather speaks of responsibilities. Also in comparison with the other NGOs, the issue of duties of the rich is much more explicit in the case of NCA.

The policy document further identifies five core values of the organisation: 1) compassion, 2) justice, 3) participation, 4) responsible stewardship of God's creation, and 5) peace (PD:7–8). These are seen as expression of the basic belief

> [...] that human beings are created in God's image, as equals with the same basic rights and obligations. We are each citizens of a global community, and our lives are bound together through our mutual dependence on one another. God calls us –

> regardless of our religion, gender, culture, ethnic origin or traditions – to work against the destructive forces which threaten humanity and the whole of creation. (PD:7)

Here the Christian basis for the NCA is explicitly related to a discourse of rights and obligations. Again it is made explicit how the universal scope for aid is the basis for the work of the organisation.

The core value of compassion refers to NCAs stated commitment to 'giving unconditional help to people in need' (PD:7). Justice on the other hand 'means that all people shall have an equal right to life, food, health, education, work, free religious expression and protection under the law' (PD:7). Thus, justice here is seen as the universal realisation of human rights. This is also the case for participation which is seen as 'the basic right of all human beings' (PD:8). The implication is that NCA's work should be 'aimed at empowering people to participate freely in shaping the social, economic and political development of their own society' (PD:8). Responsible stewardship of God's creation refers to the belief that 'human beings have a duty to manage our natural resources and the global environment in a sustainable and responsible way, so that we do not jeopardise the lives of future generation' (PD:8). Thus, environmental and cross-generational considerations are articulated as key concerns to NCA. Finally, peace is defined as 'a society in which individuals and groups can resolve their conflicts, or learn to live with them, without resorting to violence or the force of arms' (PD:8).

4.3 Save the Children Norway

Save the Children was founded by Eglantyne Jepp (1876–1928) in England in 1919. The First World War had left large parts of Europe in ruins, and Jepp was committed to helping the millions of suffering children in Central and Eastern Europe. The following year she established the Save the Children Union that would coordinate international aid efforts. Soon after she had also drafted the Children's Charter. This would later be the Geneva declaration on Children's Rights, adopted by the General Assembly of the Peoples' League in 1924. This declaration anticipates the UN Declaration on Children's Rights, adopted by the UN

General Assembly in 1959, and the UN's Convention on Children's Rights adopted in 1989.[42]

A number of other Save the Children organisations were soon established, with Save the Children Sweden (*Rädda Barnen*) as one of the first, also in 1919. Save the Children Norway (SCN) was established first in 1946, and its initial projects aimed at alleviating the post-WWII suffering in Europe. However, SCN soon targeted groups in Norway, and later projects in Third World countries also became part of the project portfolio. This meant that SCN developed into a relief and development organisation. Over the last 15 years this has been supplemented by increased involvement and participation in strategic and political discussions concerning children's rights and living conditions world wide. Thus, also SCN has developed into a multi mandate agency. Today SCN runs programmes in Africa, Asia, Europe, and Latin America.[43]

The first paragraph in SCN's *Statutes* (Save the Children Norway 2005b) states that

> Save the Children Norway is a voluntary, member governed, rights organisation that is party-politically and religiously neutral. Save the Children Norway's values are based on the UN's Convention on Children's Rights and the Universal Declaration of Human Rights. (Save the Children Norway 2005b:1)

Similarly, in its *Strategy for 2006–2009* SCN states:

> The basis for the work of Save the Children Norway is the UN Convention of the Rights of the Child. Save the children is a brave and pronounced advocate for children's rights locally, nationally and internationally. (Save the Children Norway 2005a)[44]

42 This convention is available at <www.ohchr.org/english/law/pdf/crc.pdf>. It has been signed and ratified by almost all member countries of the United Nations. Exceptions are Somalia and USA.

43 For recent studies on the work of Save the Children Norway, see Flem 2001; Helland and Deresse 2004; Brehm, Tanner, Padrão and Harris-Curtis 2004 and Dahl 2006. A popular presentation of the organisation can be found in Thrane 1998. A written account based on the experiences of one SCN staff is Rustad 2005. See also <www.reddbarna.no>.

44 Save the Children Norway regards its strategy as an internal document and accordingly does not publish it in its entirety. I refer here to the presentation of the strategy available on the organisation's internet site (<www.reddbarna.no>). Accordingly page reference is not given.

Clearly, 'rights' is a key word here. However, being a rights organisation is combined with being 'party-politically and religiously neutral'. It seems then that the values that are seen to be based on human rights are not regarded as related to any specific party-political position or religious tradition.

In SCN's *Strategy for 2006–2009* the organisation's values are explained as two-fold: 1) 'The good of the child is our first priority', and 2) 'All human beings have equal value, all children have equal rights' (Save the Children Norway 2005a). SCN's vision is also stated. It reads:

> Save the Children Norway works for a world where children's rights are fulfilled, which respects and values each child, which listens to children and gives children influence and where children live in freedom and security. (Save the Children Norway 2005a)

This vision explicates SCN's understanding of rights. Note that having one's rights fulfilled is made dependent on being respected and listened to. Emphasising children's influence, SCN seems to highlight their participation and active involvement in a similar way as NCA and MFA stress recipient participation. Similarly, the strategy states three working principles for the organisation: 1) children's participation, 2) strengthening local capacity, and 3) influencing causes (Save the Children Norway 2005a). Note again the emphasis put on children's participation.

4.4 Norwegian People's Aid

Norwegian People's Aid is a membership governed organisation founded in 1939 by the Norwegian Confederation of Trade Unions (LO), Norway's largest labour organisation, in response to the wars in Finland and Spain. Until the 1970s, however, NPA's activities focussed on Norway, beginning with reconstruction in the 1940s and followed by health programmes, vocational training for the disabled, summer camps for children, etc. An important part of the organisations work is still in the domestic arena, but since the early 1980s its international operations have grown extensively. NPA focussed initially on Southern Africa and Latin America, but is today involved in programmes in Africa, Asia, the

Middle East, Latin America, and Europe. In terms of programme activities, NPA is a major player in the fields of refugee work and mine clearance activities.[45]

The first paragraph in the *Policy and Strategy for NPA's International Humanitarian and Development Work 2003–2007* (Norwegian People's Aid 2003b; abb.: PS) is titled *Long-term objective and immediate development objective.* The expression 'immediate development' is explained in this way: 'Rights-based organisations, working in areas of conflict and oppression, have strengthened their ability and capacity to mobilise for democratisation and social and economic change' (PS:5). A footnote, however, seems to position NPA away from a purely humanitarian role (relief, emergency work), emphasising long-term development. It reads:

> Areas characterised by conflict and oppression is an 'active' term when NPA decides to start operations in a new country. But at the same time it does not imply that NPA should phase out in post-conflict situations. Long-term development implies presence throughout and beyond the immediate conflict period. (PS:5)

In the paragraph titled *Humanitarian Aid* it is explicitly stated that 'NPA's main focus is long-term development' (PS:9). In NPA's policy document *Solidarity* (Norwegian People's Aid 2003a)[46] NPA is defined as a 'humanitarian organisation for solidarity'. The term humanitarian is not explicitly explained, but the notion of human worth is addressed and defined as 'the same rights for everyone'. In other words, the rights language seems important also in this context. Still, solidarity here comes across as even more fundamental.[47] 'Solidarity and human worth have always been fundamental for Norwegian People's Aid', the policy paper points out. Solidarity is said to be 'built upon mutual support between different forces fighting for the same goals'. Interestingly, in the same way that human rights was contrasted to the concept of charity in

45 For recent studies on the work of Norwegian People's Aid, see Shanmugaratnam 2003; Ryen 2005; Knudsen 2006 and Isaksen, Samset, Pacheco and Norsk Folkehjelp 2006. A popular presentation of the first fifty years of NPA's history can be found in Lyshagen 1989. See also <www.folkehjelp.no>.

46 This document is unpaginated.

47 For a discussion of the idea of solidarity in recent European history, see Stjernø 2005.

MFA's *Fighting Poverty Together*, solidarity here is contrasted to the same. The policy paper states:

> Solidarity is the opposite of charity. Whilst charity implies that the giver has control over the recipient, solidarity means showing respect for the partners' integrity and their right to set their own conditions. (Norwegian People's Aid 2003a)

Note how the dissociation from charity is explained with reference to the issue of respect and the partners' integrity.

NPA's values are explained in the second paragraph of this strategy and are stated as 'national and international solidarity, human dignity, freedom and equality' (PS:5). Solidarity seems to be the core value among these, as this is the one that is explained in the document. Solidarity is said to be 'based on support and loyalty between people of mutual understanding and shared interests' (PS:5). Further, empowering people to 'voice their own interest', respect for the integrity and rights of the partner organisation (groups), and their 'initiatives to combat injustice, uneven distribution of wealth and to promote a human right culture where political and civil rights are respected, and economic, social and cultural rights are fulfilled' (PS:5) is accentuated.

The third paragraph, however, articulates how NPA sees itself as a rights based organisation. It programmatically states: 'For NPA and the partners NPA work[s] with, the acceptance of the Human Rights is a basis for our co-operation' (PS:6). The universality of these rights is stressed, and in this case too being human rights based is related to the concept of human dignity and international declarations and conventions. 'The international human rights instruments are the written documents that form the basis for a definition of what it implies to be a rights-based organisation' (PS:6).

Interestingly, however, a distinctive feature of NPA's use of rights language is how it is used to argue in favour of a specific method in development work, both in terms of adopting a long-term perspective, as well as a partnership strategy. The strategy states how a

> [...] right-based approach, as a method to achieve political, economical and social changes is a prerequisite to achieve a lasting change in the power structures, which in turn ensures the rights of all. NPA and its partners will as rights-based organisations struggle together to secure human rights for all. (PS:6)

The role of the partners is also highlighted as one of the ways NPA implements its international cooperation. The policy documents states that NPA shall work

> [...] in close cooperation with local popular organisations so that they can themselves gain control over their own development – it is their programmes and projects and their voice which should be decisive. Our role is to be arranger, advisor and network builder. (Norwegian People's Aid 2003a)

This issue of participation is also related to the concept of rights, as '[f]or NPA, popular participation and organisation are [...] important measures for promoting and securing people's rights' (Norwegian People's Aid 2003a). Further, NPA makes it a feature of their support to people that the organisation 'will take up a clear position on relevant social questions through public debate' (Norwegian People's Aid 2003a).

4.5 Concluding reflections

Based on an analysis of policy documents, this chapter has identified key features of the moral discourse of NDA. Both similarities and differences between the agencies studied have been noted, but four interpretative repertoires appear to play central roles in their policy papers: human rights, responsibility, justice, and recipient participation. Among these the rights discourse in particular appears to constitute a nodal point in the moral discourse of NDA.

In the case of MFA the human rights discourse is explicitly contrasted to a charity discourse. In addition, MFA emphasises Norway's responsibility to provide development aid, and construes this as a matter of justice.

NCA distinguishes itself by using language with religious (Christian) connotations. In this case the work of the organisation is explained as diaconal service and an expression of God's love. Here the notion of human dignity is emphasised and human rights is closely linked to every individuals' God-given dignity. There is also an emphasis on donor duties and the attitudes of the rich. Further, as in the case of MFA, here too the concept of justice seems to play an important role.

SCN comes across as an agency that very clearly makes human rights, and more specifically children's rights, the value basis for its work. The notion of participation, children's participation in particular, is also emphasised.

Finally, NPA also makes use of the rights language, but this is combined with a discourse of solidarity. Here popular participation is emphasised.

Part III

Self-presentation

5 Function

If it is in our power to prevent something bad from happening,
without thereby sacrificing anything of comparable moral importance,
we ought, morally, to do it.

Peter Singer in *Famine, Affluence, and Morality*
(Singer 1996 [1972]:28)

After having discussed the wider context and the way the aid agencies present themselves in the previous chapters, I turn now to the individual interviewee and her self-presentation. Different aspects of the interviewees' experience and understanding of their professional roles as development workers will be addressed, including their tasks and responsibilities, work satisfaction, frustrations, and challenges.

5.1 The development worker role

When asked if she would call herself an aid worker (*bistandsarbeider*)[1], one of the embassy interviewees in an intermediate position says: 'Yes, I would do that. I have worked with aid for many years'. One of the NPA interviewees in a senior position responds to the same question in a similar way, although somewhat more hesitantly. She says: 'No… Well yes, in many ways I am'. Also another of the embassy interviewees in an intermediate position accepts the aid worker label, but addresses the issue of how this is understood:

1 The Norwegian term *bistandsarbeider* is used both as a generic term for people working with different kinds of international aid (relief and development) and more specifically to denote those working with development aid (as opposed to being a relief worker, *nødhjelpsarbeider*).

> Yes, I suppose I have to. [laughing] I hesitate a bit. Yes, I suppose I am. Aid worker, whatever that is. […] But yes… I suppose I am. But it sounds a bit technocratic in a way, because an aid worker (*bistandsarbeider*), that is… Without the commitment I talked about and the various aspects of it, being an aid worker would be a bit uninteresting, in a way. I could be just about anything, in a way.

It seems here this interviewee wishes to distance herself from a certain understanding of the aid worker role, one that is 'technocratic' or lacking 'commitment'. The aid worker role she wants to be identified with should have this element of commitment, and this would distinguish it from other professional roles or positions.

Note how these interviewees relate more or less positively to the term aid worker when describing their professional roles. However, when one of the NCA interviewees in a senior position is asked if she would describe herself as an aid worker (*bistandsarbeider*), she says:

> I have actually pondered over that myself. If I were to describe myself, would I say aid worker? I assume others would give me that label… and in Norwegian terminology I kind of doubt if I would find another word to use. But, actually, I think it's time to look for other concepts, other words, because there is something about aid, something about what aid traditionally means…

It seems this interviewee is somewhat more dissatisfied with the term aid worker than the previous interviewees. The connotations of the term make this interviewee search for new terminology. One of the NCA interviewees in an intermediate position says the term aid worker (*bistandsarbeider*) is not the way she prefers to describe herself. She says:

> I think I have never introduced myself as an aid worker. But I think that when I talk about myself as an aid worker, it's when things are a bit difficult or tense. Then I can sometimes say that 'Yes, we aid workers…' [laughing] Yes, but I don't have a very strong identity as an aid worker.

When challenged to elaborate more on what kind of circumstances would make her speak of herself as an aid worker, she says:

> It's when I think I see that aid has a lot of dilemmas and I find that we end up in a lot of difficult situations. Sometimes I question the whole idea of giving aid. And it concerns… I think I often use it when I see myself in contrast to [local nationals], for example. 'We aid workers can afford to go to the restaurants'; 'We live in nice houses', things like that…

The term aid worker is used here to make a distinction between aid workers and local workers. The label 'aid worker' seems to distinguish between those who can afford to dine in restaurants, and those who cannot. Thus, 'aid worker' indicates wealth and resources, and that one belongs to the donor side of the aid relationship. This leads this interviewee to avoid this label.

Similarly, when asked to explain her understanding of the aid worker label, one of the embassy interviewees in a senior position says: 'No, I am not comfortable with that term. I would never call myself an aid worker'. And she continues: 'I feel maybe there is something negative about it. But I don't know… I cannot explain it any further'. Compared to the embassy interviewees quoted at the beginning of this section this interviewee expresses a much more articulated scepticism towards this key label of her profession. By implication not only does there seem to be a discursive struggle related to the concept of being an aid worker, but also the very understanding of aid seems contested. The idea of being someone who works with aid seems to be on the one hand accepted, but on the other hand avoided or rejected, and some of the interviewees offer discursive alternatives.

5.1.1 Aid or development worker

When one of the embassy interviewees in an intermediate position is asked if she would call herself an aid worker (*bistandsarbeider*), she responds:

> Er… No. I wouldn't do that. Not aid worker. I would rather emphasise development worker (*utviklingsarbeider*). But I am more of an MFA bureaucrat. And this implies that it's a profession […] and a field that of course interests me, which makes me continue doing it. But it's not a mission.

Note how this interviewee first explains how she prefers the label 'development worker' rather than 'aid worker'. As with several of the interviewees above, aid seems to be something this interviewee does not want to be associated with. This interviewee, however, concludes by calling herself 'an MFA bureaucrat'. Explaining this choice she makes a distinction between profession and mission. When asked to describe how she understands the difference, she says:

> Yes. No. It's not a calling. It's not a calling. We choose the fields where we think we are competent, where we think we can contribute, where our concern is to help someone…

Here it seems this interviewee's main concern is to distance herself from 'a calling'. She also makes it clear that she could have done something else. When asked to elaborate on what she means by saying 'it's not a mission', she says:

> […] No, it's not a mission in the sense that this is something I have to do. I can do other things too. I could very well work with other things. Absolutely, I have been thinking about it…. that I don't have to work with development aid. But I find it interesting. I have lived in Africa for many years and I find it all right. But I don't plan to stay on. I don't plan to settle, it's not like that. It's not that type of… as I see others, in different ways… Some settle here because they think it's a nice place to live, others settle because they can make a contribution. I don't have that…. I could just as well have stayed at home.

This interviewee makes a distinction between seeing oneself as obliged to work in a specific field ('I don't have to work with development aid'), and having an interest in that field of work. Regarding her own case, she says her motivation is derived from the latter. Further, she adds that she enjoys it. Although she has 'lived in Africa for many years', she points out that this is not something permanent. She does not plan to settle. Further, she clearly distances herself from other expatriates or aid workers. As noted from the first quote, she rejects any notion of having a calling. She could just as well have worked with something else, and does not want to spend a life time in Africa.

The characteristics this interviewee does not want to be identified with can all be said to belong to the traditional missionary role, where the missionary is one who is called by God to a specific task and a life time service for Him. Instead this interviewee emphasises how she could have done something else, and that she could have been at home. And rather than having a calling, her motivation is derived from personal or professional interest and satisfaction. At the same time she seems to downplay a commitment that is specific to this line of work.

One of the SCN interviewees in a senior position also makes this distinction between being an aid worker and a development worker. When asked to explain why she prefers the term development worker to aid worker, she says:

> Aid is sort of like looking at charity, as if someone cannot help themselves. That is the way I look at it. There you are. You know it all, which unfortunately is some of the mentality that I see in some of my colleagues from outside… that they have all the knowledge. These people are poor, and we have come to help them. And yet, that is not how it is. Yes, they are poor but how have they been surviving? That is what we say when we go into a community. We know it is a poor community, but these people have been here for years. They have some skills. They have some knowledge. And what is that knowledge? What are those skills? How can we enhance that? Because for them to survive in this harsh environment, it means there is something that they are doing that is correct. And that is what we want to build on. So that is why I feel like a development worker. I am not an aid worker. I am a development worker. Development means you are working on something that is already there. All you are doing is maybe cultivating, nurturing, so that it can develop its full potential.

Note the discursive link this interviewee makes between aid and charity. She seems to equate the two, and makes aid an expression of charity. One element of this charity is expressed in the phrase 'you know it all'. This 'mentality' of being omniscient she relates to the motives that make some want to help, and she finds this to be the case among some of her colleagues. The discursive link between aid and charity appears thus to be extended to the expert aid worker. The expert disregards the knowledge, competence, and skills of the recipient (see section 14.2). This interviewee, however, is eager to challenge the assumption that knowledge is only on one side (the donor side) of the aid relationship. From the fact that they have 'been surviving' she concludes that the recipients (too) have knowledge. In expressing an alternative understanding she seems to see her role more as enhancing the knowledge already present in the community or this knowledge as something 'we want to build on'. Rather than prescribing solutions from her own knowledge as an aid worker, the development worker makes 'something that is already there' the starting point.

5.1.2 Humanitarian worker

The development worker label is not the only alternative some of the interviewees say they prefer to the aid worker label. One of the NCA interviewees in a senior position initially says she calls herself an aid worker (*bistandarbeider*), but when asked to explain her understanding of the term she says she prefers the term humanitarian worker (*humanitær arbeider*).[2] She says:

> [...] In fact, humanitarian worker is a better expression than aid worker. Because, as a humanitarian worker you have some basic principles for the work you do, and a few principles often based on human rights, and also based on some laws and conventions that you as a humanitarian worker should and must be acquainted with. And these are about how aid should be independent of religion, independent of race, independent of gender and being able to assess aid in regard to respect and equality and dignity.

Explaining why she prefers humanitarian worker to aid worker, this interviewee points to the principles that govern humanitarian work ('human rights', 'laws and conventions'). In this she draws on concepts and terminology often related not primarily to development work but to relief work. However, the principles she mentions seem not to be in any direct conflict with what development aid agencies often say should govern their work. All of the agencies studied here emphasise that their work should be to the benefit of all, independent of religion, race, and gender. It therefore seems like this interviewee's preference for the humanitarian label rather than 'aid worker' must be understood as an insistence on the importance of 'respect and equality and dignity', as well as on ensuring a certain quality to the work by abiding by some agreed principles.

When asked to explain her distinction between aid worker and humanitarian worker in more detail, the same interviewee says:

> [...] Well, aid (*bistand*). Then one has to look at the word. What is it, when one says aid, well, meaning that one gives some kind of aid, one...? The word implies that aid comes as a type of help, to assist (*bistå*) someone else. And preferably keep them going, give them a stick, or preferably carry them on your back. While in the term humanitarian (*humanitær*) there is something humanitarian (*humanitært*), something human (*menneskelig*). And that has something to do with us humans doing something together. And there is also more of a kind of respect for other

2 One of the NPA interviewees in an intermediate position indicates how she can use different professional labels according to the context. She says: 'I always have a problem when I'm supposed to fill in those forms when entering a country. It says "occupation", sort of, but I don't know what to... Sometimes I write humanitarian worker, sometimes aid worker, and at other times [title]'.

cultures, for other traditions, and of other peoples' ability to manage by themselves. So that is a better word. It says more, really, about what we are actually doing.[3]

Note how this interviewee explicitly expresses how she understands aid as related to wanting to assist someone else. However, she seems to ridicule this notion of helping. Helping and assisting is understood as to 'keep them going, give them a stick or preferably carry them on your back'. She seems to speak ironically of the way helping and assisting is an expression of wanting to take control, as much as possible, over the one being assisted. The contrast is conceptualised as being 'human' and having 'respect'. The implicit assumption seems again to be that helping and assisting is something disrespectful which rejects the agency of the other. Accordingly, this interviewee prefers to speak of humanitarian work. The dissociation made from aid here repeats some of the elements noted above. Aid is associated with disregarding the resources of the recipient, while the idea of being humanitarian carries positive connotations of a common humanity, cooperation, and respect.

Having noted how the interviewees use different discursive alternatives, I will in the following primarily use the term 'development worker' to describe the individuals working in the development field.

5.2 Tasks and responsibilities

The agencies studied here and the development workers interviewed work in a wide range of thematic fields. One of the NCA interviewees in a senior position comments: '[...] this role, this kind of job is a bit special. On one day it can range from being in a shirt-and-tie-culture to standing in shorts in the mud somewhere. Yes, that's it. It's a vast

3 One of the NCA interviewees in an intermediate position similarly questions the concept of development aid, arguing that the consequence of a human rights approach would be not to demand anything back. She says: 'When you give something, you demand something back. Again, this relates to conditionalities etc. If we really want to do human rights based development aid, then... then maybe we should get rid of the word too. Development aid (*bistand*)...'.

variation'. Asking the interviewees to elaborate on what their tasks and responsibilities are within the development field makes it possible to draw a richer picture of who these interviewees are and the role they play in the aid agencies.

When asked about her main responsibilities, one of the SCN interviewees in a senior position makes a detailed statement. She explains:

> My main responsibility is, one, the strategic thinking. In terms of direction and making sure that we are moving according to the objectives of the organisation, that we find the right parties and partners to work with. That is really one of the issues, the long-term strategic thinking, and making sure that we are in line with our objectives. The other aspect has to do with relationships with governments: Liaising with government and liaising with other non-governmental organisations, making sure that we are aware about what is going on inside [the country]. We should relate to the development, and otherwise, so that we are moving alongside the others. And we are so small, so we can collaborate on different issues. So that is another area. The other is in terms of control, in terms of finances, to make sure that we are in line with approved funds that we get from… I am thinking of the funding we get from the Norwegian embassy, and the funds from Oslo directly. To make sure that we are in line with approved budgets. I have some accounting people, but I have to oversee what is going on according to the guidelines. According to what is set out for us to do as an organisation, and to approved plans. Then there are issues to do with staff and motivating staff and making sure that people are happy and that they are doing a good job so that we can achieve our goals. […] Those are some of the major areas, I would say, for my job.

This interviewee points to four core areas: 1) strategic thinking, 2) networking with governments and NGOs, 3) financial supervision and 4) work satisfaction. I will comment on these respectively.

5.2.1 Strategy

The phrase 'strategic thinking' seems to refer to the 'objectives of the organisation' and the identifying of 'the right parties and partners'. This is a responsibility one of the NCA interviewees in a senior position also highlights. She makes a distinction between administrative and financial matters on the one hand, and what she names strategic management on the other, understood as translating the organisation's 'global strategy to the reality in the region and the country level'. This latter interviewee also talks about strategic networking and partnerships as being key elements of this, and that 'the strategic work is maybe some of the most important in my work here'. Thus, this category of responsibility clearly links the work of the individual development worker to the plans and priorities of the organisation.

Similarly, one of the ambassadors interviewed explains her main task as having overall responsibility for the embassy's work in the country. She says:

> I have the general responsibility, no matter what field we work in, I will be responsible. And I will be the one who signs agreements on behalf of the Ministry and the Norwegian government, you know. So as an ambassador, head of mission, I have the overall responsibility to follow it all up, together with the person responsible for development aid on a day to day basis…

To have 'general responsibility' for the work of the organisation in the country in question is an expression used by most of the ambassadors and resident representatives interviewed. As one of the NPA interviewees in a senior position puts it, her responsibility implies 'the general responsibility for all programme and personnel activities in the region' which includes finances, logistics, etc. Not surprisingly, such 'overall responsibility' seems to be more the responsibility of the interviewees in senior positions, than in the case of those in intermediate positions.

5.2.2 Networking

The responsibility for networking, 'liaising with government and liaising with other non-governmental organisations', also seems to be conceptualised as an issue of representation. When asked about her main tasks, one of the NCA interviewees in a senior position says:

> It is representation – representing Norwegian Church Aid, especially in relation to the authorities, [country] authorities, but also to Norwegian authorities. But it's also to represent NCA in relation to international organisations like UN organisations, private organisations, to stay in touch with the embassy, with NORAD. These are important tasks.

The interviewees in this study are staff of Norwegian aid organisations and they can therefore be said to represent these organisations. Not surprisingly, all the interviewees working at the Norwegian embassy perceived their work and their roles as one of representing Norway. However, this is often also the case for those working for NGOs. When one of the NCA interviewees working in a senior position is asked if she feels she represents Norway as a country, or acts as an extended arm of the Norwegian state, she says: 'Yes, I feel that. And I feel it's important. This is something I point out to our partners: these funds don't come automatically'. Here, representing the Norwegian state is clearly related to the money provided by the same state. Similarly, when asked if she feels she represents Norway, another NCA interviewee in a senior position says: 'Yes, I feel I do. And I mean I do. I have an obligation to Norway. I represent Norway'. However, when asked if she represents Norwegian interests, she says:

> Yes, to a large extent I think so too. But it's clear that one has to find a balance, and then I have to tread carefully, and think through: What is more important, the Norwegian interests or the purpose of my being here, the aim of my being here?

Clearly, though she sees herself as representing Norway, this interviewee is more reluctant about her role as one of representing Norwegian interests. She indicates how this must be balanced against a consideration of the 'aim of my being here'. In her response to the same question, yet another NCA interviewee in a senior position says:

> More like Norway as a people, because I meet a lot of people at the project level. And of course Norway as the church, too, because I am a representative of the Norwegian church in [country] and I represent it, and also… yes, I represent Norway. But the distinction can be quite blurred.

Note here how this interviewee specifies that she feels she represents 'Norway as a people'. As a representative of NCA she also points to the back donors and founders of this organisation, and then concludes that she represents Norway, though in an undefined way.[4] Others specify this

4 When asked if she feels she represents the Norwegian people or the Norwegian state, one of the NPA interviewees in a senior position says 'the Norwegian soul' (*den norske sjela*). When asked to elaborate, she says: 'I mean, I mean that one can be proud of the values that we are so lucky to learn as children, that there is nothing dangerous about bringing them along, even if you shouldn't be a cultural missionary in a way… We are a Norwegian voluntary organisation, based on some values

to mean the individual donors or the organisation they serve. One of the SCN interviewees in a senior position says:

> I represent 110–115.000 Norwegian individuals in Norway, who give us money – plus all the tax payers who give money to NORAD, where we also get money from. And I have been very concerned that we must focus on results, we have to show that what we do works, because of our credibility with those who donate 100, 150, 200 kroner[5] a month to us. They are the ones I represent.

This interviewee does not refer primarily to her organisation, but rather to the back donors of this organisation: individuals and tax payers. Her primary identification seems then to circumvent both the NGO in question and NORAD as an institutional back donor, and focuses on individuals. When asked if she feels she represents Norway, another SCN interviewee in a senior position says:

> Yes, I feel I do, absolutely. And I am very proud of representing Norway, because I find that Norway has some incredibly good thoughts and ideas about how aid should be formulated and shaped. And Save the Children Norway as an organisation is also an organisation that I easily identify with and that I am proud to represent. It's a very good organisation. And I have worked with, as you heard, I have worked with many organisations. I have never worked for an organisation that I treasure as much as I treasure Save the Children Norway.

Here both Norway as a nation-state and the Norwegian organisations are important with respect to how this interviewee sees herself. And she is clearly comfortable with this situation. She finds that Norway has 'incredibly good thoughts' about development aid and that SCN is a 'very good organisation'. This interviewee is clearly proud of the organisation she works for. The same pride is articulated by yet another SCN interviewee in a senior position. This latter interviewee, however, explicitly rejects seeing herself as a representative of Norway. She says: 'I don't feel I represent Norway. I feel I represent a Norwegian organisation in the development field. [...] But I don't feel, really, that I represent Norway'.

The notion of representing Norway is accordingly perceived and evaluated differently by different interviewees. Several of them see

---

that admittedly are Western European in many ways, but are well rooted in Norway, were anyway. I don't think one should hide it, necessarily'.

5 'Kroner' is the Norwegian currency.

themselves as representatives of the Norwegian state, either directly or indirectly, while others see themselves as representatives of the Norwegian people or Norwegian individual donors. This seems to reflect both the close relationship between the Norwegian state and Norwegian NGOs, as well as a moral or humanitarian dimension in the national role conception (see section 3.3).

However, while some interviewees talk about representing Norway or a Norwegian organisation, other interviewees turn the issue of representation around, emphasising the role of representing the recipient. In response to the question whether she feels she represents Norway, one of the NPA interviewees in a senior position answers:

> […] Well, in relation to Norway and Norwegian Peoples' Aid I represent [country]… I have to report back to them. And if there is an initiative from the Norwegian side, then I am an important corrective or an enthusiastic pressure… It depends on what kind, but also, I have to look after… I become a voice from here, a voice that is important internally in Norwegian People's Aid. So that is my role. […] But at the same time I am also the opposite: An important voice for my own general secretary and my own structure at home in Norway and externally in [country]. For the guidelines etc. that have been adopted… I have my loyalty, but it goes both ways.

Note how representation is perceived as something that goes in two directions – to the recipient partners, and to the donor side. This makes this interviewee conclude that her loyalty 'goes both ways'. Similarly, one of the interviewees says about her role as ambassador:

> The role of the ambassador is twofold. Firstly, I represent Norway and Norwegian views. But I am also the listening post for what is going on in [country], for good and for bad. But I am to give a realistic account when I report back home. And of course, in a situation where we are a major donor in [country], and you have a famine like the one now on the way, I wouldn't have done my job if I did not persuade the Norwegian government to give extra funds to [country].

To summarise, the issue of networking seems to be perceived as a key responsibility for several of the interviewees, perhaps especially by those in senior positions. In their networking efforts they seem to see themselves on the one hand as representatives of the donor side in the aid relationship, and this is specified in different ways by the different interviewees. There is, however, also a discourse of representing the recipients to groups and individuals on the donor side.

5.2.3 Finances

The third issue identified above is finances. This is explained as ensuring that everything is 'according to the guidelines'. Again the relationship to the organisations' head office is addressed. The use of the terms 'control' and to 'oversee' indicate that there is a risk that funds might not be used according to guidelines and thus not in line with the intentions of the (back) donor. One of the embassy interviewees in a senior position also says her financial responsibilities are an important part of her work. She says:

> No, the main job is to make sure that the 250 million kroner that we have here now, are used according to the intentions and used as effectively as possible, and also to report back home about the use. In brief, that is the function of the job.

Similarly, when asked how she would respond to the claim that she controls the finances of the recipients of budget support, one of the embassy interviewees in an intermediate position responds:

> Yes, I am sort of like one who controls (*jeg blir litt kontrollør*). The thinking now is that the ministries themselves, or the recipient countries themselves should be in the driving seat and should in a way… and they make their own plans and their own budgets, and then the donors will have to see if they feel its seems relevant and OK, and then one approves. Then… then we have follow-ups during the year, where we get financial reports, receive technical updates, assess and approve them. And based on that, we can make another transaction, sort of. So we have to control in a way. From time to time, we say 'No, this is not OK. You have to explain more here'; or something like 'Here you have to reallocate, since it is obvious you have budgeted way off… compared to what the expenses show'… So it is sort of about controlling them. In a way, in the end I am supposed to sit here and check that it is appropriate to make the transactions. And in order to do that, I must first of all see to it that we get the reports, that they are correct, that we get what we are supposed to get in terms of monitoring, and also assess the quality of what we get. So it is sort of controlling.

Summarising, she says:

> […] So yes, it is about controlling in a way. It is. Quality checking and controlling, having the authority to say: "This will not work, we cannot accept it, and consequently we cannot transfer any funds".

The issue of controlling is particularly interesting in light of the explicit idea of how 'the recipient countries themselves should be in the driving seat' (see chapter 13). This interviewee, however, finds that she as a development worker 'from time to time' must overrule the recipients' decisions.[6] Thus, not only the need for, but also the legitimacy of overseeing and controlling the recipients finances is articulated. Thus, it seems, there are certain limits to the notion of recipient responsibility (see section 10.2.6).

5.2.4 Work satisfaction

Finally, the responsibility for staff follow up was noted above. The interviewee above relates this to both the staff being 'happy', and them 'doing a good job'. And the latter is related to good results. Similarly, another of the SCN interviewees in a senior position says her main task is to 'steer the organisation'. Elaborating, she says:

> [...] to ensure that it really addresses the issues affecting children. To provide leadership, and for me providing leadership means inspiring others so that they do their best for the children. More than anything, mobilising resources... I mean making sure that people are energised so that they really are able to analyse the issues that we are dealing with.

To both of these interviewees the issue of motivating staff (and others) to do a good job seems to be an important concern. By extension it seems they see a close link between professional content and achieving good results. Work satisfaction and delivering results go hand in hand.

Regarding work satisfaction, the majority of the interviewees in this study say they enjoy the work they do. It is, however, interesting to look more closely at what aspects they emphasise when elaborating on this issue. When asked to elaborate on why she enjoys her work, yet another of the SCN interviewees in a senior position says:

6 On the same issue another embassy interviewee in an intermediate position says: 'We are all the time... strong guard dogs all around... And that is legitimate, because we give a lot of money. We should be allowed to have an opinion when we donate a lot of money'.

> […] We have good staff, and we have an exceptionally good relationship with the authorities that we work with, and I try to strengthen all those processes. And I have had the opportunity to work with other aid and development organisations, and Save the Children Norway is special. We have a special target group […] I have a relatively independent position. I enjoy it, and I work a lot. With exciting things, and we see results when we travel around. We can show… good results.

Here several aspects are addressed. Firstly, contentment with working conditions seems to relate to having nice colleagues and good relations with partners. This I will call professional satisfaction. Another issue is the relationship to the organisation she is employed by, in this case SCN. The interviewee seems to enjoy working for this specific organisation and its special target group. This can be called organisational satisfaction. That she enjoys what she sees as a relatively high degree of independence can be said to be part of both her organisational and professional satisfaction. Finally, this interviewee highlights the good results of her work. As the focus here is on the end result of the work, this can be regarded as a third category: result satisfaction.

Some of the interviewees explain their contentment by referring to their love of and commitment to Africa and/or a specific country in Africa. When asked if she enjoys her work, one of the embassy interviewees in an intermediate position refers to the country she is working in. She says: 'There are nice people here and [nationality] are nice people you can get to know and that are social and… Actually, this is a pretty good country to live and work in'. Similarly, one of the NCA interviewees in an intermediate position says: 'And generally I enjoy being in this part of the world, in Africa. And I find it great to have this very open, social tone. I enjoy things like that a lot'. In the context of explaining what motivates her, one of the NPA interviewees in a senior position makes a comparison to everyday life in Norway. She says:

> […] I have lived enough in Norway to see for instance the time pressure that families with small children end up with. Here I find we are privileged. When I come home from work, I am 100 per cent at home. The advantage for the family is incredible… The closeness I have with my children means a lot. That wouldn't have been as easy in Norway.

This interviewee does not speak about the sacrifices of living abroad, but rather the privileges. The focus is not on the relationship to colleagues, working for a given aid agency or the results achieved, but rather personal satisfaction. This refers then to how the development worker enjoys the non-professional aspects of being a development worker.

5.3 Challenges and frustrations

The picture of how the interviewees experience their work becomes more nuanced when the issue of challenges or frustrations is addressed.[7] Being content with one's work does not preclude strongly felt frustrations.

Asked about the challenges in her work, one of the NPA interviewees in a senior position says: 'They are many. Incredibly many', and one of the NCA interviewees in an intermediate position says she finds the professional challenges frustrating. When asked to elaborate, she continues: 'A lot has to do with the system we work with, that we are strictly controlled by the authorities for any kind of activity. It limits our room to manoeuvre a lot'. Similarly, when asked to elaborate on possible challenges in her work, one of the embassy interviewees in a senior position says:

> Yes, it's not always very easy to work with human rights in a country where… where we maybe feel that the authorities aren't so open to what we mean by rights, or to have the same openness, where they have a different perspective on the issue.

The professional frustrations seem here to be primarily related to what could be called external factors, the context for doing aid work – not the cooperation with close colleagues or intra-organisational confrontations. This becomes quite explicit when one of the embassy interviewees in an intermediate position is asked about her main challenges. She says:

> I believe the main challenge is to put in place the external conditions (*rammebetingelser*) that make it possible to achieve some of the aims that we and our partners have for [country]'s development. […] So I think there is a great challenge related to further development and consolidating a well functioning democracy,

7 Generally I addressed this issue only after having first asked to what extent the interviewee enjoyed her work. In some cases, however, the issue of frustrations was immediately addressed by the interviewee.

> participation, security and safety for the people. Related to this is the whole field of human rights. And finally, [...] there is a considerable challenge related to a well functioning administration. That is, a capacity in the country at central, regional, and local levels.

This interviewee points to challenges she finds relate to the overall challenge of achieving results. Implied seems to be a risk that these results might not be achieved, and these risks involve the political conditions of the recipient country, as well as the challenges related to a malfunctioning bureaucracy and capacity issues. Several of the interviewees make similar statements. The difficulties that stem from the general difficult conditions are a recurring theme, as is an emphasis on the problems they face with the recipient side of the aid relationship. Responding to a question about the difficulties she is faced with in her work, one of the ambassadors interviewed points to the deep poverty of the recipient country. She says:

> [...] It's one of the poorest countries in the world. It says something about the challenges and difficulties we are faced with. And we face them in several fields in the countries where we are working. It's the institutional capacity on the recipient side. But, there are no easy solutions, because if this is to be sustainable over time there must be local institutions with ownership of their own development. All the experience gained over forty, fifty years with development aid shows that ownership is important. Therefore the challenge to us is alignment, using the institutions and systems of the recipient country. And that is easier said than done. So, parallel to doing this, or having such a policy, we must also develop the systems, the institutions, so that they can take on the responsibility that ownership implies. The other thing is a process that has been going on for years, which is to make it easier for the recipient countries, but also for the donors, to deliver aid. This means reducing transaction costs. This also implies alignment, it means creating a better division of labour between the donors and the authorities. This means that we will have new ways of delivering aid, meaning everything from budget support, programme support, sector support, and phasing out much of what we had before, project support.

Here, the main challenges of poverty are interpreted from an institutional perspective. The challenges and difficulties this interviewee meet, she relates to institutional capacity, as well as to the importance of local institutions' sense of ownership of their own development. The importance of these institutions is, however, not reflected in their relative strength. She regards them as too weak, making donor intervention necessary to strengthen them.

Another ambassodor highlights a different challenge. Discussing changes in development aid implementation, she says:

> [...] The biggest dilemma that I have experienced over the years is that many take on a role that you should not. That is, one goes out as a project leader, maybe in an isolated project, with relatively wide authority, and then you realise that the management is bad and weak. And maybe there is partial misuse of funds. Not necessarily by pocketing (*putte i lommen*) money directly, but somewhat inefficient use and that one doesn't get as much out of the money as one maybe should. And then one is in danger of creating one's own routines. Because one thinks with the heart and has a close relationship to some of the local colleagues, one establishes systems on weak foundations. And from the good intention one makes something worthwhile, but it's something which cannot continue. This might be just as corrupt as the traditional system, because just to get something done, you skip the routines. [...] This was one of the main reasons why we moved to what we call recipient responsibility and recipient orientation. We know that the recipient in the end must administer funds, must decide, must prioritise and be responsible for the implementation. The result was that we had all these small islands, and white elephants that grew larger and larger until they burst.

As she construes the challenge as one of taking 'on a role that you should not', this interviewee identifies the professional role as the challenge itself (see chapter 14). She explains it with an example, and it is clear that the role one should not take is characterised by 'the good intention' and to 'skip the routines'. The reference to white elephants is telling. This metaphor finds its roots in modernisation theory, and the interviewee here clearly echoes criticisms that have been directed toward this theory, for example with reference to project support, expert interventions, and lack of recipient ownership (see section 3.2).

One of the NCA interviewees in a senior position also addresses the issue of the role of the professional development worker. In the context of explaining her motivation for being involved in this line of work, she says:

> [...] I think the challenge is to have connections and to find out how to take advantage of them, and contribute yourself, so that it becomes an equal relationship. I find these are some of the things that I have found most challenging and exciting, just that, in addition to the professional aspects of the work that are also there. The development challenges: What is development? How do we relate to the complexities? What is the relationship between the purely political and the purely technical? What is the relationship between what is going on locally on the ground, what happens at the national level, and what is going on at the global level? Where

> are we at now? What is our role, and how can we actually be on that playing ground (*plaskedammen*), saying this is our role? That is were we should try to contribute to doing… making a difference. Those are some of the things that tease and trigger.

Three elements are worth noting. This interviewee identifies a challenge in having 'connections', and how one should 'take advantage of them'. In addition there are the 'professional aspects', which she relates to a series of questions regarding development aid. Most interesting is perhaps her questioning of the development worker role. Finding one's right place in the development field seems to be a main challenge, but also one 'of the things that tease and trigger'.

This interviewee also notes that linking the local, regional, and global can be a challenge. Commenting on the relationship between goals and achieved results, she says:

> […] We struggle to see the different levels, for example how we manage to see how things are important in several local communities, and are a common denominator in several local communities in many countries. And then it turns out that there are some conditions that go beyond national boundaries. How can we help create synergy effects and support and encourage actions, and bring the partners on board?

Implicitly this interviewee points to one of the main developments that has taken place in the development field, especially among many NGOs. As it has been put by David Korten, NGOs have developed through several 'generations' (Korten 1990:114). While they started out in the first generation as primarily humanitarian relief organisation, they soon started to expand their mandates and fields of concern to development aid. In the third generation this expanded further to the national level, and in the final, fourth generation to the global. All the NGOs studied here belong to this fourth generation (see section 1.3.1 and chapter 4). However, former priorities have not been abolished. Fourth generation NGOs are therefore multi-mandate agencies. They still do relief work, but have included rehabilitation, development work, and advocacy in their mandates. It is not surprising then that this becomes a challenge for the practitioners working in these organisations.

5.4 Concluding reflections

In the interviewees' reflections on their professional role there seems to be an ambiguity articulated when they discuss which title they prefer. Although most of the interviewees acknowledge that others probably would categorise them as aid workers (*bistandsarbeidere*), they vary as to whether they would use this term themselves. Some, including some of the embassy interviewees, see this as an unproblematic label and would use it to describe themselves. Others, however, are more reluctant and avoid using the label aid worker. This highlights how the concept of aid is discursively negotiated and echoes some of the development aid discussions that have taken place in the last decades (see section 3.2). Several of the interviewees prefer the term development worker, while some search for other alternatives. Furthermore, for some of the interviewees it is important to stress how they do not regard their work as a function of any divine calling. In this there seems to be a dissociation from notions related to a missionary or charity discourse, not dissimilar to the dissociation from the notion of charity noted in several of the policy documents.

Several of the interviewees in senior positions see themselves as responsible for the overall work of their respective agencies in the country where they work. This implies responsibility for planning and overseeing the work done, both internally in their organisations as well as in relation to their counterparts. An important part of their work is also to represent their organisations in relation to other organisations and institutions. However, there seems to be a tension between identifying with the recipients or with the donors of development aid, although many of the interviewees see themselves in a kind of in-between position. Several of the NGO interviewees seem to understand their role and work in terms of representing Norway, either as the state or the people (individuals) living in Norway, reflecting a national role conception with clearly moral or humanitarian aspects (see section 3.3.1). In most cases being an NGO employee and simultaneously representing Norway is not regarded as problematic (see section 3.3.2).

Further, several of the interviewees articulate a general satisfaction not only with the work they do, but also with the private or personal life that they have as expatriates. Some find great satisfaction in living abroad, maybe in a country that has special meaning to them. Still, there seem to be several challenging areas: the general conditions in the country, recipient responsibility, the issue of capacity building, etc. Frustrations often seem to be related to issues on the recipient side of the development aid relationship.

Accordingly, the interviews reveal aspects of the moral discourse of NDA that are not explicitly articulated in the policy documents discussed in the previous chapter. The ambiguity expressed reveals ongoing discursive negotiations regarding the meaning ascribed to development aid. Similarly, while recipient participation is one of the main interpretative repertoires in the policy documents, the interviewees' reflections on their roles and functions indicate how donor representation, and thus donor participation, is clearly also part of the moral discourse of NDA.

6 Motivation

For four years I have, relatively systematically, asked experts,
aid workers, relief workers, and missionaries about their motives.
Why did you go to Africa? Except for the latter,
almost none have indicated reasons anywhere near
what is stated in the mission statements
of the organisations they are affiliated with.

Tomm Kristiansen in *Mor Afrika* [Mother Africa], 1994
(Kristiansen 1994:269)

The aim of this chapter is to discuss the interviewees' stated motivation for being involved in development work. It should be noted that this is different from the issue of the justification of development aid. While motivation refers to conscious or unconscious driving forces, justification refers to an articulated explanation or defence. One can distinguish between the motivation development workers have for their choice of career, and the reasons or explanations they give for the same. However, these distinctions are analytical and are not always clearly made by the interviewees.

In the following I will primarily address the issue of individual motivation as this is expressed and discussed by the interviewees. I will firstly analyse how they articulate their motivation for getting involved in development work. Secondly, I will discuss how the interviewees articulate their present motivation, meaning what makes them continue in the line of work and in the positions they have. Thus, while the first section focuses on the past, the second is concerned about present motivation. The interviewees' perception of what initially motivated them to get involved in development work must, however, be understood in light of their retrospective character. When reconstructing one's initial motivation individuals often tend to (over) emphasise continuity, and might tend to romanticise the past.

6.1 Initial motivation

Several factors might have led the individual development worker into this kind of career. Accordingly, when asked why she is involved in this line of work, one of the embassy interviewees in her 30–40s explains extensively how she thinks several factors might have led her in this direction. She says:

> [...] It's probably because for me it has clearly been a personal commitment (*personlig engasjement*) from early on. I think it's a combination of an early fascination in a way [...] It's the pull towards the exotic, a little naïve maybe [...] the pull towards something, towards what is different. That is one thing. And then it has been to me at least a personal commitment related to... could maybe call it solidarity... an idea about solidarity, a kind of desire to use one's energy, competence for something beyond what could have been a different career... a different kind of job that would not have been satisfying in the same way. It's also about a commitment to the world in a way, where things are happening, to be closer to where things are going on. To be in a place where things are happening that seem meaningful. [...] And political and social processes are very complicated things, and they are not one dimensional and on a straight line. So when I see it also as a fascination in a way, there is more of a social science perspective on it. A fascination related to social and political processes. But, no, it's a combination. It's a personal commitment, an academic interest, and a kind of political commitment. [...] So there is a very multi-faceted answer to the question of why I am doing this. But I find that despite all the frustrations, setbacks, and time wasting that we all witness, and the resources that maybe don't end up precisely there and give the results we want and wish to see, it is still a personal commitment. And I think everyone, at least all the colleagues I have here, none of them would say that this is just any other ordinary job. It's kind of... it's difficult to say for everyone, but I think there is an element of... Yes, it is a small calling (*kall*), I think, in this kind of context. And then you can say in a way... you can give this calling different interpretations: political, humanitarian, religious, moral... but it is a kind of calling that drives you.

Explaining her involvement in development aid this interviewee refers to a combination of 'personal commitment, an academic interest, and a kind of political commitment'. The personal commitment is something she returns to several times ('pull towards the exotic', 'an idea about solidarity'), and she seems also to emphasise the same in her concluding reflection on 'a kind of calling that drives you'. However, this also seems to be something she regards as an initial motivation. What this interviewee says about professional interest ('social science perspective') and political commitment ('commitment to the world') seem closely related to her personal commitment, but highlight different aspects. Note how she finds development work to be a difficult field with both 'set-backs, and time wasting'. As a professional she seems, however, to find this complexity fascinating. Her highlighting of how she finds it 'meaningful' to use her 'competence for something beyond what could have been a different career' seems to suggest this is a motivating fascination. This fascination seems then to constitute a present motivation. Note also how this interviewee reflects on her colleagues' motives for being involved in this line of work. She thinks that 'none of them would say that this is just any other ordinary job'. Thus, this interviewee seems to highlight the unique character of being a development worker.

6.1.1 Early experiences

To one of the SCN interviewees in her 50–60s the entry into development work represents a marked career change and a break with the past. She says she became aware of a vacancy notice and realised that she wanted to spend her life on something other than 'satisfying the shareholders'. She adds:

> [...] Plus, I must admit that when I was working very hard at home, and never knew if I was waking up in Aberdeen, or if I was waking up in London or if I was in Amsterdam, because all the hotels were the same, and all the bars the same, and all the restaurants the same. And when I got up in the morning I asked myself: 'where am I now?', then I wanted to try something else. That is how it happened.

Explaining why she became a development worker, one of the SCN interviewees in her 40–50s describes a specific encounter with Third World poverty that made her morally outraged. She says:

> [...] it's crazy how the Western world can exploit people's poverty and ignorance in such an incredibly grotesque way as Nestlé's breast feeding substitution campaigns did. So I returned and decided that I had to get a kind of education that would enable me to work with these issues. [...] That was the reason. It was a kind of direct intervention (*direkte intervensjon*).

A political analysis is here combined with a specific personal experience that leads this development worker into the field. She criticises the 'Western world' and points to macro political issues.

To others, the way into development work represents more of a continuum than a break. For some, their upbringing seems to have played an important role. Explaining why she is comfortable working in development aid, one of the NCA interviewees in her 30–40s says: 'Aid is to me something that has been discussed at the dinner table all my life'. However, when asked to elaborate she also says: 'The other side of it is that I didn't like living in Norway. I didn't like coming back to Norway; it wasn't home to me…' Thus, to this interviewee the motivation to enter into the field of development work seems to be derived from both push and pull factors.

The influence of (radical) politics or of home-coming missionaries certainly seems to have been important to some of the interviewees. Explaining why she became a development worker, one of the NCA interviewees in her 40–50s refers to her radical past as well as meetings with missionaries and their tales from the mission field. She says:

> […] Well, I started with solidarity work when I was very young, and started with… Well, very early in life I had visits from missionaries in Madagascar. And already at that time […] I learnt about a world out there that fascinated me. So very early on I was motivated to learn more about it: What is this? There were stories and tales from missions that were very fascinating.

Asked about her motivation, one of the SCN interviewees in her 30–40s similarly refers to her teenage years in Norway. She says:

> If I were to explain further why I began thinking about working in this field, it was because I felt I was born with privileges. I am born with lots of opportunities in a country where I have never suffered. Already as a teenager I felt this gave me a responsibility. That I should use it in a way… Yes, that was probably the starting point for my beginning.

To this interviewee, realising the privileges and opportunities that follow from growing up in, and being a citizen of, a rich country, seems to have given her a sense of responsibility and motivation to work with development issues.

One of the embassy interviewees in her 50–60s, on the other hand, highlights a professional career path that has led her into this field. She says:

> [...] When you are working at a general policy level, then it's very interesting to see how work is done in the field. What are we actually doing? How are we implementing our development aid policy in a country like for example [country]? So that is why I have also involved myself a good deal in the work we are doing...

Here, it is the professional interest in the field that the interviewee uses to explain her route into the implementing part of development aid. The entry into the development field is not from an entirely different field or context for one's professional work, but rather a continued involvement in the field of development policy, away from a 'general policy level' and towards the implementing level.

Others quite clearly state that, to a large extent, it was coincidence that led them into this field of work. Reflecting on an expatriate career that started more than 30 years ago, one of the NCA interviewees in her 50–60s says: 'So it's maybe more of a coincidence, and so it just turned out this way. It was not planned when I left. I was very young when I left'. An embassy interviewee in her 50–60s is quite explicit on the character of her career path. She says: 'My way into aid was a coincidence, not a conscious choice'.[8]

Still, that the motivation for development work has roots in their childhood or early adult life is something several of these interviewees explicitly articulate. This can be seen as an example of how they construct continuity or tend to romanticise their past.

6.1.2 Adventurism and idealism

Early experiences of international work also seem to have led many of the interviewees into the field of development work. Asked to reflect on

8 While some of the interviewees find that their way into aid had been more or less a coincidence, some find that in the present situation their options are limited. Some of the interviewees have been involved in development aid work for decades. Aid work has become their career. One of the embassy interviewees in her 50–60s says: 'The last few years you could say there has been no other way. You have sort of chosen'.

why she became a development worker, one of the NCA interviewees in her 40–50s says:

> The first international experience came when I was an exchange student, when I was in high school. [...] When I was in high school, this was the radical period, and ideas about solidarity were pretty strong. [...] And I think that in the beginning, well, I don't think my motivation was to save the world, at least not when I came to the point of applying to Norwegian Church Aid. But I think I had an understanding of... that there was an idealistic attitude involved, clearly, that kind of motivation. Another thing, I think, was this thing about the unknown, experiencing what is different. And the third, I believe, was the professional challenge in it. And it probably was a certain mix, and what was stronger or weaker in the beginning, I cannot say too much about, but it was a combination, clearly. [...] But after four years I said: 'No, this will be a change of career.' Then the professional part of it started to fascinate me in a strong way, and to challenge me strongly.

Three aspects are highlighted here: 1) the idealistic notion of wanting to 'save the world', 2) experiencing something different (adventurism), and 3) the professional challenge. While idealism can be said to relate to an Other-oriented attitude, the latter two are in a sense first person oriented. This interviewee wants to experience something new, and the professional challenge must here be understood as a challenge she is motivated to take on and make her own. In other words, there are different kinds of motives here, and they are in part diametrically opposed to each other. This, however, does not exclude the possibility that all factors were at work, as this interviewee claims. She refrains, however, from speculating on the relationship between them.

To other interviewees adventurism seems to have been the primary driving force. One of the embassy interviewees in her 50–60s says: 'So all in all, the motivation was adventurism and a [life-partner] who wanted to see more of the world'. Another embassy interviewee in her 50–60s says:

> [...] You could say that I was interested in the world around me. I travelled first to Europe, especially Western Europe, and when I had seen Europe I became curious about the world outside Europe.

Here, the adventurism is explicitly oriented towards areas outside Europe. The same interviewee also explains how she did not have a religious motivation, but rather one based on the idea of human rights. She says: 'I was concerned with human rights, to do something about this and the unjust distribution in the world'. The way this interviewee describes her motivation makes it reasonable to call it an ethical motivation. Two elements are emphasised: human rights and unjust distribution. Some combine this kind of ethical motivation with a notion of having a calling. One of the NCA interviewees in her 50–60s says:

> The reason why I do this work is connected to the fact that I grew up in [country], and that I have acquired an interest in doing something for [country] and the [nationality] people. And that is the driving force, together with the calling (*kall*) that I feel I have from God, to let me be used within mission and church in this country.

Again, however, several motivating elements are mentioned. In this case too there is no single motivation. Note also how a divine calling is seemingly not seen as contradictory to, but rather in line with, a driving force based on upbringing and personal interest.

Several of the interviewees mention their idealistic motivation. One of the SCN interviewees in her 30–40s puts it this way: 'But I have always had a heart for doing something for the underprivileged, I always wanted to do something like that'. Note the terminology used here. The interviewee speaks of her motivation as one of having 'a heart' and the recipient is described as 'underprivileged'. Note further the repeated emphasis on this as a lasting motivation – this is something she has 'always wanted to do'. Similarly, one of the NPA interviewees in her 30–40s says:

> Yes, it probably was an idealistic position (*idealistisk ståsted*) at the outset. Because I… I think I chose it consciously or subconsciously when I started studying, in a way. The studies […] were sort of idealistic. It's, in addition to a more sort of private driving force like adventurism and the like… it's also a sort of idealism, and to me also a political background in a way. That is probably why I am with the Norwegian People's Aid and not one of the others, right now anyway.

Three elements of the initial motivation are highlighted here. Idealism seems to have been important both directly and indirectly in determining her field of study. Next, here too adventurism is mentioned. This interviewee, however, adds a third element: her 'political background'. Note how this is seen as an explanation for this interviewee's relation to NPA, and not one of the other organisations (see sections 4.4 and 7.4). Thus, it seems that the perceived identity of the organisation is in line with how this development worker perceives herself.

6.2 Present motivation

In the same way that the interviewees point to different factors leading them into development aid, they also refer to a number of factors motivating them to keep working in this field. Asked about her present motivation, one of the NCA interviewees in her 40–50s says:

> [...] I think it's satisfying (*givende*). I find it's very educating. I have travelled a lot. I have been to many places. But I still find it educational, as it gives me... well, it means a lot to me to live and work in Africa, or to live and work in Asia, or in South America. So it's more that, yes, I feel self-conscious about what I do. And I feel pretty certain when we talk about issues like aid and relief and development, of what kinds of tools should be used and what one does as a humanitarian worker. And what one should have as a basis for getting the job done. I feel relatively certain, and when I feel this certain, that's a good motivation for staying on. And I get quite a lot done. Well, we have good results. And we achieve a lot of the targets we set, simply to help others. And that is a good feeling. Well, so... It's comfortable to live and work here. I enjoy it. I actually enjoy living in [country] more than living in Norway. Not for ever, but for periods. That is probably my main motivation, I think.

Not surprisingly, several elements from the discussion on work satisfaction in the previous chapter are repeated here (see section 5.2.4). This interviewee mentions the joy of living and working in Africa, the sense of doing a good job, knowing the trade, achieving good results, and finally the personal quality of life. Similarly, one of the NPA interviewees in her 30–40s talks about a 'private motivation' and how the family can 'experience things they would not experience at home'.

Asked what motivates her, one of the NCA interviewees in her 30–40s says:

> I think I should be honest enough to say that this is in a way first of all an experience that I want to have. I learn a lot. And I feel privileged to have great colleagues and very exciting and meaningful tasks. So I would not continue here if I didn't think the job was exciting and varied and challenging. [...] And I think maybe it's a

> very meaningful setting. I question a lot of what we do, but I see that very much of what we do means a lot to individuals, and also to local communities and to organisations here in [country]. So that is motivating.

This interviewee too articulates several positive aspects of the work she does. Firstly, she sees this as a good experience for herself. The introductory note about being honest indicates that what the interviewee goes on to say is something she might not express (as clearly or in the same way) in public. The reason for this might be that the first element of her motivation is an egoistic motivation. This job can give her something she wants for herself. Some of the other elements that she mentions might be regarded as belonging to the same category. She finds her work 'exciting' and 'challenging'. Towards the end of this statement, however, her explanation of her motivation takes another direction, as she reflects on what her work means to others. She recognises the difficulties involved in development aid, but holds on to a conviction that it does make a difference. Again, result satisfaction seems important. Note also how she specifies that these are results 'to individuals' and 'to local communities and to organisations' (see section 9.6). It should be noted, however, that being motivated by factors that the individual finds satisfying or inspiring to herself should not be taken as egoism. Realising one's abilities and interests can be combined with concern for the Other. Personal and professional satisfaction are accordingly not necessarily contrary to result satisfaction.

As noted above, several of the interviewees refer to their idealism as one of the reasons for entering the field of development work. This also becomes the context for their reflections on what motivates them now. One of the SCN interviewees in her 30–40s clearly articulates her personal idealistic motivation for being involved in international aid. When asked why she is doing development work, she says:

> [...] The starting point to me was that I was an idealist, and wanted to do something to make a better world. But that is not something one thinks about on a daily basis. [...] But that is what has led me into this work. I can see how it's still important to me that I must feel that what I do is meaningful. I do this because it's meaningful work. I feel that I... One might become less of an idealist as one gains experience, but at the same time that is the driving force.

When asked to say more about her present motivation, however, she puts her answer differently. She says: 'I have become more realistic. The ideals are still there, but I think I have become more of a realist. I see… I am not as naïve, luckily, as when I started'. This interviewee seems to argue that the idealism that initially motivated her still is part of her motivation, in the sense that she still sees her work as 'important' and as 'meaningful'. However, the contrast to idealism, which she identifies as realism, now takes a more prominent place. In the latter comment, idealism is also related to naivety. It seems that this is the aspect of idealism that she has distanced herself from. She is now 'less of an idealist' than before, but the work still remains important and meaningful to her.

The local working conditions also motivate this interviewee. When asked about the frustrating aspects of her work, she returns to the issue of motivating factors. She says:

> […] It's really important that we have good partners here locally, and that we have good staff here locally which is motivating, and makes you feel that we manage to make things happen. I think that both this programme and other programmes have periods where things go up, and other periods where things go down. And now we are in an upturn period. And then it's really exciting to be part of it, and really motivating to watch. We have partners at the regional level who are very open minded and innovative, and who really want to achieve something. And then it's really fun to do this work.

Notice how this interviewee relates her motivation to local partners and local staff. These are evaluated as good, and their abilities seem to be important with regard to the results they are able to bring about. And, not surprisingly, what she sees as good work is motivating in itself (professional satisfaction).

6.2.1 Important results

The positive changes in the lives of individual recipients and beneficiaries of development aid seem to be an important motivating factor to several of the interviewees. Asked to explain what she means by characterising her work as 'meaningful', one of the SCN interviewees in her 30–40s says:

> […] I could tell you the story about a small project that we have developed and which now has become part of the education strategy for a region […], and that is

> meaningful. That we have managed to help them find a way to expand the education system in the region so that a lot more children get education […] And it's meaningful at a personal level, when you hear stories from individuals who have managed to change their lives. Girls who get the opportunity to go to school, and when parents try to have them married, they refuse and stay in school and continue their education. There are individual stories, and they are important. I think they are very important, also these stories about individuals and that the work we have done has changed their lives.

Here too the individual recipients are emphasised. This interviewee finds the works she does meaningful at a 'personal level' because of 'stories from individuals'. Still, there is a shift of emphasis. Here this interviewee stresses the numbers of individuals that benefit from the development aid programmes she is involved in. The impact is discussed as a function of the changes it implies for individuals, but the emphasis is on the aggregate effect of this.

This role of results is a feature several interviewees mention, and it corresponds to a concern for achieving results articulated also in some of the policy documents (for example Ministry of Foreign Affairs 2002b). One of the SCN interviewees in her 50–60s highlights the important role that achievements, despite limited resources, play in motivating her in her work. In the context of discussing her motivation, she says:

> […] The more we are able to push in the same direction and have the same goals, and manage it with the funds we have, the more children we help. And if I can contribute to ensuring that Save the Children Norway supports twice as many children, then I think that would be fantastic. And that has been one of the driving forces for me, very exciting.

Note how this interviewee speaks primarily in easily quantifiable terms. She talks about helping 'more children' and 'twice as many children'. Again, the emphasis is on the aggregated number of individuals.[9]

9 Similarly, when asked about her present motivation, another of the SCN interviewees in her 30–40s says: 'What motivates me today is some of the changes you see in peoples' lives. The number of children, like where we work with basic education, that might not have had that kind of opportunity to be in a classroom and to learn some things. So when you see some of those changes in their lives, and that they are learning something which will be useful, and they can be better people, they can be useful to people, that kind of motivates me. […] And I kind of feel I am making a contribution to staff as well, who then, eventually, should be reaching out to the people we work with. And in a way, when I get that kind of feedback, it kind

Several of the interviewees see their jobs and their line of work as something special and a privilege. Asked why she continues in this line of work, one of the embassy interviewees in her 50–60s says:

> It's a privilege to work with these things. Most people have trivial jobs, and this one I don't perceive as trivial. So it's something about… You get a job you enjoy, and try maybe other jobs, and see that this is more interesting.

The perception of working with development aid as a 'privilege' and not something 'trivial' indicates that something about it is important. What specifically makes it a privilege and not trivial, is not articulated. However, the fact that the work is somehow important is also something other interviewees highlight. One of the SCN interviewees in her 40–50s expresses an understanding of development work as a special field. Explaining her present motivation, she says:

> […] What really motivates me today is that I find that these issues about children and children's rights are extremely important, and that I have the kind of training and background that makes it possible for me to contribute so that one maybe in the future can change some things.

This interviewee relates her motivation to the importance she attaches to children's rights. It seems also that she is motivated by what she sees as her ability to assist and 'change some things'. Similarly, and responding to the same question, one of the NPA interviewees in her 30–40s says: '[…] it is the improvements that I find stimulating and that motivate me'.

Also responding to the question of how she became a development worker, one of the NCA interviewees in her 50–60s says:

> […] This is what I know, and I enjoy what I do. I believe in what I do. Even if one can ask a lot of questions: What have we achieved during all these years? But, if one doesn't have faith, then… then there is sort of no meaning, and one has to, the way I see it: You cannot change the world, but you can maybe do a little. I believe it's… What you can do is to help a little, and anything is better than nothing, and you have to start somewhere. And one has seen results, even though it's maybe more visible in the small and close things (*i det små og det nære*), the places you

---

of also gives me energy. And what makes me, in terms of continuing to do this work. You know, this work is not very easy. At times it's very frustrating. In terms of, you know, the kind of results you see, it doesn't come that easily. It's hard work, you have to be patient. It's the long-term kind of result that one has to look at'.

> work with. But when you see… Everybody knows that poverty is increasing, and all that. But still, one cannot be stopped by that.

To this interviewee, development work is what she knows and enjoys. And an important element in her present motivation seems to be faith in what she does. Despite signs that point in another direction this interviewee appears to hold firmly to the conviction that aid brings about results, at least 'in the small and close things'. Note again the combination of optimism and pessimism. Results at the local level are not doubted. Any improvement in the overall picture seems to be regarded as a different case.

6.2.2 Aversion and feedback

When asked about her initial motivation, one of the NPA interviewees in her 30–40s says:

> […] And we have travelled and seen a lot, and I have always felt very comfortable with it. And the more I have travelled the more narrow-minded I have found it at home. […] And this narrow mindedness, it is that I… I am blinded when I am at home, seeing how great the ignorance is and that they don't care about and don't think a little further about the damned terrible conditions other people live in. And it is the small things, like the level of prices in Norway. And when you see that five times a day, a colleague comes in with a bottle of coke that costs 25 kroner in the store, and I ask, have you thought about what it would cost if you bought a bigger bottle? 'No, I haven't thought about that.' 'But can't you do that for a week, and then you put the money aside.' It's such a waste (*sløseri*), it's a huge waste. And when I say this, it isn't because I sit on a moral high ground, because I too live with a Western background, and of course, I too like to go to the store and buy nice clothes. But still I find there should be some nuances, a kind of making a nuance (*en viss nyansering*) of one's life, sort of. And it's stimulating to me to be in an environment where I have like-minded people around me. And you find that in the aid community.

While several interviewees refer to a negative motivation based on witnessing the plight of poor people in other countries, the emphasis here is different. The source of the motivation lies here in her evaluation of Norwegian society. She seems to relate her motivation to a kind of disgust with experiences at home. The more she has travelled (to other countries), the 'more narrow-minded' she has found it 'at home'. In her elaboration of this narrow mindedness she points to 'ignorance', how too many people 'don't care about and don't think a little further about the damned terrible conditions other people live in', and the 'huge waste'. All these can be considered push-factors. Note how this interviewee, however, also stresses how she does not want to 'sit on a moral high ground'. While she does want to criticise the 'waste', she still does 'go to the store and buy nice clothes'. It is not an ascetic lifestyle she is prescribing. What she does call for is, however, a certain balance (see section 15.1).

Finally, note also the satisfaction this interviewee finds in having 'like-minded' people around her, something the development aid field can provide for her. Asked to elaborate on her present motivation, the same interviewee says:

> [...] In part it's working with people who are like-minded. And well, there is not only that kind of people, but for example [name] and I have worked together extremely well and had very good discussions. I have no sort of naïve illusions about making everything good in the world and that there will be peace and so on. But I think we can make it a little better. And that drives me... that I always want to see people's situation improve. [...]. So it's also stimulating when you feel that you can make a difference.

Having colleagues she enjoys working with is clearly important to this interviewee. Notice how she points out how she has no 'naïve illusions' and how she downplays the role and effect of development aid. Again NDA is seen as a tool that makes matters just 'a little better'. Similarly, one of the SCN interviewees in her 50–60s finds working with partners motivating. Referring to one of the partner organisations, she says:

> [...] And I have never seen such a good response, and had feedback like this on these things that we have done collectively, so I would say to them and also to the political leadership, that as long as they keep me happy, and that means following the guidelines that we have agreed upon, then I am motivated to raise more money.

Note that while this statement is put forward with enthusiasm for the partnership and the results achieved, there is a causal link that is also expressed. As long as the partner keeps the interviewee 'happy' she will be 'motivated to raise more money'.

6.3 Concluding reflections

To summarise, the interviewees' accounts of their motivation for entering into the field of development work vary from a notion of divine calling and the influence of an adventurous life-partner, to coincidental job offers. A number of the interviewees refer to their past (and present) idealism when they explain their route into aid work. Other interviewees seem to want to distance themselves from too idealistic motives. Another recurring theme is their early international experience, often related to the general political climate of their youth. To some of the interviewees the story of how they came to work in the development field is also a story of a break with a previous and different career path.

Regarding their present motivation there are also various accounts given, but some elements are recurring. Several of the interviewees say they enjoy their work. Many of them find the work they do interesting, meaningful, or challenging. Further, it seems most of them find these challenges inspiring. Among some of the older interviewees who have several years of experience in the field, the feeling of mastering this kind of work seems to add to their professional satisfaction.

Some of the interviewees who mention idealism as one motive for entering the field of development work adjust this notion when they describe their present motivation and self-understanding. The initial idealism does not always last. These reflections resonate with the discussions between political realism and idealism on development aid in general (see section 3.2.1). Most of the interviewees, however, articulate continuity between the initial motivation they had for entering the field of development work and their present motivation.

In several statements the development workers' motivation is expressed with a reference to others, for example the poor, partners, colleagues, etc. This highlights the importance of context and the relational aspect of the moral discourse on these issues. Thus these statements also indicate a link between the relationships the development workers see themselves as part of and the motivation they have for the work they do. Several of the interviewees say they are motivated by the results of their work and seem in this implicitly to respond to some of the critics of development aid (see sections 3.2.4 and 9.6). As the results are seen as important to someone (the recipients, the poor), their work is perceived as 'meaningful'. Further, motivation is also seen as a function of the differences between the rich (Norwegians) and the poor (see section 3.1), as well as of the relationship with 'like-minded' colleagues.

Two features in particular noted in this chapter add to the impression of the moral discourse of NDA. Firstly, while some of the policy documents of the aid agencies come across as largely idealistic, the notion of idealism is something the interviewees relate to in different and nuanced ways. Some downplay their idealistic motivation, others emphasise their realistic expectations regarding development aid, while arguing that they have retained their initial idealistic motivation. In other words, the meaning and role of idealism seems to be discursively negotiated. Secondly, the emphasis on results points to the importance of this repertoire for many of the interviewees.

7 Working for an agency

Development professionals have, almost all of us,
become caught in the evolution of a set of increasingly self-serving structures
whose imperatives, stakes, and incentives have snuck up on us,
sometimes so quietly that we have not noticed.

Thomas W. Dichter in *Despite Good Intentions* (Dichter 2003:xiii)

The interviewees in this study are all employed by aid agencies, and this chapter will focus on how they understand the institutional context of their work. This implies discussing both MFA and the distinctive traits of the different NGOs. As the experience and understanding of NDA is shaped by the specific institutional context, I will in the following discuss the selected agencies respectively, letting the interviewees of the different agencies comment on their own organisations. Again I begin with MFA, and turn subsequently to the three NGOs.

7.1 The Norwegian state (MFA)

The role of the Norwegian embassy in a given country is quite different from and broader than the role of Norwegian NGOs (see section 3.2.3 and chapter 4). Explaining her professional background and work experience, one of the embassy interviewees in her 50–60s states:

> […] But an embassy must look after all things, all relations with governments, be it aid, politics or social issues, and so on, also reporting and business contacts and things like that. So my role is, and has always been, an integrated part. Also here my main job is development aid, but I must frequently attend political meetings and organise political meetings, so the emphasis is on that. But things are closely connected, and we see also how Norwegian development policy is more and more closely tied up with foreign policy, and that is reflected here too.

Emphasis is here on how development aid and politics are 'closely connected' (see section 9.3), and how embassy staff consequently are involved in more than development aid projects (in a stricter sense of the term). However, it is worth noting how the work in some embassies also can be distinguished from the work of Norwegian embassies in other countries. One of the embassy interviewees in her 30–40s explains: 'This is a development aid embassy, and our tasks are relatively different from the tasks MFA personnel working in Brussels or Bonn have…'.

7.1.1 *The small state's self-interest*

Reflecting on the obligations of the Norwegian state, one of the embassy interviewees in her 50–60s highlights Norway's small state status. She says:

> […] As a small country we are dependent on other countries abiding by their international obligations (*internasjonale forpliktelser*), either with respect to development aid or in other ways. And then it's very important that we do so ourselves. We are ourselves dependent on others… since Norway is a small country… that we have an international order that works.

Interpreting Norwegian foreign policy on the basis of the small state vs. superpower dichotomy is a well established perspective in various analyses of Norwegian foreign policy (see section 3.3.1). A key element in such an analysis is often the same as the one emphasised in this statement: the interest small states have in an 'international order that works'. The fact that Norway lives up to its 'international obligations' is often regarded as a corollary of having this interest, as any other practice would undermine Norwegian efforts and appeals to others to abide by and fulfil similar obligations. To the extent that providing foreign aid is regarded as an international obligation, it will accordingly be in Norway's national interest to provide such aid.

Although there is a political aspect to Norwegian development work, this interviewee still emphasises that there are no hidden agendas in Norwegian development work. She says:

> […] large actors have a lot of different agendas. But we, at least when we have entered into peace processes and things like that, and such contacts, then… then we have been able to do this because we have no other larger ambitions, what I call a

political agenda. We have no hidden agendas or considerations or aims. That is in a way why we have been able to do what we did in the Middle East, and why we are involved in Sri Lanka, to the extent that is possible.[10] It's because we have no superpower ambitions, and we are no superpower either, that we have been able to do this.[11]

Again the small state perspective frames this interviewee's perception of Norwegian aid. She dismisses that there are any hidden wishes, considerations, or aims. In other words, the role of self-interest in NDA is downplayed.

However, when one of the embassy interviewees in her 50–60s reflects on the idealism of her employer, the Norwegian state, she points to a tension between recipient interests and domestic interests in the donor country. Asked to elaborate, she says:

> […] I choose to put it this way: the state is not an easy employer (*oppdragsgiver*) for people with a heart, because from time to time you may feel that part of what we do is maybe justified by short sighted political agendas aimed at the domestic market (*hjemmemarkedet*). You do things that have an impact on the Third World, on our cooperating partners, which are more suited to satisfying the domestic market than our partners. This has several aspects. One of them is what I would call the real aspect, which concerns ensuring the settlement pattern in Norway, that there is agriculture… that we have a system of agricultural subsidies, that I agree with, in the sense that a country must be allowed to have such arrangements. […] Another thing which is more short sighted and political, is that some interest groups put pressure on, and that can have various consequences. That is also part of my daily work. And everyone who has worked at an embassy has from time to time felt that some decisions, some directions that have come from the political leadership, are more the result of a need to be visible, a more short sighted need for increased support. Sometimes the reason is only to be in the limelight, and there has to be a new initiative every year, right? 'What are we to come up with this year?'

The professional work of 'people with a heart' is here seen as dependent on the extent to which the overall policy is aimed at the good of the

10 The interviewee seems here to refer to the Norwegian government's peace mediating efforts in the Middle East and Sri Lanka.

11 One of the SCN interviewees in her 50–60s describes Norway in a similar way. She says: 'First of all, Norway is considered as a relatively neutral country. We don't come with hidden agendas. They are generally open and honest in what they do, and Norwegians are maybe naively a bit straight forward. […] And with respect to trust, we create that too. And we are not large and threatening as a nation. We are maybe a bit naïve sometimes, but…'

recipients of development aid. And to this interviewee this is clearly not always the case. This stems from the fact that there are also other concerns involved. Dividing these in two, she speaks of the real concerns on the one hand, and short-term political concerns on the other. While the first is considered legitimate, the second is more populistic. In other words, there is a wide range of different concerns that stems not from the concerns of the recipients, but rather from the concerns of the donor.[12]

Discussing the relationship between Norwegian interests and recipient country interests, one of the embassy interviewees in her 30–40s says:

> [...] So in that sense we are put here to manage Norwegian interests (*forvalte norske interesser*), that is Norwegian defined priorities, with respect to the co-operation with [country]. At the same time, a lot of the work we do here also benefits the [nationality] civil society. I cannot say anything else. And I actually believe it. It's not something I just say, but I actually believe it does.

Working for the embassy, this interviewee sees her work as managing 'Norwegian interests', meaning 'Norwegian defined priorities'. Being employed at a Norwegian embassy, this is in line with how the role of a state's foreign mission is often perceived. As such this is not a surprising response. However, she also insists that the work benefits the recipient country. She repeats and explicitly denies this is something she 'just says', and insists on being trusted on this issue.

7.1.2 Colleagues' motivation

Explaining how she understands development work as a profession, one of the embassy interviewees in her 50–60s says:

> [...] But if we go back in time, and look at what kind of commitment we could maybe see in the old NORAD twenty years ago, then the motives for working with aid were... stronger in the way that one sort of... yes, what should I say... yes, you

12 The same interviewee continues: 'We are not the ones who should define and make the order of priorities. At the same time we have about twenty different strategies to relate to. There are indigenous peoples, female genital mutilation, agricultural strategies, strategies for health and education, etc. So we have a bag full of good intentions that to a large extent is difficult to fit into the other picture, which is home based'.

were more concerned about what you thought you could accomplish, and characterised by solidarity, and very critical of all this Norwegian interfering in development policy. It was untimely. That Norway had its own motives in the aid dimension, was something one couldn't speak about. Today, we speak openly about it. Today, it's at least a reality. At that time, no.[13]

Comparing the present situation with the situation 20 years ago, this interviewee seems to highlight two characteristics. Firstly, that the commitment at that time was 'characterised by solidarity', and secondly that Norwegian 'motives in the aid dimension' were excluded from the hegemonic discourse. This latter aspect seems then to rely on a perceived distinction between Norwegian aid policy and other kinds of politics. When Norwegian motives were excluded, it seems that the understanding of 'development policy' was understood in contrast to foreign policy, where the former is Other-oriented and the latter concerns Norwegian self-interest. Regarding the present discourse, however, this interviewee perceives the discourse to be of a different character. Norwegian self-interest motives are now part of the discourse (see section 9.4).

One of the embassy interviewees in her 30–40s reflects on the question of her colleagues' motivation in this way:

> [...] If you put this question to people in the ministry or NORAD or here at the embassy: Why are you here, why do you do what you do? ... then I think that some, after reflecting on empathy or something like that, solidarity, commitment, that such things will be a personal driving force. But it's a personal driving force, it's not transformed into a... I wouldn't say it's not transformed, that isn't correct, but it's not found in the bureaucratic or development aid policy discourse, you know.

This quote is interesting in at least two respects. Firstly, note how a distinction is made between a 'personal driving force' and a 'bureaucratic or development aid policy discourse' where the personal driving force finds no expression. In part this distinction seems to rely on the

13 Regarding the issue of self-interest, one of the embassy interviewees in her 50–60s uses Gunnar Garbo (a journalist, politician for the Liberal Party of Norway (*Venstre*) and former ambassador to Tanzania) as an example of one who became too other-focused. She says: 'It was said that he couldn't stay in Tanzania any more, because he had become more Tanzanian than Norwegian. "He forgets to further Norwegian interests, he only furthers Tanzanian interests." And of course, that was how development aid was in the old days'.

content of the driving force, which she identifies as empathy, solidarity, or commitment. Secondly, this interviewee argues that these notions do not find expression in the wider discourse she refers to. Accordingly, this interviewee finds a discontinuity between MFA's discourse on NDA and the discourse on personal motivation among MFA staff. One example of this might be the concept of solidarity. While the previous interviewee argues that the motives for working with aid 'twenty years ago' were 'characterised by solidarity', this latter interviewee believes solidarity might still be a 'personal driving force', but not found in the 'development aid policy discourse' (see section 11.3). The latter point seems to have been confirmed in the analysis of MFA's policy documents above (see section 4.1).

7.2 Church based (NCA)

Having discussed the embassy interviewees' perception of working for the MFA, I now turn to the NGOs, starting with NCA.

When asked why she ended up working for NCA, one of the NCA interviewees in her 40–50s says:

> Norwegian Church Aid, Red Cross, Save the Children Norway, Norwegian Refugee Council, and Norwegian People's Aid are sort of the same corporation. In general they work according to the same principles. They are a bit like different departments, and have somewhat different ways of working, but as Norwegian private organisations they are in the same category. And that it is specifically Norwegian Church Aid is a bit of a coincidence. Both with my situation, and it suited well that I took… […] But in that sense it could just as well have been the Red Cross or… So it's more of a coincidence.

This interviewee highlights the similarities between the different NGOs, and seems to regard it as coincidental that she has ended up working for the NCA. Thus she draws the main dividing line not between different NGOs, but first of all between the NGOs and state actors. And when one of the NCA interviewees in her 30–40s compares the organisation's role to that of the embassy, she says:

> […] I think that as a voluntary organisation you can perhaps operate more freely than as the Norwegian embassy in [country]. … I think it must be different for them to answer questions about self-interest and the Norwegian state's interests, because they operate in a different context. They are supposed to serve the king and country. I don't think I do that.

This interviewee articulates an understanding of the NGOs as somewhat more independent than the embassies. While the embassies are compelled to 'serve the king and country', this is not so in the case of NGOs. The issue of self-interest and Norwegian state interests is perceived as different in the two contexts. Accordingly, it seems this interviewee understands the moral commitment of embassy employees to be limited by the institutional context in a way that is different from the NGO context. While embassies must take self-interest into account, this is not so in the case of NGOs. As noted in the previous section, however, some of the embassy interviewees seem to downplay the contrast between Norwegian interests and the interests of the recipient countries.

When one of the NCA interviewees in her 50–60s is asked to compare the different organisations, she too highlights the similarities. She says:

> I think that the fundamental principles are relatively similar, across the different aid agencies. But it is clear that as a church based organisation, Norwegian Church Aid has some additional values based on the Christian faith. At least that is how it should be…

Initially, this interviewee stresses the similarities of different aid agencies. But on the other hand, as it is church based NCA is distinct. Interestingly, she adds: 'At least that is how it should be…', this latter comment perhaps indicating that she does not find that this is in fact the case. In other words, the distinctiveness derived from the religious basis for the organisation is contested (see section 4.2).

7.2.1 Mission and diaconal service

The difference between NCA and mission organisations can be articulated in different ways. Asked to explain how she understands this distinction, one of the NCA interviewees in her 50–60s says:

> You could put it this way, that many mission organisations do a lot of what Norwegian Church Aid also does, by being involved in aid work at different levels. But Norwegian Church Aid doesn't do what the mission organisations do through evangelisation and preaching.

According to this interviewee then, NCA specialises in a specific field while mission organisations have a wider mandate. One of the NCA interviewees in her 40–50s explains the difference between NCA and the mission organisations in a similar way, though more comprehensively. She says:

> [...] If you see the church as a house, then we enter into this house. And if you say that the church is a totality with responsibility for the whole human being, from the spiritual through evangelisation and to the diaconal, to the social beyond the purely individual and local, let us call it prophetic diaconate (*profetisk diakonat*). If mission enters through the evangelisation door, some would say yes, but it goes beyond that. It goes into the diaconal. But very rarely do you see that mission goes from there to what we call the prophetic diaconate. We enter let us say from the diaconal and the prophetic diaconate, and touch but don't exclude the spiritual. So at the core of what the church is, we have an overlap (*en overlappingsflate*) with what mission does and what we do. But, then we have fields where we are more heavily involved, and fields where mission is stronger. And this is our field. And we don't say that there is a contradiction in this, but it's something that has to do with entering into an understanding of the totality, which we at least like to think that the churches have.

This interviewee identifies an area that NCA does not share with (most) mission organisations, what she labels 'prophetic diaconate'. By qualifying the diaconate as prophetic diaconate, a more political understanding of the organisation and its mandate seems also to be articulated. Elaborating further on this issue, this interviewee also stresses the organisational similarity with other aid agencies. She says:

> And of course, but obviously, the fact that we define ourselves as Norwegian Church Aid also implies that we indicate that we have a spiritual side that goes beyond the purely philosophical, ethical. [...] But fundamentally, there is nothing called specifically Christian ethics, right, and consequently you don't have to make those artificial distinctions.

When reflecting on this distinct aspect of the organisation, this interviewee interprets this aspect of NCA in a way that downplays its distinctiveness. Having acknowledged first a 'spiritual side' of the organisation, she moves on to reject the notion that there is a distinctively Christian ethic. In what sense the Christian basis of the organisation then would imply a distinctively Christian rationale for the organisation's work remains unclear.

7.2.2 *Words and deeds*

A characteristic of NCA that distinguishes it from other aid agencies is its choice of partners. One of the NCA interviewees in her 50–60s points to the partners as a characteristic of her organisation. She says:

> And then, if you talk about Norwegian Church Aid, which is distinct because we work through the churches, right? Our partners are, where it is possible, church partners. And I think that is very important. We have an amazing network. In a part of the world like Africa especially, where there are churches... The churches are everywhere, on every corner. And when you have this opportunity, then you get a wide range and a large network to interact with. So I find that important.[14]

This interviewee speaks here about the distinctiveness of NCA compared to other development agencies, and says that it is the choice of partners that makes NCA different (see chapter 13). Note also how she clearly evaluates the distinctiveness of the organisation she works for as positive factor. However, comparing her own organisation with other organisations, one of the NCA interviewees in her 30–40s voices a somewhat different opinion. She says:

> [...] And I am not especially proud of all the decisions made in my own organisation. And I feel that the links between the general strategic plans and our value principles, and down to the reality that we relate to, there are quite a lot of missing links, frankly, which I find alarming. And then it's almost even more sickening (*enda kvalmere*) to work for an organisation that calls itself a value based organisation. We talk about building on human dignity, the principle of human dignity that we build on... And then we have a pretty complex idea of it. If you read the last five year plan, for example, Norwegian Church Aid's strategic plan, it's a

14 Another of the NCA interviewees in her 50–60s comments on the same issue in this way: 'Norwegian Church Aid still has a church identity, and should stand up for it. [...] And you could say, yes, by choice of partners... So it's clear that where there are church partners, we choose those. But there are not church partners in all countries, so then you cannot choose it. And then you choose partners that you feel, that you think you can work closely with...'.

> beautiful document. And this I have to say, if that is how we work, it's wonderful. But [...], the way the reality is where I work, it's far from it.

This interviewee points to the way NCA articulates the value basis for its work as something that makes the organisation distinct from others. However, at the practical level she says she is unable to detect any major difference. This is something she also returns to at a later stage in the interview. She says:

> [...] Norwegian Church Aid is one of those that really has worked on a kind of value basis and is concerned about it. But I don't think that is has any consequences for how we do what we do. [...] And then the difference between us and CARE or us and Oxfam or the UN, isn't too big at the end of the day. It's just on a somewhat smaller scale, and then it becomes all the more, yes, embarrassing for me. That is, not towards other people, but for me and my morality and my relationship with God. This is sort of what I do. If you say that you are not even trying, then that is sort of OK...

Note how the organisations she explicitly compares NCA with are not only NGOs, but also the UN. In this context she finds that the efforts put into articulating a value basis for the organisation becomes all the more 'embarrassing' for her personally. She seems to react against a kind of mismatch between words and deeds, maybe between expressed ideology and social practice. It would have been better not to have such an ambitious value basis. By contesting it, the distinctive religious character of NCA is downplayed again.

7.3 Children's rights (SCN)

As noted above, SCN focuses especially on children (see section 4.3). This focus is something SCN shares with for instance UNICEF (<www.unicef.org>), Plan International (<www.plan-international.org>), and other organisations. This seems, however, also to be one of the things that make many of the SCN interviewees evaluate their affiliation with SCN in positive terms. One of the SCN interviewees in her 50–60s says: 'As mentioned, Save the Children Norway is an exciting organisation to work for, because it has given me many opportunities. ... We try to run professionally, and I think that is really important'. Similarly, asked how she finds her work, another SCN interviewees in her 50–60s says:

> I love my work. Otherwise I would have left years ago. I love working… I love the values of the organisation. I think it's a good organisation. Of course, every organisation can always improve, but I think, generally, looking at how the organisation operates, I think it's a good organisation. There is space for people to speak their mind, space for people to try out new things. And you really feel that you are contributing to someone's life, with the kind of work that we do. So it gives you a good inner feeling. You might not get lots of other benefits, like those who are working in industry and all that. But it's the satisfaction of knowing that you have contributed to making a child happy. You have contributed to making a child able to go to school, or preventing abuse, or caring for someone who has been abused. I think that is what keeps us going. For me that is important.

Again an appreciation of the organisation is articulated. In this case too this appreciation relates specifically to SCN, but this interviewee also refers to the results achieved through the work they do. Thus, again, result satisfaction is highlighted.

7.3.1 Quality concerned

Describing an organisation that she finds markedly different from SCN, one of the SCN interviewees in her 50–60s says:

> […] What they call counselling is like the supermarket approach […] you do a bit of counselling, thirty minutes or what ever, it depends on if they have tested, and when they come in to pick up the results, you do another thirty minutes and then goodbye. There is no follow-up. I think that is different from us.

Two expressions this interviewee uses might summarise how she perceives the other organisation: 'supermarket approach' and 'no follow-up'. While efficiency might be a positively loaded word to describe the approach of this other organisation, it seems that her criticism is directed at an approach that is superficial both in terms of time spent and the quality of the work done. There is a lack of analysis of the perceived problems, and the follow-up is very limited. The implied positive evaluation of the work of SCN must then hinge on her perception of it as thorough and of quality, but possibly more time consuming.

In the case of SCN too there are interviewees who stress the traits SCN shares with other aid agencies. When asked if she finds a great difference between her own organisation and the other Norwegian aid agencies, one of the SCN interviewees in her 30–40s says:

> [...] I think there are some organisations that are not as concerned with questioning whether what they do is actually the best they can do for these children. If you question your own methods, and question the consequences, for example of building a small village for children who are doing relatively well, while the rest of the surrounding villages are not doing so well... That could be an example. And also... I would also question how various organisations use children in their marketing. That children are put in situations that are not... that in turn could have what we call unintended consequences. But I think that most of these questions have been addressed by the aid community and discussed by the aid community, and I think most organisations learn and change, the way we have. Because we have done things in the past that we now see were not right. So I think it's a general trend that everyone follows up these things regarding children's participation, that if you work with children, then you work with children's participation and involve children. So I think that is a general trend, and we are not as distinct from each other as we maybe think we are.

This interviewee addresses two specific issues. The first is whether or not the organisations are concerned about self-critically reflecting on potential unintended consequences. This relates to the quality concern also raised by the previous interviewee, and the example she uses is 'building a small village for children', where the children inside the village are relatively well off, in contrast to the neighbouring villages.[15] Thus the universal aspect of development aid is highlighted as a key concern. The second example she uses concerns how children are used for fundraising purposes. She does not elaborate on this example, but her worries seem to lie in the unintended consequences that might follow. Note also how the antidote against unintended consequences is the involvement of children. Working with children implies children's participation.

15 The organisation SOS Children's Villages (<www.sos-childrensvillages.org>) is not mentioned explicitly, but the view articulated echoes an often voiced criticism against this organisation, which with its similar emphasis on children must be considered a competitor to the organisation this interviewee represents.

7.3.2 Flexibility and respect

When one of the SCN interviewees in her 30–40s explains why she has chosen to work for SCN, she says:

> Save the Children Norway is a very professional and very focused organisation. That is why I have worked with Save the Children Norway for all these years, because of that aspect. They have been fairly open and flexible and in terms of development work it's an organisation that really values peoples' attitudes, values their local knowledge, and values, you know, the learning that goes on as we do things. Rather than trying to force learning on people from the North, which happens a lot in the development work we are doing. Save the Children Norway is one organisation trying to say let's work with the local organisations, let's work with the local capacities, let us see as much as possible how people do things. How can we build on that? [...] It's a flexible organisation. Willing to listen and wanting to learn, and to move on from there.

Here being 'very professional' is highlighted as an important feature of the organisation (see section 14.2). This interviewee adds also the openness and flexibility of the organisation, and how it 'values people's attitudes'. This latter aspect is also highlighted by one of the SCN interviewees in her 40–50s. She says about the distinctiveness of SCN:

> I think it's the fundamental openness to the fact that there are actually people in the countries where Save the Children Norway works who know how to find the solutions and who can articulate and shape their own future, especially when working with children. So I find there is a respect towards the countries one has the chance to work in, which is a fundamental thing for Save the Children Norway...

The distinctive trait here is how the organisation puts development in the hands of the recipients of aid and how local capacity building is a distinctive mark of SCN. Clearly this recipient focus is an important concern for this interviewee. As noted, this is also an important concern in SCN's policy document.

7.4 The labour movement (NPA)

Like the interviewees in the other agencies, the NPA interviewees too seem to have the same kind of satisfaction with the organisational context they work in. Reflecting on the frustrations of development work, one of the NPA interviewees in her 30–40s says:

> [...] There have been conflicts in Norwegian People's Aid, where I have worked, but Norwegian People's Aid has been a very good employer. And that has contributed to keeping my motivation going.

Explaining why she feels satisfied in her work, another of the NPA interviewees in her 30–40s says:

> Well, it's the opportunity to realise one's potential. Realising some of the ideas and thoughts... That is, the distance between having a dream and a vision and actually realising it is not as great as for example in the government system. I think, that, for example in NORAD you are tied up by parliament etc. You have a lot more of the slow process you have to go through. But in Norwegian People's Aid, within certain limits... We also have our own funds and can take our own initiatives. If you have a good enough vision you can also have it approved more easily.

Again, the flexibility of the organisation is highlighted, and here explicitly in contrast to working for a government agency. This echoes some of the perceived advantages of NGOs in general discussed above (see section 3.2.3).

7.4.1 Taking sides

When asked in what way she thinks NPA is distinct from other NGOs, one of the NPA interviewees in her 30–40s points not only to the characteristics of NPA that distinguishes the organisation from government agencies, but also from other NGOs. She says:

> I think that Norwegian People's Aid is different because it has chosen to take sides in conflicts, which implies that we sometimes have been able to come closer to our target groups.

And elaborating, she says:

> [...] Nobody can help everybody. Nobody can help all. And I actually think that with the resources we have, and not only the financial resources, but also the organisational capacity we have, then I think that by taking sides we get more out of it. If we spread out widely, if we... let us say in Sudan: if we had had a relief operation on both sides during the war, our resources would have had less effect than if... So we would get less, you could say, effect on both sides. So that is a sort of cost efficiency argument. I don't think it would... I think we come closer to the target groups if we take sides. That doesn't mean that we think the other side has... what do you say... has less needs.

This interviewee sees 'taking sides' as a distinctive characteristic of NPA (see section 4.4). This is not explicitly contrasted to the notion of neutrality, but justified in terms of an instrumental cost efficiency argument. This is further related to the effects this approach has on the relationship to the recipients. She argues it brings NPA 'closer to the target groups'. This seems to echo the understanding of solidarity as 'built upon mutual support' in NPA's policy document (Norwegian People's Aid 2003a). Accordingly, while others emphasise helping all (universality) as a trademark of development aid, this is not the case here. Rather, as one cannot help all anyway, it is regarded as better to take sides and establish a close relationship to one of the parties.

7.4.2 Humanitarian solidarity

As noted above, NPA sees itself as a humanitarian organisation for solidarity. When asked to comment on NPA's description of itself as a humanitarian organisation for solidarity, one of the NPA interviewees in her 30–40s says:

> I don't understand that at all. [...] There is a humanitarian element, but if that should be understood as relief, humanitarian, then I would say that what Norwegian People's Aid actually does is a lot more directed towards development, long-term development – almost to the extremes. We hardly implement anything, but we work with partner organisations...

This interviewee seems to interpret the term humanitarian as meaning relief work. Against this background and in light of the long-term perspective adopted in most of NPA's work, she seems to find the notion of humanitarian solidarity strange. Asked to elaborate, she says:

> […] I believe in solidarity. I believe in humanitarian work (*humanitært arbeid*) and I believe in development aid (*bistand*). But how? And how is that operationalised in Norwegian People's Aid? That is where I… That isn't easy. I think maybe the target goals are missing… So humanitarian solidarity… They are wonderful words and I believe in them, but you have to know what we mean by them and how we can get there, or how we can cooperate to get there.

Again, a perceived mismatch between words and deeds is articulated. And here too attention is drawn to the actual implementation of development aid. In this case, however, this seems to relate specifically to the relationship between relief and long-term development aid in the work of NPA. As noted above, this issue is also addressed in the organisation's policy documents. The documents and this interviewee seem to share the understanding of NPA's work as primarily long-term oriented. To this interviewee, however, this leads to a questioning of the terminology used in the policy documents.

7.5 Concluding reflections

The embassy interviewees tend to see the work they do in light of the interests of the Norwegian state, but several of them also stress how these are morally legitimate interests and serve the shared interest of both donor and recipient. This echoes the national role conception summarised in the phrase 'small state with moral motives' (see section 3.3.1). Some of them emphasise that most embassy staff have a moral motivation for the work they do.

The NCA interviewees consider NCA as a Christian organisation, but tend to dissociate it from the mission organisations. Rather, the traits NCA shares with other development aid organisations seem to be emphasised. In contrast to the mission organisations, NCA is seen as doing a diaconal service which has political implications. This can be referred to as a prophetic diaconate. However, an inconsistency between words and deeds is also articulated, as the plans and strategies of the organisation are not perceived as reflected in its actual work.

SCN interviewees tend to stress the organisation's long-term perspective and target group focus, and also highlight the need to ensure the quality of development work. Some of these interviewees commend SCN for being a flexible organisation, emphasising and practicing respect for the recipients of development aid.

Some of the NPA interviewees highlight the political stance the organisation takes, for example by taking sides in conflict situations. However, NPA's self-understanding as a humanitarian solidarity organisation is criticised. In light of the actual development work the organisation does, some of the NPA interviewees question how this should be understood.

In general the interviewees express great satisfaction with the organisations they work for. They seem proud of their organisational affiliation, considering their agencies to be professional and focused. Further, several of the interviewees emphasise how all of these organisations are in most respects very similar, and all do good development work. In light of the Norwegian model this is not surprising (see section 3.3.2).

To summarise, the interviewees' understanding of their respective organisations seems to be articulated in ways similar to those found in their agencies' policy documents. However, when they explicate their understanding of these organisations and the work they are involved in, discrepancies are also articulated. They articulate for example perceived inconsistencies between plans and strategies on the one hand, and the actual work done on the other, as well as a questioning of how these policies should be understood.

Part IV

The development industry

8 Governmental and non-governmental aid

> The Development Set is bright and noble,
> Our thoughts are deep and our vision global;
> Although we move with the better classes,
> Our thoughts are always with the masses.
>
> Ross Coggins, *The Development Set* (cited in Hancock 1991)

While the preceding chapters have dealt with the interviewees' experience and understanding of professional roles, motivation, and working context, I will in this chapter focus on how they experience and understand the agencies that make up the development industry in general. The distinction between governmental and non-governmental development aid is an important analytical distinction, but seems also to be important to several of the interviewees. In this chapter I will firstly address the issue of specific NGO characteristics, and secondly discuss the relationship between the various NGOs and the Norwegian state.

8.1 NGO characteristics

A wide range of NGOs are involved in international development aid. However, both the distinction between governmental and non-governmental actors in the field, as well as the advantages and disadvantages of NGO involvement, are disputed (see section 3.2.3). The interviewees of this study, however, seem to highlight especially two NGO characteristics: their grassroots orientation and increase in size.

8.1.1 Grassroots orientation

The NGOs' character of being grassroots organisations is stressed by several of the interviewees. When discussing the justification for doing development work, one of the female NCA interviewees puts it this way: 'I think this grassroots connection is important. And I think the non-governmental organisations are in a better position to do that'. Discussing the added value of her organisation, this interviewee adds another aspect to the added value of these NGOs. She says: '… we have existed for fifty years, we have experience and trust and confidence on the grassroots level and also with the authorities where we have been'. Thus, according to this interviewee not only do the NGOs have a closer relationship with the local level or with civil society actors, they also have the benefit of years of experience. Similarly, when asked about the added value of his organisation, one of the male SCN interviewees says:

> […] we are good at being out there. We understand what is going on in the rural areas. We have grassroots connections… Others cannot… The embassy here has to look at strategies. That must be the role of the state, and then they must get people who can implement these strategies, or accept the strategies they have. […] And then we have the advantage that we work in 12–15 countries around the world, which also is an added value. So we achieve learning effects and have systems with respect to that. In that way we learn from each other. When you do that, you gain lots of experience, and that experience can be used for lobbying at the international level and at the Norwegian level.

Again two NGO characteristics are highlighted. The first relates to a division of roles between the embassy and NGOs. While the embassies 'look at strategies', NGOs are more closely related to the grassroots. Secondly, this interviewee points to the NGOs' learning possibilities. Working with related issues in different contexts enables them to benefit from these different experiences and thus improve their programmes. This again enables NGOs to take on a lobbying role. Again, NGOs have an added value in the sense that they play a different role compared to the embassy. Similarly, one of the male NPA interviewees highlights this difference between the NGOs and the state, indicating his lack of faith in budget support. He says: 'I believe the Norwegian voluntary organisations are the most important tool we have. More and more bilateral development aid is budget support…'.

Embassy interviewees also articulate this understanding of a division of roles between NGOs and embassies. Asked whether she sees a great difference between ODA and NGO aid, one of the female embassy interviewees says:

> [...] normally a lot of the official development aid will go on a state to state level, while Norwegian non-governmental organisations will often be able to work more directly towards and in association with local communities or in cooperation with local voluntary organisations. And it is my experience with the organisations I have travelled with here that they work closely with the local communities, but also in close cooperation and through regional administrations. That goes for both Save the Children Norway and Norwegian Church Aid, among others. But they still work, in the way development aid is evolving, they are still working more at the project and programme level, while Norwegian development aid now in principle is more and more directed towards programme and sector level, for example. And in some cases direct budget support. So, in that way the working methods vary. [...] So they have a somewhat different approach. They work more directly with local communities than the official development aid does. But I would say we complement each other to a large extent.

While the state deals with bilateral state relations, NGOs relate to local communities and civil society. Note, however, the emphasis put on the local level. This interviewee seems to understand the arena for NGO work as being primarily at a local (or regional) level. This is further emphasised by the fact that she sees the NGOs primarily working at the 'project and programme level', while the state works with the 'programme and sector level'. Although this is not a clear-cut distinction, the tendency is clear: NGO work is small-scale compared to the embassies' macro orientation. This supports her conclusion that they thus 'complement each other'.

When asked if she would agree with the idea that NGOs have an added value compared to embassies, the same interviewee says:

> [...] It depends on how you understand the term, to the extent that they are closer to the grassroots. What has often been said is that you know that the money goes directly to where it is intended. If sent through state channels, you maybe don't know if it ends up where it is supposed to. And it's also an extra challenge when you work at that level, to see that the money reaches its end goal. So they work directly with that contact, and maybe feel more directly where the problems lie. They acquire a good deal of local knowledge, knowledge about the country. And, to return to our context here, we try to take advantage of that, and I hope vice versa. And we have regular meetings with them, the Norwegian non-governmental organi-

sations that are established here. To share experiences and views, and to share with each other what we are doing etc. So it's clear that these organisations have a certain experience and come closer to the local communities than what is possible for us due to the way we work.

This interviewee seems to understand the role of the NGOs in a similar way as the previously quoted interviewees, but also notes how this division of labour is something also the embassy can benefit from. This seems to provide the rationale for a close relationship between the embassy and NGOs.

8.1.2 Growing in size

As mentioned above, one of the criticisms voiced against NGOs such as those studied here is that they have grown so large that they have lost their non-bureaucratic traits. Consequently, if NGOs grow larger and their funding from government sources increases, the distinction between government aid and NGO aid becomes blurred.

Commenting on the channelling of government funds through NGOs, one of the male embassy interviewees says:

> [...] The main focus is to establish cooperating partners and to strengthen them through cooperation between organisations that have the same function. If you have that, it's very good. But you also have large operators that end up like mini states, Norwegian People's Aid, Norwegian Church Aid to a certain extent. Huge organisations... Norwegian Refugee Council, as it's now called, has a budget of 400 million kroner. Everything is financed. There is no member organisation in Norwegian Refugee Council that collects money. There isn't. They are purely operators, under somewhat odious labels. When Norwegian People's Aid for example has specialised in mine clearance, it could just as well have been Norwegian Church Aid, Red Cross, or Norconsult for that matter. It's a purely technical service delivery, of money, people, to do a specific task. It has really nothing to do with the ideological basis of the organisation.

This interviewee sees bureaucratisation as a process that takes place within NGOs too, and as such they develop traits similar to those of government bureaucracies. Note that the examples he uses are some of the largest NGOs in the field. Further, he compares the NGOs not only to the government actors, but also to those in the private sector.[1] His interpretation of the work of the NGOs is thus not only that they become more like the state, but also that they have features in common with the private sector. Implicitly he questions whether they can really be considered civil society organisations. Elaborating on the issue he also introduces a couple of other concerns that further complicate the role of the NGOs. He says:

> [...] these non-governmental organisations become in many ways companies, economic companies (*økonomiske bedrifter*). They are to administer money; they are to earn money for their head quarters in order to maintain an expanding bureaucracy. And if you now add everyone working in organisations, touching upon what the government does and could have done... And long-term development aid is one thing, but you have the same also in the relief industry which grows and grows over the years. So if you take the big organisations you have hundreds of staff in Norway who are to be paid, and you could ask if this is efficient management of funds in general.

Here this interviewee makes explicit his comparison of NGOs with private companies. In the following analysis, however, his comparison is with government bureaucracy, indicating that he sees them moving in the direction of the sphere of the state. It seems that his argument is based on the growing size of NGOs. The implicit argument seems to be that when NGOs grow, they also lose their distinctive character of being NGOs. He notes that this implies that they also become more professional in the sense that the employees are paid staff – implicitly indicating that NGOs lose their voluntary character. On the basis of this observation, then, this interviewee calls into doubt whether the channelling of government money through NGOs is efficient management of aid funds.[2]

1 Norconsult is one of the largest engineering companies in Norway (<www.norconsult.no>).

2 Another male embassy interviewee also addresses this issue. He says: 'It has been a kind of... that it doesn't help through the government channels. But if you give money to Norwegian Church Aid or to Save the Children Norway, there will be better development. There is not evidence for that. There is no evidence for it. There are private organisations that run their campaigns and say that here things are going well and here is no administration. That is just nonsense'.

8.2 The NGO-state relationship

Although critical comments regarding the character and added value of NGOs can be made, not only NGO staff but also embassy interviewees generally seem very positive in their evaluation of the work of NGOs. This is related both to the complementary character of their work, but also to their distinctive roots and position in civil society. Asked about the added value of NGOs, one of the male embassy interviewees says:

> […] I think that earlier we were so preoccupied with being neutral. And those times are now over, because now also people in poor countries are exposed to all kinds of influences; inter-religious groups, politics, and ethics, so there is a flow of influence. If we get the most decent of the Norwegian value based organisations to stand for something, I think it's good. […] I am positive about the value based ones, but not all… Some I find should not be supported at all, but for those that don't endorse narrow-mindedness and fanaticism, then I am positive.

This interviewee distinguishes between 'decent' NGOs and those characterised by 'narrow-mindedness and fanaticism'. In general, however, he seems to evaluate them positively, and this seems to relate to the distinct roles these organisations might play as opposed to the roles of governments. To this he also says:

> […] It's clear that some of these value based organisations can really enter into a dialogue with corresponding groups here, where they argue and explain views, which we cannot do, because we relate to the state.

It seems then that it is in cooperation with 'corresponding groups' that NGOs have a role to play. In other words, they have a role to play within civil society.

8.2.1 Independence

Regarding the relationship between the NGOs and the Norwegian state, one of the male SCN interviewees describes a close relationship between SCN and the Norwegian embassy. He says: 'We have the full support of the embassy in what we do. They see us as a Norwegian cooperating partner, and are proud of what we do. The Norwegian aspect of this is important'. However, when asked to comment on the possible problems related to having a close relationship to the Norwegian state, he says:

> [...] We need to retain our independence. We must have our own strategies, which NORAD may take part in, and we must ensure that individuals and private firms... [...] I think that we have to do more in the private market, and in that way we keep our identity. And I know this, if you have good projects, then you get funding.

In this latter quote this interviewee insists on securing the independence of the organisation vis-à-vis the Norwegian government. He seems to view the strengthening of SCN's relationship to the private sphere (individuals or companies) as a way to strengthen the organisation's independence and identity. Elaborating, he says:

> [...] Because NORAD trusts us, they look at our strategies, they are involved in assessing things, and they learn from us and we learn from them. It's clear that we get our freedom, and it's also a great responsibility for us. And I think that is... and then we get the freedom we should have. But if NORAD comes with 50 million kroner that can be spent on whatever it be, but 'We want you to support that country' or do so and so in [country], I wouldn't have liked that... if it wasn't in line with what we do, but drew us in a different direction. Many run after the money, to get the money... We should make sure our programmes are good, and then the money will follow. That is a different philosophy, than just going around applying for money...

Although he is positive about a close relationship to the state, this interviewee articulates here how there are certain premises for this relationship that are important to him. One such premise is the mentioned independence of the NGO, and he points to two different ways in which it can be tested. Firstly, the freedom of the NGO is challenged if the back donor, here NORAD, dictates the work of the organisation. Secondly, it is tested if the organisation itself is 'going around applying for money'. To avoid these threats to the independence of the NGO, he emphasises the need for the organisation to formulate its own policies and, within the framework of these policies, to make good programmes. The rationale seems to be that government funding is no threat (or at least less of a threat) to the NGO if this funding is in line with already agreed organisational strategies and priorities.

Responding to the argument that since SCN is heavily funded by the government, development workers in the organisation could be considered bureaucrats of the Norwegian government, another of the male SCN interviewees says:

> Yeah, but in a way, in terms of policy, one could say that that is right. Because if you look at some of the policies we have, they are really from NORAD [...] But on the other hand, Save the Children Norway is an organisation, I think, that has put itself in a good position by not accepting too much funding from the Norwegian government. [...] And I think that is the good thing that Save the Children Norway has done, not relying too much on Norwegian government funding. Though, I think the opportunities have been there. But the organisation has said no, we need to do our own fundraising so that we can remain independent. We are a non-governmental organisation, so we are not government, but we can take on board government policy. But we want to remain independent as a non-governmental organisation.

It seems that this interviewee initially accepts the proposition made. Contrary to the views of the previous interviewee he says that 'the policies we have, they are really from NORAD'. This is, however, qualified in the following, where this interviewee too highlights the independence of the organisation, primarily in terms of 'not accepting too much funding'. Thus, he shares with the previous interviewee a concern to protect the independence of the organisation.[3]

Similarly, when asked about the relationship between the NGOs and the Norwegian state, one of the male NCA interviewees says:

> [...] We have experienced that we can do two things at the same time. That is, we can be quite critical towards Norwegian authorities, and we can also cooperate with the same person on relatively large projects. When there is a problematic issue, we have to be very aware. When we say, or ask the question: 'How can we position ourselves in order to get as much as possible for the development aid funds from the state?', instead of saying: 'What is it Norwegian Church Aid wants?', and within that framework, 'how can we get as much as possible from the state?' If we all the time first ask where it is NCA strategically has decided to go, and what are our priorities, and then you can ask the state: 'How far are you willing to follow us? What can we get out of it?' And this is not an easy matter. And I think that sometimes we balance it. Sometimes we balance it. We can be asked to take on a task, and yes... 'Is that really what it is?' And then you could say, 'Well, that is not necessarily a priority, but at least it's not against our values and principles, and does it hurt then?' And then you could say, 'Are we then an extended arm of the state or

3 One of the male embassy interviewees says about the Norwegian NGOs: 'I would not characterise them as our extended arm, by no means... We have no professional follow-up, no professional directions and no budget control'.

> are we not an extended arm?' But at the moment we make compromises with what are actually our priorities and our values, then we are clearly on the road to being co-opted.

Although reflecting critically on the close relationship between NCA and the Norwegian state, this interviewee's conclusion is positive. Summarising his experience, he says NCA has not been too influenced by the Norwegian state, but rather been able both to remain 'critical towards Norwegian authorities' and to cooperate 'on relatively large projects'. He clearly believes it is possible to retain independence and cooperate closely with the government. Still, he remains aware of the challenges and problems that arise from retaining this close relationship. It seems that keeping an independent agenda is of critical importance in this regard: 'what is it Norwegian Church Aid wants', where is it 'NCA has strategically decided to go' and 'what are our priorities'? Accordingly, and in a similar way as the previous SCN interviewee argued, the state and NCA as an NGO are not seen as inherently conflicting entities.

8.2.2 Coordination and dialogue

When asked to reflect on the issue of coordination between his organisation and other organisations and embassies, one of the male SCN interviewees says:

> Yes, I think it's necessary. Otherwise we end up duplicating efforts and running up and around and becoming competitors, rather than saying we all are in the same, we have the same goal. We want to improve the situation for the people. It's better that we coordinate ourselves.

This interviewee is clearly very positive about coordination. Coordination between different aid agencies is here perceived not as an option, but rather as something 'necessary'. It is necessary for reasons of efficiency, but also because 'we all are in the same, we have the same goal'. The differences between the organisations are downplayed and having shared goals becomes the relevant way to understand NDA. This is probably not to say that all the aid agencies do the same things, but rather that in a more general way they do work to achieve the same goal. When the same interviewee later describes how he perceives the actual ongoing cooperation between Norwegian aid agencies in the country where he is working, he is also very positive. He says:

> The cooperation has been good. The embassy has tried to bring us together. We had a meeting this year. […] And they are trying to make that an annual meeting. And it's going to increase now. We are discussing a new period starting from next year. I think we could have a lot more coordination meetings for sharing, where we could come and learn from each other.

In light of the statements quoted in the previous section, this positive evaluation is maybe of no surprise. Note, however, that this interviewee sees the embassy as having a key role in establishing the cooperation. It is the embassy that 'has tried to bring us together'. This seems primarily to be a descriptive statement, but also indicates the interviewee's approval and call for more coordination.

One of the female NCA interviewees also emphasises the importance of coordination. Reflecting on the challenges of development work, she says:

> You must coordinate. That is at least something I have tried to do as well as I could. So that you don't duplicate, and if you coordinate with others, then you can at least have a wider range, so that Norwegian Church Aid does one thing and Save the Children Norway does another thing, and Norwegian People's Aid another thing. […] At least the big ones, we generally get money from the same source. And I believe in that. And if you can do this as well as possible, and to the greatest extent possible, then I think we have come a long way. I believe in coordination.

Coordination appears to be this interviewee's philosophy or creed, at least among the major agencies. One main reason articulated is to avoid duplicating each others efforts. An underlying assumption seems, however, to be that the work these agencies do and the aims they have are fundamentally the same, or at least that they are not in conflict with each other. In other words, there is a fundamental trust in a shared understanding. Again the differences between NGOs are downplayed.

When asked how he finds the cooperation between the Norwegian agencies, one of the male NCA interviewee also regards it as a 'close cooperation'. He says:

> Yes, it's a close cooperation. As mentioned, we work more or less with the same type of thinking, and it's cooperation. It's not a competition. It's cooperation. Even if we go to the same bakery to get money, we can still fight about funds and things

> like that. But in terms of implementation and working principles, we work very closely together.

Again, the perception is clearly that there is a predominantly harmonious relationship between the different agencies. Both the basis for their work and their implementation are more or less the same. Note how this interviewee moderates the potential conflict that might arise from several agencies going 'to the same bakery to get money'. When asked about the independence of NCA, the same interviewee says:

> We clearly make our own plans and new priorities. Of course, we enter into negotiations about what kinds of fields we will work in. It's more like an interaction (*samspill*), yes, it's a lot more like interaction. Where is it that we actually can be of value and where is it we can do a good job? So there are negotiations, and a lot more cooperation, because we are not a consulting firm (*konsulentvirksomhet*) for the Norwegian state. No.

The independence of the organisation is here articulated by the emphasis on how NCA makes its 'own plans' and is not a 'consulting firm for the Norwegian state'. The relationship between NCA and the Norwegian state is described as 'interaction' and 'cooperation'. Again, it seems that a relatively close relationship to the state is not regarded as inherently incompatible with retaining one's independence as an NGO.

This positive evaluation of the relationship between NGO and embassy is articulated even more strongly by one of the male NPA interviewees. When asked if he feels he represents the Norwegian state, he says:

> In part. That is, in Norway we are blessed: the Norwegian state, the official Norway, involves civil society to a large extent. Also, MFA and NORAD and the Norwegian civil society have a very close dialogue (*tett dialog*), so that it is a… to a far larger degree than in other countries I know. It's pretty exceptional what is happening in Norway both in terms of the dialogue Norwegian civil society can have with the Norwegian authorities, and the acceptance (*få gjennomslag for*) they gain for it. It's quite special. So when Norwegian Church Aid or Norwegian People's Aid or Save the Children Norway works internationally, then it is also in many ways… as they receive government financial support and accordingly they are representatives, but they… And also in terms of policy they are part of a system where they have a clear understanding of their respective roles, which are defined as complementary or supplementary to the Norwegian state.

While such close cooperation between the state and NGOs in another context and with other actors might be seen as a curse, this interviewee sees how the state 'involves civil society' as a blessing. This interpretation should be understood in light of the interviewee's explanation: it implies there is a 'very close dialogue'. It seems then that the state's involvement is not seen as any infringement of rights or abuse of power. Rather, it enables dialogue, a dialogue that makes it possible for NGOs to find government support for their ideas and programmes. Again, this close relationship is seemingly not seen as something threatening. Regarding the large degree of government funding and the organisation's independence, the same interviewee says:

> [...] It's maybe an illusion, but in principle we are independent. But we play on the same team or dialogue with the Norwegian authorities, so we are not really independent. But neither is the Norwegian state. So this goes both ways.

Note how he dismisses that any of the actors can be independent. While the NGOs clearly are dependent on funding, his claim is that the Norwegian state is also dependent. On whom the state is dependent is not explicitly stated, but from the context (it 'goes both ways') it seems it must be the other aid agencies he has in mind. When asked to elaborate, he says:

> Well, the official Norwegian foreign policy is also influenced by inputs from Norwegian People's Aid, Red Cross, Save the Children Norway, Norwegian Church Aid, so it's... it goes both ways. There is reciprocity in it. So we represent also the interests of Norwegian civil society, be it human rights or other types of rights, so that what we work on, also the Norwegian authorities are influenced by that. And that is what is quite unique to the Norwegian cooperation, and I think it's very good.

Again, the important factor seems to be that the close relationship between state and NGOs is not a threat. Rather it is a positive resource.

8.2.3 The role of the state

In the context of discussing the element of self-interest in NDA, one of the male NCA interviewees compares ODA and NGO aid. He says:

> And I mean that discussion is really strange: 'What is better, official development aid or private?' It's not a matter of what is better. Official development aid must necessarily be far larger and more comprehensive and relate to states either multilaterally or bilaterally. Like Norwegian Church Aid, of course, we also have a few contacts and connections in the government structures, but most of our cooperation is with civil society. And that cannot and should not in a way be compared. Because the state should have a primary duty (*overordnet oppgave*), and if the state doesn't have a primary duty, then you can forget about the whole human rights regime, which is based on the state assuming the main responsibility.

Here too the harmonious relationship and cooperation between NGOs and the state actors is emphasised. Setting the one up against the other is dismissed as 'really strange'. However, the complementary character of this relationship is stressed as he points out that these two arenas 'cannot and should not in a way be compared'. One interesting corollary of this line of thinking is expressed at the end of this statement: the state has a crucial role in the 'human rights regime'. To this interviewee, human rights clearly imply a focus on the state's tasks and responsibilities.

When asked about the added value of NGOs in development aid, one of the male embassy interviewees says:

> [...] I would say that these are important players. But they can never replace, or they can influence and lobby and things like that, but they cannot play any larger role, to put it that way. I am a strong defender of the state, and not least in a developing country. The state, a good (*god*) state, a kind (*snill*) state, is important, and an alternative system with many strong private actors, either in the business sector etc. And, I am, when there are no regulations for it, I am very sceptical about it. So I think that to try to make a strong state, and also a good state, is important, as one part of it. [...] And I believe that some countries go too far, and also donors go too far in using civil society as a deliverer of goods and services. Really. It only makes a mess, if you ask me.

Being an embassy staff this interviewee's emphasis on the importance of the role of the state in development is not surprising. However, note how this interviewee characterises the state. The state, which development depends on, is described as 'good', 'kind', and 'strong'. Private actors, on the other hand, he says must be regulated, because if civil society is given too much importance 'it only makes a mess'.

Asked about the relationship between relief and development aid, another male embassy interviewee argues that the NGOs in contrast to the government are governed by a short-term relief perspective. In this he sees one of the important advantages of government aid. He says:

> The long-term purpose is avoiding relief. But Norwegian public opinion, and non-governmental organisations live by relief. [...] So that's an advantage of the state-to-state aid, as I mentioned earlier, that you are not as exposed to the whims of the moment that you do something for these poor children, but you work long-term so that there will be a form of government that is so good that you avoid future famines. You work with education, so that children five or ten years from now will have good education.

Here the NGOs are not primarily perceived as locally oriented bodies. Rather their focus and dependence on relief in crisis situations seems to be the basis for understanding their role and function. Thus, while some NGO interviewees stress their identity as development workers, a different perception is articulated here. While NGOs are considered to have a short-term perspective, the embassies are seen to have (and are in a position to have) a long-term perspective. This quote thus represents an interesting background to the earlier discussion of aid and development work (see section 5.1). Again, competing discourses about the work of the NGO development workers are articulated. While one discourse stresses their involvement at several levels, not only local and individual, there is another discourse that relates NGOs to more limited relief efforts.

8.2.4 Strategic instrument

Against the background of this division of labour between the state and the NGOs, some interviewees express an instrumental understanding of the embassy-NGO relationship. Asked about her tasks and responsibilities, one of the female embassy interviewees explains the strategic thinking of the embassy (see section 5.2.1). She says:

> [...] So the embassy looks at this as somewhat strategic, as we then channel some support to the non-governmental, and that we channel support more directly down to the school system, a lower level, and through this also get insight and reports and feedback about what is going on at the grassroots level, in a way. Because, it can easily become very abstract really, it turns into a kind of Ministry-talk in papers and strategies, but never any true reality check with regard to what it's really like to be a teacher or what it's really like to be a pupil at a small school in the rural areas in

> [country], sort of. We have a little better opportunity to understand this through the small agreements we have with the non-governmental organisations.

According to this interviewee, the state-NGO relationship gives useful 'feedback about what is going on'. It provides the embassy with a 'reality check'. Thus, the relationship has an instrumental aspect. Note that the reality check is not about the NGO, but rather the country in question. To one of the male embassy interviewees this instrumental aspect is more comprehensive and more explicitly understood as a lop-sided relationship. In his perspective, the character and content of the state-NGO relationship is (at least primarily) defined by the funding government side. When asked why the embassy chooses to channel funds through the NGOs, he says:

> [...] And then it is we who decide what should be done, and they take on a task and implement it. It's not based on applications. We are the ones who want to use Norwegian Church Aid, it's not Norwegian Church Aid that wants to have money from us to do it this way.

Note how this interviewee says the embassy wants 'to use' NCA. Again an instrumental understanding of the relationship between the state and NGO is articulated. To this interviewee the NGO is a subcontracted partner doing what it is told and as such is used by the embassy. This is, however, not an expression of distrust, but rather an acknowledgement of NCA's knowledge and capacity. The same interviewee also says: 'We look at Norwegian Church Aid as a professional partner who can deliver the products that we want, and who can give us the results we need'. Note the language used. NCA is considered a 'professional partner' that can 'deliver the products' and 'give us the results'. As it is considered a subcontracting relationship, this market influenced rhetoric is not surprising. It does, however, stand in a certain contrast to the rhetoric used by other interviewees who stress the mutuality of the state-NGO relationship.

8.3 Concluding reflections

Three NGO characteristics are highlighted by the interviewees. Compared to the embassies, the NGOs have 1) closer contact with civil society organisations and grassroots, 2) the benefit of experience from other countries and from involvement over a long period of time, and 3) the opportunity to lobby the powers that be. To some extent this corresponds to the advantages often ascribed to such organisations (see section 3.2.3). Although some interviewees question the gains won by channelling funds through the NGOs, many acknowledge a pragmatic division of labour between Norwegian NGOs and the Norwegian state.

Regarding the relationship between the NGOs and the Norwegian state, the cooperation and coordination discourse seems to be important. To many of the interviewees this relationship appears to be a fruitful, complementary relationship where both the embassies and the NGOs can benefit from a close relationship based on different roles and areas of expertise. In this sense the Norwegian model seems to be a key element of the discourse (see section 3.3.2).

Several of the interviewees emphasise and positively evaluate the role of the state (both donor and recipient) in development work. The donor state, represented by the embassies, is by some of them considered a key facilitator of coordination between the agencies, as well as holding a key position and primary duty in the context of the human rights regime. The issue of cooption is recognised as a potential risk, but seems not to be perceived as a real threat. A relatively harmonious understanding seems to be fundamental in their understanding of the state-NGO relationship. Similar notions are also articulated by embassy interviewees, but the strategic use of NGOs (subcontracting) is also referred to.

Accordingly, while the policy documents primarily explain the policies and programmes of the individual agencies, and how they relate to other agencies is mostly only implicitly referred to, this relationship is explicitly addressed in the interviews. As the analysis in this chapter shows, this seems to be widely understood as a relatively close relationship. A harmonious understanding of the relationship between NGOs and state actors seems to be part of the moral discourse of NDA, combined with an emphasis on the key role of the state in securing human rights.

9 Understanding development aid

Everything is difficult because firstly salaries are so very low.
And secondly because inflation is too high.
We are living from hand to mouth, like animals.
People here are as poor as animals.

Mandi, engineer in Zimbabwe to BBC, 14.03.07[4]

This chapter addresses how the interviewees interpret development work in general and NDA in particular. This will be explored from different angles. I begin by discussing development aid understood as transfers from one country to assist another. Secondly, the distinction between relief and development aid is addressed, and this leads to a discussion of the relationship between aid and politics. This relates to the issue of self-interest in development aid, which will be discussed in a separate section. Popular support for NDA in the domestic arena is also addressed and, finally, the last section focuses on how the interviewees respond to some of the criticisms about development aid.

9.1 Transfers to assist

When asked what she thinks development aid is all about, one of the female NCA interviewees says:

> Development aid is about some people in terrible conditions having their situation improved a little (*får det litt bedre*). And it's about transfers of capital and knowledge and resources from one country to another, from one organisation to another organisation, because the aim is to make life better for some.

4 See <news.bbc.co.uk/2/hi/africa/6450621.stm#mandi> (accessed 29.03.07).

Several features of this statement should be noted. First, the use of the word 'improved' indicates a normative understanding of aid, as its 'aim' is to make 'life better'. This implies an understanding of aid as playing a role in changing a given situation which is regarded as bad, and that a change in a certain direction will improve this situation. Another feature of the statement is the limited scope of aid that seems to be implied. The interviewee says development aid is about making things 'a little' better, and repeats twice that it aims at helping 'some'. Accordingly, the implicit understanding is neither that aid is helping many or all, nor that it will have a dramatic impact on the beneficiaries' standard of living.

Further, this interviewee seems to understand development aid as constituting two pillars: improvement of living conditions and a transfer of 'capital and knowledge and resources'. Focussing on the transfer of various kinds of resources from one country (or organisation) to another echoes modernisation theory (see sections 1.2 and 3.2). Aid and the intended improvement of living conditions is then made dependent on an external input. Accordingly, focus is here on external resources, not primarily on internal resources in the recipient country.

When asked what she thinks development aid primarily is all about, one of the female embassy interviewees similarly says:

> [...] It's about how the rich nations ease (*døyver*) some of their bad conscience (*dårlige samvittighet*) with regard to the great inequalities that exist in the world. And that is why they give a percentage of, or micro percentages, of their budgets to help countries in the South, sort of Third World countries. So it's about a transfer of resources, basically. Transfer of resources and in part transfer of competence, technical... to try to assist the social economic and political development in the area.

This interviewee too defines aid as the transfer of resources to 'try to assist'. The motivation for these transfers, according to this interviewee, is a wish to ease a bad conscience. Similarly, when asked how he understands development aid, one of the male embassy interviewees distinguishes between the idealistic character of NDA and the intention to bring about development. He says:

> [...] if you take idealism as the starting point then of course development aid is a matter of lifting poor people (*løfte fattigfolk*) in the poorest part of the world out of poverty. [...] It's a large support programme, and sometimes there are elements of pure social support. That is, to help people survive from one day to the next. And

> sometimes it's that too. And sometimes it's about starting processes of growth in different ways. Economic growth or in other areas that make it possible to sustain oneself. But it's a contribution from countries and groups etc., to make a leap in development (*hopp i utviklingen*). And often it becomes clear that to take a leap forward in development terms is difficult. It isn't... It's the small steps that are really needed. But you really want countries, not least in Africa that often don't make it; you want them to make the great leaps. And we are not able to do that.

From 'idealism as the starting point' this interviewee sees development aid as a matter of 'lifting poor people'. He labels this a 'large support programme' and identifies two elements of it: 'pure social support' and 'processes for growth'. The former seems to refer to short-term humanitarian aid, as it concerns making sure the recipient can 'survive from one day to the next'. This is what I have called relief or humanitarian aid. The other element, however, is clearly about a long-term perspective. These 'processes of growth' are specified as 'economic growth' enabling the recipients to improve their living conditions in a sustainable way. This interviewee describes this as a process that leads to a 'leap in development'. In this he too seems to draw on terminology that is used in modernisation theory.

In the latter part of the statement this interviewee reflects on some of the problematic aspects of his understanding of development aid. It seems it is his own use of the phrase 'to make a leap in development' that leads him to make these reflections. From this reflection he goes on to make a distinction between taking 'small steps' and making 'great leaps'. Although the donor would like to see great changes, he finds it is the 'small steps' that are really needed.

Responding to the question of what development aid is all about, one of the male SCN interviewees sums aid up in the phrase 'filling gaps'. He explains:

> The way I see it, it's about filling gaps. Developing countries are unable to... [...] for instance if you look at the [country] government, there are so many wishes and so many things they would like to do in terms of policies, but then there are not sufficient funds. So you need to fill gaps. [...] But it's also at times about, where appropriate, an exchange of knowledge and information. But I think, this has to be taken kind of carefully, because it's not just a matter of transfer. The recipient has to be able to do the analysis and find out what is appropriate in terms of knowledge and skills that they can use in their own context.

Again notice how it is the lack of resources in the recipient country that is emphasised and provides the rationale for providing development aid. The lack of resources constitutes a need to 'fill gaps' and development aid functions as a vehicle to transfer resources to do this. Again, development aid is defined as an external input. This interviewee also explicitly stresses how this is not limited to a transfer of capital, but also of 'knowledge and information'. Note how the focus is turned away from the donor and towards the recipient towards the end of the statement, and how he then dismisses the notion that this is 'just a matter of transfer'. Towards the end of the statement the emphasis shifts from the donor towards the recipient. Both analysis and interventions should be in the hands of the recipient. This change of perspective might indicate an element of indecisiveness or ambiguity. It seems this interviewee's understanding of development aid has at least two elements, articulated by two different interpretative repertoires. Firstly, development aid is 'filling gaps' with resources. Secondly, however, he stresses that these resources do not necessarily need to be transfers arriving from outside the country. This latter condition seems to be important in order to protect the involvement and decision making capacity of the recipients of such aid.

9.2 Relief and development

One of the criteria for selecting the agencies for this study is their involvement in development aid, as opposed to for example only purely relief efforts. This is reflected in statements by the interviewees as they emphasise the development work of their own agencies. Regarding the relationship between relief and development aid, one of the male SCN interviewees says:

> I think one has to find a balance. Because you kind of need both – and a good thing is that there are organisations that have specialised in dealing with emergencies when there are food aid issues. And from our side, as Save the Children Norway, we have kind of tried to move out of that, and tried to move in to long-term development and tried to specialise in that. And I think it's a decision. Though, we don't completely say we cannot deal with emergencies. We have a stand by team

for Save the Children as an alliance. When there are emergencies we can move in and support each other. But we are not trying to build so much of our skills and capacities within the emergency area. We are not saying this is because it's less important, but because we have made a choice, and we want to make a choice to work with more long-term development issues around children who are weak. In one way or the other we contribute in the long run to maybe stopping some of these emergency food shortages that we see.

Here it is clear that the emphasis on development aid is not perceived as devaluing relief as such. Rather, it is seen as 'a choice'. While relief is necessary in emergency situations, development aid is necessary to avoid repeated crisis. To this interviewee the emphasis on the long-term perspective therefore seems important.

Discussing the work of his organisation, one of the male NCA interviewees says: 'Norwegian Church Aid as an organisation has said that we work with three different approaches: relief, long-term development aid, and advocacy'. One of the female NCA interviewees, however, describes her work as being predominantly about development issues. She says:

[…] But here in [country] we primarily do development work, long-term development work. I am a bit surprised that we don't do more relief. […] And [country] with frequent crisis situations with respect to food deliveries. So I might have thought that this would have been a larger part of the work. So here the emphasis is clearly on long-term development aid.

Similarly, one of the male NPA interviewees says: 'Yes, and that is a global strategy for Norwegian People's Aid, that we try to get out of the role as a relief operator, and to be working more with development aid'. Also one of the female embassy interviewees emphasises the need to prioritise long-term efforts. She says:

[…] It's difficult to work for the long-term… that is, here this goes hand in hand. But if you constantly face serious droughts, then that is very damaging for the long-term development aid. Because then money will have to be spent on the acute relief efforts, and in addition people become exhausted and many die. Cattle die and all this. So it undermines the long-term assistance. So we try to find solutions so that you can have buffers or structural changes, so that you can handle these repeated droughts, so that they don't need to be as severe as the last one.

This interviewee speaks from the point of view of a development worker. It is the damaging effects of recurring crisis (drought) on the long-term development efforts that she is concerned about, and she sees this work as an effort to limit and/or avoid such crisis.

9.2.1 Long-term perspective

Although there are clear differences between relief and development aid as I have defined them above (see section 1.2), there are also links that can be made. This is articulated by several of the interviewees, and three of them can serve as examples. Asked what he thinks about the relationship between the two, one of the male NCA interviewees highlights the continuum from relief to development work. He says:

> No, there is no contradiction. [...] If the people don't have food today, we must help them get their daily bread today. But at the same time we must make sure that they can develop and create their own future... long-term development.

When asked the same question, one of the female SCN interviewees similarly says: 'I feel they are connected'. Discussing SCN's involvement in an ongoing food shortage crisis, one of the male SCN interviewees, however, articulates more explicitly a critical stance towards relief efforts. He says:

> [...] Personally I don't believe very strongly in free food distribution and things like that, because it creates a kind of dependency, a dependency syndrome among people. We had a situation where we went to a community during the last time we were involved in a bit of this emergency relief, and it was one of the communities that had a good crop. They had had a good harvest. They were selling everything. Then we said: 'Why are you selling everything? This is early in the period; you still have six months to go to the next harvest. Why do you sell it?' They said that 'one of these organisations will come and give us food.' So you don't have to create that kind of dependency among the people. It's a very difficult balance.

The very last comment ('It's a very difficult balance.') shows how this interviewee is not dismissing the relevance of relief work altogether. However, he is clearly worried about the kind of dependency food distribution can lead to. Thus, these three interviewees all acknowledge the need for and importance of relief work. They are, however, also concerned about the negative effects relief work might have.

In contrast to the interviewees above, however, another of the male NCA interviewees makes a clear distinction between relief and development work. He says:

> These are two totally different schools, and to… And the purpose of development aid is to construct, to construct not only buildings, but to build institutions over a long period of time. In relief it's almost the opposite that happens. One tears down the institutions that are there, in order to put up short-term, but functioning ones, to save lives, to distribute food, to distribute water and health. So they are inherently contradictory, and the greatest challenge is precisely to try to see the connections, because it's possible to build a connection in a relief operation if you manage to adopt a somewhat longer perspective. It's rarely done, because there are so many changes of people and expertise.

The contrast this interviewee sees between development aid and relief is expressed as to 'build' up rather than to 'tear down'. These expressions do not, however, refer to any general destructive character of relief work, but to 'institutions'. It is not argued that relief is good and development work is bad, but rather that their means and tools are different. Or as this interviewee puts it, they are 'inherently contradictory'. His conclusion is, however, not to dismiss either, but to take up the challenge to 'try to see the connections'. This seems to mean being able to include a 'longer perspective' in relief work. The implied criticism is again the lack of this longer term perspective. This interviewee insists, however, that although this is difficult, it is still possible.

The emphasis on long-term development aid is not only a descriptive claim regarding the work these interviewees do, but also something several of them emphasise as normatively required. Asked to elaborate on his understanding of development aid, one of the male embassy interviewee says:

> […] And I think we are too kind (*for snille*), to put it that way. We are not cynical enough in this, unfortunately. … We… It helps us ease our conscience (*samvittighet*), both the conscience of the Norwegian people and our own, with lots of relief and short-term aid for health and education. But it's still a lopsided distribution in the development of a country, and also in the Norwegian context. We have always tried to strike a balance between the long-term investments in roads and industry and things like that, and where we could have distributed the resources in a different way, had we been kinder to ourselves. And it sounds heart breaking to say that in a country like this, to say: 'No, we should not continue giving aid to people. We should build a road or something…' That is not what I mean, like… But there

> is something about the balance in this which I find we could perhaps be more concerned about. It's this long-term perspective...[5]

This interviewee frames his answer as an issue of being kind or being cynical. The former seems to refer to short-term relief efforts, while the latter describes an approach emphasising long-term interventions. His claim is that 'we are too kind' and 'not cynical enough'. Elaborating on this criticism, it seems that he relates kindness to 'our conscience', indicating that relief might be more popular than development aid in the donor country. On the other hand, emphasising long-term efforts, like building a road, is to be cynical. Thus, while he seems to believe an emphasis on the long-term efforts is necessary, he finds this not sufficiently appreciated by 'the Norwegian people' (see section 9.5).

9.2.2 Ridiculing relief

One aspect of the comparison between relief and development work is the amount and type of attention given to relief work. Commenting on the relief workers in the country where she works, one of the female NCA interviewees says:

> That is an interview in itself, because that industry is a cowboy industry. It's a circus [...] It's relief, and at any rate it's all about feathering your own nest. There are big flags and vehicles and... 'Look who is the world champion in being kind. See how many I have helped today.' Sort of: 'Compared to you. Look at me! How kind I am!' and that sort of thing... [...] Everybody wants to be where the video cameras are, and to have their posters so that they are visible on television. That we were there, and how many refugees we helped, and the cowboys running around down there... [...] For them it's fast and quick and they don't listen, because they don't have time. And you certainly don't have time to ask questions. It's just to charge off with plastic sheets and whatever. And there are no political guide lines. That is... At least the rest of the aid industry has to work with certain structures, but in relief... nothing. It's just band-aid. And if there is inflammation under these band-aids, then they aren't worth much, really.

5 Similarly, one of the male SCN interviewees says: 'We have also been clever at peeing in our pants when it is cold. But we have a strategy, which I fully support, that when there are difficulties and when children are involved, then we should be there, and maybe among the first. But when the rest of the gang leaves, with the TV teams and things like that and... and the professional relief workers... then we stay and make sure there are lasting results'.

There is a sarcastic tone in this interpretation of relief and relief workers. The comparison with a circus and cowboys indicates a sense of show and showing off. The expression 'big flags and vehicles' points to a kind of festival. Further, in using the expression 'feathering your own nest' the interviewee seems to identify selfish interests as an important element of such undertakings, though it is not clear if this applies to the individual relief worker or to the relief organisations. The sentence following this expression refers to 'flags and vehicles' and might indicate that it is (primarily) the agencies she has in mind. In the latter part of the quote the attention seems, however, to be directed toward the individual relief workers. Commenting on what she sees as a competition in 'being kind', she seems to ridicule those implicitly boasting of their own efficiency and capacity: 'Look at me! How kind I am!' Here the focus is on the first person singular. It seems that an important element of what this interviewee is ridiculing and thereby implicitly dissociating herself from, is a kind of individual and collective boasting.

When reflecting further on this issue the same interviewee continues to ridicule relief work, but this time the target is the attention relief is given by the public. She says:

> Yes, the world thinks that is a lot more exciting, a lot more exciting. Because we look a lot more like Mother Theresa if we do that, than if we come while the children are still nice and chubby. Or take them to school and play with them. That isn't as... everyone can do that. Compared to going into the bush, the sweat, and the heat and... and to take the small children and treat them intravenously. And then they might die next week. Or tell the children who still aren't undernourished enough, because we only give food to those who are very undernourished. So you have to come back next week. That is actually how it is.

This interviewee seems to claim that 'the world' wants to see the aid worker as a 'Mother Theresa'. And to accomplish this, 'the world' prefers the more dramatic emergencies and the most destitute of the poor, in order to have their own kindness accentuated. The implicit comparison seems to be that while relief workers focus on the starving, development workers relate to children who are 'nice and chubby' and play with them in the school yard. Mentioning 'the bush, the sweat, and the heat' contributes to emphasising the extremity of relief work, as opposed to the comfort and control of development work. Accordingly, while relief seems not to need justifying, the opposite is the case for development work.

Again, however, notice the shift in emphasis in the middle of this statement. From having reflected on how 'the world' perceives relief and development aid, the focus is turned to the work of relief organisations. Mentioning 'small children' and treating them 'intravenously' draws attention to the medical aspect of humanitarian work. Two comments are worth making. Firstly, having mentioned the feeding of small children, this interviewee goes on to say: 'And then they might die next week'. This seems to point to the futility of this kind of work, or a kind of disillusionment with the long-term effects of it. Secondly, she points to the priority given to those in the most extreme conditions, and the dismissal of those not 'undernourished enough'. It seems it is this focus on extremes, followed by a lack of focus on long-term effects as well as a self-centred concern about one's own kindness, that makes this interviewee ridicule the relief industry.

However, one of the male NCA interviewees seems to have a somewhat different approach and understanding of this branch of the aid industry. He says:

> There are some myths about being involved in relief too, and you easily get a cowboy image and things like that. But as a professional relief worker you have to oppose that kind of image [...] because it isn't a cowboy enterprise. It's serious work which is very, very complicated. And it's very, very difficult work (*håndverk*) to do. And that is what it's really about. But sure, you do get more attention, because you have access to the cameras.

This interviewee exposes what he considers to be myths about relief work. Note how he also uses the term 'cowboy' to describe the relief workers. However, while the previous interviewee goes on to ridicule relief work, this interviewee dismisses such an interpretation. He thus makes a distinction lacking in the statements made by the previous interviewee, namely between the 'professional relief worker' and the others, who by implication are not as professional, possibly regarding relief as a cowboy's activity.

9.3 Aid and politics

As noted, governments have become increasingly involved in development aid in recent decades. To some this merger of aid and politics represents an illegitimate integration of two domains that should be kept apart. The argument is often that while politics is dominated by real political considerations and self-interest, international aid is, or rather should be, driven by idealism and concern for the Other. If politics and aid are made part of the same whole, the latter is corrupted by the former (see section 3.2.1). However, several of the interviewees in this study argue that politics and development aid should be closely related. One of the male NPA interviewees describes the organisation he works for as 'a political voluntary organisation', and as noted above, one of the male NCA interviewees regards 'prophetic diaconate' as a key feature of NCA (see section 7.2.1). Discussing the rationale for NDA, one of the female NCA interviewees says:

> [...] But I think we should start thinking about transitions, start thinking a little more creatively in development aid. Relate it more closely to economic structures, trade. We could relate it a lot more closely to political work. It seems like MFA thinks along those lines, as more development aid is placed under their authority, not under NORAD. That political conditions are set for development aid, and that more income generating activities can be done etc., which is starting to be integrated into development aid... but moving more into that kind of field.

This interviewee draws aid and politics closely together. The change in this direction is both something that she believes is starting to take place and something she would like to see happen more. Asked to comment on the criticism voiced against such integration, she says:

> That is what they would say. 'It should not be about politics.' But, why are the refugees there? It's because of politics. Yes, I have often had that discussion with Médecins Sans Frontières, for example. They are like that. 'It's not about politics.'

Note the example this interviewee refers to. MSF is a medical, humanitarian organisation (<www.msf.org>). Accordingly, its mandate is much more specific compared to that of NCA. This difference might explain some of the disagreements this interviewee refers to regarding aid and politics. One of the female embassy interviewees similarly argues that aid is political. She says:

> Development is highly political. It's not un-political if you do health work. It isn't un-political. You come into a local community and you do something to it. So, whether it relates to the environment or health or whatever, no matter what, it isn't un-political. And you want to see change, and you want to see people changing attitudes.

The use of the term political seems here to refer to the controversial character of development aid. Development aid seeks to bring about change and to see people change their attitudes.

Regarding the relationship between aid and politics, another of the female embassy interviewees says: 'You can't separate development policy (*utviklingspolitikk*) or development aid (*bistand*) from a general whole. It's part of a comprehensive policy where development aid is one of many elements'. Notice how this interviewee links the terms 'development policy' and 'development aid' closely together. Thus, even the terminology indicates a close relationship between aid and politics, where politics in this case refers to government policies. Further, note how this field of development aid policy according to this interviewee is clearly an integral part of and only 'one of many elements' of a 'general whole'. Elaborating on this issue, the same interviewee says:

> The thing is that politics and development are more inter-twined than they used to be. And at least that has been the policy in Norway. And that is the case whether you talk to the Minister of International Development or the Minister of Foreign Affairs. Both fully agree on this, not to mention the Prime Minister, that this should be seen as more connected and interpreted as different parts of… that development aid is part of a comprehensive foreign policy.

Two things should be noted here. First, when she elaborates it becomes clear that this interviewee sees the close relationship between politics and aid as a relatively new phenomenon, and also as something that characterises Norwegian aid. Next, the agreement between different ministers is emphasised. On the one hand this refers to the distinction that is made between foreign policy and development aid policy through the institutional division of the two, as there are two ministerial posts in the MFA: Minister of Foreign Affairs and Minister of International Development. On the other hand, this statement downplays this distinction, as the agreement between the two is emphasised. This refers to the already mentioned consensus in Norwegian development and foreign policy. Ever since its beginnings, NDA has largely been characterised by a broad consensus across the political spectrum (see section 3.3). However, when development aid becomes part of a 'comprehensive foreign policy', it could also become more controversial. While there has been a consensus on development aid, foreign aid issues such as EU and NATO membership, international trade regulations, immigration, the war on terrorism, etc., are all disputed issues in Norwegian political debates.

9.3.1 Macro policies

Responding to the claim that more aid would give more results if it addresses the issue of capacity, one of the male embassy interviewees stresses the importance of the right policies (e.g. social policy) in the recipient country in order to be able to provide qualitatively good development aid. He says:

> Yes, I agree. But it presupposes a couple of things. It presupposes that there is... that there is institutional capacity. That there is administrative capacity and that there is policy making in the recipient country. That there is a social policy... This is something we don't talk much about. Policy making in recipient countries is sort of a non-issue. No, it isn't a non-issue, but it isn't something we are involved in much. But it is a very interesting question. How much do we insist on what we see as a need for a social policy that recognises the needs of the people (*tilgodeser menneskenes behov*)? It's about priorities, right? It's about the political priorities in the recipient country. In that... I am afraid that the focus on those priorities is not made explicit enough... these premises aren't discussed well enough for us to transform one per cent into good results. That is, that one per cent of GNI presupposes that those things are in place. The problems related to governance, as we could call it, in the broadest sense, in everything from policy making to managing money, corruption, human rights protection, participation.

Through this statment this interviewee clearly makes politics an important part of development work. Note, however, that the politics this interviewee calls for is politics and policies in the recipient countries. He mentions institutional capacity, managerial capacity, and social policy. The thrust of the statement seems to be a call to put more emphasis on such issues, as, he argues, these conditions must be in place if one is to be able to achieve good results. At the end of the statement these policy issues are referred to as governance issues, and thus the interviewee places himself in what can be called a good governance discourse. Here, good governance is defined by the donors of foreign aid, and thus made a condition for giving aid and a criterion for being the deserving needy. Thus, while this interviewee starts out by focussing on the politics of the recipient state, this turns out to be implicitly a matter of Norwegian politics in the field of development aid.

Asked to comment on the claim that development aid should be increased, the same interviewee says:

> [...] But I don't think development aid is the only answer. It's about everything else too. It's about having a coherent Norwegian policy. It's about trade, the general economic conditions internationally for a country like [country] to actually improve. It's about the price of coffee, if you want to be specific. It's about Norwegian subsidies, if you want to be specific. It's again about the general conditions. It's about the political priorities made internally in [country]...

The role of politics in the recipient country, the donor country (Norway), as well as internationally, is here made a determinate factor. Therefore, if one is concerned about development aid, one must necessarily also be concerned about politics on several different levels.

Several of the interviewees emphasise the need to deal with macro political and economic issues in order to solve the structural problems that aid addresses. One of the male NCA interviewees says:

> [...] I don't think development aid is the solution. I hope nobody thinks so. But it's a combination of the right policies: global policies, regional policies, and national policies. And the need for development aid to bridge the gap that at least temporarily is... [...] I believe that if we managed to put in place a comprehensive policy, which was coherent, both economically and otherwise, then development aid would be a transitional phenomenon.

Again, the importance of politics at various levels is highlighted. Note, however, that this interviewee, while emphasising the importance of politics, still maintains the need for aid. Aid seems to be necessary to 'bridge' a temporary 'gap'. In the bigger picture, with the right policies, aid will be a 'transitional phenomenon'.[6]

6 The same interviewee also says: 'Yes, we helped five thousand, or a hundred thousand people in Darfur to survive. But what will tomorrow bring if you don't also work politically? Or in Ethiopia... We saved a hundred thousand from star-

One of the male embassy interviewees says about increased funding:

> But to think that to pour money in will have an effect, I don't think so. But maybe in ten years time, a massive increase in support could lead to the results that we want. But improving this country is not primarily about money. There are other things that must be put in place for them to modernise their country. So I could say from my heart that I would like to double development aid ten times. But I don't think it would produce any results.

While the call for more development aid is well known, this interviewee places little confidence in transferring more money into the system. To him, the issue at stake is 'not primarily about money', but rather 'there are other things that must be put in place'. As long as this is not in place, any increase in the aid transfers will not give a corresponding increase in the results. This interviewee does not argue at what level aid should be, but argues only against a relatively large increase in aid. Further, his focus on 'other things' could be interpreted in different ways. However, it does not seem to imply a rejection of financial aid. His comment that he 'would like to double development aid ten times' speaks against such an interpretation. Rather, it seems that what is being disputed is a one-sided focus on money transfers which neglects other important aspects of development aid.

9.3.2 Aid versus politics

The call for a closer relationship between aid and politics seems not to be evident to all of the interviewees in this study. Reflecting on how he understands development aid, one of the male embassy interviewees discusses how development work should be defined. He says:

> [...] If you give it a very broad definition and say that all international agreements, trade treaties, have to do with development aid... Even EU's farming subsidies are

---

vation. But what happens two years from now if nothing is done with the fundamental general conditions for the people living there? That is, you use a short-term measure for relief, and we know that relief in the long-term maybe have made situations worse. It has rapidly led to dependency on external help. And that postpones or delays necessary reforms or drastically needed remedies in terms of national policies or international reflection on a few things'.

> an important tool for economic stability… The cost of this is carried by African farmers, to put it simply. Does that have anything to do with development aid? Is that how you define development aid? It might not be purposeful, because it would, if you mix everything into one pot, be difficult to handle.

This interviewee seems to lean towards a more limited understanding of aid, excluding issues such as international trade, farming policies, etc. Asked to explain his understanding of the relationship between aid and politics, another of the male embassy interviewees refers to how development aid and foreign policy have become more integrated, but still emphasises the distinctive character of development aid. He says:

> […] I believe that… the aid aspect (*bistandsdimensjonen*) should not be abolished. It's after all the most important one. But there are a few premises about development aid that politics address. So I would not exclude it, on the contrary. I too, when we were cultivating pure (*rendyrket*) development aid, I too stood and called on the politicians to get involved in development aid. So I am more worried that the combination will be wrong. By putting too much emphasis on peace and peace mediation, and that money is used for purposes with no future (*perspektiv*), but which seem like short-term tactical considerations. Like giving money to something, so that the sides will meet etc., but… I have seen enough of those kinds of measures. I am not sure if that is a sensible use of money. I don't think so. So I think that maybe… that development aid funds… We should think that they should benefit the poor, really. And we shouldn't be afraid not to think long-term all the time… conditions for good political development, with the idea that the poor eventually will benefit from it. We have to work with the poor as we go along, or else it will take a long time before the money reaches them.

This interviewee begins by articulating the concern that the distinctive character of development work must be retained. As he continues, however, it becomes clear that his concern is not to totally separate politics and development work. Rather, it is a matter of being aware that 'the combination will be wrong'. Further, the criticism he voices is not directed at the concerns expressed by the proponents of a close relationship between aid and politics quoted above. The examples of unfortunate practices are rather 'peace and peace mediation', or short-term undertakings which may be motivated by 'tactical considerations'. Interestingly, it seems that this interviewee's concern is to ensure that aid actually reaches the poor, as opposed to more long-term projects where the rationale is that 'the poor' will benefit in the long run, but too long, according to this interviewee. In this, the concerns of the basic needs strategy are articulated here (see section 3.2).

One of the male NPA interviewees also disassociates aid from politics. When asked what he thinks development aid should be about, he says:

> The first thing development aid should be concerned with, is to… it must either be to contribute to peace, or it must be to secure peace. Maintain peace. That is the first thing. The next thing is that in the long run it isn't really about politics and political theories, but it concerns peoples' everyday lives. It's about people living peacefully without being afraid of being attacked, neither by the government nor by a guerrilla army. And that people can live with the prospect of their children having a better childhood than they had themselves, both in terms of school and education in general. After a while there will be other needs: freedom of expression and such and maybe after a while democracy. But the most fundamental is not about state models or democracy or parliamentary models. It's about creating a society where people can live in peace, and the children can have, like I said, a better childhood than their parents had. School, health, yes… livelihood.

Explaining how he understands development aid this interviewee initially points to two factors: firstly, ensuring and maintaining peace, and secondly, securing people's everyday lives. While one could argue that politics is about both of these, this interviewee emphasises that aid is not 'really about politics and political theories', as it is about 'people's everyday lives'. He then goes on to mention several related concerns (education, freedom of speech, etc.), but the most important is to him peace and 'a better childhood than their parents had'. Again, the emphasis is put on people's needs, not primarily on political or structural issues.

9.4 Self-interests

Most of the interviewees acknowledge that development aid could be seen to be about self-interests (see section 3.2.2). This is, however, not perceived as being contradictory to seeing aid as also benefiting others. Rather, an important notion seems to be that of coinciding or shared interests. When asked if there is an element of self-interest in his argument to provide funds for international aid, one of the male NCA interviewees confirms this. He says:

> Yes, I think there is. And this is the whole argument of this boomerang thinking. And I don't see… I don't see anything wrong in it. There is self-interest involved. But it's then a long-term self-interest. Maybe not my generation, but the next generation, will see the effects of it. And then of course you have the purely moral imperative in a way, that is on top of, and beside it, and should not be limited to whether or not I personally or those close to me have a self-interest in it. The one doesn't oppose the other, right? It isn't a contradiction.

An important part of this argument rests on an empirical claim, referred to in his statement as the boomerang thinking. The metaphor seems to refer to the backlash that will occur if the poverty and suffering in some parts of the world is not dealt with. This would eventually also impact the present day donor part of the world. Note how this interviewee also recognises a parallel moral imperative to assist. He emphasises, however, that these do not contradict each other.[7]

9.4.1 Doing business

The interviewees mostly dismiss the role of Norwegian business interests as a justification of NDA. Commenting on the claim that Norwegian aid is a matter of defending or promoting Norwegian interests, one of the female embassy interviewees says:

> No, actually I don't agree with that. When I compare this with other countries that I believe to a larger extent try to further their own interests. […] Norwegian businesses and Norway is actually involved only to a very limited extent in for example Africa.

It seems the argument that there is no self-interest involved in NDA is here based on a comparison with other countries. The lack of interest on the part of the Norwegian private sector is seen as an indication of the

7 Similarly asked about the role of self-interest, one of the male embassy interviewees says: '[…] It's not possible. One cannot make a clear distinction between altruistic and self-motivated actions. It's both, all the way. […] This is one of the fields in politics and in the world where altruism and self-interest actually can meet, right?'

limited role business interests play in Norwegian aid. Again a perception of Norway as unique is constructed.

Regarding the role of self-interest in NDA, one of the male NPA interviewees says:

> [...] I think for example that in a country like Angola, it shouldn't be that Norway has a commitment in Angola because we have a state owned oil company called Statoil drilling for oil there. It shouldn't be, and the same in Sudan for example. We don't have economic interests. [...] But I find it of great value that we do it without having to pump oil out of Sudan.

Angola is one of the countries in Africa where Statoil, a Norwegian state owned oil company (<www.statoil.com>), has significant involvement. By contrasting Norwegian involvement in Angola with the situation in Sudan, this interviewee highlights that such involvement should not rely on Norwegian business interests. Elaborating on this issue, he says:

> [...] If it's supposed to secure Norwegian industrial jobs, then I think... that is a too cynical approach. It's in our interest to secure the Norwegian pension fund by pumping oil, but in many of these countries it will be in our interest that they develop in the right direction, even though we don't have any concrete Norwegian economic interests.[8]

Clearly, to understand Norwegian aid as a tool to 'secure Norwegian industrial jobs' is something this interviewee rejects. At the same time, however, he acknowledges that there are common interests, in the sense that it will also be in Norway's self-interest if developing countries develop in a positive direction. He does not elaborate on why this is in Norway's interest, nor on what the consequences a different scenario might be.

Responding to a question about how Norwegian interests are met through development aid, one of the female NCA interviewees discusses the cooperation between her organisation and a private company. Referring to a meeting with this company, she says: 'And they were quite open, that they were here to improve their reputation at home. They are here in order to show that they assume social responsibility as a com-

8 The 'Norwegian pension fund' seems to refer to the Norwegian state's Government Pension Fund (<www.regjeringen.no/en/dep/fin/Selected-topics/The-Government-Pension-Fund.html?id=1441>, accessed 07.05.07).

pany'. When asked to elaborate, she explains why she initially found this joint venture problematic. She says:

> I was very critical. I was very much against their coming here. Because I thought that it certainly isn't our task to give [company] a better reputation at home. And I was really critical in a way, and I thought we let ourselves be bought, in a way. But they came, and it was a very nice group of people that have good intentions and who were very open, and that helped. That they were very open about, well, 'we need to change our policy at home' [...] So, now I find it difficult to say definitively that this is something I don't want to be part of.

In this quote, this interviewee explains how her earlier scepticism has been replaced by a more positive attitude. This is due to the transparency she experienced in her meetings with representatives of this company. Note how the 'good intentions' are here regarded in positive terms (see section 9.5). Still, as representatives of a business company, these visitors are associated with profit and this is seen as problematic in terms of reputation. Explaining why she considers such cooperation problematic, she says:

> [...] I feel it's really problematic if we become connected to a company that doesn't do business in an ethical way. But even if they say quite explicitly that they do this in order to improve their reputation at home, I don't like the fact that this is their motivation for becoming involved in [country]. Of course, I am a little worried that we will end up in a situation where we lose our ability to criticise (*vår kritiske distanse*). How easy will it be for Norwegian Church Aid to publicly challenge [company] if they do something we think is wrong?

Here the need to retain NCA's independence, to be able to criticise such companies and this company specifically, is emphasised.

Interestingly, this interviewee is much more positive about receiving money from the government than from a company such as the one referred to here. She says: 'I don't have any problems with getting money from the Norwegian government. Because, where else would we get it from? To me, that is not problematic'. Responding to the suggestion that, for example, the mentioned company could be a source of finances, she says:

> No, it's very different. It's the connection between business interests and aid that I haven't found a good way of relating to. Because the Norwegian state also has budgets that must balance and should produce a surplus, but it has at the same time in a

> way so many other duties and tasks, that I think aid is more in line with what a state does, more so than private businesses, whose first aim is to create profit.

As she summarises her reflections on the relationship between business interests and aid, some important elements of her understanding of development aid are also indicated, especially in the last sentence. Aid is dissociated with private business interest, where the goal is profit. Rather, the goal of aid is more in line with 'what a state does'. Two factors seem to be at play here. On the one hand, this interviewee seems to express scepticism in relating development aid to profit. This makes her hesitant about receiving funds from a private company. On the other hand, her evaluation of the role of the donor state in development aid is explicitly positive.

9.4.2 Immigration and terrorism

Another issue that highlights possible motives of self-interest underlying NDA is the issue of immigration. In the context of discussing the justification for NDA, one of the female embassy interviewees says:

> I know that many nowadays use the security argument. If people aren't happy where they are, then they will come and will want to share our affluence here at home, which is worse. I don't buy that argument.

This interviewee refers to aid as a tool to halt immigration from developing countries to developed countries. This is an argument of security, as such immigration flows would disturb the present societal order. Again, however, such arguments of self-interest are rejected. Referring to the same argument, one of the male embassy interviewees similarly says:

> [...] I feel that the main problem with the argument is that it puts our own situation first (*vår egen situasjon i høysetet*). And I think that's not the point. At least, that's not the point to me, and many agree with me. Rather, the situation here is the most important thing. It's not our own problems we are supposed to solve with development aid. That would be wrong.

Again it seems that the main concern is to avoid 'our own situation' being given any central role in the justification of NDA. The distinction between 'our own situation' and 'the situation here' seems to be fundamental, and is here construed as contradictory. And thus, in contrast to what was noted above, self-interest and other interests are here perceived as opposing interests.

Reflecting on the rational for development aid, one of the male NPA interviewees says:

> [...] some of these countries will become ticking environmental or terrorist, potential terrorist... Or not terrorist, I don't want to use it because so many do, but they will become potential liabilities, that is... various risk elements, both with respect to the environment and other people. There will be some people who become desperate in one way or another. So there is an interest there too, I think. ... Yes, I think that is better. I think that is a lot better in the fight against terrorism, if there is a fight, to try to get people out of pure desperation.

This interviewee addresses the issue of development aid as a tool, not to counter immigration, but terrorism. His starting point seems to be that the recipient countries might become threats to international security as people become desperate. He refers to this as an issue related to terrorism, but note how he immediately corrects this way of framing the issue, criticising explicitly the use of terrorism in this regard. Still, he returns to the issue of terrorism later, pointing out how aid 'is a lot better in the fight against terrorism'. Note again the terminological criticism he expresses when he questions his own use of the term 'fight'. It seems this interviewee is reluctant to be caught in a war on terrorism discourse. This might relate to the notions of self-interest that seem to be implied, but it is also in line with a critical stance toward superpowers' use of aid to support self-serving interests (see section 3.2.2). The same interviewee also says:

> Yes, if it's self-interest to think that the world should be a safer place to live for everyone, then it is so, of course. I don't believe I would be involved in using development aid to develop markets for Norwegian products or something like that, but to try to make the world into a bit safer and a more sustainable place both with respect to the environment and humans, then it's self-interest, of course. But it's a relatively broad concept, I feel...

This interviewee seems to be making a distinction between different kinds of self-interests. He distinguishes between developing 'markets for Norwegian products' and making 'the world into a bit safer and more sustainable place'. The former corresponds to the issue of commercial self-interests, discussed above, and the second to the issue of immigration and/or terrorism. Thus he distinguishes between a narrow self-interest he rejects, and a notion of common interest of which he approves.

9.5 The Norwegian people

Reflecting on development aid, several of the interviewees refer to traits they ascribe to the Western world or the Norwegian people. Reflecting on the humanitarian imperative to assist people in need, one of the female NCA interviewees says:

> […] from a relief perspective, I can buy that. They sit there, and they are displaced, they are refugees from their own regions and they have nothing at all. Of course, then they must receive, then we must both from a Christian understanding of man (*kristent menneskesyn*), but also from a humanist point of view (*humanistisk menneskesyn*), of course do everything we can to give them what they need in a crisis situation. […] Development work, on the other hand, I think should be based on other premises. And I wonder if it is. And I wonder what the premises are and if they are articulated. I think they are often mixed into a big bowl with a lot of other intentions. Where politics, national interests, not least capitalist interests, play a very large role. In addition to a very, sort of… yes, in addition to this… The good intentions that we suffer (*lider*) a lot from in our part of the world… We want the best for these poor Africans, or Asians, living in dire conditions. And then we want to do our best, seemingly, but without taking the context or the culture as our starting point. That is why I am quite critical to my work, my profession, with respect to the extent to which it integrates the long-term perspective.

Here this interviewee relies on the distinction between relief and development aid discussed in section 9.2, but she elaborates on this distinction by discussing the moral rationale for the two. She relates relief to the humanitarian imperative that we must 'do everything we can to give them what they need'. This is an understanding of relief work in line with statements that organisations such as the Red Cross and MSF make about themselves. Regarding development aid, however, this interviewee begins by claiming this should be and is 'based on other premises'. But as she elaborates on these premises, her reflection becomes vague, as she admits she wonders 'what the premises are', though indicating both 'national' and 'capitalist interests'.

Further this interviewee refers to 'good intentions' as another element of this basis for international aid. Notice how she describes these good intentions as something 'that we suffer a lot from in our part of the world'. This seems to be a metaphorical figure of speech, and it seems that it articulates scepticism about trusting in 'good intentions' as a driving force or moral basis for development work. The parallel in relief would be the humanitarian imperative which she discusses in much more positive terms. Elaborating on this suffering, she appears to be ridiculing these 'good intentions'. The expressions 'these poor Africans, or Asians' and 'living in dire conditions' seem to ridicule an understanding of the Other that overemphasises the poverty and the difficulties (some) Africans and Asians face, and that does not take sufficiently into account the resources they might possess. In other words, it exaggerates their plight and limits the perspective to poverty and difficulties, disregarding the wider picture. Her comment that good intentions imply not 'taking the context or the culture as our starting point' seems to support such an interpretation.

9.5.1 Feeling good or guilty

When asked what aid is primarily all about, one of the female NCA interviewees addresses the issue of moral conscience. She says:

> I suppose we want to feel that we do something good in the world. Ease (*lette*) the conscience a bit, the sort of uncomfortable conscience (*ubekveme samvittigheten*) with respect to us living in good conditions in Norway. And we are well off. [...] But is it... what is the context for it? Do we want to feel a little better, or is it a genuine concern for those who are not as well off? I don't quite know. Because we think it's more convenient (*greiest*) to help them down there. And better that not too many of them come to Norway and receive help there. [...] Earlier you went to church and gave donations, or in Catholicism you confess (*går man til skrifte*), and now... What does modern man do to ease his moral conscience? We give maybe 100 kroner to Norwegian Church Aid or to the Red Cross or something like that from time to time, and that helps a lot. And then you can have five beers afterwards, or whatever.

Arguing that aid is about us feeling 'that we do something good here in this world', this interviewee focuses on what aid does to or with the donor, and not on its effects on the recipient side. Further, her hypothesis seems to be socio-psychological, as she argues how being 'well off' leads to an 'uncomfortable conscience'. Note, however, that the question that is the crux of her statement primarily concerns authenticity. 'Do we want to feel a little better, or is it a genuine concern for those who are not as well off?' She leaves this question unanswered (see section 14.3).

Further, this interviewee claims that 'we' prefer to 'help them down there'.[9] This expression can be interpreted in various ways. Preferring to help them 'down there' relates to the geographical context of where the assisting intervention should take place. It could be argued that providing aid to the poor and needy in places where they already are is a sensible strategy, in order to help in the best way possible. However, a different interpretation seems more relevant here: the aim is to avoid that 'too many of them come to Norway'. The primary concern then seems to be that they should not come to Norway. Easing one's conscience is thus combined with a mechanism that makes it possible to avoid being confronted directly with the people this discussion concerns. One's conscience for the past or present is eased and a problem for the future is seemingly solved.

Responding to the question of what he thinks development aid is all about, one of the male NPA interviewees responds in a similar way. He says:

> [...] I think general aid is a question of bad conscience. That the rich countries give money to poor countries, I think that is about bad conscience. For in a way... Well, put a bit disrespectfully, but there is some kind of... I believe that is why aid has been as bad as it has been, that the starting point has been wrong. I think... But of course, over all these years there is more appreciation of the importance of environmental deterioration, poverty, that it's important to lift it up to a level, markets... There are a lot economic thoughts around it, but I feel that from the outset there is kind of a bad conscience there.

Again 'bad conscience' seems to be an important category in the interpretation of development aid and explaining its lack of success. Having a 'bad conscience' seems to be understood as something illegitimate, or at least as unfortunate with regard to the practical implementation of

9 The metaphorical use of 'down there' refers to the North as up and South as down.

development aid. It seems a bad conscience is something that should not constitute the basis for development aid, and if it is, the consequences are bad. Note, however, that this interviewee seems to moderate his own interpretation in the latter part of the statement.

Similarly, asked what she thinks development aid is about, one of the female embassy interviewees says: 'But I think that Norwegians want to feel good'. She continues:

> […] I find there is sort of a Norwegian double standard… that one should… We are very generous when it's needed […] Putting money in a donation box, for the TV campaign or things like that. Putting money in a donation box or collecting money in different ways. Or giving to a bank account when there is… The so-called CNN-effect. Then we are prepared. But when it comes to being nice to the neighbour who cooks food that smells of spices or something like that… We don't want more immigrants and we don't want more refugees, but we can very well help them as long as they stay down there. That is a little… We feel very good when we give something. But we never give… no-one gives… That is we give from our surplus, but we give… if we hadn't had it, we would have donated practically nothing.

The double standard this interviewee refers to seems to be summarised in the expression 'we are very generous when it's needed'. Note the quailfying 'when it's needed'. The generosity referred to is clearly understood as limited to special occasions either in the form of special fundraising events or a crisis highlighted by the 'CNN-effect'. The double standard becomes distinct when this generosity is contrasted to the attitudes toward immigrants and refugees. These attitudes point to another limitation of Norwegian generosity: we (Norwegians) are generous 'as long as they stay down there' (see section 9.4.2). Thus, as this interviewee sees it, Norwegian generosity is a generosity that follows from 'our surplus'. This generosity does not imply any sacrifice or lowering of living standards.

9.5.2 Norwegian values

Regarding the values of the Norwegian people, one of the male embassy interviewees draws on an often used distinction between Christian and democratic values (see section 3.3.1). He says: 'I would say that our very basis is what I would call Christian and democratic values… or maybe rather value-neutral values, as it has been phrased in the UN conventions'. Accordingly, when this interviewee tries to expound the basis for NDA, he points to three kinds of values: Christian, democratic, and value-neutral values. The expression 'value-neutral values' seems to be a contradiction in terms, but note the function this expression has in the context in which it is used. Here it refers to UN conventions. Accordingly, the basis for the work, as he sees it, is 'Christian and democratic values', as well as 'UN conventions'.

It is noticeable that these three kinds of values appear as both distinct and part of a whole. The difference between them should, however, not be disregarded. Christian values seem to refer to values rooted in and defined by a specific religious tradition. As such they are contrasted with values specific to other religious traditions, although the extent to which these overlap or contradict each other is not addressed. Similarly, democratic values seem to qualify a set of values that are not of an undemocratic kind. Therefore both Christian and democratic values seem to place the moral basis for Norwegian development work in specific traditions. It could, though, be argued that both of these have aspects that go beyond the limits of specific contexts. Being a missionary religion, Christianity claims to be relevant to all peoples everywhere, whilst the democratic tradition emphasises the equal voice of everyone. As such, there is a universal element in both of them. This seems, however, not to be emphasised in this interviewee's use of the terms.

The universal aspect is, however, clearly articulated through the third set of values – the 'value-neutral values', understood as UN conventions. The value basis for NDA seems then, to this interviewee, to encompass values of different kinds, with two of them rooted in specific traditions. It seems then that what could be considered as UN specific values are not regarded as context specific in the same way as the other two. Accordingly, he combines values that are specific with values that are universal. It therefore becomes possible in the practice of aid work to identify conditions that are regarded as unacceptable to the donor, based on the specific values governing aid work, as well as arguing that development aid is based on shared values, and accordingly dismissing any accusations of illegitimate interference or unreasonable conditionality (see section 13.2).

Similarly, another of the male embassy interviewees draws on the distinction between two traditions in Norwegian society that he sees as the background to Norwegian aid. He says:

> Well, the starting point is the Norwegian historical tradition related to the experience of injustice, which means that we in Norway generally speaking have two main traditions. It's the leftist one of reflections on justice (*rettferdighetsbetraktninger*), […] and then you have the Christian value basis (*kristne verdigrunnlaget*), which also has something of the same starting point, although they are quite different. But they end up with the same kinds of necessary measures. That is the Norwegian tradition. So the starting point is a kind of reflection on injustice, and when things are unjust, then there is a desire to do something, be it big things or small. And this is one small contribution with respect to injustice.[10]

The 'Norwegian historical tradition' is here conceptualised as being made up of two distinct traditions, one in the left labour movement and another in the Christian tradition. Again, however, it is the unity of the 'Norwegian tradition' that is emphasised.

This emphasis on unity echoes the findings of several historians and social scientists that highlight the predominant consensus that has governed Norwegian foreign policy as well as the construction of a shared understanding of development aid as part of Norwegian identity (see section 3.3). Note also how this interviewee frames her reflection on aid as a Norwegian response to injustice. He identifies a 'reflection on injustice' as the starting point and conceptualises Norwegian aid as a 'small contribution with respect to injustice' (see section 12.1). Note again the emphasis on the limited scale of this contribution.

9.6 Difficulties and critics

The difficulties implied in development work are recognised by many interviewees. One important aspect of this is the (perceived) difficulties involved in measuring results (see section 3.2.4). One of the female SCN interviewees says:

10 Yet another male embassy interviewee also traces NDA history to these two traditions. He says: 'The whole of Norwegian development aid history is based on the solidarity of the Labour movement, and then you have the humanitarian aspect through the church and other voluntary organisations, which has been the foundation for Norwegian policy'.

> […] When we are talking about relief, it's easy to say, yes, we have a feeding point here, so many children come and you can see them eating. That is easy to count. They are quantitative. But the ones that have a lasting impact are the ones difficult to measure. And I know for a donor, they want to see the quantitative ones. And yet, those are short-term effects. The long-term effects are more difficult to measure.

Discussing different approaches to development aid more generally, the same interviewee says: 'Development is not easy. We don't have one word answers'.

These difficulties lead some of the interviewees to question the very legitimacy of, and rationale for, such work. One of the female NCA interviewees says: '[…] I wonder if this is the right way to help people. I think that is a thought I have every day'. Asked to elaborate, she says:

> Well, development aid? I don't know if that is what will improve the lives of people in this part of the world. One could look around and ask oneself how many years we have been doing development work in this part of the world, and how great an impact has it had in the broader perspective. That is a painful dilemma, and I have struggled a lot with this conflict.

This interviewee does not question the aim of development work, but rather whether development aid is the right tool to reach this goal. Her question is historically motivated. Given that development aid has been provided for many years and given its lack of impact 'in the broader perspective', she questions whether aid is really working. Note, however, it's the impact 'in the broader perspective' that leads to her 'painful dilemma'.

The doubts regarding aid that these interviewees convey are fundamental in the sense that they challenge the very existence and practice of development work. In the context of reflecting on her motivation, one of the male embassy interviewees says:

> […] And there can be a lot of small, small steps and many setbacks. So many that it often can be very difficult to believe in the idea that we are on the way to a better place. Are we really? And then you have the MDG analysis, and the evaluation of the poverty reduction strategy papers, right? Everything shows that we aren't making any progress… We are struggling a lot. The counter forces are strong.

Similarly, when reflecting on a hypothetical end to international aid to the country in which she is working, one of the female embassy interviewees says:

> This is very difficult. In a way, sometimes I can be tempted to say that we should just withdraw. And then they need to clean up (*få orden på*) their own… Then they have to tidy up (*rydde opp i*) their own system and get rid of the most corrupt and try to take on responsibility for governing their own country. Not just be like: 'Oh well, now there is a new leader. Buying new planes and new cars…' Well, I don't know…

The consequences this interviewee imagines withdrawing development aid would lead to are worth noting. It would make them 'tidy up their own system', or as she puts it more generally 'try to take on responsibility for governing their own country'. She mentions problems such as corruption and misuse of funds, and it seems one important impetus for her considering ending aid is to make the recipient take responsibility. In other words, she acknowledges that development aid can have an adverse effect by making people ignore their own (personal or institutional) responsibility. Implicit is a notion that the recipients of aid actually have a responsibility that the potential donor responsibility does not negate.

The same interviewee adds: '[…] Norway has simply poured money into Africa since the 1960s. And from time to time I wonder: Where did the money go? Considering that the countries are still very poor'. The doubts articulated by this interviewee are related to what she perceives as a profound lack of results after over 50 years of NDA. At the general level she finds the recipient countries are still 'very poor', indicating that the results are very limited. She does, however, mention education as one field where some results can be identified, but in light of the general poverty she seems to doubt the gains achieved even in this field. Accordingly, this interviewee seems relatively disillusioned with the results of Norwegian aid so far. Similarly, one of the male NPA interviewees says: 'There have been quite a number of people, there have been, also Africans actually, who say that development aid hardly helps. And to a large degree, unfortunately, I agree'.

However, another of the female embassy interviewees articulates a somewhat different critique of development aid. Discussing the changes she has seen in NDA over the years, she says:

> [...] Development aid has become very academic. Lots of people with PhDs are signed on... And the people you are supposed to help don't understand anything you are talking about... [...] And then we have to attend a course, and you engage some kind of consultant from a consultancy firm that asks a thousand dollars a day, right? So when people, critical non-governmental organisations and similar groups, say... When they say that a lot of the money goes back to the donor country, then that is probably true.

Unlike the picture that other interviewees paint of the relationship between the passive recipient and the active donor, the perspective here focuses more on the donor side of the aid relationship. This interviewee's criticism of how 'development aid has become very academic' seems to refer to the competence and qualifications of professional development workers (see section 14.2). There is, however, also in this case a shift in her argument. In the latter section it seems it is not this development per se that is the problem, but rather a concern about finances. This criticism seems to have different elements. One the one hand this is a red tape argument – that the development aid bureaucracy is inefficient and expensive and as such takes resources away from those for whom the aid is intended. This is an echo of criticism voiced in the 1980s which regarded the official channels for aid as inappropriate, and favoured NGOs as the main channels (see section 3.2.3). The second point made by this interviewee concerns the flow of resources between the donor and the recipient. While the aid relationship is often perceived as one where resources go from the donor to the recipient, this interviewee claims there is a considerable flow of money from the recipient to the donor. Note that the criticism voiced here is limited to aid funds. Thus it is similar to, but not the same as, the critique from dependency theorists, arguing that the relationship between the North and the South is one of exploitation, and that aid reinforces this unequal relationship (see section 3.2). What these two forms of criticism share is the claim that substantial financial resources flow in the opposite direction, in effect serving the interests of the donor, not the recipient.[11]

11 One of the female NCA interviewees also criticises how too much money goes back to the donor side in the aid relationship. She says: 'But there is a huge apparatus before those shillings reach the ground, really. And a lot, most, of the money probably goes back to Norway'.

9.6.1 *Improving development aid*

Asked to explain why she questions the effects of development aid, one of the female NCA interviewees says:

> Before I left and before I started working for Norwegian Church Aid… Or maybe especially after I started working for NCA, I have asked myself that question: if what we do is actually what [country] needs, if development aid is the solution. And I think I will always reflect critically on this. It could be that our resources could have been spent differently and we could have achieved more.

Here too the focus is clearly on the macro level. Can development aid be the solution to the problems of the country as a whole? Reflecting on this, this interviewee considers whether the funds could have been spent in another way in order to achieve more. This addresses the issue of how aid should be improved. Thus, her continued reflection seems not primarily to reject the concept of development aid altogether. Further, she does not address to what extent aid is to be considered the one and only solution to all of these countries' problems. As noted, several of the interviewees reject this understanding of aid. Rather, development aid is one of several mechanisms that can be used to improve the situation in a given country. The same interviewee also says:

> I don't doubt that it works at some levels. It works for the individual and it might work for local communities and for some organisations. But I doubt very much if it works with regard to the larger picture, the profound injustice. But if that is what… you may wonder if that is the purpose. But that is what Norwegian Church Aid says. 'Yes, we want to work for a more just world.' Then I think you must dare to ask the question whether we actually are doing things the right way.

Note the distinction this interviewee makes between results at the individual level (including local communities and organisations) and the macro level (the larger picture). Her doubts relate not to the first, but to the latter.[12]

12 Similarly, one of the male NPA interviewees expresses doubts about some development projects, but retains faith in development aid in general. He says: 'In some cases development aid makes things worse. But I think in general… I think in general development aid contributes positively'.

Asked to comment on the critics' claim that the results from development aid are difficult or impossible to detect, one of the male embassy interviewees says:

> These questions are relevant, and... but the answer is not to abolish development aid. The answer is to think through what you do, and to do things better. [...] I would say that the reason why many countries in Africa are lagging behind in development, have a slower economic development, that the gap is increasing, is not because of development aid. It's in spite of development aid. If I had thought it was because of development aid, I would not have been sitting here. I wouldn't. It's despite development aid. And that implies that there are a lot of other things that play an even greater role. And a lot has to do with the international division of labour, trade regimes.

This interviewee explicitly rejects stopping development aid. Again, the difficulties involved are rather seen as a challenge to improve it, and again a strong faith in development aid's ability to make a difference is expressed. Another male embassy interviewee comments on the same issue in this way:

> [...] It's clear that development aid can be an obstacle for development. I think, however, that we have come a bit further in giving development aid in a way that produces results. We have become a lot more result oriented. And the countries are committed to delivering results. It's clear that if we did not give aid for immunisation and vaccination, the results would be different. We have exterminated smallpox. We are well on our way to getting measles and children's diseases under control. These are sensible investments that give visible results. [...] So, you can have a long discussion about what would have given better results in development aid. And I agree with those who say that we tend to exaggerate the role of development aid. Development aid is a contribution facilitating development. A lot more is needed than just development aid. But I disagree with those who say that it doesn't achieve results.

Here a specific difficulty in aid work is addressed, namely the possibility that aid is actually counterproductive. Note, however, the optimism expressed in the recent gains made in this field. Clearly, this interviewee believes aid has substantially changed and improved over the years. Accordingly, much of the criticism can be rejected as it does not take into account the way that present day development work is organised and implemented.[13]

9.6.2 *Communicating results*

While several of the interviewees quoted above express strong doubts about the results development aid is able to achieve, other interviewees seem strongly convinced that their aid efforts do lead to good or positive results. To these interviewees the self-criticism seems to be rather that these results have not been communicated to the public audience and donors. One of the male NCA interviewee's responds to the claims of such critics by saying:

> [...] I believe we haven't been good enough at showing Norway and many, many others the results that are there. Perhaps we use too big headlines, like: 'Help the poor!' But we don't say how many schools we have helped build, how many teachers we have helped train. We don't say how many clinics we have contributed to establishing. So, the criticism is actually turned rather towards ourselves.

Similarly, asked if he has any doubts with regards to the effects of development work, one of the male SCN interviewees says:

> [...] We have concrete results to show that it helps. [...] That is also for ethical reasons. One should not brag. But the point is that we actually can show results. We have proper statistics. We have systems for reporting. We have procedures for evaluations, and all this. This enables us to give reports. This is not something we just say. We can show it. And clearly, if you take people with you to the field, then people are impressed. Not only here, but also in other Save the Children countries.[14]

13 One of the male embassy interviewees highlights the constant discussions that take place. He says: 'Is there too much money? "Are the plans good enough? Are the staff good enough? Are the recipient structures good enough?" All this... "Are there some things here that we do too simply, not thoroughly enough (*for enkelt, for lettvint*)? No, damn, this is something they should do themselves", right... "Now this is enough." We have that discussion all the time. I would like to say that. We have that discussion all the time'.

14 One of the female NPA interviewees similarly argues that it is possible to measure and communicate the results development aid brings about. She says: 'It isn't difficult to measure progress. It's only difficult to measure progress if you don't have any terms of reference. And in this we have a responsibility towards the taxpayers'.

The imperative that 'one should not brag' seems to be an important concern for this interviewee, but also one that should be weighed against the need to communicate the results achieved. The key issue here is, however, this interviewee's insistence that development aid actually brings results. He insists that this is something 'we actually can show'. Accordingly, this interviewee clearly articulates confidence in the importance and effects of development work.

Results are clearly emphasised as important by several interviewees. One of the male embassy interviewees says this is not about showing off kindness, but about achieving results:

> [...] The most important thing is not to show off Norwegian kindness (*den norske godheten*), but to leave behind a few results that might not be very visible to the Norwegian public, but which have a greater effect for the people concerned.

The expression 'Norwegian kindness' is here contrasted with 'leave behind a few results that might not be very visible to the Norwegian public'. Accordingly, this interviewee stresses the aim of aid to be other's interests, not self-interest. However, the statement also says something about how Norwegian kindness is perceived. Promoting Norwegian kindness is seen as something that has an effect on Norwegian opinion. Emphasising Norwegian kindness seems then to be something that increases public support for aid purposes. This interviewee seems, however, concerned that this aspect stands in a certain contrast to the results that 'have a greater effect for the people concerned'.

Similarly, when asked if she really thinks development aid actually helps, one of the female embassy interviewees says:

> Well, I wouldn't have had the energy to do this work if I didn't think it helped in any way. I think it helps. But I believe that our time frames are often wrong, with respect to the time frame that we need here, especially in Africa. I can't speak for East Asia, sort of, because over there most things go a lot faster. But here I think things help over time. And the way we are doing things now, there is a greater demand that they think it through and build their own systems, and get a grip on what they want in terms of education, why they should have education and what kind of education they want to have and need. I think it makes a difference over time. But I believe that it takes more than a five year period. It takes ten, twenty years, maybe, before you have... You might need the next generation to step in and cultivate a more comprehensive idea about how the state has the responsibility for the development of this country.

This interviewee too seems to cling to the conviction that aid does make a difference. Note, however, that this conviction is followed by two reflections. The first concerns the element of time. Compared to other places where processes might be faster, she claims that one must adopt a longer perspective, 'especially in Africa'. In other words, she puts her faith in the long-term effects. Her second reflection concerns the manner in which development aid is implemented and her trust in 'the way we are doing things now'. She implicitly indicates that the earlier ways of implementing were not as good as the ones used now. Unlike previous programmes, she describes the present one as emphasising recipient participation ('that they think it through') and independence ('build their own systems'). Finally, note how she makes the state responsible. It's the state that 'has the responsibility for the development of this country'.

9.7 Concluding reflections

The interviewees of this study tend to identify the long-term perspective as a key characteristic of development aid, but dissociate from the notion that it is governed by kindness. On the contrary, one of the interviewees points to what she sees as a 'need to be cynical'. This is also articulated when several interviewees seem to conceptualise development aid in clear contrast to relief, understanding the development worker as distinct from both the 'cowboys' of relief and the charity work of Mother Theresa.

Another recurring feature is how development aid is not conceptualised as a contrast to the political, but rather as something that goes 'hand in hand' with politics, or is part of it. There is also a discourse articulated that emphasises the distinct character of aid, with a special focus on for example acute needs. Still, the main tendency among both male and female interviewees seems to be to regard development aid as a political undertaking – as something that must be understood as part of the wider political situation in the context of government policies, as well as something that must address macro political issues. When several interviewees seem to emphasise the need to adopt a wider perspective, this relates not only to the temporal issue of what will happen to the starving the next day. It seems also to imply a criticism that points to a lack of understanding of the political, economic, social, and cultural implications of aid interventions.

In discussing development aid, several interviewees raise the issue of having a bad conscience. While some explicitly reject that Norwegian aid has, or should have, anything to do with a bad conscience, others ridicule NDA by claiming that this is precisely what it is all about. In both cases, however, the interviewees invest discursively in dissociating from this notion. Further, scepticism towards any notion or reference to 'good intentions' is articulated. Having good intentions or boasting about one's efforts seems often to be interpreted as the opposite of actually doing good work and bringing about lasting results.

NDA seems to be widely perceived to be governed by either 'neutral values' or by universal values that everyone supports or should support. Further, it seems that Norway is perceived as a country without self-interest (see section 3.3.1). To use development aid as an instrument to gain access to markets and other benefits for Norwegian corporate firms does not seem to be a significant part of the moral discourse of NDA. This does not imply that Norwegian aid is seen exclusively as altruistic. Many interviewees, again both male and female, seem to reject self-interest as the primary motive for NDA, but conceptualise it rather as something that serves common interests. Although in some cases there might be self-serving oil interests, this is seen as separate from the development aid agenda. And although development aid might also serve Norway's own security and immigration interests, this is not seen as the rationale underlying Norwegian state policy in this field. In this sense, a harmonious outlook on international politics seems to frame the understanding of NDA.

There is also a discourse of aid criticism that is being articulated in the material. The lack of results, the way aid money finds its way to wealthy development workers, consultants etc., are issues these interviewees not only are aware of but also make part of their evaluation of the 'aid industry' that they are part of. On the other hand, there is also a discourse that stresses how results are actually achieved (see section 3.2.4). Some of the interviewees stress very clearly that they can show clear results of the work they do. Still, several of the interviewees express their limited expectations regarding what kind of results it is possible to achieve through aid efforts. There are so many other factors that seem to play a much more important role in creating lasting changes in the living conditions of the many poor in developing countries.

Several of the interviewees seem to perceive NDA as a 'social programme' that aims at making things 'a little better' by 'filling gaps'. In this, the limited aim and scope of development aid seems also to be emphasised. Emphasis seems to be on individual cases and the micro level. Thus, results can be identified and presented, but aid seems to be understood as a very limited tool in terms of making structural changes in the world. Accordingly, the results that can be achieved in the long run are very limited if something is not done at the macro level, through changes in the international trade system or at the level of international politics.

To summarise, although development aid is widely considered a political undertaking, the notion of idealism seems to come across as an important element of the moral discourse of NDA. As noted in chapter 6, some of the interviewees invest discursively in dissociating from the kind of idealism that characterises some of the policy documents. In this chapter, however, the perception of NDA as governed by 'neutral values', lack of self-interest, and common interests indicates an implicit idealistic and harmonious understanding. Furthermore, the concern for results is again articulated by several of the interviewees. In this chapter, however, the interviewees express their limited expectations of these results. Again an aspect of the moral discourse of NDA not articulated in the policy documents is revealed in the interviews.

Part V

Policy – ideas and approaches

10 Rights and responsibilities

The never-ending debate
about the ends and means of development
and the role of aid is by no means simplified
by the introduction of human rights.

Katarina Tomasevski (Tomasevski 1989:205)

Being employed by aid agencies it is not surprising that the interviewees are generally in favour of providing development aid. Development aid can be justified in different ways, however. By justification I mean the set of arguments, grounds, and reasons given to explain or legitimise involvement in international aid. As I am here concerned with the moral discourse of NDA, I will focus on the moral justifications the interviewees articulate. As noted in chapter 4, the concept of human rights seems to be a nodal point in the NDA discourse as it is articulated in the documents studied. In this chapter I will explore how this concept is used and interpreted by the interviewees, as well as the related concept of responsibility.[1]

10.1 The rights based approach

When asked what she thinks about development aid being described as rights based, one of the female NCA interviewees says:

> I think a whole lot about that. I think it's really smart. Because it relates to what I have already talked about. By talking about human rights you can take the dignity of the individual (*enkeltmenneskets verdi*) as a starting point. Human dignity is the starting point. We all have a natural or God-given dignity, etc. And further, regarding human dignity and the human rights perspective, you have social rights,

1 A brief discussion of these issues can also be found in Fretheim 2007.

> economic rights and cultural rights, etc., and in this way you can make it more concrete. What areas should we move into? As I already mentioned, I think that we should be much more political, and I think we should engage ourselves much more in the economy of the country etc. The other thing that is good about the rights approach is that by having it as the starting point, all of a sudden there are also expectations and demands (*forventninger og krav*). And this thing about stakeholders and… What is the other? Right bearers and duty holders. That is, some kind of version of this way of thinking. That someone has responsibility (*ansvar*) for someone else, and then you also have claims for something, as a human. Not that you are a citizen of this or that country, but by being a human. Then you can claim (*kreve*) it, and if you don't get it from your state, then you can claim it in terms of the rights you have as a human being. I think that is a nice development in the ideology of international aid, and something I feel that I can adopt.

The introductory comment – 'I think a whole lot about that' – seems to indicate that the issue of human rights in development aid is something this interviewee was familiar with ahead of the interview. This confirms the presumption that the concept of human rights functions as a nodal point in the NDA discourse. Further, this statement is framed by the interviewee's positive approval of human rights based development aid. She says it is 'really smart' and she finds it to be an 'ideology' that she can 'adopt'. Further, she clearly relates human rights to human dignity. As noted above, this corresponds to the language in *Fighting Poverty Together* and the UN Declaration of Human Rights, but not least to NCA's policy documents (see sections 4.1 and 4.2). Her emphasis on the value of every individual human being can also be seen as echoing this human rights discourse. However, and important to note in light of the discussion on the relationship between political rights and social, economic, and cultural rights, she explicitly includes the latter in her explanation of the human rights based approach in development aid. In this connection she also makes a normative remark, claiming that political and (macro) economic aspects should be emphasised much more in development aid work. Implicitly then she criticises those development aid efforts that do not take these societal issues sufficiently into consideration.

The introduction of expectations and demands is also important to this interviewee. Or as she puts it: there are not only 'rights bearers', but also 'duty holders'. This is a concern articulated also in some of the NCA policy documents (see section 4.2), and it corresponds to the important, although debated, moral philosophical insight that rights are empty if there are no corresponding duties. Note also how this interviewee relates human rights to the matter of being human, this time in contrast to a right based on national citizenship. Elaborating further on the rights based approach, however, she says:

> [...] But there are also some weaknesses. And one weakness to me is again cultural, that human rights easily become a Western concept coming from Norway, and that doesn't make much sense in other contexts, still... Because you have to take so many steps back before you can start talking about human rights, which takes me back to my main criticism of the new approach, the fact that it isn't really a new approach. It's only new terminology for precisely what we did before, and what we said before. And which again, in the final analysis, is based on our desire to do good (*ønsker å gjøre noe godt*) for other people. That is initially (*i utgangspunktet*) about us and not so much about them. That is what I think. If you go back to the human rights perspective again, then you have the equivalents to all those concepts, just in other jargon.

Here this interviewee mentions two objections to the rights based approach. The first is an often cited objection to the concept of human rights: that it is a 'Western concept' and as such is rooted in a specific context. By saying it 'doesn't make much sense in other contexts', she voices a criticism of human rights as a universal concept. While she thus points to epistemic difficulties in transferring a concept from one context to another, this transfer can also be criticised for moral reasons, arguing that it is illegitimate and imperialistic to impose concepts from one context onto another.

This interviewee also voices another criticism of the human rights based approach, however. Her main criticism, she claims, is that it is not a new approach. 'It's only new terminology for precisely what we did before'. Further, she argues these aid efforts in the end are 'based on our desire to do good for other people'. It seems reasonable to read 'to do good' as referring to a positive activity. However, note how this interviewee explains the basis for development aid: 'That is initially about us and not so much about them'. Although this is phrased in moderate terms, a key element in her interpretation seems thus to be the self-centeredness of development aid.

10.1.1 Universal rules or rhetoric

The interviewees articulate different interpretations of the concept of human rights and the rights based approach in development aid. When asked if she finds that NDA implies interfering with domestic policies in the recipient country, one of the female embassy interviewees says:

> Of course it does, if the authorities don't agree and think other things are more important. I have seen this several times, if we are discussing human rights for instance. Then they would say, 'you shouldn't compare us with a Western country or with the West', and 'there are so many things that are more important or as important, and we have a long way to go until we reach that point.' … And I have always felt that it is not without reason that the human rights declaration is called the Universal Declaration of Human Rights. Because there are some absolute elements that you cannot run away from, I think.

This interviewee clearly understands human rights as something universal, but also articulates a concern for the importance of contextual issues. As the question prompting this statement might be leading in this direction, the confirmation of NDA as an external factor interfering in domestic affairs is not surprising. The way she legitimises this, however, is noteworthy. Referring to the universal character of human rights, she insists they are relevant in the recipient country.

Asked to respond to critics of NDA, one of the male embassy interviewees says:

> […] There are those who…, of course, many people question and ask questions about the human rights declaration and if human rights are universal, and that is a philosophical question. And of course we can ponder over that. My conclusion is relatively straight forward. It has been made by people and can be revised by people. But when we have said that this will be the basis for our interaction, well then we have made an agreement. And if anyone breaks this agreement, then we have an intellectual collision. A collision. And we will be sanctioned, because we have agreed on the rules of the game (*spilleregler*)...

This interviewee questions the universal character of human rights but argues that since 'we have made an agreement', the rules should be followed. On the one hand he says human rights have been 'made by people', and thus argues that they can be changed. Human rights are accordingly not perceived as an inherent characteristic of man, but are rather ascribed and agreed on. On the other hand, this interviewee argues ‘we have agreed’ to make human rights the ‘basis for our interaction’. This ‘we’ seems to refer either to the international community at large, or possibly the more specific agreement that governs NDA in a given recipient country. In any event, this interviewee assumes an agreement has been made. So breaking the rules is not acceptable. Thus, while human rights are relative in the sense that they can be changed and could have been different, they are universal due to this contract.

However, explaining how she understands human rights based aid, one of the female NCA interviewees says:

> [...] Because I think that the changes in Norwegian Church Aid have been very positive, by turning more towards rights and a reflection on justice. That what we do is not only charity. That is what I am really sceptical about. We are still very much at a stage where we work very traditionally. On paper we are up in front, I think, in Norwegian Church Aid, with relatively progressive thinking about how development work should be done. But after I came here I was quite surprised to find how traditionally we are still working.

This interviewee addresses the practical impact of adopting the human rights approach. Note the distinction she makes between the traditional approach and the rights based approach. She seems, however, to question to what extent the shift from the traditional to the new has been implemented. On the one hand she makes a positive evaluation of the changes taking place, but she is still surprised at ‘how traditionally we are still working’. Just as in *Fighting Poverty Together* she seems to downplay the novelty of the human rights approach, at least in any practical terms (see section 4.1).

One of the male NCA interviewees puts it this way when asked if there are any problems with the human rights based approach:

> Yes, there are problems. There are problems in terms of learning it. Because often it becomes rhetoric and often it becomes just words that are used in academic contexts only. Taking it down to the operational level is very, very difficult.

This interviewee seems to find it hard to grasp what the human rights approach actually implies, perhaps primarily in operational terms. It seems in his view that the human rights based approach is at risk of becoming rhetoric without practical implications, and thus mere rhetoric. When similarly asked if she sees any problems with the human rights based approach, one of the male SCN interviewees says:

> […] When we talk about rights, it's kind of distant from people's reality, from the day-to-day needs of what they want. Because here you kind of take it at a higher level, and then you try to have dialogue with those […] who are the primary duty-bearers to try to afford that right to the one we support to get it. And when we talk about these issues, then at times people confront us and say that, but our immediate need today is that my child is sick. And they want their child to go to school too, but they have nothing.

Here a different criticism of the rights based approach is articulated. This time it is the lack of closeness to people's reality or sensitivity to their needs that seems to be the prime concern behind the criticism. The 'talk about rights' is considered 'distant from people's reality'. The development worker's perspective is at a 'higher level'. Further, addressing the issue of responsibility and who the duty-bearer is seems also to be a distinctive feature of how this interviewee understands this approach, although this aspect seems to be ambiguous. While it is often considered of prime importance, the understanding here is that there is a lack of focus on 'immediate needs'. In other words, the criticism seems to be that the rights based approach fails to sufficiently take into account the concerns that are often considered the primary concerns of the needs based approach (see section 3.2). Addressing structural issues should not be at the expense of immediate needs.

Explaining NPA's understanding of human rights based aid, one of the male NPA interviewees says:

> […] You can take it a long way and say that people have a right to food, so when we deliver food we have a rights based… But that is not the thinking. That is to stretch it too far, really. Because, the way the strategy states it, it is to make local organisations, civil society, able to raise its voice and make claims on the authorities, on behalf of the oppressed. That is not what you do when you distribute food. Or save someone's life. So to make it out as rights based according to the definition Norwegian People's Aid uses, that doesn't work.

This interviewee discusses the rights based approach in the context of the kinds of activities it refers to. Referring to NPA's strategy, he places enabling civil society 'to raise its voice' clearly within his understanding of the rights based approach. Distributing food on the other hand, is not part of a rights based approach. Note how this interviewee dissociates her work from that of relief workers, and how he emphasises the political aspect. Thus, it seems relief falls outside its remit, while advocacy falls within it (see sections 9.2 and 9.3).

10.1.2 Rights and needs

Despite examples indicating a relatively vague understanding of rights based aid, most interviewees are clearly enthusiastic about the human rights approach. This enthusiasm cannot, however, be taken as an expression of shared understanding. As noted in the previous section, some of the interviewees are concerned about problematic or challenging aspects of human rights and the rights based approach, and in this regard differences in interpretation are also articulated. Such differences come to the fore also as the interviewees contrast the rights based approach with various alternatives.

As noted above, one of the female NCA interviewees makes a distinction between the traditional approach and the more recent rights approach. Explaining further how she understands the difference between the traditional and the new rights based approach, she says:

> […] I think it has a lot to do with the way of thinking and the focus. It doesn't necessarily become very different in practice. But I think it means that you have to view the recipients of our help as people who have rights, to clean water, to health, to education. In this context it's about basic needs. Instead of thinking: poor people, they don't have what they need… They are actually people who have claims on something, the right to something. And that implies that there is also someone who has the responsibility to provide water and health services and schools. And that is what I believe is the difference between this approach and the more traditional approach, that you actually make someone responsible for the situation being as it is. Not only that there are some people who don't get what they should have, but that someone has failed somewhere, and needs to be made responsible (*ansvarliggjøres*). So I think it must imply working on more levels than has maybe been the case. I am not saying that people were not made responsible before, but I think that with this approach you cannot escape it.

The new rights approach is here conceptualised in terms of the right people have to receive 'our help'. In this interviewee's view this leads, or should lead, to a different way of viewing them as recipients. Further, making 'someone responsible' seems to be regarded as a distinctive characteristic of the new approach. Recipient rights and responsibilities seem to go hand in hand (see section 10.2). Further, rights are here understood as rights to have basic needs fulfilled. The reference to needs again echoes many of the concerns and characteristics of the needs based approach (see section 3.2).[2]

Several other interviewees, however, emphasise the contrast between needs and rights based aid. Three interviewees provide examples of different ways of understanding the human rights approach through such a contrast with the needs based approach. Like many others, the first, one of the female SCN interviewees, expresses a positive evaluation of the rights approach, but then goes on to articulate a difficulty in understanding what human rights based actually means compared to needs based approaches. She says:

> We understand what it means – what rights mean, but how do we make a project and ensure that it's actually rights based…? The distinction between needs and rights, it isn't… When you are running a practical project it's not easy to distinguish between the two and to be entirely sure that what we do is rights based and not… That is, rights based and needs based. Because, it's the needs we try to meet. This is something we are working on. Nobody has found the perfect way of doing rights based aid work.

This interviewee refers to and makes use of the contrast between rights and needs, but it appears that she finds it difficult to apply the difference in practice. And, although she prefers the human rights approach, it is still 'the needs we try to meet'. Again, the novelty of the rights based approach is downplayed. Elaborating further on the difference between the two approaches, the same interviewee says:

> […] If I think about needs based, then I think about these children. They don't have enough food and they don't get any schooling. So I will help them get it. And then I am kind, and I help them. But I don't necessarily have to help all, because I should really be content if I manage to help some of them, because I don't have to help all of them, because I am doing as much as I can. So if I have a project… […] and I manage to help the children in that project, then I am content. But if I think rights, then I think that all the children in [country] have a right to this. And it's my responsibility, and others' responsibility, to ensure that they get these things. And then I can't work only with a few children, I could do that, but I must also do something to influence the system causing these children not to have their rights met. So then I

2 Explaining the difference between rights and needs, the same interviewee says: '[…] Earlier we talked of needs, basic needs. And that is in a way also legitimate, because we do have needs. As human beings we do. But it has another ring to it when you talk about actually having rights to something. Because then, the way I think about it, somebody also has responsibility…'.

have a greater responsibility, and I have to think differently about how I develop the project.

Maybe the most explicit difference between the needs based and the rights based approaches in development aid expressed here is indicated by 'I don't have to help all' and 'to help some of them' on the one hand, and 'all the children [...] have a right to this' and 'can't work only with a few children' on the other. It seems that universality in the case of needs based aid lies in the notion that all could be helped, but that needs based aid will still be marked by a degree of selectivity. Not so in the case of rights based aid.[3]

Note also how this development worker speaks in different ways about the two approaches. In the context of the needs based approach, she finds that the development worker can be satisfied if she has assisted some, not necessarily all. Within the framework of rights, however, this option is not there, since she must also do 'something to influence the system'. This macro political aspect then comes across as an important feature of the rights based approach that distinguishes it from a needs based approach. Further, there is a change in terminology worth noting. Explaining her understanding of the needs based approach, she uses the verb 'to help' in the first person singular repeatedly. She says 'I manage to help the children', 'I am content', and 'I don't necessarily have to help all'. In contrast, when explaining the rights based approach, she does not use this term, but seems to prefer the term 'responsibility'. And when using this term, she highlights that this is not only her (first person singular) responsibility, but rather a shared one: 'my responsibility, and others' responsibility'. Clearly the issue of responsibility is perceived as an important aspect of the rights based approach.

When asked in what way she regards the distinction between needs and rights as a contrast, another female NCA interviewee says: 'not contrast, but maybe rather a development of the way we work', indicating a continuum between the needs based and rights based approaches. Still, she too makes the same distinction between the 'old way' and the

3 One of the female embassy interviewees articulates a similar understanding of rights based aid. She says: '[...] But what I am most concerned with regarding rights based aid is that these rights are for all groups. No groups are better than others. Whether the group is men, be it of the old or the young, ethnicity, religion, etc. It's very important that all have the same opportunities'.

present rights based approach. Encouraged to describe the 'old way of working', she replies:

> Yes, the old way was much more sort of need based, we came and built schools, not that this isn't something that also should be done, but it's really something the local government should do. And as non-governmental organisations we should not take over the job of the local government. So it moves sort of in that direction, that you make the local government take on its responsibility. And that one could also… I mean, you cannot deny it…. I have worked so many years in this, that when you work the way you have been doing, and maybe earlier, you create sort of an oasis, a little oasis, small local communities around where you work, and they benefit from it. But then there are local communities a bit further away… So there are great differences, and you create differences.

Using the example of building schools, this interviewee implicitly articulates the continuum between the old and the new way, in the sense that education not only has been, but still is a key priority in NDA. Further, this interviewee, like the previous one, highlights how the work done in the framework of a needs based approach is not wrong in itself. Her critical remark, however, goes in a somewhat different direction. While the former interviewee was concerned about the satisfaction achieved when having assisted some, this interviewee highlights the role of the local government. Within the needs based approach the aid agencies risk taking on the role she claims the government should have. In contrast, in the framework of the new approach 'you make the local government take on its responsibility'. In this case then the notion of responsibility primarily refers to the responsibility of the recipient government.

One of the male NCA interviewees also explains the human rights based approach with reference to the needs based approach. When asked about the difference between the new human rights thinking compared to the old way of thinking about aid, he says:

> Among other things, you talk about needs based and rights based. And there is a conceptual difference in looking at the needs, because the needs can be many, a lot, and big… But it doesn't say anything about, well, what you do about it. You just fill some gaps, where there are needs...

Elaborating further on the contrast between a rights based and a needs based approach, the same interviewee says:

> Yes, there has been the traditional, where you say that there is a need for food, so give food. There is a need for education, provide education. And it's a matter of how many and where etc. But there is no sustainability in it because you define things with need, and for instance not by what resources are actually there and what the potential is. You focus on the need, and not on the resources and the obligations (*forpliktelsene*) implicit in the systems.

This interviewee too emphasises the selective aspect of a needs based approach referred to by the previous interviewee. But while the interviewees above are concerned about helping all and about the risk of disregarding the responsibility of the recipient government, this interviewee's criticism of the needs based approach underlines its lack of sustainability. In explaining this lack of sustainability, a criticism of the implicit understanding of the recipients of the aid also seems to be indicated. His argument is that with the emphasis on needs, the issues of local resources and potential, as well as obligations, become less important. It seems reasonable to see this statement in the context of the discussion on how the recipients of international development aid are perceived. If a focus on needs leads to a disregard for the resources and potential of the individual recipients, this has implications for how the recipient is perceived by the donors. Having needs is then interpreted as being in need of external help, and not having the resources or potential to help oneself. This leads to a lack of agency of the recipient.

The comment that not only the resources and potential, but also the 'obligations implicit in the systems', are disregarded in the needs based approach is also worth noting. The implication seems to be that the needs based approach does not take obligations (sufficiently) into account, although this interviewee does not state how or to what extent this is taken into account in the rights based approach.

10.2 Responsibilities and duties

The interviewees generally endorse human rights as a key element in the moral rationale for international aid, but as noted above, the understanding of rights and rights based aid differs between interviewees. A further difference is the degree to which, or in what way, donor responsibility is seen as an integral part of the rights approach. Some of the informants emphasise donor responsibility, others the obligations 'implicit in the system'. Similarly, reflecting on the issue of rights and responsibilities, one of the female NCA interviewees says:

> [...] Accordingly, from a human rights perspective, if you really are to adopt the core of human rights, then you can forget about these state things. Because then you only have the human being, and it doesn't matter at all where you were born. That is something we can't control by ourselves. It's entirely coincidental where we were born. Lucky for us, because then we get the most out of life, compared to many others. So, on the basis of a really profound human rights perspective, I believe that there is a global responsibility – global moral responsibility that we have. And then also the claims that the poor in the world have, they can put them forward to the world. And they are increasingly doing that, fortunately.

According to this interviewee, the human rights perspective leads to cosmopolitanism in the sense that national citizenship has no moral relevance. She speaks of a 'global responsibility'. Thus she also says that 'the poor in the world' can put forward claims 'to the world'. To whom these claims can be made is not specified.

However, when the interviewees are asked why they think Norway as a state or Norwegians as individuals should provide or support international aid, they give different answers. One of the male NCA interviewees responds in this way: 'Well, I believe that Norway as one of the richest countries in the world has an obligation to assist countries at the other end of the scale'. And when asked if he thinks Norway or Norwegians have a duty to give international aid, one of the male NPA interviewees says:

> [...] We do have a duty. We have been given a resource to share, and a gift from nature and our own cultural heritage, the puritan heritage that we have, which has in many ways contributed to our industrialisation. And that is something which gives us an obligation. Absolutely, an obligation.

Here, this interviewee emphasises ability, as discussed in *Fighting Poverty Together* above (see section 4.1). The argument is that if you are in a position to help people living in poverty, you should do so. Norway can also be said to have a special ability, and therefore a correspondingly greater responsibility, not only because of its financial strength but also because of a 'cultural heritage'. However, the notion that providing aid is a duty of the donor appears not to be evident to many of the interviewees.

10.2.1 Voluntary giving

When asked if he thinks Norway as a state or Norwegians in general have a duty to be involved in development work, one of the male embassy interviewees says:

> That is a difficult question, but I think I will answer it with a yes and no. Yes, meaning that we must be involved internationally. Contribute in developing and maybe implementing good principles when it comes to human co-existence, human rights. So that is the yes perspective. No, it's not because of… it's not a function of the human rights perspective that Norway has a duty to give 15 billion Norwegian kroner. I don't think so. I don't think so. Then it's maybe more morally as a function of equality… that the one who has a lot should give to others. But that is a somewhat different dimension than the human rights dimension.

This interviewee, who elsewhere emphatically emphasises human rights as universal and thus adopts a cosmopolitan perspective on the moral aspects of international aid, is ambiguous about the idea of a moral duty. To him the duty is to 'be involved internationally', but he refrains from making this duty a corollary of human rights. Repeating 'I don't think so', he distances himself quite distinctively from this idea.

Several of the interviewees similarly dismiss the idea that providing aid is a moral duty, at least in a strict sense. They rather emphasise the voluntary aspect of giving aid. When asked whether Norwegian international aid is, or should be, motivated by a moral duty (*moralsk plikt*) to share, one of the female embassy interviewees answers: 'Maybe more a desire (*ønske*) than a duty...' And when asked to explain this difference, she says:

> Duty is maybe something I feel as somewhat burdening, something that weighs on you. Something you have to do. A desire is something … because it's a desire to contribute and help others. And it has a more positive value, compared to duty. … Because this is not something we have to do. It's something, as a part of Norwegian foreign policy, we have chosen to do, and something we still find support for. And… in part increasing support in the population, as far as I can remember from surveys and opinion polls that I know have been made.

The idea that the Norwegian state or the Norwegian people have a positive duty to provide development aid is dismissed in this statement. Rather, it is a responsibility one assumes quite voluntarily. Thus while NDA in this interviewee's understanding might be rights based, it is not duty based. NDA is not regarded as a function of any positive duty to assist the distant poor, hungry, or needy. Assisting the needy in far away countries thus amounts to something which is praiseworthy, but not required.

Similarly, when asked if he thinks it is a moral duty for Norwegian individuals to be involved in development aid, one of the male SCN interviewees says:

> [...] But I can't say that it's a moral obligation (*moralsk forpliktelse*) for all to do it. It has to be up to the individual to decide. But it's up to us to illustrate this in a proper way so that they at least see what can be done. The morality to us, I think, is to show that the money that is given to us, that it helps, that it makes a difference and that we can report back on it in an inexpensive and sensible way, so that they can see that the help they give makes a difference... But to try to promote at home that it is a moral obligation for all Norwegians... It has to be an appeal, rather than something you should say that everyone must take part in.

This interviewee is clearly reluctant to make any moral prescriptions for others. To support aid or not is described as an individual question, and the moral demands he is willing to make concern himself (to do a better job). Any statement directed to others must be in the form of an appeal. Note also how he discusses the issue in terms of marketing. This becomes even more evident when he is asked more specifically about the voluntary element. This interviewee then says: 'Yes, in a way. If not it's coercion, and then it will certainly not work. But it's our task to show how good we are. And when you do that, people will want to join in'.[4] Asked to elaborate on the distinction between the duty of the donor state and the donor individual, one of the female SCN interviewees similarly says:

4 Similarly, one of the female NCA interviewees stresses how forcing people is not an option. She says: 'But on the other hand, you cannot force people. That is why it's so important that you work sort of... Yes, like I said, I feel there has been a change of attitude at home. And then it's important to work on a feeling of solidarity, and to work with such issues at home too so that people can see beyond their own daily lives. But you cannot force people. I mean, I am not in favour of that'.

> […] I say it's a duty for every member of a society to enter into the political arena, whether one believes in it or not. This is what we have, and then one must try to influence in a way that is… But apart from that I don't want to place a duty on any individual, because duty leads to a bad conscience, and that is a feeling that is neither creative nor productive in any way for anyone. And that is why I don't think there should be a duty on individuals to give.

Thus, several interviewees reject the idea that Norway or Norwegians have a duty to provide development aid. Instead they stress its voluntary character.

10.2.2 Contractual state duty

While there seems to be a relatively strong tendency among the interviewees to argue against any moral duty of the individual, several interviewees express themselves differently regarding the state's duty. When asked if she would say her work is based on a moral duty, one of the female SCN interviewees says: 'I wouldn't say that everyone has a personal duty to do something, but I would say that as a nation Norway has a duty to do something'. She adds:

> An individual might just as well decide to do something else in Norway in order to… Because, there are needs there too. An individual has the right to decide for herself what she wants to do with her own life and her own resources. And she doesn't have a responsibility to the same degree as a nation, meaning a state, has. It depends on the resources of the individual, her opportunities and interests. I don't think we can say that everyone in Norway has a duty to donate money to Save the Children Norway, for instance.

Here the notion of individual freedom seems to be fundamental. Note, however, the relative term used when this development worker points out that the individual 'doesn't have a responsibility to the same degree as a nation, meaning a state'. Thus, while dismissing the notion of individual duty, this interviewee seems to imply that a residual of responsibility on the part of the individual might still be there. Her emphasis is, however, clearly on ascribing responsibility to the state, not the individual.[5]

5 Similar views are also articulated by other interviewees. When asked to reflect on how much development aid Norway or Norwegians should provide, one of the male

Another of the female SCN interviewees points to the difference between the state and the individual's duty. She says:

> I think that if you are to talk about duty, then it is the state. Because, even if those who are in decision making positions today are not the same ones who made decisions earlier, it's still part of the general responsibility in a way. And you cannot put that on the individual human being. But at the same time I find it is interesting how a lot of individuals in a country like Norway take such an interest in contributing. I don't see that as a duty, I see that as… I look at that with admiration.

Again the notion of duty is related to the state and not to the individual. This interviewee clearly regards the state as a morally responsible entity. Individual donations she looks at 'with admiration', but not 'as a duty'.

Interestingly, however, many of the interviewees see the Norwegian state's duty to provide international aid as depending on commitments made by the Norwegian government. Three interviewees can illustrate this. In response to the issue of having a moral duty to assist, one of the male SCN interviewees says:

> Yes, we have signed international conventions. And a lot of countries do that, because… the government gets a good reputation or something like that. But when we have done it, then we are committed to the demands made in these… That is a moral matter.

Here the duties Norway might have are made dependent on Norway's signing of various conventions. Thus, the state's duty to assist is expressed in the form of a contractarian argument. The moral duty to provide development aid is determined by what conventions Norway has ratified. In other words, the duty is made dependent on the voluntary commitment already made. Secondly, when asked if he would say Norway has a duty to provide development aid, one of the male embassy interviewees says:

> Yes, we have a duty if we enter into international cooperation. And when we commit ourselves to give development aid and we go public saying that we will do so and so, and we have reports to the Storting [Parliament] that say this and that. Then

---

NPA interviewees says: 'So I would like to see more individuals, and see a true commitment and an interest in what is going on outside Norway, what is going on outside our own wage settlements, for the individual. While I believe the state must assume economic responsibility for development'.

> there is an obligation, and you could say it's partly legally binding. If we make agreements and sign treaties, then it is, then there is an obligation.

This interviewee relates the duty to provide development aid to rights, which in turn are based on 'international cooperation'. Thirdly, one of the male NCA interviewees refers to the UN but seems to put more emphasis on societal interconnectedness and UN membership, rather than the signing of conventions. When asked how he would justify development aid, he says: '[...] But I think it's also a purely, let us say nation to nation, society to society, there is something with an obligation that ties us together'. Asked to elaborate on his understanding of these societal relationships, he says: 'If you take the UN Charter seriously, where we are members, and use it as a framework, then there is clearly an obligation'. Thus, while there seems to be a discourse that emphasises the state's duty to provide aid, for these interviewees this duty has a contractarian basis.

10.2.3 Popular commitment

Discussing the issue of a state's responsibility, one of the female NCA interviewees says:

> [...] We should be doing development work because so many people in the world live in terrible conditions. And as a state you have to make priorities affecting all Norwegians. And I think that actually the Norwegian people also have a moral responsibility for living in a world where resources are distributed very unevenly. So then you might say that the state has a moral responsibility. The state consists of human beings.

This interviewee seems to see the moral responsibility of the state as a function of the moral responsibility of the Norwegian people. The collective obligation can be considered an extension of the individual's obligation, and is therefore only a practical arrangement for living up to the individuals' obligation.[6]

6 Similarly, when asked to explain why he thinks Norway should provide development aid, one of the male embassy interviewees says: 'Because I feel there is a responsibility. And that is of course not only about Norway being a rich country, and how we have resources and the opportunity to contribute, but also because... and then we return to the issue of the value based and humanist

One of the male NCA interviewees articulates a similar concern. On the issue of the relationship between altruism and self-interest and the role these play in NDA, he comments on the role of the state, and thus public opinion, in this regard. He says:

> [...] We have elected politicians and we make political propositions, for example one per cent development aid or two per cent development aid. That is part of a political programme that requires public support, at least in the kind of political system that we have in Norway. And if we then manage to gain acceptance for two per cent, then this doesn't happen without people wanting it, precisely because it's a political process. Hence, there is no such thing out there called the state. It's just that the state administers it on behalf of us.

The role of the state in development aid is here made dependent on popular support. The effect is that the role of the state as an independent moral actor is toned down, and it is the people who are held responsible for its choices in this respect.

Similarly, when asked if he would argue that there is a moral reason to provide international aid, one of the male NPA interviewees says:

> And I think that Norway as a rich country, we have a responsibility to share some of our surplus. But we cannot share equally, if not... well, we cannot from Norway share equally with all the inhabitants of the world. That wouldn't be possible. And the Norwegian population would not accept that, right? It's not realistic.

(*verdibaserte og humanistiske*) commitment. It's about a kind of solidarity between people, or responsibility if you want. And it's personal... if you ask whether the state, that is the Norwegian state, should provide development aid, then yes. But the state is only a tool, in a way. It's a tool to achieve the kind of change that we were talking about. And Norway is very well positioned as a state, to be such a tool. So my answer is definitively yes. But it's not necessarily like... well... the state is to me in this regard a tool for something that I feel, at least in Norway, I believe there is general agreement about, a popular commitment. That is a problematic statement, because I don't think the Norwegian people in general actually know much about what development aid in 2004 is actually all about. I don't think they do. But a commitment related to a kind of notion of inequality, injustice, humanism, solidarity does exist. And this can be transformed into a field of work with people like us. [...] As long as that commitment is there, and this can be transformed into a field of work that achieves results, then it is important. Anything else would not be morally right'. Thus, this interviewee makes the state's responsibility dependent on public opinion and popular commitment to development aid.

Here Norwegian responsibility is construed as a matter of sharing a surplus. Thus, it seems this interviewee does recognise a responsibility, although he does not regard this as something that might involve a threat to existing welfare or living standards. It is only the surplus that must be shared, not the savings. When he argues it is impossible to 'share equally', it seems that this expression refers to a situation where the surplus is divided equally between everyone and every nation-state globally. His argument is not a principled one, however, but clearly pragmatic and relates to popular commitment. He thinks the Norwegian people would not accept it. Being a democratically elected government, the Norwegian government is restricted by what the electorate will accept.

However, when asked if he regards it as optional to provide international aid, the same interviewee speaks of the voluntary aspect for individuals, but dismisses this with regard to states. He says:

> If we talk about individuals, I would maybe say that. But if we talk about a state like Norway, then I don't think it's a voluntary matter. I think the Norwegian state has a duty, to use that term, to contribute to healthy development in many countries. Individuals do it in part via the tax return… So I think in a way the Norwegian state must assume responsibility.

While the first statement highlights the democratic basis for the state's duty, it is a non-voluntary duty that is accentuated here.

10.2.4 Realistic or unrealistic duties

Such considerations regarding the voluntary aspects of giving and popular commitment seem to affect how the responsibility to provide aid is perceived. Asked how he understands the obligation to provide development aid, one of the male SCN interviewees says:

> So… We have chosen to have 1 percent as some kind of goal, and no-one else has achieved that. […] So maybe we can take the lead and show a good example. But just as I said to you… if you say three percent, will you find support for that? It has to be politically acceptable. You cannot force people.

This interviewee hesitates to proscribe a specific moral level of development aid compared to the GNI, or to give a precise definition of the moral demand on the state. Similarly, when asked to comment on the claim that NDA should be substantially increased if it is to be based on the notion of universal human rights, one of the female SCN interviewees says:

> That sounds right. But of course, again it's about what is realistic. That is, I mean that we can give a lot more than we do, that we can improve and increase development aid from Norway. But Norway is a small country. It would be unrealistic to think that Norway could bring every country up to the same standard of living as in Norway. So I think it's more important to emphasise international cooperation – to use Norway's position to influence other resourceful countries to take development aid just as seriously as Norway does. And of course there are different opinions within Norway too. Some think we give too much, and others think we give enough… I don't think the principle of equality (*likeverd*) needs to imply that we in Norway should give a certain amount to a specific country, but it has again to do with rights and justice. We have to care (*bry oss*). If there are people suffering around the world, then we must care about that. We have for example a tendency to... that the media cover… We don't think it is as serious if 200 people die in Pakistan as if 200 people die in Sweden. I think it has to do with that. I don't think it can be transformed into a question of resources and a responsibility to give half of what Norway earns to developing countries, because I don't think it's realistic. But we have to have an active role in international cooperation and we must have an active influencing role to increase the resources for… And not least change the trade systems, fair trade, and such things…

Note how pragmatic considerations frame the way this interviewee reflects on the stringency of the duty to provide development aid. Three considerations are highlighted. Firstly, since 'Norway is a small country' she stresses that international cooperation should be prioritised. The implicit argument seems to be that if more countries contributed the effect would be greater than if Norway alone does it. Secondly, she refers to the 'different opinions' in Norway. Thus, she sees popular support as being limited. Thirdly, this interviewee reflects on how she normatively thinks 'we have to care', but more descriptively says that there is 'a tendency' to care differently for different people. Accordingly, this interviewee ascribes responsibility not only to the state, but also to the international community. Anything else is not regarded as realistic.

Asked about the stringency of the moral duty to assist, one of the male NPA interviewees reflects on public opinion. He says:

> Well, in Norway we have a democracy and we are not able to give more, to share more, as long as people in Norway don't think they have a positive development at home. I don't think we will be able give so much that Norwegian citizens find their

> standard of living diminishing. I don't think that is possible. I don't think it's feasible. Because, then we would be talking about a model of absolute sharing (*full delingsmodell*): that what we give to international development aid work will lead to a reduction of Norwegians' standard of living. That wouldn't work. It wouldn't be politically feasible.

Here too the perspective that defines the response is what would be realistic. Norwegian aid is seen as dependent on people in Norway experiencing that 'they have a positive development at home'. Accordingly, continued popular support for NDA is something this interviewee regards as dependent on increased economic growth.

However, when asked about the stringency of this duty, one of the female NCA interviewees, however, gives a different answer. She says:

> [...] I believe that such a duty comes – it should come from the heart. And then you don't think in a calculating way, I think. Then you give more than you maybe are able to. Because if you, and then I would like to relate it to the concept of love. And most of us understand love very well. When it's about ourselves, and how we love and how we would like to be loved. And then, if I love someone, if it's my husband or my father or whoever, then I am generous. Then I can give a lot. And if you really love someone, then often you give more than you should have. And you are left a little poorer. And in the Bible, that is how the widow did it. [...] How much would a father give to his child? Well, he gives a lot. How much did God give for the whole world? Well, he gave his own son. How much am I willing to give so that my brother in Africa, whom I don't know, can have better living conditions? I don't know. A dollar? The moral duty is higher, if we take our morality seriously.

This interviewee articulates a quite different discourse on moral duty compared to what is articulated by most of the other interviewees. Here the concept of moral duty is constructed independently of pragmatic considerations. Duty it 'should come from the heart' and out of limitless love ('How much did God give for the whole world?'), at least if one is to take 'morality seriously'. This universal perspective becomes quite explicit when the same interviewee continues:

> [...] I think that the family, the nation is just an extension of the family. So why should you not think that the world is an extension of the nations, so that every family member is taken care of by the family? Then every country and every human being would be part of it, if you really were to adopt the human rights perspective or a perspective of love as I like to say. To me it's not any stranger to think about my own son, than about my son here. If I see a boy on the street here, then he too should be my brother. That is at least how Jesus said it should be. And it's like that in most religions.

Note the starting point this interviewee takes for her reflection: the notion of family. She uses the idea – with connotations of closeness, care, and community – as a paradigm to understand first nations and later the whole world. The implication seems to be that in the same way that the family takes care of every family member, the human community globally should care for every human being. Note how she argues that she sees this perception as a corollary of the human rights perspective. This perspective, articulated in this way, is radically cosmopolitan and stands in contrast to the state system in international politics. In her understanding there are not separate families, nations, or states – but one global family. Further, it should be noted how she also labels this perspective a 'perspective of love'. This seems to be in line with her understanding of humanity as one global family.

10.2.5 Universal or national

When asked to comment on how she sees the relationship between Norwegians' responsibilities for other Norwegians as opposed to citizens of other countries, one of the female SCN interviewees says:

> Obviously, Norway has a responsibility for its own citizens first of all, but we also have a global responsibility. For example Save the Children Norway does work in Norway and abroad. We don't see our role… We cannot work to improve conditions for children in other parts of the world, while children in Norway are in pain. So we think we have to work actively to improve conditions in Norway for the children who are not faring well. Whether they are refugee children, or poor children according to the Norwegian definition, or children that are abused or whatever it is. So of course, we have to care… A person or an organisation cannot do everything, and it's just as important to make sure that there are no human rights violations in Norway, and that there are some doing this, and some who should work in other countries.

The responsibility Norwegians have for other Norwegians is here articulated as a primary responsibility. A global responsibility is also acknowledged, but seems to be secondary to Norwegian needs. The upshot of this argument seems to be that needs in Norway must be secured first. The responsibility of the donor state to provide international development aid is thus moderated by an emphasis on a special obligation towards the people and needs of Norway. This is not, however, articulated as an argument against aid.

Similarly, when asked to comment on the claim that NDA should be substantially increased if it is to be based on the notion of universal human rights, one of the male NCA interviewees says:

> […] And of course, I would have liked to see Norway contribute more. I would like to see that. But it's limited… I also understand people in Norway… And that is so paradoxical, that Norway has its own economic problems and social problems that we are not able to deal with. And when individuals are affected by this, like lack of senior citizen housing or social care etc., then you can understand those who are against sending that much money out of the country, when we can't even look after our own… But still I think Norwegian development aid could be increased. I hope that we will reach 1 per cent, and I think it's nice to have such a goal, and hope that we can make it.

In this case the position articulated is that both the needs of others and Norwegian needs must be met.

While considerations regarding Norwegian needs thus seem to modify the stringency of the duty to assist, the universal character of this duty seems important to several of the interviewees. The latter interviewee rejects the idea that the poor are too far away in order for Norwegians to have any responsibility. When asked to comment on the claim that Norwegians have less responsibility for those who are not Norwegians, he says:

> For me, that is not good enough. But I very well understand those who actually think like that. And I understand also those who are committed to working with Eastern Europe. Over the recent years, that has become very… because that is sort of a lot closer. It's a misery that is closer and not so far away. And then it becomes somewhat easier… it's easier to donate and contribute to it.

While this interviewee explicitly rejects the moral relevance of distance, he can 'understand' the psychological basis of this notion. He seems thus to refer primarily to the motivational factors. The same applies for a female embassy interviewee who does not accept that distance is relevant to states' duties. At the personal level, however, it is different. Asked if she thinks the obligation to provide aid becomes greater with diminishing distance, she answers:

> No, not for me, I don't think so. Not when we are talking about what Norway should do to help others. But what you do personally, that is sort of something else. Because, when it's closer to you, you feel the burden (*mer tyngende*), but... No, I don't think so. But by being close, then your eyes are opened to how terrible the situation can be for some people, of course. When you're at home, then...

Note that the rejection this interviewee articulates is at two levels – the state and the personal. It seems, however, that again it is the psychological considerations that lead to this distinction. In contrast, one of the male NCA interviewees dismisses 'closeness ethics' as a moral principle. When asked if he thinks there is a moral duty for Norway or Norwegians to be involved in development aid, he says:

> But if I too am to retain my dignity, then I cannot close my eyes to the fact that other people's dignity is being pushed around. And then it doesn't matter – geographical distance is philosophically and ethically of no interest. A thing like the ethics of proximity (*nærhetsetikk*) and the like, OK, but I mean if you start digging into that, then I think... it would be... It has to do with proportions. Of course, ethics of proximity would make you see and feel a greater responsibility for those who are close, but objectively and philosophically you have the same responsibility.

Note the distinction this interviewee makes between what you 'see and feel' on the one hand, and the objective and philosophical on the other. While he acknowledges the psychological implications of seeing and feeling, this is in his view irrelevant. It seems this interviewee relies on objectivity and detachment as core values in ethical reasoning. As such he is a representative of a typically modern approach to ethics, an approach that has been criticised by feminist and post-colonial ethicists and others (see for example Gilligan 1982).

Responding to the view that there are so many tasks at home that should be taken care of first, and that allocations for development aid should therefore be minimal, one of the female embassy interviewees responds:

> Yes, but it's all relative. And if you compare the tasks Norway has at home with some of the countries where we contribute with development aid, then it becomes really... It's just peanuts, really. All is relative. And of course, if you relate primarily to the Norwegian context, then it may seem like there are huge problems. But if you take the wider perspective, then the problems in Norway aren't really

> that terrible. So given that we have a relatively good capacity, both financially and in terms of personnel, I think we should be able to handle both.[7]

This interviewee seems to make a qualitative distinction between the needs in Norway and those in the recipient countries. However, she expects that 'we should be able to handle both'.

10.2.6 Recipient responsibility

The idea that the Norwegian state or Norwegian individuals should take responsibility for other states' citizens is further restricted by the view that the primary responsibility lies with the developing state itself. When asked who she thinks has the responsibility for securing the rights of the poor, one of the female NCA interviewees responds:

> Many people have that at different levels. We often talk about how our partners have a responsibility, and that we as Norwegian Church Aid and a donor have a responsibility. But also that the public system in [country] has a responsibility, and this is often where things go wrong, at various levels: district level, regional level, or national level, and also internationally. I don't think we are good enough at thinking internationally when we in a way analyse our applications and try to find out who has the responsibility. I think first of all we must concentrate on the local and national conditions. But I think we could be better at seeing things from an international perspective. Now I am thinking of large structures like the UN and our trade system and… We don't work in relation to that at all. And I am not sure that we should either.

Note first how this interviewee points out that there are many who carry such responsibilities. Both donors and recipients are considered to hold responsibility, and perhaps not surprisingly as this is an NGO interviewee, the partners are described as being better than the 'public system'. This interviewee is clearly also concerned about the international level of responsibility, exemplified by 'the UN and our trade

7 Similarly, one of the male embassy interviewees says: 'There are unsolved tasks in Norway. Yes. But if you compare us to a country like [country], then this is like a ripple compared to a large wave. And the basis for it is that we are one globe, we are, and with the same human dignity. And you cannot have one world; it will not be sustainable over time with a world where large parts live in extreme poverty and some live in extreme affluence'.

system'. She seems concerned that one should 'try to find out who has the responsibility' at this level, but is ambivalent about the extent to which she or her NGO should address this. It seems then that this interviewee rejects making either the donor or the recipient responsible for aid and/or poverty, but seeks to find a nuanced expression and understanding of this issue. When asked explicitly about her understanding of recipient responsibility, the same interviewee says:

> [...] But the way I think about it, is that it's in a way quite in line with a human rights based approach that the recipients are made responsible. That is what it's all about when people have rights. They don't only have rights, but they also have duties, as mentioned earlier, and a certain responsibility for their own situation.[8]

Here recipient responsibility is made a consequence of adopting the human rights approach. People not only have rights, they also have duties, and accordingly they have 'a certain responsibility for their own situation'. This statement should probably not be read as a statement blaming the victim or giving the poor sole responsibility for their own destiny, but it does, however, emphasise a certain responsibility to participate and is as such part of the partnership ideology (see section 13.1).

One of the female embassy interviewees also points to the responsibility of governments to provide for their own citizens and populace, and the consequences this has for aid agencies. When asked what it would imply for her work if development cooperation were rights based, she says:

> [...] It takes as its starting point the rights of individuals. And within a nation-state you must try to make conditions favourable for the individual to have the scope to use his abilities (*individet får utfoldet seg*), and have his rights protected. And through our development aid we must try to adjust for this, and support the work the government does on its own, right? It's the authorities' responsibility to take care of their own citizens and their own population. But that we through our development aid try to support the work that they do themselves, or try to move them in the direction they should go. [...] And that is what we try to do all the

8 Similarly, one of the female embassy interviewees limits the range of the donors' duties. She says: '[...] I think Norway has a duty, through our membership in the UN, and... so I think we... yes. But more of a duty to follow them up, the government of the country and such things, not a duty to go in and start building new schools and see to it that rights are delivered. I don't think so'.

> time… to support the work for democracy, human rights, and good governance. And it's to support and to push them (*å støtte opp under og å pushe dem*), I would say that too, in the direction where the international community in general thinks is… well, the declaration of human rights, the human rights conventions, what has been declared and adopted.[9]

While the SCN interviewee above seemed to regard aid as a mechanism to be used when someone does not assume responsibility, this interviewee rather sees it as a supplement where responsibility is assumed. However, this supportive role has another agenda, as it aims at supporting certain aspects of the government's policies, but not others. Thus, there is both a matter of support and a matter of pushing them into line with the international community.

The emphasis on the state rather than the individual noted above seems to apply to the recipient country as well as to the donor. One of the male NCA interviewees highlights the role of the state. He says:

> […] the state should have a primary duty (*overordnet oppgave*), and if the state doesn't have a primary duty, then you can forget about the whole human rights regime, which is based on the state assuming the main responsibility.[10]

While, as noted above, the concept of rights in some statements leads the interviewees to articulate a characteristically cosmopolitan understanding of rights and duties, and therefore to limit the role of the state (see section 8.2.3), here the concept is used to focus on the state, specifically the recipient state. This interviewee also emphasises very clearly the role of the recipients in bringing about change, something he argues is not sufficiently addressed by a human rights approach. Asked to elaborate on what he sees as deficiencies in the human rights based approach, he says:

9 Similarly, one of the male NPA interviewees highlights the responsibility of the state. When asked to comment on the claim that development aid is the responsibility of the developing country, not a responsibility of Norway or Norwegians, he says. '[…] Our role will always only be to a limited extent to support our partners, to contribute to development either in the form of money or in the form of competence or in the form of solidarity, to the extent that we give them moral support and political support. But I agree, it's clear that the responsibility for the development in a country belongs to the citizens of the country and their elected bodies'.

10 The wider context of this statement can be found in a longer quote in section 8.2.3.

> […] This thing about me being my own change agent (*endringsagent*) can be translated into an understanding of society and the local community – that society can become its own change and development agent. And that is not necessarily related to rights, but actually has to do with your own opportunities or your desire to create a world which is a better place for me and my local community. And so, you have potential for change, a social change potential. I don't think this is fully captured if you only think in terms of human rights based aid. […] And I also believe that the rights based approach would be enriched by including this perspective. […] But you also have situations where it's difficult to say who is the oppressor and who is the oppressed. Because there are people opposing each other in a conflict of interest, and for people working against each other in a conflict of interest, it's not always a matter of… or it's not so easy to tell who the oppressor is and who the oppressed are. This can change in the various phases of a conflict. Consequently, you have to include other concepts. You have to include the idea of consensus building. You have to include an understanding of what the conflict is really all about. Is it more about conflict of interests, or values, right? What values, and conflicts of values, which is difficult to relate directly to a human rights approach. But you could enrich the human rights approach if you include this.

Note the distinction that this interviewee makes here between social change and human rights based aid, and which seems to constitute the basis for his criticism of the human rights based approach. The notion that 'society can become its own change and development agent' is something he sees as 'not necessarily related to rights' and which in his opinion is not 'fully captured if you only think in terms of rights based aid'. Thus, the agency perspective is not only something this interviewee finds missing in what he sees as the rights based approach, but also something he wants to include in it.

In the latter part of the quote it seems to be the complexity of real life situations that begs for an approach that is more comprehensive than the human rights approach. It seems as if this interviewee finds the human rights approach unable to grasp these complexities, and he thus calls for a more multifaceted approach. Concepts he mentions are consensus, understanding, and values. It seems like the human rights approach is considered too technical and that it needs to be supplemented by approaches that are more qualitatively oriented and able to sense the specific situations and nuances missed by the rights based approach.

10.3 Concluding reflections

Most of the interviewees, both male and female, express their approval of applying a human rights based approach to development aid. In this, they seem to be in line with the policy documents of the aid agencies they represent. In their interpretation of what this approach implies, many of them emphasise universality, all human beings' equal worth and equal rights, as well as the challenge to reach as many as possible. In other words, development aid is seen as a response to the rights of people everywhere.

The analysis reveals a strand in the Norwegian aid discourse that relates human rights to the concept of human dignity, understanding them as referring to political, economic, social, and cultural rights, and in some cases also to corresponding duties. Another and more dominating strand within this discourse seems, however, to have only a vague notion of human rights and what a human rights based approach in development aid implies. In particular, what the expression human rights based aid means and the practical and moral implications thereof seem to be unclear to some of the interviewees. Thus, though the concept of human rights is widely acclaimed, the implications of adopting a rights based approach in development aid remains unclear.

That Norway has a responsibility to contribute in the field of development aid is articulated by many of the interviewed development workers. However, their understanding of the implications of this responsibility is far from uniform. Often it is derived from Norway's relative wealth and corresponding ability to share its resources. This is seen to be in line with widely shared values in Norwegian society (see section 3.3.2). However, when asked to comment on the responsibilities Norway and Norwegians have for those they share nationality with, compared to the responsibility they might have to those living in poverty in the South, some of the interviewees emphasise the primary responsibility one has for one's own fellow citizens. Similarly, the recipients' responsibility for their own development is articulated by most of the interviewees.

Many interviewees find it difficult to comment on how strong the duty to provide aid should be, and a striking feature in some of the interviews is a reluctance to make clear statements on the demanding character of this duty. This reluctance must be understood in light of the relationship between donors and NGOs. While independence is one of the characteristics often ascribed to NGOs, there clearly is an element of dependency in the relationship between aid agency and individual donors. With their pragmatic appeals for support from donors and the electorate, both governmental and non-governmental aid seems to derive its legitimacy from popular support.

Further, the moral reflections of these interviewees are marked by an emphasis on individual freedom combined with the idea that the state should take the burden of aid. Several of the interviewees are more inclined to ascribe a duty to provide aid to the state rather than to individuals. This is articulated by both male and female interviewees. Accordingly, although the responsibility to provide development aid is widely acknowledged, the duty to assist remains unspecified in terms of the who, when, and how. Several voices actually express an understanding of this duty that corresponds to the kind of voluntary, supererogatory action often associated with the charity approach, although that approach (or terminology) is explicitly dismissed by most of them (see section 11.1).

To summarise, this chapter identifies the interviewees' interpretations of two of the dominant discourses articulated in the agencies' policy documents. The human rights discourse is widely acclaimed, while the discourse of responsibility seems to be interpreted in a way similar to notions often associated with the charity approach in development aid (markedly dismissed in the policy documents). Further, this chapter shows how contractual and pragmatic considerations play an important part in the interviewees' interpretations of responsibilities and duties in relation to NDA. This element of pragmatism contrasts with the principled and programmatic statements relying on the notion of universal human rights in the policy documents, as well as with the emphasis put on the donors as duty-bearers by NCA.

11 Charity, compassion, and solidarity

There's a world outside your window, and it's a world of dread and fear.
Where the only water flowing, is the bitter sting of tears.
And the Christmas bells that ring there are the clanging chimes of doom.
Well tonight thank God it's them instead of you.
Feed the world! Let them know it's Christmas time.
Feed the world! Do they know it's Christmas time at all?

Bob Geldof and Band Aid, 1984

As noted above, the concept of human rights is frequently contrasted to charity. In this chapter I will discuss the concept of charity, as well as two other concepts that seem to be on the margins of the moral discourse of NDA: compassion and solidarity.

11.1 Charity

When one of the female SCN interviewees is asked to comment on the use of the terms charity and compassion (*veldedighet og barmhjertighet*) to describe development work, she says:

> Charity and compassion… We really don't use these terms so much any more. At least in our organisation they have become sort of…, politically incorrect. That is not how we should think any more.

When this interviewee refers to a certain way of speaking as 'politically incorrect', this indicates a hegemonic discourse that excludes other competing discourses. Those defining what is politically correct are not identified apart from the rather vague reference to 'our organisation'. When asked to elaborate on her understanding of the concept of charity, the same interviewee replies:

> Well, charity… The way I interpret the word, there is less responsibility in it. It's something you do when you feel like it… to feel a little better. I have contributed with something. But it sort of takes away the responsibility. That is my interpretation of the word. […] Somebody with lots of money, who just gives some of it away to ease his or her conscience.

Charity is here understood as a term that conveys 'less responsibility', though the comparison that is implied is not explained. Further, there is an intentional aspect ascribed to charity – to make one 'feel a little better'. Finally, charity is related to easing one's conscience.

One of the male SCN interviewees also stresses how he and the organisation are not involved in charity. He says: 'We don't do charity. We don't do charity'. When asked to elaborate on his understanding of charity, he says:

> […] If someone comes here, for example a mother, and asks for one-off support… then we say no. We have to work more with the systems… We cannot… […] I try all the time to take a helicopter overview (*helikopter oversikt*) on this. We can't be involved in charity for individuals. […] Like the priests still do, which is very popular… They go out and hand out money to people on the streets, which is the charity part of it. That doesn't work in the long run. If you want to give away fish, then you must teach them how to fish.

For this interviewee charity refers to acts directed towards individuals. In contrast to this he wants to adopt a 'helicopter overview'. This metaphor seems to indicate a systemic approach which does not focus on individuals. Note also how charity is implicitly understood as something random and occasional. When approached by an individual, 'for example a mother', support would be denied. And towards the end of the statement he relates charity to the practice of the priests, who 'go out and hand out money to people on the streets'. The main element of the critique seems to be the lack of sustainability implied in such an approach. Accordingly, this interviewee highlights the long-term perspective of development aid, and sees this as markedly different from charity based aid. While the charity approach to aid is concerned with the individual, development aid should adopt a more systemic approach. When asked how he understands rights based aid, the same interviewee says:

> Yes, that is the difference… on the one hand that children have a claim, and we are kind and give to them. It's sort of… It has taken Save the Children Norway several

> years to understand the difference, and we are still a bit stuck in the charity thinking. That is why we don't have individual sponsorships at home. So that, if a child here in [country] is lucky enough to get help, he or she should not have to thank anyone in Norway for being kind to them, because there are rights in this. […] The difference is that this is something they are to have and almost all countries, except Somalia and USA, have signed the children's convention. So it is a duty to deliver. This also has to do with justice with regard to children's rights.

Note how the distinction between charity and rights based aid is constructed. Charity is understood as being 'kind'. Rights based aid on the other hand is recognised as being based on international conventions that imply a 'duty to deliver'. Further, this approach seems to imply that the recipients (here children) do not have 'to thank anyone in Norway'. Finally, the rights based approach is understood in terms of justice, although the relationship between rights and justice is not explained.

From this statement it seems that the position of both the donor and the recipient is regarded as different within the framework of rights based aid, as opposed to charitable giving. With rights based aid the recipient has a claim, rather than being an object of pity, and the donor has a duty, rather than a choice to assist. Accordingly, this interviewee distinguishes the rights based approach from other approaches, but also indicates two things: firstly, that it has taken time for the organisation to understand this difference, and secondly, that although there is a difference (between rights and charity), the one approach has not fully taken over for the other. Rather, he finds that Save the Children Norway is 'still a bit stuck in the charity thinking'. Accordingly, regarding development aid as rights based does not fully exclude charity. This seems to echo the rather vague understanding of rights based aid discussed above (see section 10.1.2).

Asked to comment on the claim that people in SCN are involved in development aid because they want to be kind, the same interviewee says:

> […] Do-goodism (*snillisme*) relates to charity, which I know we are not doing. When we say we are a rights organisation especially, that aspect becomes less significant. But there is always something… of course.

Clearly, kindness and charity are not concepts that constitute the basis for how this interviewee understands his work. His understanding of SCN as a rights based organisation seems to exclude such terminology and/or notions. However, although this distinction and mutual exclusion is stressed, there is still some room for kindness, and charity is still retained. The role such notions play is 'less significant', but 'there is always something … of course.'

11.1.1 Humanitarian hand-outs

When asked to comment on the claim that development aid is charity, one of the male SCN interviewees says:

> Defining charity, it's like, you are out there and you are just giving out things to people, either food or clothes or things like that. Yes, one can say that. But from our side, we try not to define what we are doing as a complete charity as such. Because we try doing it in such a way that people contribute a lot themselves, in terms of their time, in terms of their own resources, in terms of their own opinions. And to me, charity is based on… Like out there, and you just give out, and people walk away with whatever you have given them. But the way we see it, that's not the way we try to work. We try to work with people's capacities. And we build on resources to try to encourage them to do things by themselves.[11]

The random and occasional character of charity is emphasised in this statement. However, this interviewee introduces an interesting concept, that of 'complete charity'. In this there is an implicit recognition that the work he is involved in can be described as, or at least perceived as partly charity, but also an understanding that it should be more than this. In other words his work is not 'complete charity'. He underlies how people themselves contribute: 'We try to work with people's capacities.'

Also one of the female embassy interviewees articulates scepticism about these terms. When asked to explain why she does not want to use the term charity to describe Norwegian aid, she says:

11 Similarly, one of the female SCN interviewees says her organisation does not do charity, because 'we don't do hand-outs'. She admits, however, that in certain situations they do 'do hand-outs'. And her comment on this is that: 'There are some times when you have to take a short-term approach, where you give food, so that children can participate in the long-term program that is more developmental, instead of the charity. So yes, to a certain extent you can say during emergencies there is some charity work'.

> Yes, it has to do with goodness and kindness (*godhet og snillhet*) and such things… To me charity is that you sort of give, and hand out money. It's an old fashioned way of thinking. And with the guidelines and framework now in place for Norwegian development aid, it's not like that any more. It's very… Again back to realism. You consider very carefully which countries to work in, which fields, and what programmes or projects. Actually, we are not involved in projects at all, mostly. So very thorough considerations are made before you get involved in a country or a field, so… No, to me, I would not use the word charity.

Again, charity is interpreted in terms of being random and occasional. The lack of planning and strategic choices seems to be considered a distinctive mark of charity. She finds strategies and plans to be the distinctive mark of NDA, and therefore does not regard it as random giving. Further, it seems that charity is here seen as something naïve or idealistic, belonging to an earlier phase in the history of aid. It is contrasted to the realism and thorough planning made before embarking on a development programme today.

When asked if he perceives the work he does as charity, one of the male embassy interviewees says:

> No, I don't think so, really. I find that we are working in a mutually binding cooperation, more than charity. If you by charity mean hand-outs in way, we don't do that. I think humanitarian aid is closer to charity.

Again charity is contrasted with present day development cooperation, but this time with a reference to mutual commitment. While charity is regarded as donor led, defined by conditions set by the donor, modern development aid is marked by cooperation.[12]

When asked which values should constitute the value basis for NDA, one of the male NPA interviewees says:

> […] We should base our development aid on something which is not charity, where we come as white people with our values that are supreme or better than for

12 When elaborating further on this point, the same interviewee says: 'But development work, as it's done in 2004, in a country like [country] is not characterised by charity. It's a very political agenda, which involves the recipient side in questions that are very real to them. And it's not about receiving charities (*gode gaver*), but it's about a binding dialogue about questions that are important to us or to them, which we can disagree on. So it's a lot more… I find it a lot more of a political process than doing charity'.

example those of the Africans. That we have respect for the values African societies have too.

Describing charity, this interviewee uses a terminology that alludes to colonial times. Asked to elaborate on his understanding of charity, the same interviewee says: '[…] If we collect money, maybe motivated by a desire to ease our own hearts more than what we contribute on the ground, then I think this is charity'. Again note how the problems associated with charity seem to relate to the implied motives of the agent. Charity seems to reflect bad motives rather than a concern about good results. In this, however, it seems that different aspects are conflated, in the sense that motives are set against results. It seems then that a general scepticism about virtues and motives is set against a general positive concern for results.

When asked to comment on the claim that Norwegian aid in many ways amounts to charity, the same interviewee says:

> I don't think so. To me charity… It's about simply giving, just like that, putting money into something without being involved. I don't think that is what we do. […] But I think maybe it's charity to fill a few boxes with worn-out clothes, put it in a container and send it to Poland. That is charity.

In this case it seems to be the lack of commitment that is regarded as the problematic aspect of charity. This might indicate that there is a lack of authentic involvement that is addressed. Note also the example he uses to explain the charity approach. This is an example that carries several of the characteristics often associated with hand-outs. The political assessment of the situation is lacking, and there is no long-term involvement or structural perspective. On the contrary, the intervention is limited and in many ways technical.

11.1.2 Christian charity and gratitude

When asked to explain her understanding of the statement in *Fighting Poverty Together* that says NDA is not charity, one of the female embassy interviewees says:

> If anything is rights based it's in a way that everyone has a right to a decent life, be it schooling, housing, food. Being helped in having your rights fulfilled, that is a

> universal claim you have (*universelt har krav på*). If it's charity and compassion, then it's more like: 'Oh poor you. We feel so sorry for them. Oh, yes. We should share a little and be kind (*snille*).' It's more like handing out alms. And in a way it has an element of... what is it called... that you... are made an object of pity (*stakkarsliggjort*), when you receive alms. Probably one doesn't want to put the recipient in that role. It's a very unfortunate position. Not a very dignified (*lite verdig*) position to be in.

Regarding how the rights based approach is understood, several of the same features as noted in the previous chapter resurface in this statement. The phrase 'everyone has a right to' indicates a universal concern. Note also how charity and compassion here are both contrasted to a human rights based approach, and they seem to be associated with being 'kind' and offering limited or selective assistance, here expressed by 'we should share a little'. Further, this interviewee seems to understand charity and compassion as something which makes the recipient of aid pitiful. This she explicitly evaluates as negative, referring to the lack of dignity of being in such a position.

One further term this interviewee uses to explain the charity approach in development aid, and which it is worth considering more closely, is the term 'alms'. This is clearly used to indicate a contrast to the rights based approach. It also serves as a metaphor for the mechanisms involved in the charity approach that lead to the recipient of aid being in an undignified position. The concept of 'alms' has strong ties to religious discourses. In several religions the giving of alms is an important expression of piety and understood as a religious obligation. The same can be said also of charity and compassion. These too are terms loaded with religious significance. As such it seems that the human rights discourse here is contrasted to discourses that are marked by their religious associations. This does not imply that the rights discourse is atheistic or agnostic, but rather that it does not rely on any religious motivation or rationale, and even less on any specific religious worldview.

Another corollary of the charity approach seems to be the expectation of gratitude. When asked to comment on the distinction between the rights based approach and a charity approach, one of the male embassy interviewees says: 'No, this has actually been the thinking all the time. Many of those who support development aid, they have a charity approach. But it has actually been rights based…' Implicitly this interviewee here makes a distinction between those involved in aid, and those supporting it. He seems to claim that while supporters of aid might have had a charity approach to it, aid has actually been rights based 'all the time'. When asked which supporters he has in mind, he answers:

> Many of those who belong to […] the Christian background…. I think for example Bondevik went a long way in a speech he gave in saying that it's good to see that poor people are so happy when they receive development aid. It warmed his heart to see their eyes when they received aid… Like that. You become very popular when you give gifts. It's a very good feeling to give gifts, and to see that it matters. That is, there is clearly a combination. It's not either or, but that part is often pretty strong.

Here this interviewee makes a connection between Christianity and charity. This is in line with the historical roots of the concept. The example he uses is worth noting. The Prime Minister of Norway at the time of the interview was Kjell Magne Bondevik, representing the Christian Democratic Party, and a politician who on numerous occasions presented himself as a supporter of foreign aid. The criticism voiced here concerns, however, not his political views but rather how he expressed them. It seems he expressed a certain satisfaction in seeing poor people being 'happy when they receive development aid', and some degree of personal satisfaction to himself. It seems that the perceived problem with the charity approach is not so much that people have such motivations, but rather that it implies an inappropriate focus on the donor.[13]

When asked what he would consider to be the benefits of adopting the rights based approach and not charity, the same interviewee says:

> Then you will be able to dissociate a bit more from your own needs. Well, many of those who work in the charity industry (*veldedighetsbransjen*) do it partly because they get a good conscience from doing things. It's sort of ego-supportive (*ego-*

13 The same concern is put forward more as a kind of self-criticism by another of the male embassy interviewees. Discussing how he regards the motives of others, he says: '[…] The joy of giving could maybe have been… Or, I would maybe have liked to see it less articulated. And less visible, if you… Because… Yes, I would have liked to see that it wasn't a charity permeated programme (*gjennomsyret veldedighetsprogram*) we were running'. The main objection this interviewee has seems to be directed toward the instances where 'the joy of giving' becomes too pronounced or visible. He is objecting not to the private sense of satisfaction, but rather to the public, conspicuous display of goodness. It seems he identifies the latter as a characteristic of 'charity permeated programmes'.

> *oppstøttende*). You expect gratitude, to get gratitude from those starving... But if you have a right, then you might be a little more cynical with regard to the ambitions, but maybe more concerned about results and not your own personality... A little distanced from the experience of things changing from bad to better... I am not saying that charity only leads to bad results, but I am saying that too many have gone too far with regard to their own conscience, and with respect to seeing it as a tool for achieving something else. Therefore I am very pleased that rights are made the basis.

It seems that one of the advantages this interviewee sees in the human rights approach is that it enables the development worker to distance herself from her own needs. Again, charity (as the implied opposite to the human rights approach) seems to be related to a (primary) concern for oneself, not to the needs or rights of the Other. The issue of distance seems, however, also to be at work in the donors' relation to the recipient. It even makes you 'distanced from the experience of things changing from bad to better'. Notice, however, that this interviewee is not entirely negative about charity, but appears to be worried about a lack of concern for results.

Further, two important assumptions about 'those who work in the charity industry' are articulated in this quote. Of course, the assumptions about how other people think must be regarded as expressions of this interviewee's understanding of others, and thus as expressions of how he understands himself and his work as well as the work of others. This interviewee seems to think that people in the 'charity industry' do it 'because they get a good conscience from doing things' and that they 'expect gratitude'. Implicitly the question of legitimate and morally commendable motives versus those that are not, are addressed here. Note the terminology used: the aid industry is referred to as the charity trade, and the claim is that many are involved in this just to ease their conscience. The interviewee's evaluative comment is that this is 'ego-supportive'. It seems reasonable that he primarily sees self-interest serving motives behind their involvement, and thus is sceptical about it. This is contrasted with the rights based approach. The rights-worker 'might be a little more cynical', while charity-workers 'expect gratitude'. It seems that the tendency to use or understand one's role as a 'tool for achieving something else' is an important aspect that makes this interviewee prefer human rights as the basis for aid.

This criticism of development workers who expect gratitude seems to assume a purity of heart. It seems to indicate that it is not the well-being of the donor that should be the primary motivation or goal, and even if it was just one element or aspect of one's motivation, it would be damaging to aid efforts. Interpreted in the strictest sense, this seems to be an unrealistic demand. The notion that a rights worker needs to be 'a little more cynical' is an interesting statement in the sense that being cynical often has negative associations. However, the interviewee is not advocating total cynicism in aid work, but is rather acknowledging that a certain degree of cynicism is desirable. By defining charity in this way this interviewee focuses on effect, in the same way that several other interviewees are concerned about the lack of emphasis on results as a feature of charity. However, when this interviewee is concerned about 'results', it seems to be the long-term results he has in mind.[14] Similarly, one of the male NPA interviewees says: 'Charity is to give resources without having an opinion of the effects of the resources spent'.

11.1.3 A loaded term

When asked if he would describe the work he does as charity work, one of the male NCA interviewees says:

> Charity is a very loaded term, often used politically. And I would maybe say that this is where those on the political Right would like to see us, seeing us as charity workers, because that is relatively convenient and non-political, according to their

14 When asked to describe in more detail how he understands the charity approach, this interviewee returns to the example of the Prime Minister's speech. He says: 'I have to say that when I heard the Prime Minister speak, about Norwegian development aid, and it was in the middle of that… when he told how touching it was to see… that the eyes of the recipients were shining. There was something about it that made me really react. What has that got to do with it? And it's sort of like, Norwegian goodness is made the focus and it's really good for us to do good deeds, because it makes us feel good […] and clearly, many of the mission organisations have misinterpreted the Great Commission, I think it's called. They have this thing about saying how people are so grateful for what they do, and that is what counts. And gratitude often leads to passivity and subordination, and dependency. I think that kind of gratitude is quite risky when working in a context defined by the relation between those who have a lot and those who have little. It will harm both those who give and those who receive if gratitude becomes too important'.

> vocabulary. Which of course is not non-political, but that is a different discussion. But then of course you can hope that there is some charity, namely that you want to care for people (*vil andre mennesker vel*). And through the work we do, we want to care. But the general understanding of charity, namely that I do something to improve the situation for others… that it's my own action that matters. But I hope it's actually their own actions that improve this world and their lives. So in that sense I hope we are not doing charity.

This interviewee initially articulates scepticism towards the term charity, as he regards it as a 'loaded term'. In his continued reflection on the term, however, he seems to challenge this understanding of charity, suggesting a definition of the term as wanting 'to care for people'. This interviewee clearly wants to retain this meaning of the word, and applies it also to the way he understands himself. However, he explicitly rejects the notion of charity as a self-centred approach. This interviewee also points to the apolitical connotations associated with the concept of charity.

When asked to explain how he distinguishes between compassion (*barmhjertighet*) and charity (*veldedighet*), another of the male NCA interviewees explains charity in this way:

> Well, charity, if you sort of push it to the extremes, means talking about taking away part of the reflections on human rights. We give what we feel like giving, while it really is a right to give. It's more a kind of language use. […] I am not negative about charity. It's very good. It's a very important part of civil society and in creating commitment. So I am not negative, by no means against it. But it demands a bit more. And it doesn't help with regard to development work or humanitarian work that a few ladies in Ullernåsen[15] flash their gold jewellery (*klirre litt med sine gullsmykker*) and give a thousand kroner note. That is, we can thank them for that. But it's of little avail. And we must also dare to challenge part of the wealth and part of the injustice. And it's sort of not on the charity level. It's on the rights level.

To this interviewee charity implies 'taking away part of the reflections on human rights'. However, he says he is 'not negative about charity'. His concern is that this is not enough, and he makes an interesting distinction between feeling 'like giving' and having 'a right to give'. Thus, it seems that rights is something the interviewee ascribes to the donor, not the recipient of aid. While the rights language is usually used to

15 Ullernåsen is located in the Western part of Oslo, often considered an upper-class part of the city.

stress the rights of the recipients of aid, the rights are here the rights of the donor.

Similarly, when asked to comment on his scepticism towards charity, one of the male embassy interviewees says:

> […] My scepticism is that it shouldn't be given too much room. And it shouldn't be more of… that you give contributions when the misery is really great. But you easily end up in permanent charity programmes (*permanente veldedighetsopplegg*), and that becomes negative also for the people concerned. And development aid through voluntary organisations especially, it doesn't have to be Norwegian organisations, but… Of course, it has contributed to improving people's situations, but it easily becomes a repeated exercise. 'Yes, well. Now we are out of money. Now we need more.' … 'Well, what have you done yourselves?' … 'Well, what should we do?' So it makes people passive. There are lots of examples of that here.[16]

This interviewee too does not reject charity altogether. It seems that his criticism is primarily about 'permanent charity programmes', which he seems to understand as a 'repeated exercise' where the recipients are passive.

Another of the male embassy interviewees is also sceptical of the term charity. He says: 'Charity can mean so many things, in a way. But it's a pejorative word in my book'. When asked to elaborate this statement, he says:

> No, because I find that charity implies limiting something that should be a lot broader. And often it might be more on donors' terms than it should be, if you think about modern cooperation between nations. Charity should not be the main pillar. But in some organisations it's also the bottom line. Fund raising and all this about mobilising the Norwegian people to simply… It has both positive and maybe some negative sides, by being a bit like forgiveness for sins and alms (*syndsforlatelse og almissepreg*). But it's positive that it involves people, and is very informative.

16 When asked to explain how she understands charity, one of the female NCA interviewees says: 'I understand that as help given without any expectations regarding… It's sort of speaking in very general terms, but I think maybe the problem with charity is that you don't make any demands or expectations with regard to the recipient and you give maybe with good intentions and out of the goodness of your heart, but not necessarily considering how it's done. Charity… It's maybe also related to how the one giving also gets a good feeling from giving. And that maybe the big problem is that you don't see the cause of the problem, but only treat the symptoms. You don't deal with the root causes. I think that is the biggest difference'.

> Many of these campaigns have provided good information, which is positive, and involvement.

In this statement the problem with charity is not construed as one of its inherent features. Rather, it seems it is its limited or restricted character that is the main objection to the term. Thus, this interviewee too articulates both positive and negative aspects of charity. 'Forgiveness for sins and alms' is deemed to be negative, while involvement and information are viewed positively. Note again how the religiously loaded connotations are emphasised, and how they seem to be viewed negatively.

11.2 Compassion

One of the values highlighted in NCA's policy document is compassion (see section 4.2). However, compassion is not emphasised as a key value by any of the other agencies studied here (to the contrary), and several interviewees express their unfamiliarity with the term. When asked to comment on the claim that development work involves compassion, one of the female NCA interviewees says:

> I have a very strong… I have been working and seen people come handing out some money here and some there. And I don't believe in that kind of compassion work at all. I have seen so many examples of how it creates a lot more problems than gains locally, because people come without warning to a small community and build a school and give money to some people, and it creates a split in the community. […] The intention is good, but the results are not always as intended when you're sitting in Norway and don't follow up. So I have a very clear opinion on that.

One of the male embassy interviewees offers another example. Explaining why some terms do not suit him well, he says: 'Compassion… That is a word I don't relate to at all. People who talk about that, live in a totally different world'. Commenting on the term compassion, one of the male NPA interviewees, however, indicates a somewhat different evaluation of the term. He says: 'Well, I'm not a religious person, but I clearly think there is something in that word'.

11.2.1 Personal compassion

When one of the female SCN interviewees is asked to elaborate on her understanding of compassion, she says:

> […] But, still, clearly, compassion is not something we should get rid of. I think the word compassion is something more personal and something you can feel when you meet these children who live in difficult situations. It might be part of our motivation for doing this, although we logically think that it has to do with rights, maybe it still is compassion that drives us, but charity… I don't feel… […] I don't feel that's the right word to use anymore.

Note the distinction this interviewee makes between charity and compassion. The latter she understands as something personal, and she relates it to personal feelings that arise in personal encounters and personal motivation. Still, a certain link to rights is indicated by the expression 'although we logically think that it has to do with rights'. Thus a space for compassion is allowed, but it belongs to the private and personal sphere, and is understood as being related to feelings, not logical thought. But she does not allow charity the same space.

Asked if she herself or her organisation does this work because they want to be kind, the same interviewee says:

> […] To me there are certain fundamental principles. The world as it is today isn't just. I can't just sit down and ignore that. But that Save the Children Norway as an organisation… No. Save the Children Norway as an organisation says it is rights based work. That it is because it is the right thing to do (*riktig*). That it is because these children have rights that are being violated, and therefore we have a responsibility. Then it's not only to be good that Save the Children Norway is out there running programmes.

To this interviewee the moral rationale for development aid lies in contemporary injustice and the concept of universal human rights. When asked if she personally wants to be kind, however, the same interviewee says:

> Of course we want to be kind (*snille*). Of course we like children. We want to be kind to children. And we want to help children, and all those words we don't use because we have a rights perspective. That doesn't mean… The thing about compassion is still there, even if it's not what we front as the main reason for what we are doing. But clearly, as human beings committed to this work, we do it because we want to be kind to children.

Here this interviewee takes us backstage. While the concept of charity is excluded from the public rhetoric, she reveals that it might play a role behind the scenes. Note also her interpretation of compassion. It is related to people who are 'committed' because they 'want to be kind'. Compassion is seen as something personal, and maybe even individual. The expression 'want to be' indicates a voluntary aspect.

In the context of discussing the relationship between rights based and charity approaches in development aid, one of the female NCA interviewees says:

> [...] I believe in the rights based approach, and I would like to avoid charity... But still I act as a response to someone suffering. And that I connect more to a kind of... I would not say compassion, but maybe... Yes, maybe more compassion, but maybe not charity... That compassion too is a driving force to me, in a way not only a desire to create a more just world.

Just like the previous interviewee charity is here too something one seeks to avoid. And similarly, a distinction is made between charity and compassion, allowing a space for the latter as part of the individual development worker's personal motivation.

As with charity, compassion is, for some of the interviewees, related to individualistic approaches that are not sustainable. Asked to comment on his understanding of the term compassion, one of the male SCN interviewees says:

> You have staff here who at least used to give money from their own salaries to help individuals. We have a philosophy that you shouldn't support for example [...] give to street children begging. But when there are kids standing by your car, when you stop on every street corner here, and they say they are hungry, then it's very difficult for us as foreigners, and for the locals too... [...] So it's hard to say no. But we also know that if we say yes and do something, then it could worsen the situation, as more children come on the streets, because it's a system... There are probably a hundred thousand street children here in [city]. So the compassion... it doesn't help if you can't do anything about the systems. And that is the consideration all the time: Where do we draw the line? And I'd like to say that, too... I see some people here have become involved in voluntary work on the weekends. And they hardly cope. It's too tough. You get too many individual cases. And I have also had the same thought: I could really have made a difference here, because if I spent three hours a week, then I could maybe have helped a thousand. It's that consideration all the time. I try to push it into the background and be pragmatic.

Compassion is here dismissed as it is perceived as individualistic and thus incapable of dealing with the systemic issues. This is, however, also phrased as a matter of how one should take various considerations into account. Note also how there is a 'philosophy' mentioned here with regard to how one should deal with beggars. The term indicates that this refers to a policy drawn up ahead of the actual encounter with beggars (see section 15.3), and this interviewee clearly indicates how it can be difficult to follow the given policy in concrete encounters.

The critical stance this interviewee here takes toward compassion is not only related to its individualism, but also to his emphasis on the need to keep a certain distance. Too many individual cases will be too tough. So it is necessary to keep a distance (see section 14.3).

11.2.2 Kindness and gratitude

When asked how she would describe the opposite of human rights based aid, one of the female SCN interviewee says:

> […] And to me there is a difference between someone getting something because it's that person's right, or someone getting something because somebody else felt sorry for him. So if they get something from me because I pity them, then I am incredibly kind and you have to be grateful to me, because I am kind. With rights you don't have to demand, or you can't demand gratefulness. And that has to do with personal worth, that every person has the same worth.

The distinction this interviewee makes here seems to rely primarily on distinguishing between someone's right and feeling sorry for someone. It seems that an element of dissociating people from each other is implicit in this concern. Feeling sorry is associated with being kind, expecting that the recipient is 'grateful to me, because I am kind'. Gratitude is especially emphasised. The concept of rights, however, seems to rule out the notion of gratitude. When asked what the problem with kindness is, she says:

> The problem is that if somebody wants to be kind, there may be ulterior motives. If I am kind to you, I want you to be kind in return. Or I want you to be grateful. That is why I give this to you, in the hope that you will give something back. I don't think that is right. If I give this to you because it's your right, then you can do whatever you want with it. And you don't have to give me anything back. I demand no-

> thing of you in return, because it's your right. I give my children food because it's my obligation. I have to give them food. And if at times they behave like wild animals towards me, I can be grumpy and everything, but I can't stop doing it when it's about… because they don't behave the way I want them to. That's the thing. They have a right. And to me, that is the difference.

The problem this interviewee sees in kindness seems to rest primarily on the notion of the expectation of favours in return: 'to be kind in return'. And it is precisely in this regard that she identifies an important difference from the rights approach. The rights approach expects nothing in return. The rights perspective expels the notion of reciprocation altogether from the parties in the aid relationship. Note how kindness in this interviewee's perception is expelled even from the family sphere. The concern seems to be that aid should not be allowed to depend on feelings.

Several of the interviewees distance themselves in a similar fashion from any kind of attitude that makes aid a matter of being kind or good. When asked if the expression human rights based aid is one he would use herself, one of the male NCA interviewees says:

> […] We have to put aside the idea that we are doing this because we are kind, or because we have such a good heart. Or that we feel so very sorry for them. The idea is more that this is a right we have as fellow human beings. That is, there are some who have certain rights, and there are others who give them certain rights. […] We have to get rid of this attitude that if only you are a good Christian, or just because we are in a church, and that we sort of should give tithes. It's more than that. There is a right, and the poor must have both a voice to express and the opportunity to articulate that right.

Note what this interviewee argues should be abolished: the notion that 'we are kind', that we have a 'good heart', or that 'we feel so very sorry for them'. The alternative he favours is that 'this is a right we have as fellow human beings'. His interpretation of this right is worth noting. While 'there are some who have certain rights', there are 'others who give them certain rights'. This notion of giving rights is contrary to one of the most important elements in the traditional notions of human rights, namely that they are natural or inalienable. Accordingly, the individual is in the traditional understanding not dependent upon being given these rights. Note, also the expression: 'it's more than that'. The way this expression is used, the relationship between these attitudes and the rights based approach is not construed as contradictory, but rather as supplementary. The concern is not to expel such notions fully, but rather to supplement them with another perspective. Further, as he comments on the attitudes that follow from being 'a good Christian', a distancing from religious discourse can be noted.

When asked if it is a problem that people want to be kind, the same interviewee says:

> It's not a problem. It's very, very good. And that is often the driving force. We should not condemn that. But if we are now talking about a specific vocation, then it should be anchored much more firmly. Not only to be kind. We have to know a bit about what it means to have a right to education. What it means to have the right to protection. What it means to have the right to health. And we have to know this, as a church and as development workers. And that is the difference. And if you ask what is wrong with it… What can go wrong is that if this attitude is too strong, it becomes a patronising attitude. Somebody comes along and takes off his cap. When they come to me and ask for help. And I should sort of raise my head pretty high and say 'Yes, poor man. If you behave well and are a good Christian, then you might get help.' You see? And it happens.

The expression 'not only to be kind' seems to support the interpretation of this interviewee's perception of rights and compassion as supplementary concepts. Explicating the need to supplement, he seems, however, to reveal that an important part of his concern is to fight ignorance in the field, as well as paternalism. When asked how he views the role of compassion in NDA, the same interviewee says:

> Clearly, compassion is central both in the Norwegian church, and in the Norwegian churches. It's a kind of… maybe the most important role, […] is the ability to care, and maybe also being a voice in order to make people care. And that is a great challenge, really.

That compassion belongs to a religious discourse is here confirmed, but also given an interesting interpretation. Compassion is rephrased as the term 'to care', and also 'being a voice in order to make people care'. Compassion seems then to be explicitly related to advocacy work.

When asked to elaborate on her understanding of goodness, one of the female NCA interviewees makes a distinction between goodness and misunderstood kindness. While she finds '[…] goodness (*godhet*) is something we all should strive for (*streve etter*)', she thinks:

> [...] being kind has sort of a sting to it. 'He is kind', which is sort of... Not much too kind (*dumsnill*), but misunderstood kindness (*snillisme*), maybe? Like, we are supposed to be kind. And we are not really interested in looking at what we are actually doing, or what would really be the best thing to do. It's a lot easier just to give, and then I leave. Instead of sitting down and listening to you, to seeing you first, and talking to you. Yes, to dig a bit deeper, right? And that is what I think the whole development industry is suffering from. They are not interested in going down to that level and looking at the structural causes of all this. You don't have to be an academic to know. But we are not supposed to do that, because if you mix politics and aid, and enter into that field, then aid isn't unconditional anymore. Then you have the whole issue of conditionalities, and it all becomes really complicated. So instead of venturing into that, it's easier to follow the humanitarian imperative, where you only help. You don't need to ask any questions. You don't need to make any demands.

In her reply, this interviewee compares 'being kind' to 'misunderstood kindness'. Her analysis seems to be guided by the intuitive understanding of goodness as something positive while 'being kind' is perceived as something with a certain 'sting' to it. Kindness is distinguished from being 'much too kind', and she indicates that it might be closer to a 'misunderstood kindness'. This, however, indicates that there might be a concept of kindness that is not misunderstood and that as such could be considered positive in the same way that she evaluates goodness positively. Note further the problems she sees arising from 'kindness'. She relates it to a lack of interest in 'what we are actually doing' and what would be 'the best thing to do'. In addition, she seems also to relate it to a superficial approach or behaviour – where donating money is limited to the actual donation and not followed by 'sitting down' and in depth understanding. Note how these shortcomings are ascribed to 'the whole development industry'.

Further, this interviewee argues that there will be a lack of concern for 'structural causes' if kindness is the driving force. In this she echoes the dependency school's criticism of modernisation theory (see section 3.2), as well as a number of practitioners and academics who find that the continuum between relief, rehabilitation, development aid, and political advocacy is crucial in order to achieve lasting improvements (see sections 9.2 and 9.3). Note, however, that this interviewee finds that taking such considerations into account complicates things – and thus it becomes 'easier to follow the humanitarian imperative'. This alternative is, according to her understanding, marked by its explicitly apolitical approach. And it is this reluctance she finds the development industry is 'suffering from'. The suffering seems to be an inability or an unwillingness to make political considerations. Thus, this interviewee makes making demands a key concern.

11.3 Solidarity

In contrast to the concepts of charity and compassion, solidarity seems to be widely regarded as a positive term. As noted above, NPA makes this a key concept in its policy documents (see section 4.4) and the term can also be used to describe personal motivation (see section 7.1.2). When asked to comment on the claim that development aid is based on the notion of benevolence (*nestekjærlighet*), one of the female embassy interviewees chooses to translate it into a more familiar term. She says: 'Well. I would call it solidarity. But it's approximately the same'. Similarly, when asked to comment on the claim that Norwegian aid really is charity, one of the male NPA interviewees says:

> There is a lot of truth in that. Earlier it was very true, but still there are a lot of projects I would characterise as charity. I hope and think that more and more are moving towards solidarity.

This interviewee accepts the notion that NDA amounts to charity. Note, however, that this is something he seems to dislike, as he would like it to be more characterised by solidarity. He seems to identify a change from charity towards solidarity over the years.

Asked what he thinks NDA is all about, one of the male NCA interviewees says:

> It's primarily about solidarity. It's a desire to help the rest of the world, in relation to many other countries, and what kind of interests we might encounter. But from the Norwegian side, Norwegian development aid is based on a strong attitude of solidarity. It's neither connected too much to economic interests, nor to political interests. In some contexts it might be, but not much. Other major nations do that a lot, lot more. USA. Japan. Germany. So when I sort of see Norwegian foreign policy, and also Norwegian development aid, it's a lot about solidarity and actually a desire to help the world.

Note how Norwegian solidarity here is defined in terms of its negation. Solidarity has no place for economic or political interests (although he admits there might be exceptions). Accordingly, solidarity refers to aid as not governed by self-interest. Note also how this is regarded as something that distinguishes Norwegian aid from other states' aid programmes (see section 3.2.2). However, this only applies to the 'major nations', exemplified by USA, Japan, and Germany. Again, note the understanding of Norway as a small state as a key notion. In conclusion, this interviewee then insists on 'actually a desire to help the world' as the basis for Norwegian aid. Where realist oriented analysts might seek other explanations, the idealistic understanding of aid is here not only emphasised, but also insisted upon (see section 3.2.1).

11.3.1 Distribution between classes

When asked about the arguments he would use to justify development aid, one of the male NCA interviewee says:

> I believe the notion of solidarity is not dead. And out of human decency and a notion of responsibility (*menneskelig anstendighet og ansvarstenkning*), a notion of solidarity also becomes important. And if you also think politically, from that part of the political landscape which talks about solidarity, you also think in terms of class society. And if you think even bigger, it's certainly also a global class society.

This interviewee's conviction that thinking in terms of solidarity is not dead implies a notion that solidarity played a more important role in earlier times. He seems, however, to regard solidarity as important. He explicitly relates it to the political sphere and the notion of a class society.

When asked to explain what it means to express solidarity, one of the female embassy interviewees says: 'It's to share. Just like I think one should share in Norway, too'. The same distributive concern is also emphasised by one of the female NCA interviewees. When asked how she would justify NDA, she says:

> I believe the most important argument is that we live in a world where wealth is distributed very unevenly. That we as one of the world's richest countries have an obligation to… you know what, I think… to be a state that expresses its solidarity (*være en solidarisk stat*).

Note how it is the uneven distribution of resources that constitutes the justification for aid. From this she derives a duty to be a 'state that expresses its solidarity'. Being such a state amounts to having an obligation, and it seems this obligation is to correct the uneven distribution.

11.3.2 Shoulder to shoulder

Asked what he means by the term solidarity, one of the male NPA interviewees says:

> [...] Norwegian People's Aid started with relief assistance to Spain and Finland in the thirties. It's sort of the historical legacy of Norwegian People's Aid. It's sort of assistance between peoples. A solidarity where you stand shoulder to shoulder with other people in difficult situations, where you see yourself with partly the same goals, and partly the same values, shared values, etc. Where you want to stand there and not let them stand alone in their struggle. [...] So, solidarity goes back to a sort of political, very clear political connotation.

Note again how solidarity seems to have connotations concerning interconnectedness and special relations – 'between peoples' standing 'shoulder to shoulder'. This interviewee also relates shared or concurrent values to this concept. Further, he explicitly addresses the political connotations – placing it at the left end of the political spectrum.
Asked to mention some values he thinks development aid should be based on, another male NPA interviewee says:

> [...] some of the values of solidarity, to actually choose to side with people, which I think Norwegian People's Aid has done. I think that is important. To say: 'OK, we place ourselves on their side. We will also be there when the challenges come.' We in Norwegian People's Aid have done that in Palestine and in Sudan. We haven't always done the right thing, but we have shared their burdens. So I think solidarity is important.

Here too the political aspect of solidarity is highlighted. In this case, however, it is not the party political aspect, but rather the issue of taking sides (see sections 4.4 and 7.4). Clearly, to this interviewee this is considered a key element of solidarity, as well as of how development aid should be implemented.

One of the female SCN interviewees also finds solidarity to be an important word in relation to development aid work. Asked how she understands solidarity, she explains:

> […] And when you are doing this, it has to do with solidarity. You want to stand by these people and fight together with them to improve the situation for them and to further their rights. So it's clear that there has to be a basic feeling of solidarity, both personally and in the organisation when you work from a rights perspective. And I don't think that is necessarily the case if you think in terms of charity. It doesn't have to be solidarity. But with rights I think you have to have solidarity.

As she explains her understanding of solidarity this interviewee uses expressions such as 'to stand by' and 'fight together'. Again it seems that the concept of solidarity carries notions of shared community and close relations, as well as an understanding of a conflict or tension where one is committed to take sides. Note further how the fight of solidarity is a fight to 'further their rights'. Accordingly, solidarity and rights seem to relate to each other in a positive manner. Actually a 'feeling of solidarity' seems to be perceived as a necessary precondition if one is working from a rights perspective. Note further how, in the eyes of this interviewee, solidarity seems to be related to rights, but is absent if one speaks of charity. Like human rights, solidarity seems to be a word that is contrasted to charity.

One of the male SCN interviewees also makes a connection between solidarity and rights. In this case, however, the issue of results is more markedly brought to the fore. Asked if he would describe the work he does as solidarity work, he says:

> […] If I have to make a decision, I would not think of myself, not think of the authorities and not of Norway, but of the rights we have with relation to children. So that is the solidarity in this. But we don't walk around just to express solidarity, if you see what I mean. It has to be… a businesslike basis for this, that we get results. And it must be for the children.

In this statement the term solidarity seems to be used to refer to where one's primary loyalties lie. To this interviewee the main concern is not the interests of authorities or Norway, but the rights of children. It seems that solidarity thus expresses a sense of accountability and a special kind of relationship to a specific group, in this case the recipients or beneficiaries of aid, the children. Note also, however, how he specifies his understanding of solidarity. It seems that he finds reason to dissociate from any notion of solidarity that amounts to walking 'around just to express solidarity'. Rather, in a 'businesslike' manner results must be achieved. It seems than that the consequences are considered of prime importance. A habit of expressing solidarity that lacks results seems to be rejected.

11.4 Concluding reflections

To several of the interviewees the terms charity and compassion are terms they either do not use or feel uncomfortable using. This is articulated by male and female interviewees, and by representatives of all four agencies studied here. Some feel that these concepts are altogether unfamiliar to them. Thus they become concepts in contrast to the hegemonic rights discourse, and related terms like kindness and goodness seem also to be rejected as tools for understanding NDA. In this the interviewees' language use seems to correspond to that of the various policy documents, though to some extent in contrast to the policy papers of NCA.

As opposed to rights based aid, charity is recognised by its selective and random approach. Charity is considered to help alleviate poverty in the short-term, but not in the long-term. Further, the charity approach is characterised by its stronger focus on the donor and her needs and feeling good than on the rights of poor people. Charity seems also to be understood as an approach in development aid that focuses on individual recipients and ad hoc assistance, and is associated with relief efforts. Further, it is characterised by being related to the feeling of pity, and this is evaluated negatively. Two elements seem to carry special importance to the interviewees: that the aid efforts are not primarily to be understood as a matter of good will by the donor, and that the recipients are not humiliated or made to feel that they should be grateful. Giving aid is not regarded as a matter of being kind. It is a matter of fulfilling rights. Generally, charity seems to be more closely associated with having feelings drive one's commitment, in contrast to the rights based approach where it is laws, conventions, and universal values that are made the motivating basis.

The concept of compassion seems to be used and understood similarly to the way the concept of charity is used. There is accordingly a relatively sharp contrast between its use in NCA's policy documents and how many interviewees relate to the term. In the more personal context, however, the role of feelings seems to be acknowledged, and charity and compassion are by some interviewees admitted a (limited) role in that sphere.

The concept of solidarity seems, however, to be widely perceived as a positive word. The term seems to be associated with the political left, and more than rights it seems to articulate a notion of togetherness, standing 'shoulder to shoulder', and 'fighting' a shared struggle. Some of the interviewees express a concern that the idea of solidarity should not disappear, indicating it is an appreciated, though peripheral, concept in the dominant discourse.

Accordingly, the analysis in this chapter shows both continuity and discontinuity between the interpretative repertoires that are used in the policy documents, and those preferred by the interviewees. While the concept of charity seems to be used and understood in a way that is similar to its use in most of the policy documents, this is only partly so in the case of compassion and solidarity. As mentioned, while NCA highlights compassion as one of five values guiding its work, this concept is largely dismissed by the interviewees, including some of the NCA interviewees. Similarly, while NPA makes solidarity a key term in its policy document, this appears to be only a peripheral concept in the interviewees' discourse on NDA.

12 Justice

If You're an Egalitarian, How Come You're So Rich?

Book title, Cohen 2000

In *The Nicomachean Ethics* Aristotle distinguishes between distributive and rectificatory justice (Aristotle 1980:109). The latter form of justice comes about through the rectification of past wrongs committed, while distributive justice concerns levelling present inequalities and could be based on a criterion of merit, need, or equality. Using these categories as analytical tools, I will in the following discuss how the interviewees use and understand the concept of justice.

12.1 Reacting to injustice

When challenged to explain her understanding of justice in the context of development aid, one of the female SCN interviewees says:

> Justice is very important. I feel it's a key issue. To me it's what drives me, really. Because it's the injustice that... And that is related to a word like rights. It's not just that the children in [country] live in such conditions. It's not just that my children have everything they need, and if we walk two hundred meters down the road there are children who don't have enough to live. That is not just. So I think justice is a better word than charity. It has other implications as to how you view development work.

This interviewee not only identifies justice as an important part of her motivation, but also relates it discursively to 'rights' in an explicit contrast to the concept of 'charity'. Interestingly, she also indicates that this has consequences for 'how you view development work'.

When one of the male NCA interviewees is asked to comment on the concept of justice, he says:

> Justice is a far more relevant concept, I think. Because we live in an unjust world, where there are great differences. Where there are natural disasters, where there is war and unrest and where individuals are affected in an unjust way. So it's clear that it's also about making a contribution to creating more justice and equality in the world.

Like the previous interviewee, this interviewee too evaluates the concept of justice positively and regards it as a 'far more relevant concept'. Thus, the concept of justice seems to feature as a positive term in these statements, and as an important concept in these interviewees' understanding and justification of NDA. This is in line with the role the term plays in the policy documents of both MFA and NCA (see sections 4.1 and 4.2). More specifically this interviewee seems to relate the concept of justice to the issue of distribution. He regards an unjust world as a place 'where there are great differences'. The expression 'individuals are affected in an unjust way' is used in the context of natural catastrophes and war, and might, especially with respect to the latter, refer to some kind of wrongdoing, and thus to some kind of rectificatory justice. However, in the next sentence 'justice and equality' are mentioned together, and seem to support each other. Accordingly, the distributive aspect seems to dominate this interviewee's understanding of the term, although a rectificatory element may also be present.

When asked about what arguments she finds most important with regard to development aid, one of the female SCN interviewees says:

> The most important arguments are that… I think it's right to think globally in this world. And not be… well, because we are Norwegians doesn't imply that we are only responsible for Norway and things that happen in Norway. But I feel that we live in a world where… Well, how should I put it… I think it's very limiting to think that Norwegian resources should be spent in Norway and that we should only think about ourselves. I feel it isn't right. I feel that Norway has a responsibility, in the same way that I feel that I as a person have a responsibility. Because we are better off, because we have resources. Because, if you think historically about our part of the world compared to this part of the world, then the reason why Europe and North America are richer, is that they have exploited (*utnyttet seg av*) this part of the world. So I believe you have a responsibility. And that it's right that these countries with more resources should contribute to a better situation in countries with fewer resources. At the same time, it's a matter of the future and the world.

> You can't go… If one half of the world, or more than one half of the world live in extremely difficult conditions, then that will affect the situation in the rest of the world too. It's to think ahead, it's to think about the future of your children. So I feel there are lots of good reasons for doing this kind of work.

This interviewee starts by indicating the general perspective she finds necessary to apply when answering the question. She wants to think globally. This makes her emphasise how responsibility for the world's poor is something both the Norwegian state and she herself as an individual share. This responsibility is explained through a reference to 'resources', and seems thus to depend on a notion of ability to share. However, she also explains this responsibility by arguing that Europe and North America have exploited other parts of the world and that a responsibility can be derived from this historical fact. Accordingly, responsibility is based on an identification of wrongdoings in the past. Responsibility is thus derived from a perception of injustice in the past that has consequences in the present. This injustice must accordingly be corrected. Finally, an argument of common interest is made. Poverty in one part of the world will affect the rest of the world (all of us), and even the future (coming generations). Accordingly, one can identify three different ways of justifying international aid in this interviewee's reflection on the issue. Her first argument could be classified as an argument of distributive justice (affluence and ability). Her second argument is one of rectificatory justice (historical guilt/compensation), and the third one of common interest.

Later, when challenged to formulate what she would consider a moral argument for international aid, this interviewee adopts the same global perspective and stresses mutual dependency. In this context she also makes human rights the core of her argument. She says:

> Yes, well… We live in a global society where we are dependent on each other. And if we only continue and think only about ourselves, and use the resources in our own society, then there will… First of all, from a rights perspective you cannot just stand back and watch human rights being violated all the time. We have to do something about it. We cannot just stand back and watch it happening. We have to do something to change things. And we also have to consider… I feel it's very important to think about the world and not countries. Not to think from a national perspective, but a global perspective and a rights perspective.

Note here how she makes a discursive chain: the 'national' is contrasted with the 'global', which in turn is related to the rights perspective. Thus, it seems reasonable to interpret the 'global perspective' that frames her response above also in terms of a related human rights discourse. Accordingly, just as *Fighting Poverty Together* makes a human rights based policy a matter of justice, the rights perspective seems to frame this interviewee's argument of justice.

12.2 Distributive justice

The argument of distributive justice is articulated by several of the interviewees although the term is not always used explicitly. Rather than a discourse of justice, it seems therefore more reasonable to label this a discourse of distribution. When asked about what arguments he finds most important with regard to international aid, one of the male SCN interviewees says:

> To me it has quite clearly been that I see how great the differences are, and how indifferent we are when we live safe and sound at home. And we go on party trips like the teenagers to Greece, or to Spain, and we have things like… and we complain about the increased price of electricity or the tram ticket going up two kroner. And when you go out to the local villages here and see what people are lacking. So the differences… And not least when we have a social democratic society, relatively speaking, at home, then we cannot accept, with the wealth we have, that the difference is that great. And we can afford it.

There seems to be two distinct elements that form the rationale for providing international aid articulated here. One is 'how great the differences are'. This interviewee seems to ridicule the lifestyle and what he sees as a culture of complaining in Norwegian society, and compares this with 'what people are lacking' in the villages in the country where he works. Note also how the argument of ability is here expressed with reference to the great disparities in living standards. The concluding comment 'we can afford it' seems to indicate that the level of aid he is envisioning is well within the limits of our ability. It seems reasonable to understand this as indicating that what he envisions does not represent any major interference in the standard of living or in any way threaten individual life projects. Thus, as 'we can afford it' seems to be both an argument for providing development aid in the first place, as well as an argument for relatively rich Norwegians to do so.

To this he adds, however, a second pillar, namely that 'we have a social democratic society'. The societal situation and the character of the Norwegian society seems then in part to be something he finds has a bearing on what kind of development policy the Norwegian government should adopt. It seems to be a notion that there should be a certain link between domestic policy and foreign policy. Thus, it appears to be a feature of the argument that a social democratic society challenges the sharp distinction that is often made between domestic and international politics, and which makes national borders normatively relevant in issues of distribution. Rather, a social democratic society must adopt a foreign policy that corresponds to its domestic policies. The social democratic policies are often considered widely egalitarian, and thus, this argument seems to support the distributive concern that frames the statement (see section 3.3).

When addressing the same issue, one of the female embassy interviewees starts off with an argument of self-interest (security), but rejects this, and then mentions the argument of distributive justice. She says:

> [...] It has to do with trying to do your small part in dealing with distorted distribution (*skjev fordeling*) in the world. A distorted economic world order, one could say. It's about what Christians would call love of your neighbour. That is, that we have abundance and you should share with each other. [...] I think I am kind of a socialist in the sense that I think we should share the wealth. And that doesn't only apply to small Norway or in Oslo municipality, but also globally. Then you have a kind of moral obligation to share with others. But you cannot share with everyone, and you cannot... Well, yes, I think it's OK that a part of my... well, my tax money, because that is what it is, a part of my tax money goes to people in poor countries. I support that.

Again, the issue of distribution is the key element of the argument. This interviewee refers to 'what Christians would call love of your neighbour', but conceptualises her attitude in terms of her 'socialist' convictions. Note also her summary regarding abundance. She seems to think that an 'obligation to share with others' can be derived from a situation of surplus. The perspective is clearly forward looking and distributive, but national borders are also apparently made irrelevant in regard to the issue of distribution. With these assumptions one might expect a cosmopolitan conclusion, but her conclusion seems rather to limit the global relevance of sharing wealth to a principled support for ODA.

Asked to explain why she thinks development aid is about rich countries easing their bad conscience, another female embassy interviewee says:

> [...] It's a paradox when you still have a Western world with an ever increasing standard of living, and that... We are really becoming richer and richer, at least many people are anyway, and the standard of living and rights and everything has become very, very good. Since the fifties up to today, sort of... And then it's somewhat strange, it leaves kind of a foul taste in your mouth that you meet in the UN and are aware of the huge differences that exist... I don't know, between two seats in the General Assembly. Norway sits next to Nigeria.

The paradox this interviewee discusses seems to rest on two notions. One, that the Western world is getting 'richer and richer', and two, that there are 'huge differences'. The wealth of the Western world seems then both to be a relative wealth (in comparison with poorer countries, e.g. Norway vs. Nigeria), and one which provides a standard of living this interviewee evaluates very positively. Note the explicitly international character of the comparison made. Clearly, NDA is seen as and justified as a tool to level uneven international distribution. The latter seems to echo what was referred to above as being in a position to 'afford' it, and thus having the ability to provide aid. This is an interesting emphasis in the way that it focuses on our situation, the wealth of the (potential) donor, rather than the plight of the poor or suffering. It seems then that the notion of distributive justice, at least to this interviewee, is related to a notion of the Norwegian society having reached a level of sufficient satisfaction. To continue 'becoming richer and richer' seems consequently to produce a certain discomfort.

Asked if he thinks Norway or Norwegians have a duty to provide development aid, one of the male embassy interviewees is also mostly concerned about how wealth should be shared. He says:

> [...] To me it's... and it's not necessarily only out of goodness to put it that way, but it's also in your own interest to share with your neighbour from time to time. [...] No, we are really wealthy, and we should take a large portion of our wealth and share it, but we are also a little concerned about the way we share it.

In this statement, however, the sharing 'with your neighbour' is given legitimacy through a reference to 'your own interest'. Thus, self-interest is seen as a legitimate part of the rationale for development aid (though with a temporal limitation). Note also the priority this interviewee gives to the 'how' of international aid rather than the 'how much'. The part of the wealth that should be shared should be 'large', but it is 'the way we share it' he seems primarily concerned about. It seems then that he avoids the former topic, and relates primarily to the latter. This can be seen as limiting one's focus and field of responsibility. While politicians, the government, or the NGO head office bureaucrats must deal with the question of how much, this interviewee focuses on doing his job. He does not question the system, but focuses on his own limited role.

12.2.1 Dangerous inequality

Asked if he would make a moral argument for development aid, one of the male SCN interviewees says:

> Of course this is about morality. And it's clear that if we don't do anything about it... We have a huge problem. [...] And the projection by the UN system is that in 2050 there will be a [...] guaranteed doubling of the number of people here today. And if we don't do anything about it, the population growth, which maybe we cannot do anything about, and then the whole world will be divided to the extent that it might be dangerous for the rest of the world if we don't do anything. And of course, when we can afford it... And if I am not mistaken, I think the military budgets in the developed world... three or four days of the military budget could have provided development and education, and better education for all the children in Africa south of the Sahara. And that is prioritising three days, so it's not that we can't afford it.

By explicitly confirming the 'morality' implicit in development aid, this interviewee points to 'a huge problem' he finds fundamental in this respect: 'the number of people'. This reference to population growth is not without preceding examples. This was of primary concern to several writers in the early 1970s, for instance in the works of Paul Ehrlich (Ehrlich 1971) and Garrett Hardin (Hardin 1968). Note also the consequences he sees resulting from this population growth – a divided world that 'might be dangerous for the rest of the world'. Thus, a global problem with global consequences is addressed, which in turn makes the morality of development aid a morality of common interest. Note also this interviewee's insistence on the ability of the 'developed world' to deal with this problem. Referring to the resources allocated for military purposes, he substantiates his claim: 'we can afford it'. Accordingly, if one is able to provide aid, there is also a duty to do so.

When asked what he thinks are the most important arguments for why Norway or Norwegian organisations should be involved in development aid, another of the male SCN interviewees says:

> I think that when you look at the world today, there is a very big imbalance, between the developing and the developed world, in terms of resource distribution. And I think Norway is one of the richest countries in the world, and I think it's an obligation that they contribute to the development of the underprivileged part of the world. To me it's a kind of obligation that I think that it is OK to do. But at the end of the day, when you look at what some of these imbalances cause, if you have a big part of the world with extremely poor education, it means that they are not utilizing resources in the best possible way, and eventually this affects everyone else in the world. If there are countries in the world where there are no proper democratic systems and no good governance, it spills over to the rest of the world. That is why you have terrorism, and people are [...] fighting for A, B, C and D, and eventually it spills over to the rest of the world. So in a way it's a contribution to minimise some of the deprivations that are so huge in the world. And that should make a better world for everybody at the end of the day. It means contributing to good governance, better democracy, people having more opportunities in terms of education and health, they can live a better life, and then you have maybe less of some of the things that are happening today.

This interviewee too makes the issue of 'resource distribution' the core of his argument for a Norwegian duty to provide development aid. He also uses this as a starting point for reflecting on the consequences this 'very big imbalance' might have, and claims that 'this affects everyone else in the world'. In this context he seems to understand aid as an instrument that serves everyone's interests. The implicit notion seems to be that poverty breeds terrorism, and forces people to leave their home countries (see section 9.4.2).

In the statements above none of the interviewees have used the term justice (or the adjective just), but have articulated distributive concerns. However, when asked what he thinks is the most important argument for why Norway or Norwegians should provide development aid, one of the male embassy interviewees makes an explicit argument of distributive justice and common interest. He says:

> Yes, my main reason and my concern is a desire for a just distribution of resources. It actually is. It might sound a bit repulsive (*odiøst*) or a bit... well, 'you can't really mean this', but yes, I do. I believe that development aid is one of several ways to distribute wealth and make sure that the planet survives the next hundred years. The last point could be turned on its head, saying that development aid is something we really give in order to secure our own future, if you think about pollution and natural resources and deforestation and all that... Then you could deduce from that a second argument: you could say the humanitarian idea, with distribution of resources and such things. And the other thing is to secure the existence of the earth. That we have to cooperate, make sure deforestation stops, etc.

Note how the notion of justice is related to distribution. It is distributive concerns that constitute this interviewee's main justification of international aid – 'a desire for a just distribution of resources'. It seems reasonable to understand his insistence on being trusted on this ('It actually is.') in the context of his position as embassy staff and the distinction between idealism and realism. He makes an explicit idealistic claim, and seems therefore to find a need to stress his trustworthiness. This functions then as a reply to realist suspicion (see section 3.2.1). Further, note how this interviewee also refers to the issue of distribution as the 'humanitarian' argument. He seems to also use an argument of common interest, and this again makes him discuss the relation between common interest and self-interest. The emphasis is, however, clearly on common concerns ('the existence of the earth').[17]

17 Similarly, when asked what he thinks are the most important reasons to provide development aid, one of the male NPA interviewees highlights both distribution and self-interest. He says: '[...] You could think along two lines. The first is more of an ethical or humanist starting point where we as a wealthy nation with considerable abundance have an ethical responsibility to share some of the surplus we have, and that we as fellow human beings have a responsibility to contribute so that other countries not in the same situation can have a positive development. [...] The other thing is that contributing to a healthy and positive development in the Third World would ensure that Norway can sustain its own situation. If you look at this in a more cynical way, it would be favourable for world peace and the global economy if the Third World develops positively'.

12.2.2 Wealth and poverty

When asked about his arguments for NDA, one of the male NCA interviewees says:

> Of course, when I am out in the field and know that more than eighty per cent of the population in a country like [country] have miserable access to clean water, have bad health conditions, where girls who are pregnant have to walk up to eleven or twelve kilometres to go to the clinic… What they get at the clinic is an aspirin, and they have to come back again next week. When I see what kind of educational facilities children are offered, and how bad it is, not to mention the close to half a million who don't have access to schools or education, then… and at the same time hear about the huge riches we have in Norway, which we have created over the last fifty years. And we are also part of a system, I am thinking of a global trade system that excludes large parts of the world. So it's not only a moral obligation, it's actually a right to give and to share (*en rett å gi og dele*) a part of what we have.

Again, it is the difference in living conditions, the uneven distribution of wealth, that is addressed. Note, however, the conclusion this interviewee arrives at after having explained the issue of uneven distribution. He implicitly concludes that it is a 'moral obligation', but seems to want to emphasise this by adding that 'it's actually a right to give and to share'. This use of the term right seems odd, considering that the right to give aid is not usually challenged. The exception here might be proponents of alternative development, who see development aid as a tool to dominate, and something that destroys local culture or other ways of life. Within the development aid discourse, however, the issue at stake is most often the right to receive, and whether or not there is a corresponding duty to give. The use of the term right in order to emphasise the moral obligation is, however, still in line with how rights language is often used to emphasise the importance of providing aid and distinguishing the present approach from, for instance, the charity approach. As such, this use of the term is rather traditional.

When asked what implications the notion of justice has on his daily work, the same interviewee says:

> And one of the main challenges that we have is management and sharing of wealth. And now I am talking about wealth North-South, but I am also talking about wealth in my work here in [country]. I see hundreds of new Mercedes coming here. I know that an elite is about to develop here in Southern Africa.

When this interviewee identifies management and distribution of wealth as one of the greatest challenges in his context, it is a forward looking perspective that he adopts. In contrast, the creation of the wealth in question – how it was acquired and its present legitimacy – is not raised as an issue. Rather, the wealth at hand is acknowledged and recognised, and he sees the challenge to be one of managing and sharing it. Note, however, that he explicitly makes a point out of not making this an issue of redistribution between North and South. While he does not seem to want to reject this perspective he wants to supplement it with an awareness of the wealth in Africa, by what he refers to as 'an elite' and symbolised by 'hundreds of new Mercedes'. However, this interviewee too is an example of the presence of the North in Africa. And further, by pointing to this reality, he also opens up for debate about the fact that there is wealth in the South and that it is the responsibility of recipient countries to address the issue of redistribution. As long as that has not taken place, one could also question their right to, or the effects of, international development aid. Rights seem here to be something that can apparently be derived from the character of the inequality that exists between peoples' standards of living.

It should be noted that several of the interviewees are concerned to nuance the image of the poor and of poor societies. In the context of explaining his understanding of what would characterise 'the good development worker', one of the male embassy interviewees says:

> [...] Well, there is something positive about knowing these societies a bit better than from reading newspapers and sensational postings. It's that you see how the descriptions of misery (*elendighetsbeskrivelsen*) do not always correspond to reality. That is, what could seemingly look like misery, terrible, is perhaps a society with its own rules, its own standards. They might have a different... they are not in 2005, but they are in 1723 in terms of welfare etc., and in terms of standard of housing, food and welfare benefits. But if you accept that societies living in poor conditions also have their intrinsic value and maybe also positive elements, human elements, human compassion, like taking care of their own... [...] I think that the longer you work in the field and in a way manage to function and to see things, the better you accept the realities of the situation.

Note how this interviewee stresses that descriptions of misery do not always fit with reality. He continues to highlight 'positive elements' in 'these societies'. However, he also uses a model of stages to underline his argument. It becomes most explicit when he uses years to compare different societies. While some societies are 'in 2005' others are 'in 1723'. In effect this interviewee seems then to place all societies on a progressive continuum, where the level of development is indicated by a year on a dateline. While some countries have reached the top level (the present year), others are lagging behind. Thus, all countries are evaluated on the same scale, and the same goal or aim applies to all of them. Although this interviewee does not speak of stages in development, he still relies on a model that shares many of the stage-theories developed, for instance in Rostow's modernisation theory (Rostow 1960).

12.3 Rectificatory justice

In the discourse of distribution the perspective is forward looking, as the aim is to level present inequalities. In other statements, however, a different discourse is articulated. The argument here relies on the notion that any harm done should be compensated for. This is, in other words, a discourse of rectificatory justice. In the case of international aid, this argument can be invoked either with reference to historical wrongs (e.g. colonialism) or to ongoing contemporary wrongs (e.g. the international trade system). That the Third World has been exploited by the now affluent First World is a widely used argument in both political and academic debates. This is an issue that is often raised by voices in the developing world who see foreign aid as a matter of rectifying the wrongs of colonial exploitation. Severin Rugumamu represents one such voice from the South. He writes:

> [...] the argument is straightforward: the industrialized capitalist countries should not overlook the fact that they are responsible for today's appalling conditions in Africa on account of slave trade, colonial exploitation, and neocolonial haemorrhaging of resources. (Rugumamu 1997:54)

However, this argument is also acknowledged outside the South, either as an argument for reparation or that 'we must not uphold extreme inequality in social starting positions when the allocation of these positions depends upon historical processes in which moral principles and legal rules were massively violated' (Pogge 2002:203). From a moral philosophical point of view, the argument that rich countries have gained their wealth through the exploitation of other countries, and thus have harmed these countries, seems to be a relatively strong argument for a duty to provide some kind of aid.

Another version of the rectificatory argument points to the part affluent nations play in perpetuating the suffering in poor nations. The issue here is not that they have been exploited in the past, but that they are being exploited now. This is most often expressed as a critique of the present global economic system shaped and governed by affluent countries, but with continued mistreatment of the poor as its consequence (Pogge 2002:15–26). Thus, one can distinguish between the forward looking distributive argument, the retrospective argument for compensation for harm done, and finally the argument that one should stop harming in the present. Nigel Dower highlights all of these when he writes:

> What is done in and to developing countries may be seen as unjust, because of the exploitation of resources and of cheap labour. So the demand for justice is not merely a forward-looking demand that the world be so organized as to meet basic needs. It is the demand that we stop active injustice as well, and also make recompense for what has been done. Of course, most of 'us' are not directly involved in all this; but we are all part of, and beneficiaries of, the system that does this. (Dower 1991:274–275)

I will first discuss notions of rectifying past wrongs and then turn to ongoing exploitation.

12.3.1 Past wrongs

Just as several interviewees seem to justify development aid in terms of distributive justice, there are also those whose arguments refer to notions of rectificatory justice. As noted above, one of the female SCN interviewees derives a notion of responsibility from historical exploitation. Discussing what she regards as the most important arguments for NDA, she says:

> Because, if you think historically about our part of the world compared to this part of the world, then the reason why Europe and North America is richer, is that they

have exploited (*utnyttet seg av*) this part of the world. So I believe you have a responsibility.[18]

The responsibility this interviewee talks about clearly also concerns distribution of goods, but is still a different kind of responsibility than that discussed above. The key issue is how she explains European and North American wealth. Firstly, note how her explanation is historical. Secondly, wealth is considered a result of exploitation. Accordingly, responsibility is based on a retrospective orientation that links wrongdoings in the past with present consequences. Responsibility is thus derived from a perception of injustice in the past that has consequences in the present. This injustice is regarded as something that must be corrected.

Similarly, asked why she thinks Norway or Norwegians should be involved in development aid, another of the female SCN interviewees says:

> [...] The way I see it, the riches of the world have been distributed wrongly because it's the people who have had the strength to begin with who have somehow had the upper hand. And if you look at European development, it's to a very large extent founded on the exploitation of Africa and the natural resources in Africa. [...] I think that Africa somehow has been the continent that has always been exploited as much as possible, something which has been compensated for only to a very limited extent. That is unjust and it's our darned duty to try to see to it that these injustices are somehow compensated for.

This interviewee focuses on Africa as an exploited continent, and this is seen as an unjust condition. The contemporary distribution of wealth in the world is in other words regarded as illegitimate. Clearly, the issue of justice is construed as a historical matter. This historical injustice is seen as a basis for the present 'darned duty'.

Asked to comment on the claim that Norway is one of the wealthy countries that historically exploited poorer countries and therefore should compensate them for this, one of the female NCA interviewees says:

> [...] We have a terrible history. Europe especially has a pretty terrible, a bad CV in this respect. But I am not sure if we are able to clean it up. Because it has become sort of like if you cut off the leg, then you come along and put on band-aid, sort of. That is how it works! That is, then you have to go over to the person and see what it

18 The context for this statement is presented in a longer quote in section 12.1.

> is that will actually get him on his feet again. Give him a new leg or a wheel chair or… It has to be something structural that in a way can make him well again. Not bits of band-aid.

This interviewee clearly subscribes to the historical argument. Stating at the outset that 'we have a terrible history' she then turns to a metaphor: to 'cut off the leg' to express European treatment of poor countries. Clearly, this points to the dramatic consequences of European interaction with countries in the South, and not least the blameworthy character of (earlier) European policies. That cutting off the leg demands compensation seems therefore to be a basic premise when she expands the use of the metaphor by comparing aid with putting on band-aids, thus expressing the inadequacy of aid as compensation. Note that she considers the proper response to be structural. Development aid in this statement is perceived as lacking this structural element and is rather regarded as superficial treatment of symptoms (see sections 9.2 and 9.3). Thus, although she seems to accept the historical argument, and therefore argues in favour of rectificatory justice, her emphasis is on what she sees as an adequate response. She discusses aid implementation, not its rectification.

Similarly, asked to comment on the historical wrongs of wealthy countries, one of the male NCA interviewees says:

> […] Now you could say that Norway hasn't contributed much in colonial history, but if you look more closely, it's clear that this is a story where we are not innocent either. Because, I assume that for example the Norwegian shipping industry didn't lose money from the kind of traffic that was going on at that time. So we shouldn't be too naïve with respect to that. And if we think collectively beyond our own limited perspective (*ut over våre egne nisseluer*), it's clear that there is a historical argument. And that is just as much an argument for radical political changes, or economical-political changes… because this was economic exploitation (*økonomisk utplyndring*).

While the previous interviewee refers to Europe, this interviewee applies the argument explicitly to the Norwegian state. He acknowledges that Norway's colonial history is very limited, but is still not willing to rule out Norwegian guilt in this respect. Further, the reference to the Norwegian shipping industry highlights the international character of important parts of the Norwegian economy, now and in the past. Thus, the notion of Norway as a country secluded from international power politics and exploitation is challenged (see section 3.3).

Note further that it is the economic side of the colonial exploitation that is emphasised. Any positive aspects of the colonial era are clearly downplayed. Further, this 'economic exploitation' seems to be regarded as 'an argument for radical political changes, or economical-political changes'. In this, elements of the so-called dependency theory are articulated (see section 3.2). The relationship between the North and the South is perceived as one of exploitation at the structural level. Accordingly, there exists an obligation to abolish, or at least reform, the ruling structures. However, while dependency theorists tend to view development aid as a tool for continued exploitation and to uphold an already unjust and exploitative system, the same analysis is here used to argue in favour of development aid that also includes advocacy for structural reforms.

12.3.2 Uniqueness and pragmatism

In contrast to the arguments discussed in the previous section, several of the interviewees reject the notion that Norway or Norwegians have committed past wrongs. Asked to comment on the claim that Norway should have a bad conscience for enjoying a wealth which is the result of exploiting others, another male NCA interviewee says:

> I am not so sure that applies so much to Norway. It's clear that the colonial powers in their time, that they might have exploited (*utnyttet*)... the rich countries... that is probably a relevant discussion. But that Norway as a country, seen by itself, has been part of that. I cannot agree with that.[19]

19 Similarly asked to comment on the claim that Norway should have a bad conscience for enjoying a wealth which is the result of exploiting others, one of the male embassy interviewees also dismisses the relevance of the historical argument. He says: 'With respect to Norway, I would say that I don't think it is... I don't think it's a correct description. True, Norway was a trading nation and a shipping nation, but we have only been a colonial power to a limited extent. So I don't think we have any old debt to pay in that connection'. Also asked to comment on the claim that Norway should have a bad conscience for enjoying a wealth which is the result of exploiting others, one of the male NPA interviewees places Norway on the fringes of this discussion. He says: 'Well, I think that... Norway is on the edge of

Contrary to what was noted above, the uniqueness of Norway is here made the core of the argument. While the colonial powers might have exploited others, Norway's case is different. Thus, while acknowledging the historical argument, its relevance in Norway's case is rejected. This argument is also articulated when one of the male NPA interviewees is asked to reflect on the same issue. He says:

> I am a bit uncertain about that. It's also used frequently here in Africa, in view of the colonial heritage. Colonial powers have a responsibility for what was created then, and the imbalance… everything from the drawing of national borders to the various economic systems that were established, from Bretton Woods, WTO, etc., and all this, a kind of colonial heritage that is thrown in as a kind of global guilt (*en sånn global skyldgreie*), which you often have to relate to. Er… I am not sure if that is healthy, really. Norwegian exploitation of various situations, that probably happens all the time. There are Norwegian oil companies, for example, that are heavily involved in Angola, so that kind of exploitation, sure. But they are not there for charity; they are there for profit. So that happens all the time, but I would have thought it was… Instead of using guilt as a driving force or as moral energy (*moralsk energi*) for sustaining development aid, I would rather use the active global cooperation, that we have been given a bigger part of the wealth and that we have the opportunity to play a good constructive role in various contexts as the driving force. Not that we should sit and be guilty… that is a little… There is an element of paternalism in it. It's sort of humiliating for the other party, that once… […] There is no equality (*likeverd*) in it. I don't think, when reflecting on it, I am not so happy about that kind of driving force.

Clearly, the historical argument is something this interviewee is somewhat ambiguous about. He refers to it as something which is used in his context and acknowledges the possible relevance it might have, but still he does not want to use it as 'moral energy' to sustain development aid. The reasons he gives for his scepticism are informative. First, he points to what he sees as an 'element of paternalism', which he explains as the historical argument being 'humiliating for the other party'. Accordingly, equality or respect seems to be the standard for evaluation. Using the historical argument seems to this interviewee to imply an understanding of the colonial power as being strong and the colonised as weak. And making this argument relevant in the present situation seems to be something he perceives as also making this strong-weak distinction an issue

---

that discussion, since we haven't had, we haven't been colonisers. And we are not like France, England or Portugal which have been active in that way'.

today. His ambiguity concerning this argument seems then to rely less on the validity of the argument than on the function it has in the contemporary situation. An element of pragmatism in the reasoning can thus be noted.

Similarly informative is the alternative this interviewee outlines. He argues that we (Norwegians) should 1) be part of the 'active global co-operation', that we 2) have been given a 'bigger part of the wealth' and that we 3) have the 'opportunity to play a good constructive role'. Of these three expressions, the first and the latter are forward looking. The second shares the retrospective orientation of the historical argument but lacks its concern for causal explanations. It seems that this interviewee is content with stating that unfair distribution exists, and he refrains from discussing how the rich (or powerful) might have caused other people's poverty. Again, the contemporary situation is prioritised at the expense of history. This also seems to be the case when the same interviewee elaborates further on the issue of compensation. He says:

> No, then we should rather look more at precisely those systems that maintain this situation. We must not end up with a tax system to compensate in a way, and which can't by any means compensate for the losses actually inflicted. Rather we should look at the systems that have been created, WTO for example. [...] So I would rather look at those systems, rather than us... rather than using guilt as a reason for giving some compensation.

Again the reference to historical wrongs or historical guilt is dismissed and a clear preference for contemporary issues expressed. Similarly, taxation as compensation in a system that creates the need for something to be compensated for is also dismissed. Thus, the emphasis is on addressing contemporary systems, present day structural issues.

When asked to comment on the colonial argument, one of the female embassy interviewees says:

> I am not a strong supporter of a kind of, what do you call it, paying indulgence or... First of all, Norway was no colonial power, although we were in on it, because we were... When we were colonised by Denmark we took part in the slave trade in the Caribbean. [...] So we were certainly in on it, although maybe we didn't have a choice, as we were under Danish rule. But really, no, I am more... I think that if the Jews are to have compensation for what was taken from them during the Second World War, why shouldn't the Africans be compensated, that is those who were slaves or the descendants of slaves today, for the slave trade that took place, which involved a lot more people and lasted for a much longer period of time? But they

> are not organised in the same way and not as clever at claiming their rights, plus it's a bit further back in time. And it might be difficult to assess who should get what etc., but... But that it has... well, I think that there are, that the colonial period is one of many, but one reason why Europe became rich. I think so. And the exploitation that maybe started as adventurism, or I don't know what, exploitation of natural resources in other parts of the world. I think so.

Initially this interviewee seems to dismiss the argument on historical grounds. She considers it a form of 'indulgence', and rejects it on the grounds that Norway was not a colonial power. As she continues to reflect on the issue, however, she develops a different position (although she continues to articulate uncertainty on the issue). First, she moves on to acknowledge Norwegian participation in, and benefit from, the slave trade. Then she compares the descendants of slaves to descendants of Jews, and argues that compensation (for harm done) should be paid equally in equal cases. She also discusses the practical difficulties in implementing such a compensation scheme, but concludes by confirming that the colonial era is an important reason why Europe became rich. In this way she moves the focus away from Norway to Europe, but maintains the historical perspective in order to understand present wealth. She consequently downplays the application of the historical argument in Norway's case. Note further the pragmatic perspective this interviewee adopts. Compensation is difficult because it might be 'difficult to assess who should get what'. This perspective becomes even more explicit when she later elaborates further on this issue. She says:

> There is something to that argument, but it doesn't work. It doesn't work. It's just like, you can't accuse... If I meet a German, thirty years old, today, then I can't say that your dad put my dad in jail. Really, that is not how the world works.

The repeated 'it doesn't work' explicitly expresses the pragmatic character of this interviewee's reflection on the issue. Further, note how the reasoning here is characterised by its focus on the contemporary situation and the related dismissal of historical factors.

When asked to comment on the historical argument, one of the male embassy interviewees says:

> [...] there are good reasons to learn from history and to analyse the situation, if it's necessary to correct a development in the wrong direction. Yes, I agree with that. But, today the main argument cannot just be history. It has to be today's situation.

Note again the ambiguity and the pragmatic considerations related to the historical argument. Finding practical problems in basing aid on historical wrongs, this interviewee rejects the historical argument on the grounds that one must take 'today's situation' as one's starting point. When asked to comment on the historical argument, another male embassy interviewee similarly highlights the complexity of the historical compensation issue. He says:

> […] This is a complex picture. Who has exploited what, and why have some developed fast and some slowly? If there hadn't been any colonialists in Africa at all, Africa would have been different. I think that a nuanced assessment of the grounds for development, that there has been a fast development in some countries, while other countries have had a development at a normal pace, and then you end up in a situation where those who are lagging behind, they will think they don't have very many opportunities, when other countries for some reason or other have developed fast. But the old Marxist theory, I don't think anyone emphasises that any more.

Pointing to the complexity of the 'picture', this interviewee implicitly rejects the historical argument as he considers it to be too simplistic. Together with the democratic argument, that hardly 'anyone' supports 'the old Marxist theory' anymore, he in effect rejects this line of argument.

One of the female NCA interviewees also dismisses the historical argument, but on somewhat different grounds from those noted so far. Commenting on this argument, she says:

> […] It's quite clear that the systems we have for interaction between countries, maybe especially economically, are unjust. But I find it hard to say that the prosperity we have in Norway has come at the expense of poor countries. That we are lucky enough to have our backyard full of oil is not at the expense of anyone else. We could have shared our oil billions in a better way, for sure. But it's difficult to make a direct connection between us being well off because they are worse off. I don't know if there is evidence for that. I think it's a negative starting point. But I understand that you can argue in that way. And I understand that a lot of what has been going on through history, through colonialism and imperialism, that there has been exploitation. And I can maybe partly agree that the trade system we have today is also a kind of exploitation, but that is not the starting point I would use to legitimise development work.

Here, Norway is again perceived as a special case, and is thus freed from the guilt others have. While this interviewee acknowledges that the present international trade system might be inherently unjust, she dissociates Norwegian wealth from the poverty of others. She explicitly rejects the notion that Norwegian oil resources come at the expense of others and does this by rejecting the causal relationship between wealth and poverty. Thus, she does not question the legitimacy of these resources. And accordingly, any sharing of these resources is not conceptualised as a matter of correcting a wrong but rather as a matter of distributive justice. Here too the historical perspective is dismissed: the discussion must take the present situation as its starting point.

Note further how, though she 'partly' acknowledges historical exploitation, this interviewee also acknowledges present exploitation through the trade system. She rejects taking this as a starting point to 'legitimise development work', however. One of the reasons she gives seems to be that she considers this to be a 'negative starting point'. She does not explain what she means by 'negative', but from what she actually does reject, one element seems to be the issue of exploitation. This appears to lead her to the conclusion that while she acknowledges exploitation both historically and in the present, she rejects the relevance of this with respect to international aid. One interpretation of this could be that she rejects wrongdoing as a morally relevant factor. This, however, would be contrary to fundamental moral intuitions. Alternatively, the concern might rather be to retain a positive understanding of development aid and as part of this a positive starting point for debates about aid. This would appear to be another example of pragmatic considerations defining the perspective adopted.

12.3.3 Contemporary harm done

The issue of contemporary wrongdoing is most often expressed as a critique of the present global economic system, shaped and governed by affluent countries benefiting from it and with continued mistreatment of the poor as the result. When asked how he regards the impact the international trade system or Norwegian oil policy has on developing countries, one of the male embassy interviewees says:

> That is something I appreciate more. It has to do with learning from the past. Well, that is something we… Yes, I think we have great challenges. And the trade system doesn't work well. It works first of all for those who are strong and rich.

However, several of the interviewees reject the idea that Norway exploits the South today. When asked to comment on the claim that Norway should compensate for having exploited other countries, one of the male SCN interviewee says:

> I mean… What has Norway taken out of [country] for example, the last thirty years we have been here? We've had close to no industry here; we haven't had business people (*forretningsfolk*) here. Business people are afraid to be involved in developing countries. They are afraid to lose their money. How much have we taken out of these countries? […] I don't think we have… We are starting to get Statoil and others dealing internationally, so you might say there is something to it… but I don't think that is the main argument in the Norwegian context.

As Norwegian industry and business people have been mostly absent, this interviewee argues that Norway as a society can not be said to have taken anything 'out of these countries'. However, the activities of Norwegian oil companies are mentioned as an exception to the general picture painted. Regarding these companies, one of the male NPA interviewee says:

> There are Norwegian oil companies, for example, that are heavily involved in Angola, so that kind of exploitation, sure. But they are not there for charity; they are there for profit.[20]

The work of Norwegian oil companies is here described as 'exploitation', and this interviewee thus articulates both a negative evaluation of their activities and possibly also a more general scepticism about the private sector. Note how charity here is used as the contrast to profit concerns. Thus, charity seems to be used in a positive sense, referring to something these companies do not engage in, which is partly why their activities amount to exploitation rather than legitimate concerns. Thus, the common interests of profit making companies and countries seeking development seem not to be something this interviewee finds plausible.

Several of the interviewees explain Norwegian wealth in terms of the country's oil resources and related oil industry. A recurrent expression used in relation to this issue is how Norway 'earns tons of

20 The context for this statement is presented in the longer quote in section 12.3.2.

money'. Also commenting on the issue of historical exploitation, one of the male NCA interviewees says:

> [...] If you take the increase in the price of oil over the last couple of years and how Norway has earned tons of money (*tjent grovt*) from this development, and if you look at what the increase in the oil price means for this country, for example, it's incredibly distressing. There are businesses that have to close, just because the oil price increases too much in comparison with the general development.

The tension in this statement is primarily between those who earn money, and those who lose. While Norwegians earn not only some money, but 'tons of money', developing countries experience increased problems. Thus, this interviewee points not only to a stark, but also an increasing contrast. The legitimacy or illegitimacy of the money Norway earns is not discussed, but the expression used ('tons of money') points to the significant amounts involved. As such, the issue seems to be construed primarily as one of distribution, not one where wrongdoing should be corrected.

Another male NCA interviewee argues along the same lines and points to the enormous income Norway generates from its oil industry. As part of his discussion of reasons why Norway or Norwegian organisations should be involved in, and provide money for, development aid, he says:

> [...] We earn tons of money from the trade we do with both Africa and some of the countries in the South, and in part the resources in other countries are being exploited: Angola, for example. Where we have Norwegian interests, Norwegian companies, like companies in the international oil industry, taking out huge resources. And we in Norway, also in the oil sector, we take huge resources back to Norway, from a world that is very, very unjust. That is where we have to plough something back (*pløye noe tilbake*). [...] This is really... actually, it has to come to an end, the fact that people have to stand cap in hand and ask for help. And that applies both to state leaders and also to people in general. We have to get together and actually create a few mechanisms so that we can have a more just world. And we have to work more on that.

The argument put forward here is not historical, but relies on an assessment of Norwegian trade in today's context. By using the example of Norwegian oil companies' involvement in Angola, emphasis is put on the present day situation and the oil industry that is a cornerstone of Norwegian economy today. Further, this interviewee's starting point is the

Norwegian trade 'with both Africa and some of the countries in the South', which he sees as one of exploitation since it implies earning 'tons of money'. The key premise in the argument, however, seems to be that where people take out 'huge resources' they should also 'plough something back'. Here too then the injustice seems to primarily depend on the inequality implied: what Norway gets is enormous while the other countries in question remain poor. The concern about justice seems again to be one of distribution, not rectification.

In light of the call for 'a few mechanisms so that we can have a more just world', the implication seems to be that attention should be given to the structural level. As such, the obligation that arises from making a profit in an unjust world is apparently not primarily to give money in return, but rather to change the rules of the game, the market mechanisms. Responsibility seems primarily to be at the international, not national, level. Thus, this interviewee seems to accept the structural argument of the dependency school. He points to how Norwegian oil industry is restricting Angola's development as it extracts resources from this country. He is concerned about Norwegian exploitation in poor countries, and relates this specifically to the Norwegian oil industry. Asked to explain how he thinks Norway is exploiting other countries, he says:

> Yes, or… it's Norwegian companies that do this. So it's not the Norwegian state doing it. Norway as a state is actually pretty… clean in a way. But it has to do with Norwegian companies, and a few Norwegian partners in the oil sector, because the oil sector as a system is very unjust…

Note how the wrongdoing is located in the private sector, in Norwegian companies, while the Norwegian state is acquitted.

12.3.4 Bad conscience

Several of the interviewees reject the idea that Norway or Norwegians should feel guilty or have a bad conscience for their wealth. Asked to comment on the claim that NDA is an expression of bad conscience, one of the male NCA interviewees says:

> No, I am not so sure we should have a bad conscience for being so well off (*har det så godt*). Because… it has ended up this way that we have… we have been given a resourceful country, which we have managed to develop (*klart å bygge opp*), and I don't think we should have any bad conscience about that, I don't think so… But rather that we with openness and appreciation… precisely because we have so much and are so resourceful, we should share with those who are not.

This interviewee rejects the idea of having a bad conscience on the basis of two different factors: First, Norwegians have 'been given' a land full of resources. This seems to indicate an understanding of Norwegian natural resources as a gift from someone/-thing – either God, nature, history, forefathers, etc. The other element is that this country is something 'we have managed to develop'. In this expression it is not the gift but rather Norwegians' labour or effort that is addressed. Accordingly, Norwegian wealth belongs to Norwegians, either in the sense that it has been given to them or because they have worked for it themselves. The point seems, however, to be the same: Norwegian wealth is legitimate, the premise being that it has been rightfully acquired. Legitimacy is then derived from the rightful procedures that have led to the result – Norwegian wealth. That the oil resources belong to Norway is not questioned. This is rather perceived as a matter of fact.

Asked if she thinks Norwegians should have a bad conscience, one of the female embassy interviewees expresses a similar notion. She says:

> […] But I don't think Norway should have a bad conscience because we in a way have oil. We could have managed (*forvaltet*) the oil wealth very differently than what we have done. So in terms of that we should thank, I don't know who to thank with respect to that, but in this we found a model or a system that has worked. It could very well be that there are other models that would have been better, but of the systems known today, it's Norway that has succeeded the most in using and managing the oil resources. And…, I don't think that Norwegians should have a bad conscience about that. Norwegians work very hard and a lot, and they are clever and often sort of logical in many ways.

Again note how there is an emphasis on human efforts to manage oil resources. Thus, Norwegian wealth is explained by referring to oil, and specifically the managing of this natural resource. In effect then, the issue of ownership of these resources is not critically discussed, and further, the effort and activity of Norwegians is emphasised. Accordingly, Norwegian wealth is portrayed as a function of working 'very hard' and being 'clever'. Implicitly, the poverty others might experience is either because they were unlucky (and did not get the same resources) or because they are lazy or not as clever.

Also asked if Norwegians should have a bad conscience for being rich, another of the female embassy interviewees points to the contrast between Norwegian wealth and the poverty in the country where she works. She highlights that there is no need to feel bad about it. She says:

> [...] when you live and work in a country like [country], one of the [...] poorest countries in the world, and when you come home to Norway on holiday, and see how well off we are, and sort of what it is people complain about at home, then... It gives you a certain perspective: that we are very well off at home. But, you know, I don't think there is any reason to have a bad conscience because of that. I don't think so. We have, after all, worked for it.

However, when also asked if he thinks Norwegians should have a bad conscience, one of the male NPA interviewees has a different interpretation:

> They should have a bad conscience for their trade regime, but that is not something people in general... that is, in an extended meaning of democracy I suppose we are all responsible for it. But that is too technical, I think... So apart from that I don't think Norway should have a bad conscience. We have been lucky and have found oil, but we can't have a bad conscience for that for the rest of our lives, sort of.

Note how there is a change of argument in this statement. At first he argues that Norwegians should have a 'bad conscience', but this is initially related to 'their trade regime'. However, he seems to limit this line of argument and instead concludes that 'apart from that I don't think Norway should have a bad conscience'. This is then explained by the fact that he understands oil resources as something 'we have been lucky' to find. To this interviewee, Norwegian wealth seems to be a function of pure luck. This is more in line with the idea that it is a gift, and less with the idea that it is a function of hard work or Norwegian cleverness.

12.4 Concluding reflections

The concept of justice is a key word in the policy documents of both MFA and NCA (see sections 4.1 and 4.2) and is also a term many of the interviewees use in their interpretation of NDA. However, while some of the interviewees have a degree of sympathy for the argument that rich countries (and people) have historically harmed others, and should therefore compensate for harm done, the majority seems to reject this as a basis for Norwegian development aid. This rejection is articulated by both male and female interviewees. The reasons for this seem largely pragmatic and include the complexity of the issue, for example calculating possible compensation, and the argument that this is not relevant in the case of Norway. There seems to be a tendency to draw attention away from the issue of historical wrongdoing toward the present and future. The argument that Norway benefits from the present trade system is accepted, but most still refuse to see development aid as compensation for any harm done through this system. In other words, development aid is not viewed as a matter of rectificatory justice. Notions of compensating for harm done or rectifying wrongdoing are certainly present in the material, but are either downplayed or rejected.

The activities of Norwegian oil companies are addressed by several of the interviewees. Accordingly, the international activity of these companies seems to have an impact on the NDA discourse, as it leads some of the interviewees to reconsider the notion of innocent Norway and Norwegians (see section 3.3.1). Critical tools borrowed from Marxist analysis seem to inform the same discourse. Accordingly, there is a discourse that questions the activities of Norwegian oil companies and considers at least parts of their international involvement as wrongdoing. In the dominant discourse, however, emphasis seems to be put on the enormous differences created through these companies' otherwise justified activities. The discourse of distribution seems to be more dominant than the discourse of rectification (see section 3.1).

Accordingly, while several of the policy documents refer to the concept of justice, the analysis in this chapter shows how NDA seems to be understood primarily in terms of distributive justice. This discourse of distribution emphasises the ability Norway and Norwegians have to share resources internationally, and includes a notion of a responsibility to do so. However, this is a distributive argument which, although it has a parallel in domestic policy, still does not seem to imply a notion of redistribution internationally to the same level or degree.

Part VI

Donor – recipient encounters

13 Partners in development

In these closing years of the twentieth century
the time has come for the lords of poverty to depart.
Their ouster can only be achieved, however,
by stopping development assistance in its present form
– something that might prove to be in the best interest both
of the taxpayers of the rich countries and the poor of the South.

Graham Hancock in *Lords of Poverty* (Hancock 1991:193)

In this chapter I will discuss the moral discourse related to the dominant strategies for implementing NDA. A key concept in the discourse on development aid implementation is the concept of partnership, and I will discuss how partnership and related concepts are used and understood in this context. I will argue that the concepts of recipient responsibility, conditionalities, and respect are key elements in this discourse. I begin by analysing some general statements regarding the partnership paradigm, and then move on to discuss the interviewees' perceptions of the partners they work with. The second main section of this chapter concerns development aid conditionalities.

13.1 The partnership paradigm

When asked what she considers her main tasks, one of the embassy interviewees in her 50–60s describes today's development aid by contrasting it with that of the 1970s and 1980s. She says:

> I would say that development aid has partly changed its character, in the sense that we in the 1970s and 1980s implemented different types of aid projects to a much larger extent. More or less initiated and governed (*etter initiativ og styrt*) from Norway, or by Norwegian experts abroad. Then, what I would call a paradigm shift took place early in the 1990s, and Norway was one of the first to be involved in

> this. And this was the realisation that development has to happen on the terms of the cooperating country. The governing must be done there. We can contribute to a certain extent, but not all the way, and… so this thing about recipient responsibility (*mottakeransvar*), recipient orientation, and partnership (*partnerskap*), this idea about partnership. We are partners, development partners. And this is the term I would use, and I mean this is dominant now – that our role is to be a partner for the authorities, and also to make demands, but we have to listen. It's the country's own plans we should support.

Although the contrast between the old and the new is toned down through use of the word 'partly', this interviewee emphasises the changes that have taken place in the field of development aid. By using the term 'paradigm shift', the comprehensive character of these changes is accentuated.[1] The new mode of development aid is labelled partnership. According to this interviewee, one of the basic assumptions in the partnership paradigm is that development aid must be based on premises set by the recipient country. Thus the role of the donor is downplayed and a shift of emphasis from intentional to immanent understanding of development aid seems to take place. Being a partner is not seen as incompatible with making demands or setting conditions, but it is regulated by a focus on the need to 'listen' and 'the country's own plans'.

This interviewee seems to understand what she sees as a paradigm shift in the field of NDA as a shift from a situation where the donor is operational to one where partnership is the dominant strategy for implementing development aid. Accordingly, it seems to be part of the partnership ideology that the Northern development agencies are not operational. Thus they are not as close to the field as they otherwise would have been, but rely on their partners. Further, the former way of doing development aid was, according to this interviewee, characterised by its emphasis on 'aid projects'[2] and the way the donor agency implemented the projects. These were 'initiated and governed' from Norway or by 'Norwegian experts abroad'. When the recipient is responsible for defining the terms of aid, the donor no longer operates in the same

1 The 'paradigm shift' that introduced the concept of partnership is here placed in the 1990s. This corresponds to most commentators' conclusion and is reflected in the academic attention the issue received in this decade (for example Crewe and Harrison 1998, Lister 2000, and Dahl 2001).

2 The concept of 'aid projects' is often, though not explicitly here, contrasted with 'aid programmes' (more comprehensive interventions compared to projects).

way. Elaborating further on this paradigm shift, the same interviewee says:

> [...] We have moved from giving money to specific purposes, to giving money to the country's budgets, budget support. That is also a paradigm shift. It might sound simple, but it's also more challenging, for both parties, because the authorities must deliver in certain fields. There has to be a satisfactory financial management, there must be a functioning audit system, and there must be a state budget where not too much is spent on the military. So it's dialogue, and it has a small element of control (*en liten kontrollfunksjon*) if you like, which requires us to be prepared to answer to how we can accept that the money goes into a big black hole, that there is corruption and misery. And the only way to meet this is by ensuring that the routines are good enough, and by assisting in establishing routines that are good enough. They are never really good enough, but based on the country's development and the given situation, there must be an evaluation and a risk assessment of what is good enough. So that is the challenge all the time. What is enough in a country like this? And of course, if we are too strict, we can go home tomorrow. They don't have Norwegian standards of financial administration at the district level.

While it was the ideological basis for partnerships that was addressed in the preceding statement, it is here rather the practical implications that are addressed. The interviewee argues there has been a move from 'specific purposes' to 'budget support'. Further, while the premises of the recipient were emphasised above, here it is rather the conditions he or she must fulfil that are highlighted. Giving budget support is demanding 'for both parties' because the authorities in the recipient country must 'deliver'. Three issues are highlighted, and they all relate to financial matters. The financial management must be 'satisfactory', the audit system should be 'functioning', and 'not too much' of the state budget should be allocated to military expenditure.

Note also how this interviewee retains the recipient orientation emphasised above through the term 'dialogue'. On the other hand, the issue of setting conditions that has only been alluded to above is here addressed more explicitly. She talks about a 'small element of control', and discusses at what level this function should be exercised. One of her main questions seems to be precisely what 'good enough' means in the context of a developing country – and, by extension, in comparison to what it might mean in a western welfare state. It seems then that the relationship between recipient responsibility and conditionalities is an important issue in the partnership discourse.

Several interviewees articulate this shift of paradigm.[3] Such emphasis on difference is fundamental in the construction of identity. These interviewees construct an identity as development workers, and a sense of belonging to a time and an ideology that is different from the former. One interpretation of such identity building could be that it is a strategy to avoid the criticisms that have been raised against aid and development work as it has been implemented in former times. Thus, by renewing terminology and consequently reinventing its discourse, development workers and the aid industry gain credibility and thus legitimacy, despite even well founded criticism (see sections 3.2.4 and 9.6). For our purposes here, however, it is sufficient to note the key role the notion of partnership plays in the contemporary development aid discourse. Although the term partnership is widely used, that does not mean its use is acclaimed in all circles nor that its use is precise or accurate. This gives reason to explore further the use and understanding of the term.

13.1.1 Difficult partnerships

Most of the interviewees fully endorse the partnership strategy. In the context of explaining her main tasks, one of the SCN interviewees in her 50–60s says:

> […] And we have chosen new ways of working, related to the fact that we don't implement the projects ourselves, but that we work through local partners, a strategy that I fully agree with.

Like this interviewee, several others also say they not only endorse the partnership strategy but articulate satisfaction and pleasure at having this strategy guiding their work. Asked about the frustrations she might have in her work, one of the SCN interviewees in her 30–40s points out how she finds working in partnership inspiring. She says: '[…] We have partners at the regional level who are very open minded and innovative,

3 Asked to explain her different tasks, one of the NCA interviewees in her 50–60s provides another example as she tells the story of how her organisation moved away from traditional project orientation towards partnerships. She says: 'In previous years Norwegian Church Aid was directly involved and directly operative both in relief operations and in rehabilitation and long-term development projects, but in recent years we have changed and work through local national organisations'.

and who really want to achieve something. And then it's really fun to do this work'.[4] Note how the positive experience of partnership is here clearly related to the interviewee's evaluation of the partner in question. They are regarded as 'open minded and innovative' and organisations that 'really want to achieve something'. The experience and evaluation of the partnership strategy seems then to rely not only on the donor, but also on the recipient. In the process of bringing about change, this development worker sees herself as dependent on good partners. However, what it implies to be a good partner is not evident, and it is clear that the interviewees in this study evaluate their experiences with partners in different ways.

On occasion, the recipient partners are evaluated as relatively strong, and this can lead to some specific challenges. Asked to characterise 'the good development worker', one of the SCN interviewees in her 50–60s says:

> […] Now the recipients are becoming very professional too, setting people up against each other, and all this, and have other agendas than we are used to from back home. You have to stand firm (*være fast i fisken*).[5]

Note the understanding of the recipient which is articulated here. Contrary to the image of the weak and helpless recipient, he or she is here portrayed as 'very professional, setting people up against each other'. This image resonates with that of the unreliable recipient, not because of ignorance but rather the opposite, because of ingenuity.

Discussing her experience of having strong and independent partners, an embassy interviewee in her 30–40s says:

> […] And internationally Norway says very clearly that the recipient country should be in the driving seat, and in a way be leading the policy making, setting their own priorities, etc., and that is very good, but there are some challenges there. When a country really is in charge that also puts the donor countries suddenly in a different situation, compared to where their governing is not altogether real, that is where it's the donor country that is in fact doing the policy making.

The former of these two interviewees describes the partners as not only strong but also manipulative, and her response seems to be summed up

4 The wider context of this statement is quoted in section 6.2.
5 The wider context of this statement is quoted in section 14.1.

in the expression 'to stand firm'. On the other hand, the latter interviewee indicates the novelty of having a relatively strong partner that is actually 'in charge'. While the former thus indicates mistrust, the latter indicates that the more common scenario is the relatively weak partner. The latter seems to be the perspective that most of the interviewees adopt. The partners are considered weak, and this in turn complicates the realisation of the partnership model of development work.

Asked what she means when she says it is necessary to make demands of aid recipients, one of the SCN interviewees in her 50–60s addresses the issue of money and acknowledges that she represent the powerful. She says:

> [...] But of course, this is not simple, because at the end of the day we are in a way holding the power, we have the money and all this. [...] Like someone said to me, not here but somewhere else: 'You can say what you want, but you have the money.' We try as much as possible to avoid this, but we also set conditions for our partners and the people here. If they are not able to add value to the partnership, or derive value from the partnership so that it becomes mutual learning, then we have work to do. It must work both ways.

Here, the relationship between money and power is made quite explicit. The partner who holds the money also holds the power. This interviewee implicitly indicates how the weakness of one partner is related to the strength of the other. However, while on the one hand stating that this as an unavoidable fact, this interviewee then goes on to say that this is something 'we try as much as possible to avoid'. The demand she then goes on to mention is the demand that the recipient of money also manages to 'add value to the partnership' or 'derive value from the partnership'. This will in turn make mutual learning possible. Thus, she clearly stresses how partnership must be mutual, working 'both ways'.

Against this background it is not surprising that several interviewees see working in partnership as being very difficult. Asked to reflect on her experience of working in partnerships, one of the NCA interviewees in her 40–50s says:

> Partnership is incredibly difficult. Because, we say that we are going to help people, and we are going to help weak groups and the most vulnerable. And we are not going to do it ourselves. And we are going to ask others to do it. And going down that route, which is our partners, can be very frustrating and difficult, because many of them are very weak, especially within the church. We have a good partner network.

The difficulty of partnerships seems here to have at least two different aspects. On the one hand, the art of helping someone and not doing it oneself seems to be an important factor. Another element seems to be that the 'route' for providing one's help is not suitable. In contrast to the interviewees who are more positive about partnerships, finding support and inspiration in their partners, this interviewee regards them as 'very weak', although the group of partners as a whole is described as 'a good partner network'. In this context the same interviewee also describes the partnership idea as one with dilemmas. Elaborating on the issue, she says:

> And we have dilemmas within partnerships. And it's important to be aware of these dilemmas, because what we mean by it… it's often not problematic to talk about it and define it, but it's often difficult in practice, the way it works. Because, if we have a partner, that is something genuine (*det stikker ganske dypt*). That is to say that we have to have someone here who we can have confidence in and who we trust and who has the capacity to do what we want. And that is not always the case. And then it often boils down to who is able to be a partner. Who has the resources and sufficient power to be a partner? And within the church structure here, that is really difficult because they are very weak churches.

The dilemmas this interviewee is concerned about seem to stem from the very nature of what a partnership should be. Note how she speaks of partnership as 'something genuine'. This in turn makes it necessary to evaluate the partners according to the extent to which they are organisations 'we trust' and that have 'the capacity to do what we want'. Not all potential partners have this capacity, according to this interviewee.

Other interviewees express similar views when they make trust a precondition for setting legitimate conditions for partnerships. Asked to explain how she understands the issue of partnership versus the notion of making demands, one of the NCA interviewees in her 30–40s says:

> […] If you have a relationship based on trust in a partner, then I don't think it's a challenge, really. I don't think there is a tension between making demands and challenges, and having a good partnership. On the contrary, I think it's more difficult if you can't. But it presupposes a large degree of transparency and trust. And that isn't always there.

Notice how established trust is considered to defuse many of the other issues, and if trust is there then 'making demands' and being able to challenge is compatible with having a 'good partnership'. Asked to explain what she means by trust, she says:

> [...] At times things have gone wrong (*skåret seg*). So we do experience that. It's a kind of continuous process really, and sometimes we forget... Again, because we are so concerned about action and we have deadlines and... And I have felt it myself... Especially we, as efficient Norwegians who want results, and maybe we rush processes at times, because things take longer than we are used to.

This issue of weakness or lack of capacity is a recurring concern in several of the interviews. Thus, although the partnership paradigm implies a shift in operational responsibility and an emphasis on the participation and involvement of the recipient in the aid relationship, the recipient partners' lack of capacity seems to be perceived as something that limits the impact of this change. When asked if she considers partnerships an efficient way of doing development work, one of the NCA interviewees in her 50–60s responds:

> It's not obvious that it's more efficient. Maybe the implementation of a project would be more efficient if Norwegian Church Aid itself had the operative responsibility. But still, at the end of the day, it's not certain that it would be right.

Asked to elaborate, she says:

> No, because it could be... When I think about more efficiency, then it can be in order to get, to have more done, maybe in the shortest time possible. But it's not certain that so much will be left in the local communities, other than some results which may look fine and good in an annual report, but which possibly, but which will not have long-term effect, as they would have had if done in a not so efficient way, that it would take longer, but the long-term effect would be better.

Clearly, efficiency is not the only or even the decisive consideration for this interviewee. Rather, she accentuates the long-term perspective of development aid. In the short-term, effectiveness could have been better had the donor agency kept its operational responsibility. The right thing to do, however, is defined by the long-term effects, and from this perspective she prefers the partnership model. In this perspective then, the partnerships primarily have an instrumental value.

Other interviewees, however, talk of an intrinsic value of partnership. When asked to comment on her main professional challenges, one of the NCA interviewees in her 40–50s says:

> One challenge is the fact that we ideologically, and we also say it in our plans, that we are a partner organisation that is not operational on the ground, meaning with our own staff on the ground implementing things, which I in principle agree with. [...] But, then there is also the fact that we have our own priorities which are not necessarily in line with the partners' priorities. It's not given that they have the resources and the capacity for it. And then the question is, how do we manage to balance this with partnership as a value in its own right which we want to develop, from the perspective of the global church, and on the other hand, partnership as an instrument for implementing our own agenda. And I don't have a problem with saying that we have our own agenda, because this we do very transparently. [...] But the question is, to what extent do we use our partners as an instrument, and to what extent do we give our partners the opportunity to use us as their instrument? That is a pretty big challenge.

Again, an endorsement of the non-operational partnership strategy is expressed, together with an awareness of the difficulties of trying to implement this ambition in the field. This is where this interviewee locates her main challenges.

In these statements an inherent inconsistency in much development aid discourse is implicitly addressed. This is the issue of trusteeship. The concept of partnership emphasises the participation of the recipient, and thus relies on the notion of immanent development. However, international development aid implies intentional development, that somebody knows the goal for the development and guides it in this direction. Michael P. Cowen and Robert W. Shenton labels the holder of this knowledge the trustee (Cowen and Shenton 1996:26). If the people have this knowledge themselves, they can be in control of their own development. On the other hand, if they do not know what the goal is, then somebody else must be there to guide them. In development aid the donor is often considered the one who has the money, who evaluates development, and who knows what it implies to be a good partner with the right capacity. Thus, it is the donor, not the recipient partner, who holds the knowledge and the trusteeship necessary for development. This is an aspect that not necessarily becomes explicit in the partnership discourse, but which becomes articulated when the difficulties and challenges related to the partnership agenda are addressed.

13.1.2 Equal partners

Asked to explain her understanding of the concept of partnership, one of the NCA interviewees in her 50–60s says:

> […] Of course we are in partnerships, but that we are on the same level, as was maybe the intention from the outset… that I don't believe. Because those who have the money, they have the power. That is how it is. And I think it's an illusion (*glorifisert*) to believe anything else.

Here too the relationship between money and power is highlighted. Note also how this interviewee dissociates from an 'illusion' of such partnerships. On the one hand she confirms that partnership is fundamental when doing development work, but on the other hand she emphasises how this partnership is not between equal partners.

Regarding this issue of being equal partners, several of the interviewees argue and admit that this is something they are not able to achieve. In the context of reflecting on the work of her organisation in terms of rights and charity, one of the NCA interviewees in her 30–40s voices an even more critical evaluation of partnerships. She says:

> […] So, are they partners? Are they equal partners? No, I don't know, really. I don't think so, and I work with several of our partners. And they don't think so themselves. And that is something that should be recognised. But perhaps you can never be equal partners when the balance is such that I give you money, and then you and I are partners. I don't know. Most of us are in relations where we give and receive, and we know in a fundamental way that if we only give, then the one who only receives will feel a little… uncomfortable until he is able to give in return. So I mean, why do we think that this is so different for those who are poor?

The main thrust of this interviewee's criticism seems to concern the use of the term 'equal partners'. She does not think it is an equal partnership, and claims neither do the partners she is working with. She further identifies money as the factor that makes equality so difficult, or impossible; at least it distorts the balance of the partnership. It becomes clear how mutuality is the key concern. She compares this with other relationships which are characterised by to 'give and receive'. And she describes as a fundamental characteristic of giving that one does not feel right until the gift has been reciprocated. So 'why do we think that this is so different for those who are poor?'

Asked whether she thinks there might be a tension between regarding the aid recipient as a partner and making demands, one of the NPA interviewees in her 30–40s highlights the comprehensive character of partnership. She says:

> [...] I believe one should be aware of this, that it's not necessarily so that the partner organisations that I work with, are not necessarily only of the kind that sit and bow when we come, because these are people with a higher education and lots of experience. But they lack the means to achieve things. But, since it's we who are the ones with the money, then we have enormous power. And then we have the problem that sometimes the partnership turns into a form where we contract someone to do a job for us. And that is not partnership, where you go in and define what should be done, and then you make a contract, and you do this on our behalf. Then it's not partnership. [...] But if you go out with the partner and go out and do a joint assessment of what the needs are, and together meet the target groups, and discuss and debate and agree on an action plan, and then the partner implements the action plan and afterwards we together evaluate how it went, then it's a partnership.

Again, emphasis is on cooperation, process, and recipient participation. The aid relationship is clearly regarded as something more than the simple transfer of money, or a relationship where the donor simply subcontracts the recipient. In such cases the aid relationship is defined by the transfer of money from donor to recipient, together with relatively detailed instructions from the donor about how the money should be used. When asked to elaborate on the role of making demands, the same interviewee says:

> I can demand that we do what we have agreed to do. Based on the fact that there has been a process where we did agree on what they should do. Not that I am simply ordering (*kommanderer*) them to do what I want, but that both sides have an obligation. This was a result of a comprehensive process where there was considerable involvement, both from the partner and from the target group.

Here 'what we have agreed to do' is a key phrase. Notice further the stress on process and participation. When this interviewee highlights the possibility of setting conditionalities in aid, this is combined with an understanding of development aid as a process of discussion and dialogue aiming at consent. And from consent follows obligations. Further, this interviewee is clearly concerned with ensuring that partnership amounts to more than simple transfers of funds. This makes her stress the need for processes as a key feature of partnerships. When asked to say something more about the process element of partnerships, she says:

> If there isn't a process, if there is only… if the assessments of needs, need assessments, and project design only takes place with us as an aid agency, and is in a way delivered to a partner organisation, then it's not, then it's subcontracting. Then they have become sub-suppliers of the services.

Again the notion of equality seems to be important. Rather than being a donor and a recipient, development aid implementation is now a matter of both being partners. Being in a partnership implies making joint assessments, rather than being in a subcontracting relationship and simply transferring money.

13.1.3 Respect and responsibility

Reflecting on how she thinks contemporary development aid is being implemented and the issue of partnership, one of the embassy interviewees in her 50–60s says:

> […] We can't do practical development work. We are not supposed to be operational. That is up to the countries themselves. We can only help them. I used to say, when this new concept of recipient responsibility came in, I think it was in the 1990s… I used to say to my children that you will have twenty kroner pocket money per week. You have to manage (*styre med*) the money yourself and spend it the way you want. But you are not allowed to spend it on sweets, not allowed to spend it on porn magazines, and you are not allowed to spend it on comic strips. You may spend it on poetry and carrots. That is more or less how we treat the recipient countries, or how we used to do it… Now we think we have improved a lot, but we haven't. That is, we don't trust… and there might be reasons for that, but we don't trust the recipients enough. That is, in a way we say: 'You should manage the money. We leave the money to you, please. We should not interfere.' But still we do. That is… in some countries we pay straight into the national budget. But we say you are to do A, B, C and D. And we want reports and accounting, and we want audits… and… In a way we surrender control, and at the same time we want to be in control. It doesn't add up.

The parallel this interviewee makes between the recipient governments and her own children is informative. She makes the parallel in order to explain the role of the donor towards the recipient when (budget) support is given. Note again how the issue of trust is the critical point. She seems to argue there cannot be trust when there is tight control. Thus she can describe the contemporary aid modality as sending out a mixed message. 'In a way we surrender control, and at the same time we want to be in control. It doesn't add up.'

The same interviewee compares the field of development work with diplomacy, and sees the former as one lacking the respect that she finds characteristic of the latter. Commenting on the issue of charity, she says: '[…] There is a mutual respect between diplomats that sometimes fascinates me a little, where no development aid involved. Because development aid easily becomes unbalanced'. In contrast to aid, diplomacy is, according to this interviewee, largely characterised by mutuality. This mode of interaction seems, according to her perception, to be threatened as soon as this relationship becomes one between donor and recipient. A relationship between equals then seems to become distorted and lopsided.

This is an issue several interviewees address. When asked to comment on the issues of partnership and recipient responsibility, one of the SCN interviewees in her 30–40s says:

> […] I believe the danger is that you become an extra link in the chain – that you only become a money donor, and let the partner do the work. Also that… And then you could just as well take away that intermediate link, and then the development funds could just as well go from the Norwegian state, for example, or the Norwegian donor directly to these organisations. But in partnerships…. we put more into the word. We try to have what we call an added value. That we, together with the partner, explore what is the problem, what needs to be done, and that we also include children in partnerships. Because they are the recipients, we feel it's important that they have a say in what needs be done, how it should be done, and what changes they want.

Here this interviewee points first to what she perceives as a risk: that the donor becomes nothing more than a 'money donor'. The relationship between the donor and the recipient is then reduced to the transfer of money. However, she wants the partnership to have an added value. This is explained as a more comprehensive cooperation with the partners, which in turn relies on a much stronger involvement of the partners.[6]

6 This interviewee highlights in this the inclusion of children in these processes. This is not surprising as she works for SCN. Translated into a more general language, this articulates the need to involve the target group for the resources transferred. Thus, a distinction is made between the partners (or recipients) and the target group.

Emphasis seems to be put on having a more inclusive approach, or on a process together with the partner, not only in the implementation of aid efforts but also in the planning. Reflecting further on this issue, the same interviewee says:

> [...] But at the same time, it's very easy when you are the one sitting on the money, that you become a controlling partner. So, again, this is something we are working on, to have mutual respect. At the same time we have to make demands on our partners. As you say, recipient responsibility. We have to demand that they use our resources in a way that..., that we see that the money is spent in the right way and that they don't disappear here. So we have to make demands. And we have of course; we do, of course, set up certain guidelines. 'This is what we are interested in supporting.' So it's a balancing act. I don't think we can say that we have a fully equal partnership with a local non-governmental organisation, because we are the ones sitting on the money. And we are the ones who say no. 'This we will not support, and this we would like to support.' And you notice how the non-governmental organisations turn things around in order to get the support. But we have to be quite convinced that what we do is right. Because I think it's difficult to avoid that role. We can't only be naïve and give money to everyone who asks, either. We do have principles we... In this we also have a responsibility towards those who have given us the money. Because we have said that our support will go to this and that. So, we also have a responsibility in that direction.

This interviewee here articulates some of the same concerns for recipient responsibilities and conditionalities noted above. Just as other interviewees argue that conditionalities are necessary, this interviewee points to the need to ensure that 'the money is spent in the right way'. However, while others downplay the difficulties that arise in partnership relations, this interviewee seems more concerned about highlighting them. She points to the danger of becoming a 'controlling partner'. This would imply an inequality in the partnership relationship, a barrier to 'mutual respect'. This tension is, however, not absolute. She also talks about 'a balancing act', and seems thus to interpret this primarily as a practical dilemma.[7]

To this interviewee, partnership implies involvement not only by the (intermediate) partners, but also by the target group (participation).

7 Reflecting on the difference between the two parties involved in the partnership one of the embassy interviewees in her 50–60s says: '[...] I don't feel that this is either a practical or a moral dilemma, that one part is more powerful than the other. What it needs, is to take it into account'.

Further, this interviewee also concludes that in the work she is involved in they do not have a 'fully equal partnership'. She gives two reasons for this: it is the donor who is 'sitting on the money' and it is the donor who defines the partnership. Interestingly, she then highlights the importance of the donor being confident that 'what we do is right', and 'not only be naïve', in light of the responsibility that the aid agency has to donors back home. Note how the right way for the money should be used appears to be an issue for the donor to decide upon. Thus, the conditionalities set are perceived as normative conditionalities, in the sense that they follow from a normative consideration made by the donor. Accordingly, this interviewee seems also to regard them as legitimate conditionalities.

Asked to elaborate on her understanding of partnership, the same interviewee says:

> [...] If one partner holds the money, then it's not a fully equal partnership, no matter what you do. You could just as well say that. Idealistically, you could think that this is how it should be, but it's more complicated than that, also in relation to what I said about having a responsibility towards those who have given us the money, and we have a responsibility towards to the children. We have a responsibility to ensure that the partner we are working with does what we actually believe in. ... But we train our partners in order to increase their capacity and enable them to get resources from other organisations too. We assist in capacity building in connection with the development of projects, and reporting, and evaluations and... So we try to strengthen these partners so that they can get to a level where they are not as vulnerable with regard to various organisations like us. So we have a responsibility to give them a stronger role too.[8]

From this statement, three stakeholders can be identified. Firstly, the partner with the money is responsible to the back donors ('those who have given us the money'). Secondly, this partner is also responsible to the target group of the resources in question ('the children'). Thirdly, the

8 Similarly, another of the SCN interviewees in her 30–40s says: 'I think that is what has been lacking in development. A lot of decisions have been made on the other side of the globe. But of course it's like, we have the money, we will tell you what to do. Irrespective of whether it is what you think is the best thing to do. And to me, that is wasting a lot of resources. It's best that the recipients sit, discuss their situation, analyse why are they in the situation they are in, where do they want to go, how do they want to get there, what do they have in terms of their own resources, what are they lacking, what can they get from the outside, for them to move to where they want to be'.

money holding partner has a responsibility to the recipient partner ('the partner we are working with'). This is, however, a two-fold responsibility, as it is both to control the partner and to strengthen the partner. Of course, the weight one gives these responsibilities in relation to one another has a strong impact on how the partnership is implemented.

Some of the interviewees also interpret the concept of recipient responsibility in light of previous aid practices. When asked if she feels comfortable with working in partnership, one of the embassy interviewees in her 50–60s says:

> [...] earlier many donors moved too far into the recipient's territory (*banehalvdel*), which made a mess of (*forkludret*) this other ownership. We cannot have responsibility for delivering results. This is something the recipients must do, their institutions. We can take part; enable the recipients to deliver. But we cannot take the responsibility for results away from them. Because Norwegians have... they must take responsibility for development in their own country – the ownership. And we as donors have been relatively eager to make special constructions which have not been sustainable, in order to get quick results. This era I think, at least for Norway, came to an end several years ago. And for most donors it has come to an end.

This way of phrasing the issue of partnership puts an interesting emphasis on how the partners are responsible for the results. This recipient responsibility for results, however, should probably not be interpreted as a refusal to be accountable for results oneself, but rather that results must be owned by the recipients. Note again how the impatience of the donor is regarded as a problem, and how this interviewee thus also emphasises long-term, sustainable results, and perceives these in contrast to quick results.

This interviewee's concern seems to be to confirm how it is the recipients who 'must take responsibility for development in their own country'. This could be read as a discourse that blames the victim, implying that the recipients have not assumed this responsibility earlier. However, this is not how the statement is framed. Rather, this interviewee's criticism is directed toward donors who have made 'special constructions'.

13.2 Conditionalities

The issue of conditionalities has already been touched upon above. In this section I will discuss how the interviewees of this study experience and evaluate the role of conditionalities in the implementation of development aid. The term conditionalities refers to the conditions that donors set for the recipients to fulfil as a precondition for being partners in an aid relationship.

As noted above, some of the interviewees emphasise the need to 'stand firm', to have conditions apply when development aid is provided. In the context of reflecting on arguments for doing development aid, one of the SCN interviewees in her 50–60s says:

> […] I also believe we should be tougher in development work, and make demands on people. That is to say, we should not just give, but we also have to make tough demands (*sette tøffere krav*) in terms of governance and leadership and… […]. So we have in a way a moral duty to… to do something. But what we do has to be good. Both the state and we as organisations can make demands.

Interestingly, this interviewee constructs a discursive chain between moral duty, quality, and conditionality. The moral duty to 'do something' is not to do just anything, but to do something which is 'good'. For this reason, the donor in the aid relationship must make certain conditions. Implicitly then, it is the donor who knows what is good or not. The considerations the donor makes are clearly of fundamental importance, as this defines the space in which the aid project or programme can be implemented. Thus, conditionality is seen primarily as a matter of securing efficiency and quality in development aid efforts.

Asked to reflect on her role in light of the concept of recipient responsibility, one of the embassy interviewees in her 30–40s says:

> […] The way I understand recipient responsibility, it's a bit like us financing their plans and budgets. We don't come with, here is a budget and this is what we want to finance. […] There are some conditions to it though. We cannot just continue paying blindly, and just say: 'Yes, oh you poor ones, you have such low capacity', and 'Yes, we give you another round of…'. A certain responsibility goes with receiving something. When you receive someone else's money to spend it on something, then you must in a way make sure that it's used as far as possible according to guidelines.

As it is explained here, recipient responsibility refers on the one hand to what the donor finances. It is 'their plans and budgets', not donor shaped projects or programmes. On the other hand, recipient responsibility seems here to be defined in terms of the responsibility that arises from 'receiving something'. There are strings attached, and the conditions and guidelines that are applied must be followed. Recipient responsibility thus means doing what you are told, if you choose to accept development aid in the first place.

Asked if she understands conditionalities as part of the human rights based approach in development aid, one of the NCA interviewees in her 30–40s confirms this, and elaborates:

> [...] You can't say to the authorities: 'If I am to give a school to those children, then you have to tidy your closet.' Because, then we won't have... Those we hurt by that are not the ones given the conditional terms.

This interviewee discusses the issue of conditionalities from a human rights perspective. Note how she restricts the use of conditionalities to a use that does not hurt those who are meant to benefit from the aid given. In her perception then it seems that the state must be bypassed, and aid given directly to the recipient group. Note here how the criticism voiced by the basic needs strategy against the modernisation theory is articulated again (see section 3.2). In other words, the human rights perspective makes it legitimate to bypass the state.

13.2.1 Normative conditionalities

While the concern for achieving results – and good results – is one way of legitimising conditionalities, another strategy seems to be to give them a normative strength.[9] Asked to comment on the claim that there is a

9 One can distinguish between conditionalities of two different kinds. The first generation of conditionalities were emphasised in the neo-liberal marked economy oriented policies of the 1980s, and were conditionalities regarding the economic policies of a developing country. In order to be allowed to get support from the World Bank or the International Monetary Fund (IMF), developing countries were required to adjust their economies according to the market-liberal policies of these institutions. The second generation of conditionalities followed in the 1990s. This time the focus was not on economic policies but rather on good governance and

tension between partnerships and conditionalities, one of the embassy interviewees in her 50–60s reflects on the norms that govern the international arena. She says:

> [...] We have to be able to make demands on the partners, so that... that we fulfil what is internationally considered... there are a number of conventions, for example, that are normative... So that you could say that a partner operates, that is, the partner who makes demands doesn't operate in a vacuum, in the sense that the one who makes demands has come up with something smart. You operate in an international community where you have norms, which at least in our society, the Western world, the Christian Western world, are accepted as a basis.

The same interviewee is not reluctant to give conditionalities. Elaborating further on this issue, and reflecting on tensions and dilemmas she faces in her work, she says:

> [...] This is a condition which isn't related to inequality, but a condition that has to do with... human rights. And I would call this a normative condition (*normative krav*): that everyone has a right to education, everyone has a right to health services, and everyone has a right to clean water. And we have to assist the authorities in making sure that there are plans to cover every part of the country. This is the reason why I certainly defend our development work, although I see the dilemmas. In the end I believe we are justified by the fact that we support the authorities in fulfilling what I would call the normative conditions of development of a country, based on human rights.

Again, the conditionalities that this interviewee sees as legitimate are those that are related to human rights. This makes them 'normative conditions'. Thus there are some rights that must be fulfilled, and to make this a precondition for further aid is therefore not regarded as problematic. Still, even normative claims are not necessarily undisputed. Asked to comment on the potentially contradictory interests of donors and recipients in the aid relationship, another embassy interviewee in her 50–60s addresses the discussions about conditionalities in development aid. She says:

---

human rights. Thus, the second generation of conditionalities could be regarded as softer than the first. However, the second generation could also be said to be more comprehensive, and intrudes more into what would earlier be considered the domestic policies of the government.

> So then there is a certain discussion about the conditions for development aid. [...] And we might have an interest which maybe contradicts the interests of the other side, and we have different understandings of what is right and wrong. And we encounter this all the time. And that is where we have the difficult discussions. On what terms should we invest money in this country?

Thus, although the claims are normative, in light of international human rights (as these are interpreted by the donor), there might still be conflicts of interest and 'different understandings of what is right and wrong'. So who then is to decide on this matter? It seems that there may be two possibilities: one option is to insist that the conditionalities are based on internationally recognised human rights that are so fundamental that they are also human rights any given government has a positive duty to fulfil for its citizens. The other option is of course to make this a matter for further discussion and dialogue. Thus, the issue of conditionalities is transformed into a practical challenge (or maybe a rhetorical or strategic one).

Regarding the relationship between donor and recipient, one of the embassy interviewees in her 30–40s describes this as being regulated under the umbrella of human rights and democracy. In the context of discussing the interests of both Norway as a donor and the recipient country, she says:

> [...] Everything is defined under a wider umbrella of human rights and democratisation. But it's a long and difficult process, because that is not where the [country] authorities themselves make an effort. This is a typical issue (*innsatsområde*) pushed (*drevet fram*) by the donors. We engage in dialogue with them about it, but in this too we move in a rhetorical space and a discursive reality that is very... which is easy to be stuck in (*fanget i*). Because concrete results in terms of allocating resources, results in the field of human rights or democratisation are more difficult to see on the [country] side than they are for health and education. But that also implies... I am not saying we sit administering Norwegian interests and that this isn't right, because in this case I am convinced that it is actually important. That is, these issues that Norway has decided to push in [country] are actually important. Although the [nationality] would prefer something else, I believe that human rights are important, obviously. We can't just put this aside and make [country] priorities decisive when we actually see there are issues that are not addressed, and which are important to Norwegian development aid policy.

This interviewee expresses how the hegemonic discourse of human rights regulates the social field in which NDA is carried out. Note, however, how this is also something this interviewee empathetically endorses at the personal level.

13.2.2 Respect and conditionalities

As was noted above, several interviewees understand partnership as a deep-rooted relationship based on trust. However, several also see this threatened by, among other things, the recipient's lack of capacity, and others also stress the necessity and importance of conditionalities. This makes the very concept of partnership a challenging one, as ideals and rhetoric meet reality. As noted, some of the interviewees understand this issue as a matter of respect. One of the SCN interviewees in her 30–40s says: 'We have to respect the competence and the sovereignty of the countries in which we work. We can't come as Norwegians and say: "Now we will show you how to do this".'

When asked to elaborate on her understanding of 'the good development worker', another of the SCN interviewees in her 30–40s says:

> The way I see it, it's the attitude of believing that people, however poor or backwards they are, they have something to offer. They may not be able to read and write, but they have managed to be where they are. Because they have the skills, they have the knowledge. And for one, we can build on that. And to be able to utilise the resources and the skills they have, to move on. And..., because at times, what puts people off is that when a young development worker comes into the community and meets the old people, and brushes their knowledge and skills aside. You know how they would feel. 'I have managed to live my life for the last forty years, and someone comes to tell me how I should live my life now. But I have managed to survive all these years.' To me it's that attitude, to appreciate that even if people are poor, even if people are in a so-called backward state, they have a lot. [...] So to me, those attitudes are being able to acknowledge that people, however poor they are have knowledge and have skills. That one can see this, is extremely important to me.

A respectful attitude towards the recipient is again stressed and contrasted to an approach that disregards their skills and know-how (see section 14.1).

When asked about her main professional challenges, one of the NCA interviewees in her 30–40s says:

> […] In a way this whole idea of giving development aid is a very challenging project. I think that it is us, as a donor organisation, who should no longer be implementing in a way, but that perhaps first and foremost we should work through partners. And that is a good idea, but to run a partnership in a good way, I find that challenging. I find that we easily end up in a position where we in a way have our priorities, concerning rights, gender equality, and very fine and important values, but which we then are to convey to our partners. And I don't always think that we are able to do this in a good way. It can easily become a bit of a top-down attitude and a communication that implies that we know how we want things. So I think it's a very big challenge to respect people for what they stand for and at the same time hold forth our values, because sometimes these don't go well together.

Warning against a 'top-down attitude', this interviewee calls for respect in development work. Respect seems, however, to become a challenge as she wants to combine it with holding 'forth our values'. Prompted to elaborate on the issue, she says:

> […] We end up in a lot of discussions which are exciting and interesting and all this, but which… I get the feeling that our partners are left with a bit of a feeling that we don't respect them one hundred percent, because we want to create change, which they are not entirely in on.

Arguing partnership 'is a good idea, but to run a partnership in a good way, I find that challenging' this interviewee highlights the manner in which the concept of partnership is realised, and she finds the ideology or the ambitions inherent in the idea of partnership not easy to fulfil. The result is a discrepancy between ideals and reality, ambitions and results. Further, note how this interviewee evaluates partnership as a 'good idea'. As in many other cases, the interviewee endorses the ideals of aid, but at the same time questions key aspects of it primarily related to its actual practice. The potential pitfall seems to be that the inequality in the relationship results in a patronising attitude, incompatible with respect. This then leads to another challenge, that of respecting the partners on the one hand, and at the same time being transparent about one's own values. And 'sometimes these don't go well together'.

This feeling of lack of respect seems to be the most disturbing to this interviewee. When asked what she would do to improve these matters, she says:

> I think maybe we should have spent a little more time talking with each other, going a little deeper. We are very action oriented. A lot of the time is spent on the

> practical work. […] I think that to have a little more openness about this is not very easy, with our partners, but together try to find out how we can relate to value issues, to the difficult dilemmas. Then maybe we could progress a bit further.

This interviewee would like to see partners 'talking with each other, going a little deeper'. It seems that the conflicts that arise when the donor sets certain conditions for providing aid is something she finds difficult to handle.

When asked to compare relief and development work in terms of results, one of the embassy interviewees in her 50–60s points to the issue of conditionalities. She says:

> […] But it's a problem in [country] that over the last twenty years things haven't improved, despite lots of development aid. And then you could pose the question: Why is the situation like this? And maybe we haven't been insistent enough in terms of governance. We have been too polite. We haven't been sufficiently, I was about to say, cultural imperialists in terms of making demands. […] But if the money we give in support is not spent in a proper way, then we see that results are bad. And that is perhaps part of the situation, that we have shown too much respect. […] Everyone agrees when I put it like this: 'You have to respect.' But you cannot do that and get results. So then you have to strike a balance so that you behave in a proper way towards the decision makers, but you have to say that certain conditions accompany Norwegian development aid.

Here achieving results is contrasted with respect. Achieving results is related closely to being 'insistent enough in terms of governance', while showing 'too much respect' is perceived as a potential problem. This interviewee also says that one might not have been eager enough to use conditionalities earlier. Implicitly, she argues in favour of the legitimate role of conditionalities in development aid. Her explanation for why they have not been sufficiently expressed earlier relies on the assumption that 'we have been too polite', and not sufficiently 'cultural imperialists'. However, this interviewee is also very enthusiastic about orientating development aid towards the recipient. When asked how she understands the issue of recipient responsibility, she says:

> No, recipient responsibility is really, that is the most important concept we have, because responsibility, that means that from time to time we must let go of some of what we would like to control, and from time to time give up some of our views, and from time to time we have to contribute to decisions that we don't agree with. Then we have the discussion. How far are we willing to go?

Quite explicitly this interviewee here articulates some of the conesquences implied if one were to fully embrace the ideology of partnership. It would involve letting go of control and even contributing to decisions one does not agree with. And she puts the question pointedly: 'How far are we willing to go?' The same interviewee also refers to an example where this became an issue, and where she felt she had to put her foot down. Commenting further on this experience, she says:

> [...] It was OK, it was very good, I would say. But, that is to say that we took some of the responsibility away from them. And it's like that all the way. But I support delegating responsibility to a large extent, and then a dialogue about how it's practised.

For this interviewee, the way forward when one of the partners (in our discussion it would most often be the donor) has to use its power in order to get its own way, is dialogue. In times of conflict, she turns to discussions (in an atmosphere of trust) to sort out such differences of opinion. Thus recipient responsibility is delegated but can also be overridden. As such, dialogue does not take place in a power vacuum.

13.3 Concluding reflections

Partnership is clearly a key concept when the interviewees discuss development aid implementation. It also seems to be a concept that is used to distinguish contemporary development aid from that of earlier times (see section 3.2). An important element of partnership seems to be an increased involvement of the recipient in the aid relationship, and several interviewees regard the comprehensive character of partnership as one of its prime features. The partnership idea thus stands in the tradition of making development aid more recipient oriented, something also highlighted in several of the policy documents. The ambition is to have a partnership between equals, where mutual respect and processes that go 'a little deeper' are fundamental.

At the same time interviewees from all of the agencies studied here see the idea of partnership threatened, either because the partnership is limited to the transfer of money or because the power of the money holder (the donor) threatens the intended equality between the partners. Parallel to the concern for recipient participation there is also an emphasis on the need to 'make demands' of the recipient. Recipient participation seems to be closely related to the notion of recipient responsibility, and as the recipients have responsibilities donor conditionalities are perceived as reasonable. Such conditionalities are regarded by most of the interviewees neither as illegitimate nor as contrary to the notion of partnership, but rather as a legitimate, integral aspect of this kind of cooperation. Accordingly, they can be referred to also as normative conditionalities.

The need to make such demands is also legitimated in terms of the perceived weakness of the partners. The aid recipients' perceived lack of capacity makes it difficult to trust them in the way a 'fully equal partnership' assumes, and leads the donor into the role of a 'controlling partner'. Similarly, conditionalities do not seem to be regarded as contrary to being respectful, but rather as an expression of respect. The concern for respect can also be seen as something that must be weighed against the concern for achieving results, however. Accordingly, the concept of partnership seems to imply a wide range of partly contradictory notions, but seems still to be a widely approved of and acclaimed concept in the moral discourse of NDA.

The findings in this chapter thus supplement the emphasis on recipient participation identified in several of the agencies' policy documents. Not least are the challenges and contradictions implied in the notions of partnership and participation highlighted, for example as articulated with reference to conditionalities and the recipients' lack of capacity. The notion of respect seems to be an especially important interpretative repertoire to the interviewees when relating to these challenges.

14 Facilitating development

Fifteen thousand people dying needlessly every day
from AIDS, TB, and malaria.
Mothers, fathers, teachers, farmers, nurses, mechanics, children.
This is Africa's crisis. That it's not on the nightly news,
that we do not treat this as an emergency – that's our crisis.

Bono, in his *Foreword* to *The End of Poverty* (Sachs 2005:xvii)

In this chapter I take as my starting point the expectations and ideals that the interviewees associate with the development worker role. This leads to a discussion of professionalism in the second part of this chapter. In the third section I will address the personal characteristics that seem to be associated with being a good and professional development worker.[10]

14.1 The good development worker

In order to provide an opportunity for the interviewees to express their thoughts on the implementation of development work at the individual level, they were asked to describe 'the good development worker'.[11] The

10 The next chapter will address aspects of the private lives professional development workers lead. As will be noted, this can also be regarded as an important aspect of being a good development worker.

11 Responding to a question on how she would describe 'the good development worker', one of the NCA interviewees in her 40–50s criticises the question given, saying: 'The question is whether it's possible to describe a good development worker. Because it's sort of like asking: what is a good economist, what is a good farmer, right? There are a lot of different kinds of farmers, and a lot of people working with economy, but it varies so much'. In the sense that the question disregards the various roles aid workers of different kinds occupy, this interviewee

answers indicate not only the ideals interviewees seem to have regarding how 'the good development worker' should act or be, but also how they understand the role of the development worker, both descriptively and normatively.

When asked what characterises 'the good development worker' (*den gode bistandsarbeideren*), one of the SCN interviewees in her 50–60s says:

> [...] It has to do with being open and honest, and not having any hidden agenda, but also being structured. You have to be willing to make demands, since you could be too naïve and be fooled. Now the recipients are becoming very professional too, setting people up against each other, and all this, and have other agendas than we are used to from back home. You have to stand firm (*være fast i fisken*). And not least, you have to be open and attentive and flexible.

According to this interviewee 'the good development worker' must not be naïve, and she highlights traits such as openness and honesty, as well as the need to be 'structured' and 'willing to make demands'. In addition, however, she emphasises that he or she should be attentive and flexible. This indicates that there can be many and different expectations associated with the development worker role.

14.1.1 Relating to the recipient

When asked to describe 'the good development worker', one of the NPA interviewees in her 30–40s defines 'the good development worker' simply as a fellow human being. She says:

> No, it's to be a fellow human being (*medmenneske*). And to behave in the same way you behave towards your own family and your own friends – your own society, be it Mandal[12] or [capital] – that you are a good fellow human being, nothing else. I don't think there is a course for becoming a good development worker… well, yes, there are… There are a lot of courses and PhD studies and stuff, but really… the fundamental is about being a good human being. It will translate from the micro level to the macro level in some way or other. I think that is the fundamental thing.

---

correctly points to an inaccuracy in the way it is posed. On the other hand, as it is phrased it challenges the interviewees to focus on the shared features within the profession.

12 Mandal is the name of a Norwegian town.

This interviewee sums 'the good development worker' up through a reference to his or her personal character. Also asked how she would describe 'the good development worker', one of the NCA interviewees in her 40–50s says:

> [...] At the same time, it's clearly a fundamental premise that you are curious, professionally; to know where you are and what context you are in, with respect to culture, with respect to sociology, with respect to politics, with respect to topography... the lot. When I say curious, you don't have to have it all when you arrive, but it's a gradual development. But to be curious, and have awareness about it and a wish to develop it, that is important. It's very important.

Note the emphasis on being curious. Contrary to emphasising knowledge and expertise which the development worker brings from her home country, emphasis is here on the context in which she works – culture, politics, etc. This seems to refer to something this interviewee understands as a process of learning. One of the NCA interviewees in her 30–40s makes a similar point when she is asked to describe 'the good development worker'. She says:

> [...] It's a person who spends time and energy trying to understand the country and the people he or she is asked to work with. And who at the same time works on the basis of explicit values and priorities. And who is willing to enter a role where you challenge everything from cultural norms to public systems... That is, so that you don't end up with a relativistic attitude of only understanding all the time, but that you have to strike some kind of balance between knowing the cultural context you are in, and at the same time daring to make some choices and follow some strategies.

This interviewee identifies elements in the recipient country's culture that might be challenged – cultural norms and public systems – and indicates that a kind of balance must be struck between cultural sensitivity and making 'some choices'. Similarly asked how she would describe 'the bad development worker', she says:

> [...] I think the greatest danger is that we become know-it-alls (*bedrevitere*) who forget the kind of humble attitude that maybe has to be there, although we challenge them. I think I have seen a few examples of that.

Here this interviewee issues a warning against becoming 'know-it-alls', and explains this as one who forgets to be humble. Note how humility is stressed 'although we challenge them'. It seems that this interviewee understands 'the good development worker' as one who manages to combine these two traits, being humble and challenging.

When asked how she would characterise 'the good development worker', one of the NPA interviewees in her 30–40s stresses similar concerns. She says:

> Well, the good development worker should be a person who can contribute something, in the way that it's a person with skills and capacity relevant to the target groups. But that is not enough. You must also have your heart in it. You have to be able to identify with the needs of the target groups, and you have to have a heart for what you do. But you can't only have a heart for it, because then you end up like, excuse the expression, the happy Christian amateurs (*glade kristne amatører*), where there is only goodness (*godhet*), sort of... It's not only: 'Now we want to be kind (*snille*).' It has to be someone capable..., a good development worker who is skilful in his field. [...] So it's not a limited technical exercise, but it's a person who can see that his competence can contribute to development.

A nuanced stand is articulated in this statement. There are elements both of an expert discourse and a recipient discourse. Characteristics of 'the good development worker' are presented as the opposites of expressions such as 'only goodness' and 'now we want to be kind', and are combined with emphasising that 'you must also have your heart in it'. Thus, the sharp distinction between rights based professional development aid and charity oriented work seems to be challenged. Professional qualifications are emphasised, but also here in combination with having a heart and being committed. Again, however, a warning is issued against too much, which would cause the workers to end up as 'happy Christian amateurs'. Further, this interviewee stresses that aid work is more than a 'technical exercise'. Elaborating further on this issue, she says:

> A good development worker also makes demands on partners and target groups. You are mean if you don't make demands. Some use the phrase that you are kind if you don't make any demands. That you are too kind with the local staff and things like that, and they can do whatever they want. But you are not kind (*snill*), you are mean (*slem*). If you let local staff get away with misuse of money, or partners not doing their job, but still have money transferred, then you are not kind. Then you are mean. They say the same thing about children in Norway, right, that granny is kind and the kids are allowed to eat sweets all day, right, so their teeth fall out. Then you are not kind, you are terribly mean to the child. It's sort of like that here too. So not being able to stand firm, not... without character. That is not a good development worker.

The underlying understanding of the aid relationship seems here to be pedagogical. The development worker is, or represents, the educator, and the role of the recipients of aid is understood as analogous to that of the child. There seems thus to be a paternalistic element in this statement. Note the contrasting language used, as this interviewee takes the labels 'kind' and 'mean' to characterise different ways that development workers act. Together with the child-grandmother metaphor, this is a use of language that puts the recipient in the role of the child. Consequently, the development worker is conceptualised as the grown-up, adult trustee.

14.1.2 Competent donor representative

When asked what she thinks would characterise 'the good development worker', one of the embassy interviewees in her 50–60s identifies several important issues. She says:

> [...] I think a good development worker primarily needs to be competent. There has to be a professional competence. And competence could be anything from management to knowing a specific field, like education, industry, etc... and the other way around. I don't think the development worker should be driven by a calling or excessive solidarity (*overdreven solidaritet*). It should be based on professionalism. But of course, there should be a positive attitude to the work you do. You need that. You need a positive attitude to it, and you need to be optimistic and to think with a long-term perspective. Because the moment you start to be cynical and frustrated and negative, and getting the 'we have seen this before' attitude, then you can quit. [...] I don't want to recruit anyone with too much enthusiasm. It goes wrong. It goes wrong. I think that is the general trend. You would probably find great enthusiasm primarily in some of the voluntary organisations, but I think there too they have come to realise that the world is as it is. And we must do the best we can, with optimism...

This interviewee clearly emphasises the professional qualifications of 'the good development worker'. It seems that this is regarded as a constitutive aspect of being professional. The repeated 'It goes wrong' markedly warns against the danger of 'too much enthusiasm'. In the eyes of this interviewee, this would be incompatible with being professional. Of course, when she warns against great enthusiasm, she indicates also a legitimate role of enthusiasm. I take this to be summed up in the term 'positive attitude'. Still, an important thrust of her argument seems to be warning against an overdose of such involvement.

When asked what kind of attitudes should characterise a Norwegian development worker, another of the embassy interviewees in her 50–60s says:

> The first word that comes to mind is integrity, for some reason or another. And by that I mean that you are aware of what you want to achieve, that you are honest with regard to what our views are and what we want to achieve: Managing money, returning to that, because we also have considerations in that regard, towards Norway and not only the recipients. That we stand by what we say, that we have a clear and honest attitude and relationship to our cooperating partners. Quality and knowledge is also important, of course. To have the right people in the right places, and all this, but… And what we say about ourselves is transparency and accountability, these are not only slogans. But I think it's important, also in the case of individual development workers. With respect to the work they do, be it critical questions or praise (*ros*) or… Clearly, we often have programmes where you have to criticise and be strict (*streng*), because, as I said, there are other obligations too. Then we can't just be kind and say that the reports that never came don't matter anyway…

In her response this interviewee touches upon several issues that will be discussed more closely below. At this point, however, note how she situates the work, and thus the role, of the development worker. The role of the development worker is understood in light of 'Norway' on the one hand and 'the recipients' on the other hand. Thus, she situates the development worker role in a position where she must take different, possibly conflicting, interests into consideration. However, when explaining her immediate response – 'integrity' – she stresses the importance of 'our views' and 'what we want to achieve'. Her emphasis appears to be on the need to take donor considerations into account, implicitly criticising those who identify too closely with the recipient. In this sense she seems to position the development worker primarily on the donor side of the aid relationship (see section 5.2.2).

From 'integrity' follows honesty toward the recipients as an important quality of a development worker, but also the ability to 'criticise and be strict'. One cannot 'just be kind'. In other words, the donor is the one who makes demands, gives criticism, and leads the way. Compared to the partnership discourse, it is a quite different discourse that is articulated here. Here it is the donor, the trustee, and educator that take the lead. Further, this interviewee emphasises quality and competence.

To summarise, these statements indicate that there are a number of different traits the interviewees emphasise when trying to describe 'the good development worker'. While there is an emphasis on skills and knowledge on the one hand, there is also an emphasis on personal characteristics. Similarly, there is a concern both about being interested in, and understanding, the local context and a strong emphasis on the need to challenge the local situation. One of the main traits of 'the good development worker' can thus be summarised as professionalism. This raises new questions, however. How is professionalism perceived in the field of development work, and how is the good, professional development worker role constructed?

Exploring these issues implies making a distinction between the professional lives and the personal or private lives of the development worker. By personal I mean the character, attitudes, and views of the individual development worker, and by private I am referring to the life of the development worker that to a lesser extent relates to her professional work, and more to her leisure time, the family sphere, etc.[13] These are, however, only approximate definitions, as the character of the relation between the personal and private and the professional is one of the topics to be explored. Thus, the terms professional, personal, and private function here as analytical categories. They are introduced in order to assist the analysis, but remain distinct from the emic categories present in the material being studied.[14]

In the following section I will structure the analysis first around notions of professionalism. As noted, 'the good development worker' is also described in terms of more personal characteristics. In the third and last section of this chapter I therefore address the personal.

13 I make this distinction although I am aware the problematic aspects of it pointed out for example by feminist critics.

14 When asked about the bad development worker, one of the NCA interviewees in her 50–60s emphasises the attitudes and lifestyle of the aid worker, and thus indicates that she sees the professional life of the development worker not entirely distinct from her personal and private life. She says: 'Lack of love for the people you are working with, spending a lot of money, leading a wild life... Such characteristics are bad examples...'.

14.2 Professionalism

How do these interviewees understand the concept of professionalism in the context of development aid? Robert Chambers has made the point that although realities are changing, the dominant thinking in the development profession remains relatively stable. This he calls normal professionalism. He claims: 'Normal professionalism is embodied in the norms, methods and behaviours which are taught, learnt, and rewarded' (Chambers 1993:4). Students are taught from old textbooks, and practitioners devote themselves to the correct observance of methods. He argues development debates thus risk becoming incestuously North-North. Consequently, normal professionalism is inherently conservative, understanding the development worker as an expert bringing knowledge to the field and thus bringing about development. Chambers finds that the weakness of this paradigm lies in its rigidness – a rigidness that leaves gaps between areas of specialisation not addressed, and that leads to both a misuse of methods and a bias regarding priorities.

As an alternative to normal professionalism, Chambers proposes a new development paradigm. This implies a reversal of power relations – thus his famous phrase 'putting the last first' (Chambers 1983; see also Chambers 1997). He distinguishes between four interacting levels. Firstly, at the normative level, development should be people-centred. In other words, professionals are here not experts, but learners. Secondly, conceptually, this means that development is a process of continuous adaptation and problem solving, as opposed to progress in a given, single direction. Thirdly, empirically, the new development paradigm states that conditions are diverse and complex, rates of change are accelerating, and poor rural people are knowledgeable and capable of self-reliant organisation. Fourthly and finally, at the practical level, these three levels are integrated (Chambers 1993:9–14). Accordingly, there is a call for new skills and a new professionalism.

Chamber's normative starting point is that development must be 'people-centred'. This implies further that development work becomes a process of trying and failing, where the direction is not predetermined. In addition he assumes that poor people also have relevant knowledge and competencies, and that this must be included in practical development work. In other words, there is reflection on what development is and what furthers this kind of development, and this has a bearing on how professionalism in development work is understood. Normal professsionalism can be considered part of the tradition in which modern development work started, in other words in modernisation theory and its development and scientific optimism (see section 3.2). On the other hand, new professionalism is an expression of the break with this tradition of colonial heritage and paternalism. At the same time there is not a total rejection of development, neither as a term nor as a phenomenon. It is the discourse of alternative development that is articulated here, rather than the post-development discourse. Still, it is a clear break with what has been perceived as expert dominance and an (arrogant) Western know-it-all attitude.[15]

14.2.1 Make a difference

When asked to explain what it means to be professional in this field, one of the SCN interviewees in her 30–40s says:

> [...] We move into areas of work, not for sentimental reasons, but because it's right to do that in that area. So we build confidence and capacities in that area for us to be able to make a difference in children's lives. And we are not in this for the sake of competition, or to flag up Save the Children Norway's name. But we want to do a good job. And we want to be able to make a difference in peoples' lives. And that is what I mean by being professional. And having those professional ethics is not a matter of moving around because it's Save the Children Norway. It's moving around and listening to people, and moving with their ideas, but being able to contribute in a professional way, in a more sensible way.

In the first half of the quote above, two contrasts indicate this interviewee's understanding of 'being professional'. Firstly, the motivation

15 One of the embassy interviewees in her 30–40s addresses the above mentioned increased professionalisation of the field and indicates how she understands professionalism. In the context of reflecting on the attitudes that should characterise development workers, she says: '[...] If you see this over a long period of time, there is no doubt that development cooperation has become a lot more professionalised, and you could very well say bureaucratised, right? And more technocratic in a way, many would say. It doesn't have to be so, but I think there's a risk that it is. And then there is a struggle, in a way, between commitment and bureaucratisation. It's not necessarily a contradiction, but it can be'.

for the work is not 'sentimental reasons' but 'because it's right'. Secondly, another contrast is made regarding the motivation or rationale for doing aid. In contrast to being involved 'for the sake of competition' or to 'flag up Save the Children Norway's name' (see section 9.2.2), the interviewee claims her organisation wants to do 'a good job' and 'make a difference in people's lives'. The reference to a competition between aid agencies is not unreasonable. As a result of the multitude of aid agencies, there is clearly an element of competition in the relationship between them. In this quote, however, this aspect of the aid industry is toned down (see chapter 7 and section 8.1), and excluded from the notion of being professional. Rather, professionalism is understood in terms of quality and making a difference. The implicit claim is of course that there are aid agencies that have a different agenda, not related to quality and not too concerned about making a difference. As noted earlier, these elements are also discursively linked to the concept of charity.

Having explained then what she means by 'being professional', the interviewee moves on to give a more substantive explanation of what this implies in positive terms. Here focus is on 'listening to people' and 'their ideas' which is clearly in line with what Chambers calls a new professionalism. The notion of professionalism seems to lean towards the recipient side of the aid relationship. This is, however, qualified at the very end of this quote. Being professional is clearly not only to be 'moving around', but also to 'contribute in a professional way'.

Looking more closely at how the notion of professionalism is contrasted with other concepts or ideas, a number of similar tensions appear. Professionalism is clearly viewed by some interviewees as a contrast to a charitable approach to development aid. Asked if she sees a tension between being professional and being a voluntary organisation, one of the SCN interviewees in her 50–60s says: 'We need to have a fully professional leadership, to be able to defend the way we spend the money. Volunteerism and charity and such, doesn't work'. When asked to comment on the claim that SCN staff do development work because they want to be kind, the same interviewee says:

> I have given talks for business leaders, and I have said: 'We are probably at least as professional as you are. You think that we do charity, but we don't. We are professional. We have systems, we have strategies, and we have evaluations. And we adjust things as we go. We are flexible and we are result orientated.' So the do-

goodism (*snillisme*) which everyone thinks development aid amounts to, at least we have to show that the do-goodism, to what extent is it all naivety, because do-goodism is also related to that, but that we also want to be result orientated.

Professionalism is here quite explicitly interpreted in terms of having a systematic approach, and this is contrasted with charity. Further, this interviewee not only compares herself and development worker professionals with business managers, but even declares that development workers surpass them in terms of being professional. Implicit in this is not only an interpretation of what it means to be professional in the field of development work, but also a positioning against perceived prejudices of others.

14.2.2 Addressing the wider picture

Discussing charity, one of the SCN interviewees in her 50–60s says: 'We have to adopt a wider perspective. That is what I mean. Then you have professional development'. The main issue here seems to be that a 'professional development' implies adopting a macro perspective of the issues at hand. Asked if she thinks it is possible to be professional and compassionate at the same time, she says:

> [...] I wouldn't say that we are without compassion when we do this... There is a driving force in this, seeing that you can do something. But if we don't manage to do it professionally, you could just as well go down to the street corner and hand out money to the poor. And you don't know the underlying causes for their being poor... We hear rumours that families are renting a house here in [capital] and place thirty children there. They go out begging on the streets, as income generation for the family. So they suffer. So, if you are not professional in this, and only compassionate, then you too can be fooled and make the system worse. So the combination, having a feeling that this is right, and that you have something that drives you. But you have to be professional when you make decisions, and many decisions can be very difficult. [...] If I am to think long-term, and think about whom I should prioritise when I make a decision here, it isn't necessarily the board or Save the Children Norway in general, it has to be in the interest of the child. And that is where rights come in. I try to be professional. ... It's about finding a balance...

Here beggars (see section 15.3) are used as a case in point, and professionalism is contrasted with being compassionate. Note also how compassion is referred to in terms of personal motivation. The overriding concern seems, however, to be professional, interpreted as being distanced and thus able to make difficult decisions. The ideal seems to be that the development worker should be detached, neutral and thus distanced in order to make good decisions.

The professionalism of the development worker is here explicitly interpreted from a systemic and structural perspective. What is more striking, however, is how this interviewee presents her work as very different from charity and compassion, and she does so with considerable pathos. Several times during the interview she repeats that this is neither charity nor compassion, it is professionalism. This seems to echo how the rights approach in development aid is presented as being in distinct contrast to the charity approach. While the rights approach is understood in terms of principled thinking and a concern for the whole picture, the charity approach is related to feelings, coincidence, and a perspective that sees only the individual recipient in the present. The rights approach seems also to be the professionals' approach. Charity is the domain of amateurs. And in the same way that it seems important for many of the interviewees to keep a distance from the charity approach, it is important and necessary for this interviewee to present herself as a professional in her self-understanding as development worker (see sections 11.1 and 11.2).

When asked how she would describe 'the good development worker', one of the embassy interviewees in her 30–40s says:

> It's someone who has a really good overview of the field he works in, who both knows the specifics of a given field and also has the ability to lift it up to a higher level, sort of. Not to immerse himself too much in specifics and details, but who can see what is being done in one field in a wider context, on a national basis. Possibly be able to make some connections to the international field. That would be an important characteristic of a development worker. That you don't become too focused on your little… but see yourself in connection with something bigger, the plans and strategies and the national context, sort of.

In this way of describing 'the good development worker' this interviewee too emphasises professional knowledge and competence. This emphasis seems to draw on the concept of the expert in the field and is shared by several of the interviewees. Another aspect worth noting is this interviewee's emphasis on being aware of 'a higher level' and the 'international field'. While several interviewees repeatedly draw on ideas echoing the basic needs approach in development, this emphasis on the larger context seems rather to draw on more structurally oriented theories. In this can be seen a kind of macro discourse articulated with roots in both the dependency school and more recent debates on globalisation. These are approaches that are concerned with, and deeply sceptical about, development aid (see section 3.2).

The issue of relating one's work to plans and strategies is even more strongly emphasised in the description of a bad development worker one of the NCA interviewees in her 50–60s gives. When asked to describe someone she would consider a bad development worker, she says:

> [...] Because I have seen development workers who hand out some money here and there and who maybe build their own... Well, you sort of don't have a concrete plan... [...] it's a little here and there, and I have seen several examples of this. It creates a lot of problems. To me, that is not the way to do things. That is what I call charity.

Aid work done in a casual manner seems here to be the prime example of how things should not be done. Further, the labelling of this as charity seems to be in line with how charity is understood as in contrast to the human rights approach.

14.2.3 Being present

Interestingly, one of the NCA interviewees in her 30–40s responds to questions regarding professionalism in quite a different way from those referred to above. In her reflection on 'the good development worker', she chooses to tell a narrative – the story of a development worker that comes across as close to the perfect development worker in her mind. She says:

> [...] He was sitting in a village. He enjoyed it, and he felt it was great to be there. And he achieved a lot. People trusted him. They came to him and told him about everything that was going on, and he managed to make the best assessments of what the actual needs in the area were... He sat a lot outside his hut – sat there. And he made lots of things happen, really amazing. There are so many schools he managed to establish and actually make them work, and the number of teachers still teaching etc. It's really incredible. So he is an example of the good development worker. And every Sunday when he was off work, he got up at the crack of dawn and went out to the plains and up to the mountains. Oh, he had a good time. And then he came back, sweaty, just in time for the fire and the slaughtering of the

> goats. Oh, he enjoyed it. He thought it was tragic to go back home. That is a good development worker. If he also had made an effort to learn the language, I would have…

The emphasis here is quite different from what can be seen in the other interviewees' statements above. 'The good development worker' is here not primarily the expert with knowledge, but one that listens and wants to understand. Here making demands or setting conditions is not emphasised, but rather just being there (he 'sat there'). This is the development worker who has plenty of time, enjoys herself and is involved in the local social life. The description of him has several traits in common with what Robert Chambers refers to as new professionalism, in contrast to normal professionalism.

An important element in this interviewee's description of this development worker appears to be the simple fact that he was present. Not only did the development worker described enjoy being there, he also spent lots of time outside his house. One gets the impression that this development worker had plenty of time. He spent a lot of time with the locals in this village. Note the detailed and descriptive language this interviewee makes use of. 'The good development worker' is sweating, sitting, and walking, clearly present and part of the community he works with. Similar aspects are, however, also emphasised when the same interviewee describes 'the good development worker' in more abstract terms. She says:

> The good development worker, I think that is someone with plenty of time. It's someone who comes, and who sits down first and talks with people. And who greets people and who observes. One who will hear, and listens for a long time before doing much else. And who doesn't have a lot of advice to give. But who is very willing to step in when people are needed. […] Ideally a development worker should be in the same place for several years, also out of respect for their co-workers and their fellow human beings who also live in a very difficult context, with lots of replacements. I see this in my own organisation. You notice it with the staff that have to relate to a change of leader every second year. […] So a good development worker has time, at least gives that impression. Greets people, looks people in the eyes… eats with them.

In this quote too being present seems to be a key concern. It seems to be valued not only out of instrumental considerations, but also for its intrinsic value. It implies talking with people, observing, and listening 'for a long time'. However, in this latter quote this interviewee also indicates how this understanding of 'the good development worker' is challenged in real life. She would like to see development workers spending several years in one place, although actual practice is that most are replaced every second or third year. A similar comment can be made about her perception of a good development worker sitting outside his house in the village. Only a few development workers in general, and none of the interviewees of this study, actually live in such villages. Rather, they work in city centres a long way from people in villages. Similarly, most of the interviewees find they have very busy work schedules and are often short of time. There are reports to be written and deadlines to be met. The ideal of listening, taking time, and being present seems then to carry certain romantic elements. They are ideals that refer to situations that do not apply to many of the expatriate professionals involved in contemporary development aid.

Further, this interviewee emphasises taking time. In this the contrast is with another group of aid workers, the relief workers. Their task and mandate is precisely not to be patient, to take time, or to listen to people. On the contrary, their task is perceived as being fast and efficient. This contrast is confirmed explicitly when the role of 'the good development worker' is compared to that of the relief worker (see section 9.2). When asked to elaborate her understanding of 'the bad development worker', the same interviewee says:

> He is pretty boring. Just sits there. That's exactly it. But that cowboy is quite cool. And he becomes a hero when he goes back home, too. Tanned and starved, right? He didn't have time to eat. He didn't have time, not for this or that. But the slow development worker, he enjoys being in the field, and takes walks with them and comes back and…

While the relief worker is a 'cowboy' – cool, enduring hardships and always in a hurry, 'the good development worker' is slow, sitting there, and enjoying her stay and company.

This ability to be present is also stressed by one of the SCN interviewees in her 30–40s. When asked how she would describe 'the good development worker', she says:

> Yes, to me a good development worker is someone who is able to go out to someone in the field, and be able to relate to people, be able to appreciate the way people live their lives, and be able to contribute to that and support peoples' ways of doing things, and analyse this. And where possible support them to change, according to

their will, through the development worker facilitating that process, without the development worker necessarily doing things for people. An aid worker should be in my opinion, should be a facilitator. Be able to facilitate for people who are poor, by helping them to think, by helping them to analyse their situations, so that they are able to improve and to change them. That is the way I see it. But it has to do with attitude. One has got to have the right attitude; one has to be able to listen to people… because often people don't do this. They think they know everything. When they come they want to tell people what to do. Aid workers should be able to listen. To be able to listen […] to help them to analyse the situation they are in and to move with them. To me, that is the kind of attitude that is appreciated in an aid worker.

Here, the concern appears in many respects to be the same as noted above: to relate to people, facilitating but not doing, etc. This interviewee summarises key personal qualities of the development worker in terms of having 'the right attitude' and being 'able to listen to people'. The explicit contrast is with those who 'think they know everything' and 'want to tell people what to do'. In these statements the art of listening is contrasted with the habit of telling people what to do. The issue of listening vs. telling is, however, also related to the issue of knowledge. 'The good development worker' should listen, and she should not think she has all the solutions.[16]

14.2.4 The qualified facilitator

Having noted the emphasis put on professional qualifications as a key feature of development worker's professionalism, and now on listening and taking time, the relation between them needs to be addressed. What is the role of the professional competence of the listening development worker? One answer to this question is found in a statement made by one of the NCA interviewees in her 40–50s. Like the SCN interviewees above, she understands the role of the development worker to be that of

16 This dissociation is something expressed also by another SCN interviewee in her 30–40s, who articulates this explicitly in her description of 'the bad development worker'. She says: 'A bad development worker… A bad development worker is someone who comes to [country] thinking that he has all the solutions, and who begins by telling the locals how things should be done. And doesn't listen and doesn't try to understand the situation. Someone who brings his own fixed ideas about how we should help. That is what I call a bad development worker'.

facilitator. Reflecting on how she would describe a good development worker, she says:

> […] And I think that another good thing, a must for being a development worker, is to say: 'Yes, what I do is important', but on the other hand to say that 'It's not what I do myself that is the important thing', if you understand that distinction. Because, it's important what I do but what is actually going to happen, that is up to what other people are doing. And sometimes I use the image that if I want a merry-go-round to move and I am in the middle and try to make it… then it doesn't help much if I stand there and just turn around my own axis, right? It looks like I am really active, and doing lots of things. But that doesn't mean that the wheel around me is moving at all. And that is why what I do is important. But what is important to do is done by others, and to have that as a fundamental attitude… Because we see, even today, that too many people come out to save the world with their own ideas. It has a lot to do with professionalism because you shouldn't be without ideas. But you should be open to how your ideas could fit in with, or slowly blend in with the ideas of others. Because it has to do with, development has to do with… Nobody else can develop me. And it's always like this: nobody but the local community can develop the local community.

The work of the development worker is here explicitly related to the actions of the recipients of development aid. This is highlighted by the phrase: 'what is important to do is done by others'. Development is here seen as something that can only take places as an immanent process, as 'nobody but the local community can develop the local community'. The primary concern is what in other contexts is referred to as local ownership, often regarded as a prerequisite for sustainable development. What then is the role of an external development worker? This interviewee's answer is that 'you should be open to how your ideas could fit in with, or slowly blend in with the ideas of others'.

When asked what values she thinks should characterise the Norwegian development worker, another of the NCA interviewees in her 40–50s says:

> Yes, I would say that respect is a word we should take a closer look at. And that means respect for other fellow humans, other cultures, other traditions, and others' opportunity to develop themselves. We too often come with the view that we have the answers to a great many things. And I see that we don't have those answers. They lie elsewhere. What we often can do from Norway is to facilitate if you like, or we can assist in and moderate or push forward (*moderere eller dytte litt på*) some of the processes, but development really has to come from the people themselves. And then we can be conversation partners and someone who motivates. […] That

is, we too often come here with the answers and all the solutions and that doesn't work. I am not saying this is easy. Often this has to do with power. As soon as you come with money you come with power. So it is demanding. It takes a lot of tolerance from those exercising this power, and we who represent this power: that you are able to listen, and able to include. And it's difficult, because we are all very different.

Clearly, and quite explicitly in this quote, the issue of respect is of critical importance to several of the interviewees (see section 13.1.3 and 13.2.2). In this case it seems as if this concern arises from an experience of colleagues having a notion of having the answers to too many things. In this interviewee's mind 'we don't have those answers'. Again, note how local knowledge is emphasised at the expense of the knowledge the development worker has. To this interviewee, the role of the development worker is 'to facilitate'. She explains this as one who can 'moderate or push forward some of the processes'. And quite explicitly she emphasises development as an immanent process. Thus, the role of the development worker is in this respect ruled out, and of course the issue of which role she then should have assumes critical importance. In addition to being a facilitator, this interviewee refers to her as a 'conversation partner' and 'someone who motivates'.

One of the SCN interviewees in her 30–40s is also concerned that development workers should not act as experts. Rather, they should respect the recipients. When asked what values or principles she thinks should characterise NDA, she says:

I think we easily come in and think we are the experts. And it's really important to respect. At the same time we shouldn't be naïve, and think that everyone we meet in these countries is an honest person who seeks the best for their country. Of course we must keep our eyes open, to corruption and... But we shouldn't from the outset come in and decide what is to be done. But this should be cooperation.

Again note how the notion of the development worker as an expert is criticised, alongside the reminder 'to respect' while not being too 'naïve'.[17]

17 Also asked how she would describe 'the good development worker', one of the SCN interviewees in her 40–50s says: 'I think it would have to be a person with no prestige of his own, who hasn't got a very big ego and has to be seen and heard on every occasion. I think it should be a person who is humble. And who sort of has the desire to facilitate, but not necessarily be the one who performs or directs or is

14.3 Personal qualities

In addition to the professional qualifications, several interviewees highlight the importance of the development worker's personal qualities. It is not only a matter of having the right competence, but also of personal commitment. As part of a discussion of the rationale for development aid, one of the embassy interviewees in her 50–60s says:

> [...] and the idealism implicit in the desire to do something for someone poorer... If that isn't the driving force for what we are doing, we could just as well have done something else. I feel that by far the majority of those I have worked with over the years have had this in them. A lot of committed experts and others in the administrations, Peace Corps volunteers over the years... a lot of committed people who have generally been motivated... Adventurism, sure, it has to be there, if not... stay at home. But the humanitarian aspect of it... that you actually want to do something positive for other people, if that isn't there, it will be rough going. [...] I think money is only a small part of development aid. Money is only a small part of development aid. It's the personal commitment. It's to be present. [...] Be there for people who are oppressed etc. That is an important part of development aid.

This interviewee's reflections are primarily descriptive. However, in the second half of the quote, she also makes her own normative assessment, emphasising the positive effects of idealism and commitment of individual development workers in the context of their professional work. The personal commitment is further stressed at the end of this quote as it is contrasted to the role of money in aid. While 'money is only a small part of development aid' – and this is repeated – personal commitment is seen as an 'important part'. Compared to an understanding of development aid as a transfer of resources, this is an explicitly different understanding. The role of money might still be constitutive of the aid relationship, but it is seen as only a small part.

---

in the frontline, sort of. And I think he should have lots of patience, because things take time. I often meet frustrated people who maybe have a short-term contract and really would like to feel that they have achieved something'.

14.3.1 Having a heart

An expression that also seems to refer to the concerns about personal commitment, is the metaphor of 'the heart'. One of the NCA interviewees in her 40–50s uses these expressions in her discussion of what constitutes 'the good development worker'. She says:

> I think that if a doctor becomes a technician, he is no longer a doctor. Because... a doctor works with people, and I think it doesn't have to be the fact that you work directly with people but most of what you do in your profession will have consequences for people. And if you don't have a heart for that, then the whole profession loses something. If you strip the profession of its human side, then I think you can hardly talk about a profession... At least in the field we are... But it's dangerous if the heart governs. It's not the heart that should govern, but the heart should be there. Because if not it will be difficult to relate to a holistic understanding of people, because the heart, the emotional, is actually a very important part of being human. It has nothing to do with sentimental emotionalism or things like that, but it has to do with how, if you are not aware of the emotional part of a person, you will definitely misinterpret that person and his behaviour, and then you will go wrong. So just by thinking professionally, you have to consider that. Where is the heart in this?

This interviewee relates having 'a heart' not to development aid as such, but to the development worker profession. And not only is it seen as something positive or valuable, it is constitutive. 'If you strip the profession of its human side, then I think you can hardly talk about a professsion.' The thrust of the statement seems to be precisely this emphasis on the key function of bringing one's heart, defined at one point as 'the emotional part of a person', into the professional work of development worker.

In the comparison this interviewee makes with the medical professsion, having a heart is contrasted with being a technician. Implicitly she compares the work she does herself with that of a medical doctor. This is a contrast one of the NPA interviewees in her 30–40s also makes in her description of 'the good development worker'. But even more than the NCA interviewee, the NPA interviewee is concerned about how 'the heart' should be balanced against its contrast. When asked how she would describe 'the good development worker', the latter says:

> The good development worker has a big heart, but not so big that it overshadows his or her ability for logical, rational thinking. [...] That is, I have to say that I have

> never in my life met so many big hearts as within the aid community. But in some cases, maybe more than I had hoped, this sort of overshadows the ability to sit down and analyse things. I don't think it's necessarily a good idea to replace development workers with professional managers and business people. Because I think you need to have your heart in it somehow. But it should not be so big and beating so hard that you are not able to look at things in a rational way. Are there such people, do you think?

Asked if she knows of such people, she says:

> No. Unfortunately, I don't think so really. But as I said in the beginning, there are a lot of very able development workers, don't misunderstand me. But I think there is a danger, clearly, that the heart disappears in favour of realism, or what some call realism, and that is what I call cynicism. And then you only end up as a shark in a suit, in a way. Then you are only a professional... a technician who doesn't have anything but technical implementation as a motive for the job he does. I think it ought to be something more.

Here this interviewee uses the same contrast noted in the NCA interviewee's statements. The argument is clearly that 'the good development worker' is not 'a technician'. There 'ought to be something more'. As noted, this something is having 'a heart'. And, just like the NCA interviewee warns against a heart that 'governs', this NPA interviewee calls for 'a big heart, but not so big that it overshadows his or her ability for logical, rational thinking'. The danger that 'the heart disappears' is, however, a new emphasis.

This emphasis of commitment and empathy can of course be understood in different ways. On the one hand, this seems to be a call for authenticity. Development work is not a technical exercise, it is not just any kind of work but something the individual development worker commits herself to. In this perspective the emphasis on personal commitment seems to be a return to the charity approach, in that it is the donors' or the aid workers' own moral qualities that are emphasised. On the other hand, this can be understood as a continuation of the concern to ensure quality in development work. Empathy is about knowing the reality and context in which one is working, and when this is stressed this relates to the fact that although one is working in a developing country, it is perfectly possible to avoid seeing, smelling, and feeling the poverty in the country. As mentioned, the development workers interviewed here are not relief workers, nor do they live in rural areas or share living quarters with the local population. They are rather administrators and managers, but still there is a clear expectation that they should know what real life is all about.

One embassy interviewee in her 30–40s makes an interesting remark in this regard. When asked what characterises 'the good development worker', she says:

> Openness… Openness. Reflexivity, I think is fundamental… Commitment, if that is an attitude. I don't know if you could say that. Actually, I do believe you shouldn't take it too far but I do believe some kind of empathy is pretty important. And to me this is related to the line I try to draw between the bureaucratisation of what we are doing… That is, a kind of empathy, a commitment that makes this job as a development worker, as you say, a personal matter (*personlig anliggende*) in a way, and that… To me that is important. I don't know if other people would agree with me, but to me that is important. Then you have all the other things with respect to the context in which the development worker finds himself. Loyalty, efficiency, flexibility with regard to our own political system, and that of the recipient, which demands that kind of approach to the work, and… But it's more like… These are ways of working or premises in order to be able to do a good job. But the personal commitment, when you ask about attitudes, then I believe that, yes: openness and a certain amount of empathy are important. But that is me… But I find it's a challenge to transform this empathy, whatever that is, into a work reality which is relatively bureaucratised, if not politicised.

Note how this interviewee too addresses the issue of commitment, or as she puts it, a 'kind of empathy'. With certain reservations she emphasises this as something that makes the work of the development worker also a 'personal matter'. It is clear that she does not want this concern to be taken 'too far', however, she too does stress its importance. Note also how she stresses that the emphasis she puts on empathy is her personal opinion. One interpretation of this could be that the interviewee is aware that this is a disputed issue – that not everyone working with NDA would agree with her on this. Another interpretation could be that it is her own reservations that are echoed here. However, later the same interviewee elaborates further on this issue, saying:

> […] And there are some aid groups or organisations, maybe where there is more room to talk legitimately about empathy. In Norwegian Church Aid I would think you can talk about empathy, in mission I think you can talk about empathy, because it's an important part of the value basis for what they are doing, if by empathy you mean a kind of committed sympathy. That is, it's committed because it should lead to things. It is action oriented. And I think that is a very good thing. That is to say,

> that it exists. I am not so sure we can as easily talk about empathy as an important driving force in our own work. We are a more bureaucratically run organisation.

Note the comparison this interviewee here makes with other aid agencies. She assumes the discourse is different within other organisations. Note also the positive evaluation of the role of empathy – and the interpretation of this as something that can be articulated as a motivation in at least some other agencies (see section 6.2).

14.3.2 Idealist or realist

Asked to comment on the moral motivation some development workers might say they have, one of the NPA interviewees in her 30–40s also gives critical comments on the nature of idealism. She says:

> […] I find that idealism… in the context you end up in, it's sort of scary, because idealism demands sort of idealistic results and that pretty quickly. And things are complex here, and they take time. And then for an idealist to internalise this reality and to realise that: OK, this idealism is maybe something you should reconsider in view of the set goals.

This interviewee seems to regard impatience as part of 'idealism'. She sees, however, a difficulty arising from such a perspective, as it might collide with the complexity of real life, and the fact that it takes time to achieve results in this field. Elaborating further on this issue, she says:

> […] So, if you come with too much idealism, that is unfortunate. I think you should bring along a certain amount of moral idealism, but… otherwise, in a way… […]. It's a problem you deal with when there is an abyss between what you experience of wealth in Norway, and what you experience here. You need a driving force to be able to contribute in one way or another, in order to, not eliminate poverty, but to be able to contribute to poverty becoming maybe just a tiny little bit smaller.

This interviewee's scepticism about idealistic attitudes is made quite explicit. She retains, however, a place for what she calls 'moral idealism'. This seems to refer to a 'driving force' she sees as necessary in this kind of work. Similarly, one of the embassy interviewees in her 50–60s contrasts realism with kindness and naivety. She says: '[…] I think you should be very realistic when you enter into development cooperation.

You should not do it just to be kind and naïve'.[18] Other interviewees also emphasise the need to balance one's idealism with other qualities. However, asked what role she thinks idealism should have in development work, one of the embassy interviewees in her 50–60s points to the risk of becoming cynical. She says:

> [...] There is a balance. You could easily end up in cynicism. When things move slowly and you become frustrated. That's where the biggest danger lies. So if the idealism... the idealist becomes maybe more easily frustrated. It's sort of paralysing when the expectations don't match reality. So I am not looking for the idealist, who easily ends up in cynicism, nor the bulldozer.

Again, the art of finding the right balance is articulated. Elaborating further on this issue, the same interviewee says: '[...] You have to play your part and not be cynical. But you have to stick to your role. And not take it all in'. The need to achieve results and subsequent frustrations requires that idealism is balanced with a certain amount of realism. If not, idealism can turn into cynicism. When asked what motivates her today, one of the NPA interviewees in her 30–40s also highlights this issue. She says: '... of course, one of the dangers of coming out here is that the idealism fades away, and you become cynical instead of idealistic after a stay here'. Idealism is implicitly seen as something that should not be lost. It should rather be protected, avoiding the dangers of being perverted into cynicism.

This issue of personal qualities is also addressed when one of the SCN interviewees in her 50–60s is asked what she thinks development aid is all about. She says:

> [...] I think there are some genuine people out there who really want to work with people, like I said, in development. But I also feel there are people who have hidden agendas, even though they claim to be working in the development arena. So it's difficult to give... You know... You have to weigh each situation, you have look at every situation and the values of an organisation. And even within an organisation that has the right values, that has the correct working principles, you still find

18 This interviewee also contrasts realism and idealism, and considers the former to be prominent among her colleagues. She says: 'I believe that also in development work it gradually... I don't know if there was more idealism earlier, but the people I have been working with here have at least to a large extent been characterised by realism in what they are doing'.

> people who are somehow attracted to that organisation because they see opportunities to exploit.

This interviewee points out that there are some 'who really want to work with people'. Thus she addresses the issue of authenticity, 'genuine people'. Note, however, that the understanding of being genuine here seems to be related to the desrie and ability to work with people. The development worker who opposes this participatory strategy might accordingly be understood as not being genuine.

14.3.3 Empathy

A recurring topic in the field of professional ethics is the extent to which the practitioner should keep a certain distance to her clients, patients, or partners, and the extent to which the ideal or norm should rather be to encourage personal involvement. This distinction and tension also makes itself present in the material of this study. As noted above, however, the issue of distance and involvement is described in terms of a tension that must be dealt with – or rather that a balance between the two is needed.

Commenting on the context of the hypothetical situation of recruiting a new staff member, one of the embassy interviewees in her 50–60s says:

> You have to be cynical in some situations to get the job done. But you also have to strike a balance between cynicism and going local, as it's called – that you are not able to stay out of it.

Accordingly, while some then stress that one should not become too cynical, others stress that it is important to be cynical enough. It seems reasonable to understand this as a dilemma, where the challenge is to find the right balance. However, asked to comment on the role and place of empathy in development work, one of the NCA interviewees in her 40–50s says:

> Well. You can come to [country], and you can stay here, I don't know two weeks, one week… And you can stay at a decent guest house or a hotel, and you can stroll around in [capital], and go down to [town] and see [tourist attraction], and have a wonderful time. And you don't have to see one hungry person or one poor child. But we have 4 million of them. And you have to be willing to go out and meet them

> and see them and talk to them and hear what the problem is. The problem is that there are children aged fourteen or fifteen who are responsible for seven or eight other children. There was this girl… Two days ago I was out there and met a seventeen year old girl who was responsible for four siblings. She was in her last term in secondary school. She could not afford to pay her school fees. She had gone 98 per cent of the way, but could not afford the last term. She lacked 320 kroner. You have to dare to see this, and dare to meet it and dare to help, really. And you can't do that to everyone, but you have to dare to act. You have to be willing to sit down in the village and actually listen, and acknowledge how people are living. And that has to do with a kind of empathy and something like compassion (*barmhjertighet*)… This means we can live in our own world if we want to. I don't have to see anything at all. So, some of those steps… And that is sort of a part of Norwegian Church Aid's message, which we should take on… We should go out. We should not just be a voice on their behalf, but we should actually go out and see, and we should try to communicate some of it.

This interviewee highlights how it is possible to avoid seeing the poverty and suffering of others, but emphasises how this is necessary in order to be a good development worker. In other words, rather than keeping a distance, she stresses the need to share the experiences of the recipients, at least to a certain extent. Again the idea of the development worker as someone who sits downs and listens is articulated, and this in turn is related to the ability to empathise and be compassionate. Similarly, asked how she would describe 'the good development worker', another of the NCA interviewees in her 40–50s says:

> Well, if you don't have, for example, empathy (*innlevelse*) as a part of your repertoire and that has to do with the heart, but it also has to do with a fundamental value, then I think you… And sometimes you should feel sympathy, although sympathy often is pretty useless (*nytteløs greie*), but that is also a part of us. But if you don't have it, then it can be difficult to have empathy.

Again the ability to (sympathise and) empathise is explicitly highlighted as a key characteristic of 'the good development worker'. When this interviewee is also asked about her encounters with individual recipients of development aid, she says:

> When you come to the larger contexts and sometimes you are in a hurry and you meet the big schemes, it could be a refugee camp, a camp for internally displaced people, or other kinds of schemes… Sometimes I find that quite difficult, because it's hard to relate to individuals. You relate to a group. And then they are only sort of numbers. They are only black heads. And you see ragged clothes etc. Often you end up thinking: All right, what is my responsibility with respect to seeing to it that

> what happens here is done in the best way possible? Then it's the strategic, professional aspect that comes up. I am not able to relate to all the individuals here, but I must at least see if what we do here is the best way possible to serve the people here. That becomes part of the strategy in larger groups. [...] But of course you try, as far as you can, to sit down with individuals or smaller groups to at least have a conversation and go beneath... This is far from thinking that they see you as an equal, but at least a willingness to sit down and listen.

While this interviewee in the previous statement underlined the role of empathy in development work, emphasis here is rather on keeping a professional distance. However, at the end of this statement she articulates a kind of balance between the two, expressed as 'at least a willingness to sit down and listen'.

14.4 Concluding reflections

In different ways the interviewees of this study situate the role of the professional development worker somewhere between the donor and the recipient (see section 5.2.2). They are all employed as representatives of donor agencies, and there is an important strand within the discourse that indicates a primary identification with the donor. However, there is also a discourse clearly marked by a concern for and identification with the poor or the recipients. There is for example a discourse of closeness that highlights ideals of humility in encounters with the representatives of the recipients. This discourse is markedly present in issues regarding the personal traits of the development worker, where empathy and having 'a heart' are stressed.

Several of the interviewees emphasise the need to be professional as a development worker. To be a good professional implies being thorough, efficient, and honest. These values seem to be emphasised to mark a contrast to idealistically driven charity, but also to highlight the need to fulfil a role in a bureaucracy set up to ensure transparency, efficiency, and fairness. Being professional seems to imply having the administrative skills needed to manage aid funds, understanding the wider picture and the complexities involved in poverty reduction efforts. The ability to work strategically and to relate one's efforts to political and macro economic factors appear to be important elements of being professional. The contrast seems to be the naïve development worker, 'led astray' by her good heart and empathy.

On this issue, however, there are divergent views present in the material. While some are eager to emphasise the professional aspects as opposed to these more personal aspects, others seem to explore ways to include such characteristics into the understanding of professionalism. While some interviewees stress the professional competence and expert knowledge of the development worker, others stress her personal commitment and involvement, as they also emphasise the role of the recipients in development aid. The discourse of 'being present' is most clearly articulated by some of the younger NGO interviewees. An important tendency, however, seems to be that the development worker role absorbs several of these aspects, making it a complex and challenging role.

One of the contrasts at play when the issue of development worker professionalism is addressed is the one between the expert and the amateur. There is clearly a discourse that emphasises the role of the professional development worker as being different from the omniscient expert. This is articulated for instance in terms of being humble and understanding one's role primarily as one of facilitating. Further, in their reflections on the motivation of other development workers, there is an emphasis on being genuine and authentic (see chapter 6).

To summarise, by focussing on development aid implementation this chapter adds new perspectives to the moral discourse of NDA. Interestingly, features that are elsewhere widely downplayed or rejected seem here to be highlighted by the interviewees. While the language of human rights and justice dominates the discourse on NDA policies and approaches (not least in the policy documents), concepts such as closeness, empathy, and personal commitment seem to play a much more central role when the interviewees reflect on development worker professionalism.

15 Individual lifestyle

We are the world, we are the children.
We are the ones who make a brighter day.
So let's start giving.

Michael Jackson and Lionel Richie (USA for Africa)

The professional and private spheres of the development workers' lives are distinct, but not fully separate. The moral discourse on the professional good development worker can also include aspects of the private sphere. A statement by one of the NPA interviewees in her 30–40s provides an illustrative example. When asked to reflect on how she perceives 'the good development worker', she says:

> Lead the way by example. I thought a bit about the word moral just now… I find it difficult to see that you are a good development worker if for example you use prostitutes, if you drink and drive, and if you don't follow the set of rules that you in fact have at home. And you must perhaps actually also be very scrupulous where there is a set of rules stricter than at home. In Zimbabwe, for example, it would go damned wrong if you openly show that you are gay. And I fully support the same rights for all, but I think that if you are a development worker, then I think you should be conscious of the fact that you should follow the set of rules in that country. […] We should not just come here… And that is unfortunately something I have seen, that people here do things they would not have done at home. Drink and drive, and I must admit that I have done it a couple of times myself, and… And just outside here we have prostitutes in the evenings, and I walk past there every night, and I see a lot of white land cruisers stopping there. So, a good development worker must have an opinion about that. It's totally beyond what I can accept. But, then I think you should live up to what it is you are working for.[19]

19 Note how this interviewee lets it become evident that she in this quote is partly prompted by the earlier questions regarding morality. When she addresses issues of personal lifestyle, this might then not only be a consequence of these earlier deliberations, but also reflect her understanding of morality, implying that this is something she (primarily) understands as relating to personal or private issues.

This interviewee addresses the issue of 'the good development worker' by focussing on issues that can be said to belong to the private domain, in the sense that they are not directly linked to the implementation of development work. Still, this interviewee regards them as relevant issues when discussing the development worker role. There are certain things that one should not do if one is working as a development worker, for example drink and drive and buy sex. Further, it is worth noting how this interviewee defines such matters. On the one hand she seems to indicate that one should follow the set of rules that apply at home, but on the other hand, where the rules in the country in which one finds oneself are 'stricter than at home', then these should also be followed. And perhaps most interestingly, even those rules that contradict what she would consider to be universal human rights should be respected, she argues. Thus, following up on the example she uses, a homosexual development worker should refrain from having sex if working in a country where this is not allowed. And finally, note how this interviewee summarises her response in the form of an imperative: 'you should live up to what it is you are working for'. Thus, the normative expectations she has of development workers not only relate to his or her professional life, but also to the private sphere and the individual development worker's life-style.

In the first part of this chapter I will discuss how the interviewees of this study understand and evaluate their own personal wealth. In the second part I discuss how they describe their relationship with their domestic helpers and in the third and last section how they reflect upon their encounters with poor individuals.

15.1 Personal wealth

The social context for development aid is one of international inequality (see section 3.1). As development aid is implemented, however, this inequality becomes visible not only through a comparison of states. It is also an inequality at the individual level.

The interviewees of this study are paid staff. Generally, their salaries are set and adjusted according to the level of wages in Norway, not with that of the country in which they live. Accordingly, development workers such as the ones interviewed here generally stand out as rich individuals in a context characterised by widespread poverty. When asked what she thinks development aid is about, one of the NCA interviewees in her 30–40s highlights development workers' consumption and wealth. She says:

> [...] And we who work out here, I mean, we are really not in that a bad state, or most of us have chosen an occupation which we find a lot more exciting than the opportunities we have in Norway. And many can live a lot better out here than we can at home. They can save up more money.

Several critics of the aid industry have addressed this issue of personal wealth among expatriate development workers (see for example Hancock 1991 and Klitgaard 1991). One criticism is that a large part of funding for development aid never reaches its intended recipients, as there are so many others who benefit from these funds before they ever reach the recipients. In this perspective, development workers become rich at the expense of poor people's improved living conditions. Taken as a whole then, the aid industry does not, as it claims, serve the poor, but rather it maintains (or increases) the wealth of the already rich.

Asked what she thinks about her own wealth and opportunities when faced with poverty, one of the SCN interviewees in her 50–60s says:

> [...] I try to live as locally as possible... I have a car and I have a decent house. But I don't get a UN house. I try to live reasonably well (*rimelig bra*). And also to show it to others here... Sometimes they find it a bit embarrassing, because I am a boss... so they find it strange.

Through the strategy to 'live as locally as possible', this interviewee clearly seeks to downplay her wealth. Note the contrast that is made with the UN. In this a discourse of modesty that considers UN staff as overpaid is articulated. In comparison with the UN, there is an ideal that one should earn less and live more modestly ('reasonably well').

When asked what she thinks about her own wealth, one of the NCA interviewees in her 30–40s says:

> I think it's totally undeserved. And I feel very rich here. I have never felt this rich before. I save more money than I have ever done before because there is not so much to spend money on here. But I don't think we are overpaid in the Norwegian

> Church Aid. But it feels very unpleasant (*ubehagelig*). I experience it often myself. I don't like to go shopping with my colleagues, because I can allow myself so much more than they can… I think there is really no reason why I should earn much more than my colleagues, for instance, who I think have worked much harder than me in life… to succeed. So it is problematic. I think it is.

This interviewee seems to emphasise two aspects of being rich. She thinks it is 'undeserved' and she finds it 'very unpleasant'. Further, the comparison here is primarily with fellow colleagues. This interviewee finds that she earns 'much more' than them.[20] Still, she finds that she is not 'overpaid'. In this sense her salary does not appear undeserved or problematic, but rather legitimate. Her use of the term 'undeserved' seems then to refer to a comparison with the lower wages of local staff, being paid according to local salary levels, while she herself is paid according to Norwegian or expatriate levels.

15.1.1 Dealing with a dilemma

When asked how she feels about her own wealth when faced with poverty and suffering, one of the SCN interviewees in her 30–40s says:

> It's definitely a dilemma at times. You know, for instance, I look around me and say: I go out to the field, and when you look at the figures of what a teacher earns on a monthly basis, and it's unbelievable how these people survive. When you look at what you earn, it's so many times over. It's kind of quite disturbing when you think about it and you think about the lives of some of these poor people, out there, so many poor people, and some of them fairly educated people, for instance. But earning so little and living in very difficult kinds of situations.

This interviewee defines the issue as a dilemma. When explaining this dilemma, however, she goes on to describe how she perceives living in poverty. The 'dilemma' she speaks of seems then to be closely related to how she thinks it is to be 'living in very difficult kinds of situations'. Another of the SCN interviewees in her 30–40s also responds by referring to a dilemma. Asked what she thinks about her own wealth and opportunities when faced with suffering and poverty, she says:

20 As a rule these colleagues (local staff) cannot be counted as among those who are worst off.

> It's a dilemma. When you talk about dilemmas, it's difficult. ... Because we have sort of other expectations as to what is acceptable in terms of standards of living, and what is acceptable in terms of housing, and the food and the clothes you must have. And, the contrasts are of course huge. And we, who come from abroad, drive around in cars and have everything we need, and can send our children to the most expensive school in town – and employ people to help us in our homes. And of course, it's... Especially the first time you go abroad it makes a strong impression. When I worked in [country] this was something I struggled with a lot. It's maybe something you protect yourself from. If you start thinking about it, it easily becomes too much to handle. And I can see that the way that I try to handle it... [...] If I were a total idealist (*helt idealist*) then I could say no, I will live in a shack, and not have anyone working for me and walk to and from work every day, but I think that is going a bit too far. I have actually seen people who have... When I stayed in [country] I saw a family who came to the country, and who were very much aware of this issue. They decided that their doors should be open, and everyone who wanted could enter their home, and they would help all of them. They lasted a month. Then they couldn't cope anymore and returned home. It has to do with the fact that you must be able to cope in this work, in this way of life. And you need... especially if you come with a family, then you must maintain your own... You have to satisfy your own needs as a family in order to survive here, to be able to do this work.

While the previous interviewee explains the dilemma by describing the lives of the poor, this interviewee points to the expectations and lifestyle of foreign, rich people (of whom she is one). And following up on her descriptive account, she goes on to warn against idealism. This she explains in terms of a development worker's standard of living. Idealism would imply reducing one's standard of living, and being 'a total idealist' seems to mean a drastic reduction, exemplified by living 'in a shack'. She warns against this kind of idealism as she considers this would make her unable to function in her work. The needs of the individual development worker and his or her family must be fulfilled 'to be able to do this work'. At what level the needs of the family must be met is not addressed. Still, it is clear that for this interviewee, idealism must not be interpreted as a moral demand to share one's wealth to the extent that one actually shares the living conditions of the poor. A difference between the development worker and the poor must be upheld for the development worker to be able to perform well in her job. As such, the relative wealth of the development worker seems to be considered legitimate.

15.1.2 Reasonably rich

When asked what she thinks about her own wealth in the face of poverty and suffering, one of the NCA interviewees in her 40–50s says:

> Often I find it difficult, because in comparison we are unbelievably rich, although we only have an ordinary Norwegian average salary. And we can, sort of, afford to buy the food we want, and my children go to a good school. And we have good jobs. It's problematic. It hurts to sit in the villages and see what terrible conditions some people live in, and to see the contrast to my own conditions. And it's huge. That is often a dilemma. And then, in a way, you must start to reflect, both on how you can help others, and how you can contribute best. Because then you simply have to be somewhat more aware, to appreciate that you are able to work here, and allowed to work here, and allowed to contribute and able to contribute, and actually try to do your utmost to help. And this is what often happens to me. In a way I am not here just to have a nice time. I am actually here to help a few people. And this I have to take seriously, because it doesn't help if I pack my bags and go home. I will not help any more people by doing that. It can hurt and be very painful to see people in such terrible conditions. And I can, in a sense, feel empathy and rationally reflect on it, but it must motivate me to do even more.

This interviewee too speaks of the wealth-poverty divide in terms of it being difficult and problematic. In addition, she describes the encounters with the poor communities as something that 'hurts', and she refers to the 'huge' contrasts as a dilemma. From here, however, she moves on to discuss how she responds to this situation, with regard to 'how you can help others' and 'contribute best'. This response she articulates in different ways, but an important element seems to be to work hard. She speaks about trying 'to do your utmost' and being motivated 'to do even more'. This again, however, leads to what she sees as a dilemma: her inability to do enough. Again, personal wealth is discursively legitimised through a reference to professional work – in this case as a motivation to do an even better job. The same interviewee also says:

> I can probably do a much better job and fundraise more for the poor if I have my own resources, to be both a kind of advocate, to be the voice, and to use my background to identify and raise funds. So the solution is really not to be fully involved, because you have to find a level you can work at. And it's difficult and it's hard, but this is a dilemma we all face. You sit in front of your TV screen at home and see the misery too. So we all have it, but I have it a bit closer. And it becomes stronger. But some of the same mechanisms have to set in for me too.

Here this interviewee makes two rhetorical moves worth noting. First she frames the issue as one of a dilemma (as she did in the quote above). Second, she regards her own dilemma as qualitatively no different from that of those sitting 'at home'. Thus, she dismisses the notion that development workers have any special responsibility compared to others. The first of these seems to imply a questioning of the status quo and wealth-poverty contrast – while the second seems to be another way of legitimising one's relative wealth. In effect, this interviewee questions the moral high ground of those sitting 'at home', expecting more from development workers than from themselves.[21]

When one of the embassy interviewees in her 50–60s is asked how she feels about her own wealth, she says:

> It's always hard. It's always hard. But I was about to say… I just think about the way we live. We have nice houses and good conditions, and this is in stark contrast to how many other people live. […] You have beggars just outside your front door, and when I drive to work then there are cows and goats and everything… But, it's in a way like living in the rural districts… Well, the contrasts are huge. But still I think that you should not have… personally I don't feel that I should have a bad conscience because of this. What I feel is that when you live and work in a country like this, and you sense the poverty and misery right outside the door every day, then you are also, in order to be able to do an OK job, you need a sanctuary, and some breathing space. This is at least what I keep saying to myself. But of course, it's rather terrible when you travel around and see, in drought ridden areas and elsewhere, how people live… But I feel that I cannot go around with a bad conscience all the time. Then you are not able to do a very good job either. But I think that, and I think this applies to many people also working in humanitarian disaster situations; you must try to keep a certain distance, in order to do an OK job.

Note how this interviewee also stresses that she finds it 'hard' to be rich in a context of poverty. And again, keeping a 'certain distance' is made a precondition for being able to do one's work as a professional. Further,

21 Another way some of the interviewees legitimise their relative wealth can be found in the comparison with missionaries. In the context of reflecting on her personal wealth, one of the NCA interviewees in her 40–50s says: '[…] There are a few missionary tragedies (*misjonærtragedier*), where they have agreed to that kind of life, and when they come back [to Norway] then they have built up nothing, at least close to nothing, in terms of pension, house, everything. And there are a few tragedies in the wake of that'. In light of such 'missionary tragedies' the personal wealth of the development worker stands out as less problematic, and in that sense justified.

in order to keep one's distance, relative wealth does not comes across as something problematic, but rather as something necessary. Accordingly, although it is 'hard', she 'cannot go around with a bad conscience all the time'. Again, the development worker's relative wealth is legitimised as a necessity in order to 'do an OK job'.

From these statements, it seems that personal wealth is perceived by several interviewees as 'difficult' and representing a 'dilemma', but that it is still legitimate. However, one of the interviewees reflects on this issue in a different manner. Asked how she perceives her own wealth compared to the poverty and suffering she witnesses, another embassy interviewee in her 50–60s says:

> Now I must be cautious and not give an honest answer... I find it in many ways unproblematic. It's possible that you do some kind of rationalising or a kind of self-compensation, and close your eyes to much of the poverty. But I think that... Firstly, the wealth and the privileges that you have are relatively modest in comparison with what you have in Norway. [...] So this perception of this as a luxury life is in many ways wrong, I think. I don't identify with it. Although all the time you have that conflict between the average Norwegian civil servant at a relatively high level, with an immense difference in standard of living and to the poorest people here. The poorest here constitute ninety-five per cent of the population. Ninety-five per cent of the population is very poor. And you have to accept that, in a way. If you are morally upset by this every day and walk around pondering over it you can just as well go back home.[22]

While one of the NCA interviewees above finds her own relative wealth 'problematic' and says she has 'never felt this rich' (primarily in comparison with local staff), this interviewee says it is 'in many ways unproblematic' and compares her situation with the wealth and pleasures of living in Norway. In this perspective she finds her wealth to be 'relatively modest'. Thus, the experience or interpretation of being wealthy is quite different, although the perspective here resonates well with the discourse of modesty discussed above.

22 Asked how she deals with her own wealth when living in a poor country, one of the NPA interviewees in her 30–40s expresses a similar understanding. She says: 'Yes, I tackle it relatively well. I don't have any big problems with it in a way. I don't have any big problems with it because the cynical part of me says that those who really enrich themselves in this country are the local politicians or those who may not be too preoccupied with what I have not got, in a way. So I don't have any big problems with it'.

Two further matters should also be noted. Firstly, this interviewee begins by issuing a warning to herself. She should 'be cautious and not give an honest answer'. It seems reasonable to regard this remark as an indication of her awareness that the views she is about to voice are contested. This might indicate that there is a discursive struggle being articulated here. The vast difference in salaries and general standard of living seem to be something that in the dominant discourse should be regarded as problematic, although her own reflections on the issue lead elsewhere. Secondly, this interviewee ends her reflection on the issue by relating it to the issue of being an expatriate. If one is morally troubled by these huge inequalities, there is no other option but to 'go back home'. If, on the other hand, one is to stay, the only alternative seems to be to keep a distance so that one is not morally troubled. In this she seems to draw on the same kind of discourse identified above that legitimises the development workers' relative wealth.

15.2 Domestic help

One of the issues often raised in the interviews by the interviewees themselves, is the issue of having domestic help. Most of the interviewees say they have domestic staff, some only one, others two or more. The reference to domestic help appears to be made primarily in order to exemplify how one deals with the fact that one lives as a relatively wealthy person in the midst of poverty.

Asked what she thinks about her own wealth in comparison to the suffering and poverty, one of the SCN interviewees in her 30–40s says:

> [...] At home I have a nanny. In addition I have someone who cleans the house and someone who cooks the food. And for me... after a long day at work, I come home to a prepared meal, a clean house, and kids who are doing fine. And while she has been taking care of my child, in the meantime she has not been with her own children. That is pretty... But I know that if I said that she had to go home to be with her child, then she would be very sorry, because she needs the money I pay her. So the way I try to handle it, is first of all to give them a decent salary, and at the same time I try to... with one of them... I pay for one of them to go to school and get further training, so that she can increase her chances of getting a job after we leave, and when she has finished I will take the other one and provide further

> training for her. So I try to support them in a way to help them with their lives after I leave. At the same time I find it incredibly important to be respectful and just. There are a lot of examples of people who, when they are in this situation, treat people badly, and the children order them around etc. So I am very concerned, for example, that my children are respectful and treat them as grown ups. So I try on the one hand to help and support them and treat them decently, and on the other hand I try to teach my children to respect them.

This interviewee seems to compensate for the discrepancy in living conditions in two ways: by giving financial support and being respectful. Regarding the former, this interviewee compensates both through paying what she calls a 'decent salary', as well as by paying for education. Reflecting on what a just salary for her domestic help could be, she says:

> […] It's… not easy. I cannot start comparing what I earn with what they earn, but I can compare what they earn with what… with the job they do… and what is an average salary here in [country], and what is an average salary that they can manage well on. And at the same time I can… there are things that I don't… Yes, it's very difficult. What is a just salary? That is not an easy one. … Those who work for me think they have a very good salary and are very happy about it. But if I buy a bottle of wine costing [price], and think that that is about one eighth of their monthly salary, then that is… Is that just? Sometimes I remove the price tag, because I don't want them to see… It's not easy; it's not at all easy. Although I know that I pay more than most people do… I started from what is normal, and then I raised the salary. But still, in comparison with the amount of money we spend it's very little. So, I try… by giving them further training I try sort of to work on it… But it's not easy, and there are no easy answers. There aren't.

Note how the issue of comparison is considered a real problem. What should the salary for domestic staff be compared to? Further, having commented on how her domestic help seem to be satisfied with the salaries they get, this interviewee also adopts a strategy already mentioned above. She downplays her own wealth, for example by removing price tags. Finally, note also how this interviewee repeatedly says 'it's not easy'. It is difficult. As noted, this articulates a discourse represented in several other interviews.

15.2.1 Small extras

Asked what she thinks about her own wealth, one of the NPA interviewees in her 30–40s says:

> [...] But I have some small projects: the driver, my own housekeeper, etc., etc. And I have sort of decided to help them buy a piece of land and build a house, and that is only a small, small drop in the ocean. But it might improve their situation, and might lead them to think that there is a kind of justice in the world. And I don't do any kind of charity, but they borrow and I set up... and interests, and when it's Christmas or a birthday or something like that, then I cancel the debt. But these are small things. That I think I can afford, and that I enjoy doing.

Note how this interviewee highlights that what she does is not charity. Even though what she describes shares several of the traits that, as noted in previous chapters, are discursively linked with the notion of charity (these are 'small things' she as a donor 'enjoys doing'), she argues that this is something else. In what way, however, remains unclear. When prompted to elaborate on this, she says:

> Yes, but these are such minimal things. And for instance, she buys things for me when I have a birthday. And when I come home, she has bought flowers, and that is from her own money. So it's more... There is no doubt that I am the one who has money and that she is working. You cannot get around that. But we have a lot of mutual respect.

By accentuating that the scale of these 'projects' is small, this interviewee is actually highlighting one of the characteristics of charity. Her last comment: 'we have a lot of mutual respect' is, however, worth noting. Here the key concern of the previous interviewee seems to be reiterated. Her transfer of money from rich to poor is done respectfully, according to this interviewee, and it seems it is this feature that makes her 'small projects' qualitatively different from charity. In other words, charity given with respect and in the context of personal relationships is evaluated positively.

Towards the end of the interview, when asked if there is anything she would like to add, another of the NPA interviewees in her 30–40s returns to the issue of respect. She says:

> Yes, there is this thing that morality and ethics are not only about the way we deal with the target groups in the field. It's also about how we treat our own staff, and also how we treat those working for us in our homes. And there is another thing. That is something I have seen myself that by no means all development workers treat the people they meet in a good way. And that annoys me. The way house maids, guards, etc. are treated. So ... But I think that on average Norwegians are better than some other countries, because we are not used to having servants. We are not used to that from home in Norway. But it's also something... [...]. It's not

> only to focus on the target groups, as I was about to say, who are in the refugee camps here, but it's also the people you socialise with on a daily basis. How you treat your secretaries or driver, to the extent that you have that kind of setting around you, that you treat them too in a respectful manner.

Here too role obligations that extend into the private sphere are articulated. Note how the issue of respect is of primary importance to this interviewee and is something she finds concerns everyone. Further, note how she expresses faith in Norwegians, regarding them as better than others. Thus, a disassociation from development workers of other nationalities is expressed.

However, some of the interviewees emphasise the conditions on which these extras are provided. When asked what her strategy is for handling the contrast between her wealth and others' poverty, one of the embassy interviewees in her 50–60s comments:

> […] I have a portfolio of loans, but I want absolutely everything back, because if not, there will be misunderstandings again. Those who work in the house and the people that I work closely with, I think are OK. So, I suppose I have some things that I do that not to ease my conscience, but that I think are OK to do there and then. But I don't walk around thinking that what I do means a lot, but at least some get a few more opportunities based on the money I have sent them.

This interviewee seems to consider giving loans as a way of avoiding the giving of gifts. Note how she explains this as a way of avoiding 'misunderstandings' and that this is something she does 'not to ease my conscience'. In this she seems to invest discursively in dissociating from notions of charity. Still, this strategy of giving loans is not necessarily one that avoids the connotations of inequality that arise from the giving of gifts (see section 11.1).[23]

23 Reflecting on her own wealth compared to that of her domestic staff, another embassy interviewee in her 50–60s says: 'But it's clear what they want, and that they have a salary that is twice or three times as much as what they get if they work for a [country] national. And they have, every time they do something extra, they get an extra amount of money. But my role in this, and which they find difficult to understand, is why they cannot get a loan for this or for that. But my long experience tells me that I must try to train them for the world they want to see, or the world they want to enter, and how their behaviour must be then. And then they have to plan. Many of them have this understanding that they have one pocket, and that is what comes in. They don't use their other pocket to save for whatever they need a loan for. So I have tried many times to say: "OK, I'll be your bank".' Here there are

15.2.2 Personal solidarity

When asked how much she thinks development workers should donate to the poor, one of the embassy interviewees in her 50–60s says:

> I would clearly be against any duty to share… in a way, even out the inequalities by sharing your salary and maybe give away your car, as a kind of moral demand (*moralsk krav*). It… I think you must accept that you are allowed certain things in your private life. […] If there were to be any additional moral conditions (*moralske tilleggskrav*) in terms of sharing, it would make it very difficult. But in reality you will find that by far the majority, and maybe a bit more than what is healthy, will get involved by sharing and giving small gifts (*milde gaver*), and not only small gifts… […] I wouldn't say that I share fully my 'wealth', in quotation marks, but it's clear that when there are things coming up, school attendance fees, funerals, and various things… Both my gardeners are building a house, so they get money. I find it nice and something positive to help some of the closest ones. I think everyone does, and I find that positive. It has to do with a kind of personal solidarity, and is a kind of side effect. But to make it some kind of demand, that I find difficult. I think you must make a distinction between the more personal and private, and the more official.

Note how this interviewee explicitly rejects the notion that the development worker has 'any duty to share', and makes a distinction between the 'more personal and private, and the more official'. The practice of giving a little extra to her staff is something she allows for in the private sphere, but not in the professional sphere. She calls this 'a kind of personal solidarity' (see section 11.3). When asked if she sees this as a kind of charity, she says:

> Yes, the last thing is that. It's a kind of charity. When you have… you develop a relationship to people who earn very little, although they in many ways earn more than many others. They get a place to live and they get food etc., so that they have living conditions… The two I have working inside the house, have a standard of living which is a lot better than that of the average poor, and also in terms of sending children to school outside the home, and such things. Earn a good salary according to [country] standards. And you have a personal relationship and they get to share a little of the affluence. It's a kind of charity. It happens to most. Some are maybe driven a bit too far into it. Don't manage to sort of let go and keep on after returning back home… Pay education for the children, for the house maid, etc. …

---

clearly notions at play that are reminiscent of a colonial, paternalistic discourse. This interviewee sees her role as trying to 'train them for the world they want to see'. As part of this, and by giving loans, she takes on the role of a bank.

> But I cannot, I see it as an off-shoot of the primary task, and which is charity and which I don't have any problems with.

Out of the 'personal relationship' that is established between the development worker and her staff, and arising from certain benefits, 'a kind of charity' seems to develop. Note then that although these kinds of benefits are regarded here as expressions of charity, they are also evaluated positively as such. In the context of personal relationships, charity seems to be considered positively, at least as long as one is not 'driven a bit too far'.

15.3 Beggars

In their professional lives, these interviewees deal with issues of poverty, health, education, and sanitation, etc. However, to a large extent they deal with these issues at a macro level. Those working for NGOs might more than embassy staff actually meet poor people who lack proper health services, access to schools or clean water, but still they too primarily deal with these issues through partners. These partners function as a kind of intermediary between donor representatives and the end recipients of NDA. However, when development workers (as representatives for the rich donors) live in poor countries, direct encounters with the poor will most often occur. The relationship between the rich and the poor then becomes not only a macro political fact, or an abstract notion. In such meetings the rich-poor relationship becomes visible at the micro level, in a face-to-face encounter. How do the interviewees reflect upon these encounters?

One such encounter is the meeting between the development worker and beggars. Several of the interviewees refer to such situations and experiences when reflecting on the contrast between their own life situations and that of the poor in the country where they work. When asked what she thinks about her own wealth and opportunities in relation to the poverty and suffering she sees, one of the NCA interviewees in her 50–60s says:

> It's clear that it's a daily confrontation. Every day, several times a day you are confronted with it, simply because I drive between my home and my office, I encounter beggars. Every time I stop the car, the beggars come up to the window. And when I go out on the street, there will always be someone asking for some money for food. And of course, it is a difficult problem. You can't sort of help everyone, and… I have asked myself this question from time to time: am I becoming too hard-hearted (*for glatt*)… when I don't react?

When asked to elaborate, she says:

> I don't think, I don't find that I am too hard-hearted, but sometimes it may seem like that. But that is precisely why I am here. It's because of the poverty, it's because of the suffering (*nød*), it's because of the injustice (*urettferdighet*) that I am here. … But I have to realise that I cannot help everyone. I have to acknowledge that. Then there is a part of the suffering I just have to close my eyes to. And then I must concentrate on the part which is my responsibility to work on.

Three elements in these statements should be noted. First, this interviewee clearly articulates that this is not a peripheral issue. These are daily meetings or encounters, and her choice of words when describing them is worth noting. She describes them as 'daily confrontations', and says 'you are confronted with it'. These expressions seem to emphasise the contrasts of the situation. Second, she describes this as a difficult problem. The problem is rooted in this direct, daily confrontation, but her comment on the problem goes in a somewhat different direction. Rather than the problem being that she repeatedly meets these poor people, she defines the problem in terms of not being able to help everyone. Thus, the problem is one of limited ability, not of the actual encounter itself. And third, note the reflective question this interviewee raises: whether she has become 'too hard-hearted'. She seems to regard this as a risk, and clearly sees it as something she wants to avoid.

Asked how she thinks one should act towards beggars, the same interviewee says:

> I think that we should… I try to give to the beggars I meet every day. I do. That is the easiest way we can help them, so that they can have bread today. But it's clear that ideally we should do something far more… by helping them into a system where they could have a life they could manage, where they could support themselves.

One of the NPA interviewees in her 30–40s chooses the same response and characterises this as charity. Asked if she is negative towards this kind of charity, she says:

> Yes, the thing is that I appear so hasty in such situations. I don't have a chance to do anything else. I cannot give them a job; I cannot improve their standard of living in the long-term, enabling them to help themselves. But it becomes… It becomes moments when you meet them, and in the next moment she has driven away. And then… it's the only way, the only tool you have in that situation. And I feel very strongly that I am well off. I sit in a land cruiser which is air conditioned and everything, and things are all very good. And the feeling of guilt (*skyldfølelsen*) is not very far away at those times. If I were to try to ignore or something like that… the period that I did that, I found it was very difficult. I found it was very difficult, really. To see them in front of me and try to avoid their eyes and… That wasn't easy. I, too, know that there is an industry, many… In many cases this turns into a beggar industry (*tiggerindustri*). Kind of victims in a cynical game, especially with children who are sent out by some individuals behind them again… So I try not to be too naïve, but it… No, it's difficult.

In her account of her encounters with beggars, this interviewee highlights two aspects: first, the hasty nature of these meetings, and second, her own wealth. The second leads to what she describes as 'feeling of guilt' and difficulties in coping with the situation. She regards this situation as a cynical game and finds herself challenged not to be 'too naïve', but finds it 'difficult'. Whilst the previous interviewee issues a self-critical warning against becoming indifferent, this interviewee warns against being 'too naïve'. They both say they give to beggars, but while one seems to consider it an antidote to indifference, the other says she does it despite worries about being too naïve.

15.3.1 Keeping a distance

Asked if she thinks Norway or Norwegians should have a bad conscience for being wealthy, one of the SCN interviewees in her 30–40s says:

> No, well, as long as we take this seriously and do development work and continue to put resources into it and take that work seriously, then we shouldn't have a bad conscience for being so well off. I don't think so. No… But we would have had a bad conscience if we didn't do development work. But as it is, we give a lot more

> than many other countries. We are on the top of the list compared to our resources. So I don't think we should have a bad conscience. No.

Interestingly, however, she concludes differently at a later stage of the interview, when reflecting on the issue of wealth and poverty from a more personal perspective. When asked if she has a bad conscience herself, she later says:

> Yes, I have a bad conscience when I drive past beggars and don't give them money. And at the same time my head tells me it's not right to give money to those who walk between the cars and beg for money, and when you don't know where the money goes, and if the children themselves get it or… But I do have a bad conscience every time I say no to a beggar. At the same time, logically I know that it isn't the right way to help, yet I can see a mother with a small child and say, how can it not be the right way to help, when this woman needs it here and now, and I have the opportunity to… And then I go into the store and buy lots of food for my family. So I, yes… I have a bad conscience every time I see beggars. I do.

The expression 'bad conscience' seems here to articulate a feeling more than an intellectual acceptance of guilt. The personal encounter with beggars seems to function as a reminder of the contrast that the wealth-poverty divide constitutes and of the relative wealth of the development worker. As such, beggars interfere in everyday life, questioning the complacency of the wealthy.

Asked how she chooses to relate to 'the poorest of the poor', one of the embassy interviewees in her 50–60s refers to her 'long experience'. She says:

> No, from my long experience, you cannot take it in. You have to protect yourself in order to do your job. You can understand and observe, but you cannot do anything about it. But the insight that you get there, that is the platform for being here. … So, and it varies how people… When there are beggars, I don't give, on principle, in order to function. What I would do is to refer them, say to them that if you go to this or that place you will get help.

For this interviewee keeping a distance from beggars is a matter of being able 'to function'. Accordingly she too chooses a different approach from that of the interviewees quoted in the previous section. She chooses not to give to beggars. Encounters with beggars seem to function as a reminder of the reasons why she is in this situation. However, the plea for assistance is redirected to others and not responded to individually.

One of the SCN interviewees in her 30–40s also says she does not give to beggars. Asked how she reacts when she sees beggars, she says:

> Well it's a difficult situation. Personally I try as much as possible. I try not to give to beggars, because it's kind of… Some of them maybe could have lived a better life if they remain in communities where they are. But there are push-factors that cause them to be in that situation. But, if on a daily basis someone is giving them something on the street, then it kind of encourages them to stay there. And I don't believe in, as I said, I don't believe in […] charity. If I give a sick child something, it means that they have done something for me. Some of them come to me if I park the car, and they say: Can I take care of your car? That means that they have an attitude that they want to do something in return for something from me. And then I can give them something. But if someone comes to me today, and it's not like, and I always ask them: 'What have you done for me?', you know. There has to be some way, otherwise we are encouraging them to come out and beg, and not be able to think on their own. But it's a difficult situation, and a lot of people in terms of their religion, they are told to give to such people on the street. And to me I think it encourages the children more and more. I have been to [country], and there I think it's like a begging disease, because it's also part of the religion. It's part of the religious belief. Begging – and everyone is begging.

This interviewee too finds this to be a 'difficult situation', but her response is different from what was noted above. She is clearly worried about the effects of giving donations to beggars. In this there is a consequentialist argument. Her comment that such donations would also make them 'not be able to think on their own', however, might also be interpreted as a concern for the autonomy and dignity of the recipient. This reasoning leads her to the conclusion that her donation should be related to a service. Put in contractual terms, she recognises a duty to give to beggars if the two have agreed on some sort of transaction. If not, she worries about the consequences and chooses not to give anything.[24]

24 Reflecting on how she treats her domestic staff, one of the SCN interviewees in her 40–50s similarly says: 'And to me it is somehow part of the social network. Here there are no social security offices, there is no unemployment benefit, there is nothing, but there is a system where people work, and if you can work… I give for instance… you have to sort out your own thoughts, but I never give money to those who beg. […] But I often give to those who work. Look after the car, clean the car…'.

15.3.2 Alternative approaches

One of the NCA interviewees in her 30–40s, however, articulates a third way with regard to beggars. She first describes the same two categories I have identified above, keeping a distance (not giving to beggars) and empathising (and giving to beggars), and then describes her own way of dealing with this issue. She says:

> [...] I struggle with these questions, as I said, every day. First of all, I live in the city, and that is a choice that I have made because I don't want to live behind walls in an area where I can [...] be spared from seeing the poverty, which is possible, at least to the extent that you avoid getting it too close to your heart and thoughts and all that. And that's a choice I have made, because I want to be confronted with it daily, because I want it to affect me. I want to feel it, that I am rich and incredibly privileged compared to the majority of the world's population. And I should feel it every day, so that it makes me feel that I do what I can every day to change it. But it's hard. Every morning I walk out of my apartment and the street children are there. I live in a street with many street children. I have a close relationship with the boys who live there. I meet them immediately when I walk out the door.

While other interviewees describe their encounters with beggars as interruptions in their everyday lives, this interviewee seems to be actively seeking these encounters. She says: 'I want it to affect me', and to feel 'that I am rich and incredibly privileged'. She also makes it a point not to distance herself from their poverty. Later she says:

> [...] How do I relate to it? I'm not able to answer that in any way other than that I try to relate to it daily, and that I try not to make up my mind about how to relate to it. I don't want to have a specific way of relating to it, because these are individuals. They are individual human beings who I meet, and who are entitled to be regarded as the human beings they are, and that requires that you don't have a specific approach.

A key aspect of this interviewee's reasoning seems to be to protect the dignity of and respect for street children and other beggars. As such, she seems to articulate a call for consistency between policy papers and development work at the macro level and such individual micro level encounters. As several other interviewees she seems to find these encounters problematic, but still wants to prevent herself from becoming too removed from them. This is in some ways similar to other interviewees' reflections on how they want to guard themselves from the pitfalls of development work, striking a balance between keeping a distance and being empathetic.

A number of interviewees seem to be trying out alternative responses to such situations. Several of the interviewees seem to be more concerned about structural issues than on reflecting upon these encounters with individuals. When asked how one should respond to the beggars one meets, one of the NCA interviewees in her 40–50s says:

> […] You can share to some extent, and what you see there and then, then you can alleviate your own pain by giving them a little there and then. But apart from that it's a deficiency in the system, so you have to approach the system.

This interviewee clearly recognises that making donations to beggars is an option she has. She seems, however, to downplay this option, relating it to the donors' psychological well being. Her interest is more in the failure of the system. Thus, this statement seems to represent a macro level response to a micro level challenge.

Reflecting generally on her own wealth and the poverty of others, one of the NCA interviewees in her 30–40s says:

> I don't feel that I have found any good strategy. For the moment my strategy is to save money, have… I don't spend much money here. I don't like in a way to throw (*strø rundt meg med*) money about. I try to give the impression that I am not rich, but I am. Here, sure I am. But, I don't for example give money to street children or beggars or the like. But I can contribute when colleagues come and ask for support for funerals, things like that, but it's a very difficult distinction to make, because it's also not a solution that I come here and open my wallet for all my friends and colleagues. So what I think is that when I come home I want to manage my money in a way I find morally defensible.

Again, this is an interviewee who says she chooses not to give to beggars. Interestingly, however, she indicates that she responds differently if the question about financial assistance is posed by one of her colleagues (meaning local staff). This indicates that the choice not to give to beggars is less related to the nationality of the recipient, but rather to the perceived distance between donor and recipient. Further, she clearly makes herself a representative of a group of development workers who are financially very well off. She does not 'spend much money' and thus has a surplus she chooses to save (not donate). She seems to escape the difficulties involved in these encounters, both with beggars and with colleagues, by postponing the issue until she has returned home and settled. Again, the solution seems to be at the structural level and in this case also in the future.

15.4 Concluding reflections

A recurring aspect of these interviewees' discussions about their private wealth is how they conceptualise this as a difficult dilemma. Acknowledging that they are rich, one key strategy seems to be to downplay their wealth and rather 'live locally' in order to avoid the difficulties of being rich in a context of poverty. Further, the dilemma seems to be tackled by seeking something they can classify as a reasonable standard of living or lifestyle and some combine this with an emphasis either on how gratitude for being wealthy motivates them to work hard, or how a certain standard of living is necessary in order to do their job.

It is, however, a striking feature in several interviews that the interviewees dismiss any reason for them to feel bad or have a bad conscience for being rich (see section 9.5.1). As such it seems that the 'difficult dilemmas' they face are conceptualised primarily as a matter of contrast and distribution (see section 12.2). The difficulties are not (primarily) perceived as a moral duty to change one's status of being rich, or to correct an implicit wrong.

In their interaction with domestic staff the interviewees describe ways of relating to them that in many ways resemble the charity approach they elsewhere dissociate themselves from. Several of them say they pay more than average salaries and they also help out in special circumstances. This can be understood as ad hoc, individual interventions. When challenged to explain this discrepancy, some of them justify it by referring to the relationship as one of respect. In the case of domestic staff members the notion of respect seems to be related to the special relationship that exists between the development workers and their domestic helpers.

However, there is no special relationship between the development workers and the beggars they meet, and several of the interviewees describe these encounters too as 'very difficult'. In this context the issue of not being able to help everyone, is often addressed. Being rich and repeatedly encountering the plight of the poor and the face of the individual beggar, seems to produce both a sense of guilt as well as an aversion to the development workers' own life situation and lifestyle.

As in the previous chapter, this chapter adds another perspective to the moral discourse of NDA by addressing a field that is not explicitly discussed in the policy documents. Although the contrast between the wealth of some and the poverty of others is also the context for the documents, this is explicitly addressed only to a limited extent, and even less in terms of personal wealth and individual encounters with the poor. Further, interpretative repertoires identified in earlier chapters are articulated again here, for example the discourses of distribution and respect. This seems to confirm the key role these play in the moral discourse of NDA.

Part VII

Moral discourse reconsidered

16 Discourse of rights and riches

That we are naturally myopic and conformist enough
to be easily reconciled to the hunger abroad may be fortunate for us,
who can 'recognize ourselves', can lead worthwhile and fulfilling lives
without much thought about the origins of our affluence.
But it is quite unfortunate for the global poor,
whose best hope may be our moral reflection.

Thomas Pogge in *World Poverty and Human Rights* (Pogge 2002:26)

This study has focussed on moral discourse as articulated by staff members of four different Norwegian development aid agencies and by these organisations themselves. These are agencies with different historical roots, organisational structures, and stakeholders. To some extent they also have different partners and target groups, and articulate their value basis in different ways. The analysis has shown, however, that despite these differences there seems to be a widely shared moral discourse of NDA. Human rights is articulated and emphasised as the basis for NDA by all the four agencies studied and is similarly widely highlighted by the interviewees. Further, both in the documents and in the interviews a discourse of responsibility is articulated. A discourse of justice seems to play an important role in some of the documents, and this too is reflected in the interviews, and finally the same is the case for participation. Still, the analysis has also shown how there are different interpretations of the agencies' policy documents among the interviewees and some interviewees question how these policies (or parts of them) should be understood (see chapter 7).

In other words, there is both continuity and discontinuity between the discourses articulated in the policy documents and in the statements made by the interviewees. This can partly be explained by the fact that they constitute two distinct sources of material for this study, though they are not entirely unrelated (see section 1.3.3). The policy documents are principled and forward looking, while the interviewees' reflections are in the context of their work 'in the field'. The interactive character of the interviews also makes it possible to explore issues in more depth, for example issues that are only briefly or not at all elaborated on in the policy documents. This will account for some of the differences and points to how the interviews constitute material which supplements the policy documents. The analysis has shown how although the interviewees refer to, and thus relate to, the policy documents of their own agencies (and other organisastions), they also criticise and (re)interpret these. The discursive similarities between the documents and the interviews, however, are striking, as indicated by the shared discourse of human rights, responsibility, justice, and recipient participation.

Further, embassy interviewees stress the moral motivation and commitment of their MFA colleagues, features often ascribed to NGO staff (see section 6.2), and several of the NCA interviewees emphasise the universal scope of the organisation's work and downplay the uniqueness of NCA's religious value basis (see section 7.2). There is also a close relationship between all of the agencies, including between MFA and the NGOs, and this cooperation is highly valued by many of the interviewees (see chapter 8). Thus not only is there a shared discourse, but differences between the agencies seem also to be widely downplayed by the interviewees. Viewpoints and perceptions articulated by interviewees from one organisation are often also articulated by interviewees from other organisations.

On several occasions a demarcation against the development aid of other countries has also been noted. Self-interest seems to be regarded as playing a smaller role in NDA compared to the development aid efforts of other countries (see section 9.4). Similarly, several of the interviewees seem to argue that Norway is largely exempt from any historical guilt (see sections 12.3.1 and 12.3.2) and there is also a notion that Norwegians treat their domestic staff better than many others (see section 15.2). Thus, there seems to be a vague, but still noteworthy, shared self-understanding among the interviewees that relies on a construction of Norway and Norwegians as different from, and in part qualitatively better than, other countries or nationals (see section 3.3.1).

As noted in chapter 5, however, several of the interviewees articulate an ambiguous attitude to the aid worker label. This reveals discursive negotiations not similarly articulated in the agencies' policy documents. Although most of the interviewees acknowledge that others probably would categorise them as aid workers (*bistandsarbeidere*), they vary as to whether they would use this term themselves. Some, including some of the embassy interviewees, see this as an unproblematic label and would use it to describe themselves. Others, however, are more reluctant and avoid using the aid worker label. The ambiguity seems to relate especially to the notion of being an aid or helper. Although many of them say they are motivated by idealism, reacting against what they see as injustice (see chapter 6 and section 12.1), and although many seem satisfied with their working context (see section 5.2.4 and chapter 7), the notion of helping seems to be regarded as difficult. A preferred term for many of them seems to be development worker (see section 5.1), partner (see section 13.1), or facilitator (see section 14.2.4).

A similar ambiguity seems to be expressed when the issue of representation is raised (see sections 5.2.2 and 8.2). On the one hand the interviewees seem to identify with the poor or the recipients of NDA and are committed to working for their benefit (see section 6.2). On the other hand several see themselves as representatives of Norway or Norwegians and acknowledge their own position as privileged and fortunate (see section 15.1). Thus they see themselves in a position where they relate to rich and poor, the fortunate and the struggling poor. It is in this context that they articulate the moral discourse of NDA, just as the inequality between rich and poor is the implied context for the policy documents as well.

In this final chapter I will firstly address the key representations in the moral discourse of NDA identified in the preceding analysis. Secondly, I will discuss implicit interpretations in this discourse, and in the third section I will conclude this study by highlighting what I find to be characteristics of the moral discourse of NDA.

16.1 Dominant discourses

The analysis of the policy documents identified human rights, responsibility, justice, and recipient participation as dominant discourses in the moral discourse of NDA. In this section I will discuss how these key representations seem to be interpreted by the interviewees and thus explicate the role they play in the moral discourse of NDA.

16.1.1 *Human rights and charity*

The emphasis on human rights corresponds to contemporary trends in international politics. Francesca Klug notes how 'the post-Cold War search for new ideals and common bonds in an era of failed ideologies appears to have contributed to a growing appreciation of human rights as a set of values' (Klug 2000:147). Sarah Owen Vandersluis and Paris Yeros point out that the 'global pervasiveness of the language of rights is now irrefutable' (Vandersluis and Yeros 2000:13). However, even an omnipresent language of human rights does not imply that it has become a moral 'Esperanto' (Stout 2001:5). It is still necessary to ask how this language is used and interpreted in a given context.

As noted in the analysis, the Universal Declaration of Human Rights (UDHR) seems to play an important role both in the policy documents and when the interviewees explain their understanding of human rights, although UN conventions are also referred to. This is consistent with the close relationship between development and human rights that many scholars have pointed out. Birgitte I. Hamm contends, for example, that: 'The fact that development and social progress are indispensable for the realization of human rights is already put down in Article 28 of the Universal Declaration of Human Rights from 1948' (Hamm 2001:1008).[1] More explicitly, however, human rights and development are linked closely together in the Declaration of the Right to Development from 1986, which speaks of a human right to development and calls for international cooperation. Article 4 in this declaration reads: 'States have the duty to take steps, individually and collectively, to formulate international development policies with a view to facilitating the full realization of the right to development'.[2]

In line with the agencies' policy documents, most of the interviewees express their approval of adopting a human rights based approach in development aid (see section 10.1). At the same time, however, several seem to have only a vague notion of human rights and what a human rights based approach in development aid implies. In particular,

1 Article 28 reads: 'Everyone is entitled to a social and international order in which the rights and freedoms set forth in this declaration can be fully realized' (<www.unhchr.ch/udhr/lang/eng.pdf>, accessed 20.03.07).

2 This declaration is available at <www.ohchr.org/english/law/pdf/rtd.pdf> (accessed 20.03.07).

the meaning of human rights based aid and the practical and moral implications thereof, seem to be unclear to some of the interviewees. Thus, though the concept of human rights is widely acclaimed, the implications of adopting a rights based approach in development aid remains unclear. Accordingly, the concept of human rights seems to function as an empty signifier with multiple meanings ascribed to it, though with seemingly considerable mobilising power.

Still, when the interpretation of human rights and the human rights approach is articulated, many interviewees emphasise the equal value and rights of all human beings. In other words, they emphasise universality. Similarly, some of them stress the duty to reach as many people as possible. In such cases the human rights discourse seems to imply an understanding of rights that justifies comprehensive development policies and this provides a strong argument for the rich to provide development aid to the benefit of the poor.

Two other factors also seem to carry special importance in the interpretation of human rights. It seems to be part of the human rights discourse that development aid efforts are firstly not to be understood as a matter of the good will of the donor, and secondly, that the recipients should not be humiliated or feel they should be grateful. This becomes especially clear when rights based aid is contrasted with charity (see section 11.1). Charity, and related terms like compassion, kindness, and goodness, is widely rejected as a tool for understanding development aid. Charity is regarded as a selective and random approach. It helps alleviate poverty in the short-term, but not in the long-term. It is an approach to development aid that focuses on the individual recipients and ad hoc assistance associated with relief efforts (see section 9.2). Further, the charity approach is characterised by its stronger focus on the donor and his or her needs than on the rights of the poor, and is associated with a dismissal of responsibility. Charitable giving confirms the poverty of the poor and the wealth and goodness of the rich. Thus, both the political issue of changing this relationship and the question of any possible rights the poor might have are not really discussed. The human rights discourse, on the other hand, highlights the rights of the recipient of development aid and qualifies aid as an Other-oriented enterprise.

The analysis has also shown that while the concept of charity seems to be used and understood by the interviewees in a way that is similar to its use in most of the policy documents, this is only partly so in the case of compassion and solidarity. While NCA highlights compassion as one of five values guiding its work, this concept is largely dismissed by the interviewees, including some of the NCA interviewees. Similarly, while NPA makes solidarity a key term in its policy document, this appears to be only a peripheral concept in the interviewees' discourse on NDA (see chapter 11).

Several interviewees describe ways of relating to their domestic staff and colleagues, however, that resemble the charity approach they elsewhere dissociate themselves from (see chapter 15). Several of them say they pay their domestic staff more than average salaries, and they also help out in special circumstances, as ad hoc, individual interventions. In their encounters with beggars some try to treat everyone as equals, meaning not giving special treatment to specific, individual beggars, whilst others chose to give something to some beggars (and nothing to others). In the latter case, a key element of the charity approach is retained. Further, the role of feelings seems to be acknowledged in the more personal or private contexts and it seems that charity or compassion are admitted a (limited) role in such spheres.

16.1.2 Responsibilities and duties

Jeremy Bentham claims that 'a declaration of rights would be but a lop-sided job without a declaration of duties' (Bentham, cited in O'Neill 1986:120). Rights where there are no corresponding duties are only manifesto rights (Pogge 1992:246).[3]

The UDHR states that individual human beings have universal rights, but it is addressed to nation-states and governments. Thus, the UDHR makes nation-states and their governments the primary agents of justice 'with capacities to determine how principles of justice are to be institutionalised within a certain domain' (O'Neill 2001:181). Accor-

3 Robert Nozick and others dismiss, however, the relevance of positive rights and acknowledge only negative rights (Nozick 1974). Having negative rights means that there are duties only to refrain from interfering in other peoples life, not limiting their freedom (negative duties), but no duty to intervene with support to ensure for example economic or social rights (positive duties). Ronald Dworkin (Dworkin 1977) and Henry Shue (Shue 1980) have rejected this minimalist interpretation of human rights.

dingly, as the various states have duties towards their own citizens, the declaration seems to presuppose a global division of labour. However, in cases when states 'fail as primary agents of justice' (O'Neill 2001:182), it becomes relevant to ask whether universal rights also corresponds to universal duties, in other words, whether there are other duty-bearers, in addition to states, to act as secondary agents of justice.

Many human rights scholars argue that a rights based approach to development aid must affirm the positive rights of the individual and corresponding positive duties. Arjun Sengupta writes:

> One of the benefits of using a human rights approach to development is that it focuses attention on those who lag behind others in enjoying their rights, and requires that positive action be taken on their behalf. (Sengupta 2000:561)

As mentioned, the analysis has shown that the human rights discourse is frequently used in the policy documents and widely acclaimed by the interviewees. However, it is the concept of responsibility, and not duty, that seems to play the corresponding central role (despite the emphasis the notion of duty-bearers is given in NCA's policy documents, see section 4.2). That Norway and Norwegians have a responsibility to contribute in the field of development aid is articulated by many of the interviewed development workers (see section 10.2) and seems often to be derived from the country's relative wealth and corresponding ability to share of its resources (see sections 4.1 and 12.2). The implications of this responsibility are far from uniform, however, and its meaning often left undefined.

To some, responsibility indicates a kind of duty of the Norwegian government that goes beyond national borders and Norwegian citizens, undermining the role of the state (see sections 10.2). This seems to correspond to, for example, Peter Singer's dismissal of making borders the horizon for moral deliberation (Singer 1996 [1972]:28–29). To Singer, distance, cooperation, nationality, ethnicity, family ties, etc. bear no moral significance in respect to the obligation to provide humanitarian aid.[4] The obligation remains the same nationally and internationally.

4 Singer writes in direct response to the devastating situation in East Bengal in 1971, and it is evident that he has life threatening emergency situations in mind. However, the moral relevance of international borders becomes an issue also in the case of chronic poverty and life protecting development aid.

With this interpretation, the rights language weakens or dismisses the role of the state and thus challenges the structure of international society as it is today.

However, when asked to comment on the responsibilities Norway and Norwegians have for those they share nationality with, compared to the responsibility they might have for those living in poverty in the South, several of the interviewees emphasise the primary responsibility one has for one's own.[5] This corresponds to the notion that the special responsibility a government has towards to its own citizens is a constitutive element of being a sovereign nation-state and limits the moral obligation of a given government.

Further, many of the interviewees find it difficult to comment on how strong the duty to provide aid should be, and a striking feature in some of the interviews is a reluctance to make clear statements on the demanding character of this duty. Pragmatic considerations seem to play an important role in the understanding of the duty to provide development aid (see sections 10.2 and 12.3). This element of pragmatism contrasts with the principled and programmatic statements relying on the notion of universal human rights in the policy documents, as well as with the emphasis put on the donors as duty-bearers by NCA. In fact, several voices in this material express an understanding of this responsibility that corresponds to the kind of voluntary, supererogatory action often associated with the charity approach markedly dismissed in the policy documents.

It is, however, not necessary to make a clear-cut distinction between duties and supererogatory actions. As pointed out by Nigel Dower: '[…] appeals to kindness, charity or compassion, can all be seen as ways of stating an important duty' (Dower 1991:274). Similarly, Onora O'Neill speaks of an obligation of charity. She writes:

> Traditional religious views of charity saw it as a matter of obligation. Obligations of charity were not 'perfect' obligations, to which rights correspond; yet they were considered real, if 'imperfect' obligations. In the Western religious tradition, there was no suggestion that 'imperfect' obligations were optional. These were called imperfect only to indicate that they were incomplete. (O'Neill 1988:72)

5 In an article from 1988 Robert E. Goodin phrased the question in this way: 'What is so special about our fellow countrymen?' (Goodin 1988).

While the perfect duties refer to duties that must always be fully fulfilled, the imperfect duty is a duty that remains unspecified in terms of the who, when, and how.[6] Thus, an imperfect duty to be charitable is not inconceivable. The moral demand would then not be the utilitarian conclusion of a duty to share until 'the point of marginal utility' (Singer 1996 [1972]:30). The agent is not acting as the heroic saint when assisting the poor; she is fulfilling her duty to do good. Charity, so understood, need not disregard a realistic analysis of the situation or of the effects or unintended consequences of the intervention made. In this sense, charity based assistance too can be planned, targeted, and result oriented.

However, whilst responsibility to provide development aid is widely acknowledged in the moral discourse of NDA, the duty to assist is not. In effect, the argumentative power of the rights language is considerably weakened. As the moral discourse of NDA downplays the duties that might correspond to human rights, the discourse leaves open the extent to which a rights based approach should lead to such actions.

Further, the moral reflection of these interviewees is marked by an emphasis on individual freedom, combined with the idea that the state takes the burden of providing development aid (see section 10.2.2). Several of the interviewees seem more inclined to express that the state, rather than the individual, has a duty to provide aid. The implicit assumption seems to be that while you cannot force people to donate money individually, ODA is approved of. Consequently, the coercion involved when a government collects taxes and transfers some of these to development programmes abroad is not questioned. A notion of the state as inherently good seems to be assumed, in particular with regard to the Norwegian state. Thus, it seems there is an idealistic understanding of the state implicit in the moral discourse.

16.1.3 Justice as distribution

Another concept that plays an important role in the moral discourse of NDA is justice. In *Fighting Poverty Together*, justice is introduced as a

6 One application of such an approach could be to regard humanitarian aid as a perfect duty we all have towards everyone. In life threatening situations, the friend and stranger distinction is irrelevant (see section 3.1). In situations that call for life protection and improvement, this is not so.

corollary of viewing development policy as human rights based, and it is made a key concept in NCA's policy documents too. It is also a preferred term when the interviewees articulate their understanding of development aid. However, the interviewees generally understand justice as distributive rather than rectificatory (see chapter 12). Similarly, the concept of solidarity also seems to be interpreted in distributive terms (see section 11.3.1).

This is not to say that issues of guilt or wrongdoing are excluded from the discourse. Several interviewees raise the issue of bad conscience (see section 9.5.1). Some explicitly reject that Norwegian development has, or should have, anything to do with a bad conscience, and others ridicule NDA by claiming that this is precisely what it is all about. However, in both cases the interviewees invest discursively in dissociating from this notion. Several of the interviewees dismiss any reason for them to feel bad about being rich (see section 15.1). As such, it seems that any 'difficult dilemmas' they face being rich in a poor country are conceptualised primarily as a matter of contrast and distribution. The difficulties are not perceived as a moral duty to change one's status or to correct an implicit wrong. On the other hand, being rich and repeatedly encountering the plight of the poor and the face of the individual beggar seem to produce both a sense of guilt or bad conscience as well as an aversion to the development workers' own life situation among some of the interviewees (see section 15.3).

As the distributive interpretation of justice disregards the duty to compensate for harm done, it downplays the causal relationship between Norwegian wealth and others' poverty, and the moral discourse of NDA becomes primarily forward looking. By emphasising distribution, NDA seems to be primarily regarded as a response to present and future needs (see section 12.2).

16.1.4 Participation

Development aid involves two parties and a transfer of resources from one of these parties, the donor, to the other, the recipient. A key feature in the policy documents discussed here, however, is the involvement and participation of the recipient in shaping and implementing NDA. A similar emphasis has also been noted in several of the interviews. When the development worker role is construed as being one of a facilitator, this seems to reflect a focus on the role of the recipient and an understanding of development as an immanent process (see section 14.2.4). Similarly, the emphasis on recipient responsibility (see section 10.2.6), respecting partners and treating them as equals (see section 13.1.3), and strengthening the capacity of the recipient (see sections 5.3, 9.3.1, and 13.1.1) seems to point in the same direction.

Other aspects of the discourse seem, however, to point in a somewhat different direction. While recipient participation is one of the main interpretative repertoires in the policy documents, the interviewees' reflections on their roles and functions indicate how donor representation, and thus donor participation, clearly also is part of the moral discourse of NDA (see chapter 5). Further, the competence and the qualifications of the development worker are emphasised by several of the interviewees (see sections 14.1 and 14.2). This indicates a notion of the donor being the holder of some kind of knowledge the recipient does not have, but which, according to the donor, he or she might benefit from. Similarly, the necessity and importance of having certain conditionalities attached to NDA is addressed by most of the interviewees and widely approved of. These conditionalities seem to be justified by referring to Norwegian and/or Western values that the donor regards as universal and thus shared by both the donor and the recipient (see section 13.2). It is, however, the donor who is in the 'driving seat' in terms of defining these conditionalities. Accordingly, the discourse of participation is combined with a discourse of control and conditionalities.

16.2 Implicit interpretations

While human rights, responsibility, justice, and recipient participation are key representations of dominant discourses in the moral discourse of NDA, there are also other repertoires that seem to be frequently in use, and which thus also constitute characteristics of the general discourse. In this section these will be discussed under the headings: Respect, Authenticity, Contractarianism, Political harmony, and Micro and macro.

16.2.1 Respect

In the interviewees' reflections on their own professional role, there seems as mentioned to be an ambiguity articulated when they discuss which title they prefer (see section 5.1). This ambiguity reveals ongoing discursive negotiations regarding the meaning ascribed to development aid and the interviews thus reveal aspects of the moral discourse of NDA that are not explicitly articulated in the policy documents. One of the reasons the interviewees dismiss the aid worker label seems to be that they regard it as having an implicit lack of respect for the recipient.

Further, the interviewees are all employed as representatives of donor agencies and there is an important strand within the discourse that indicates a primary identification with the donor. However, there is also a discourse clearly marked by a concern for, and identification with, representatives of the recipients. Generally most interviewees appear to share the assumption that the development worker role is part of a relationship where both sides are present and have legitimate concerns. In other words, development aid is marked by a double accountability. There is accountability to the recipients (and a corresponding focus on their participation) on the one hand, but also accountability to back donors (individuals or governments). Considering this accountability and the partnership approach, several emphasise the importance of treating the recipients with respect (see sections 13.1.3, 13.2.2, and 14.2.4). The relationship to domestic helpers and individual beggars is also described as one where the notion of respect plays an important role (see sections 15.2 and 15.3).

In general the notion of respect seems to be highly valued and to play an important role when the interviewees discursively seek to understand and justify their professional work. This is an interesting addition to the emphasis on recipient participation identified in several of the agencies' policy documents. The challenges and contradictions implied in the notions of partnership and participation are highlighted, for example with reference to conditionalities and the recipients' lack of capacity. The notion of respect seems to be an especially important interpretative repertoire for the interviewees when relating to these challenges. This discourse of respect downplays the socio-economic differences, however, between the two fundamental parties in the development aid relationship (see section 3.1), and as such contributes to reducing the perceived difficulty of being rich. In effect, it downplays material differences and constructs an idealistic notion of togetherness.

16.2.2 Authenticity

A number of the interviewees refer to their past (and present) idealism when they explain their route into development work, while other interviewees seem to want to dissociate from too idealistic motivations. In this there is both continuity and discontinuity with the policy documents. While the policy documents of the aid agencies come across as largely idealistic, the notion of idealism is something the interviewees relate to in different and nuanced ways. Several of the interviewees who mention idealism as one motive for entering the field of development work adjust this notion when they describe their present motivation and self-understanding. Many of the interviewees, however, emphasise the continuity between the initial motivation they had for entering the field of development work and their present motivation (see chapter 6).

Further, some interviewees reflect upon the extent to which other development workers are genuine in the work they do, although they are sceptical about the role of 'good intentions' in development aid (see section 9.5.1). When some of the interviewees ridicule the notion of helping (see section 5.1), relief workers (see section 9.2.2), or Norwegian lifestyle (see section 12.2), this indirectly addresses the same issue of being genuine.

Many interviewees also emphasise the need to be professional as a development worker. Being professional seems to imply having the administrative skill needed to manage funds, understanding the wider picture and the complexities involved in poverty reduction efforts, and being accountable and honest. These values seem to be emphasised to mark a contrast with idealistically driven charity, but also to highlight the need to fulfil a role in a bureaucracy set up to ensure transparency, efficiency, and fairness. The contrast seems to be the naïve development worker, 'lead astray' by her good heart and empathy (see section 14.2). Also on this issue, however, there are divergent views present in the material. Describing 'the good development worker', some interviewees stress the professional competence and expert knowledge of the development worker. On the other hand, some of the interviewees seem to contrast this with a more personal and 'close' way of being a development worker, while others try to integrate them (see section 14.3).

Accordingly, features that are elsewhere widely downplayed or rejected seem here to be highlighted by the interviewees. While the language of human rights and justice dominates the discourse on NDA policies and approaches, not least in the policy documents, concepts such as closeness, empathy, and personal commitment seem to play a much more central role when the interviewees reflect on development worker professionalism. With the search to include empathy, feelings, and having 'a heart' in the understanding of development worker professionalism, and the call for authentic development workers, elements of what is elsewhere described as charity seem to be included in the understanding of how development aid should be perceived and implemented. Thus, aspects of the charity approach that the human rights discourse rejects seem to be implicitly brought back into the moral discourse of NDA. One such aspect seems to be a renewed concern about the personal qualities of the individual development worker.

16.2.3 Contractarianism

Several interviewees and some of the policy documents refer to international conventions when arguing in favour of NDA. The responsibility (or duty) to provide development aid relies on the adoption and recognition of these conventions. Some interviewees argue that the international society implicitly acknowledges some values, for example human rights (see section 10.1). Both of these arguments are contractarian.[7] This discourse of contractarianism, however, contrasts with

7 Contractarian arguments can be used both to support and to reject the duty to provide international aid. On the one hand some argue there is no, or at least not sufficient, cooperation between nation-states (or the rich and poor countries in question), and that accordingly there is no duty for development aid. This argument is based on the idea that moral obligation can only exist where there is interaction between people (Sumberg 1973). On the other hand, if one agrees that we live in a globalised world where we are all interconnected in a common web of ecology, history, commerce, and exchange of ideas, this might establish a sufficient degree of relationship between everyone that makes distance irrelevant. Charles R. Beitz has argued that international relationships constitute a global scheme of social cooperation (Beitz 1979).

the notion of development aid as based on UDHR also emphasised in a number of policy documents and by some of the interviewees. While human rights according to UDHR are based on the notion of an 'inherent dignity' and 'inalienable rights', the corresponding duties are here made dependent on a contract.[8]

The discourse of contractarianism is also implicit in the way some interviewees describe the recipients of development aid. The partnership rhetoric defines the recipients of development aid as partners (see section 13.1). However, being partners, the relationship is fundamentally a contractual one, where both parties are considered free to enter, or not, into a mutual contract (Dahl 2001:14). Further, in a contractual relationship the conditions for entering into a partnership are more easily made explicit. This makes room for demands and expectations, for example regarding good governance, efficiency, and accountability. These are issues which can be explicitly discussed and included in the contractual agreement between the parties.

The partnership discourse therefore allows for conditionalities and, as noted, this is emphasised as necessary and important by several interviewees (see section 13.2). Thus, the contractual character focuses on the donor (not the recipient) and makes the moral discourse of NDA not only Other-oriented, but also markedly defined by the wants and values of the donor.

16.2.4 Political harmony

In line with the call for a comprehensive development aid policy in *Fighting Poverty Together* the interviewees generally seem to regard development aid as a political undertaking, and there is an emphasis on the macro political aspects of poverty. NDA is perceived as something that goes 'hand in hand' with the political (see section 9.3). Several of the NGO interviewees also highlight the political stance their organisations take, for example by taking sides in conflict situations or doing advocacy work (see chapter 7). This corresponds to the agencies emphasis on the same.

8 See the preamble to the UDHR available at <www.unhchr.ch/udhr/lang/eng.pdf> (accessed 20.03.07).

While recipient participation is one of the main interpretative repertoires in the policy documents, the interviewees' reflections on their roles and functions indicate how donor representation, and thus donor participation, is clearly also part of the moral discourse of NDA. Further, not only embassy interviewees, but also several of the NGO interviewees seem to understand their role and work in terms of representing Norway, either as the state or the people living in Norway (see section 5.2.2). In most cases, however, they do not regard being an NGO employee and simultaneously representing Norway as problematic. Although some interviewees question the gains won by channelling funds through NGOs, many of them acknowledge a pragmatic division of labour between Norwegian NGOs and the Norwegian state. For most of the interviewees this relationship seems to be seen as fruitful and complementary, where both the embassies and the NGOs can benefit from a close relationship based on different roles and areas of expertise. Several of the NGO interviewees stress that they see coordination as necessary and important, and that they consider close cooperation between the NGOs and the Norwegian government, represented by the embassies, important too. The issue of cooption is recognised as a potential risk, but seems not to be perceived as a real threat (see chapter 8). The role of the Norwegian state in development is repeatedly emphasised, and often the Norwegian state is regarded as a kind or good partner that shares the same aims as the NGOs or the recipients of development aid.

Further, Norway is widely perceived as a small country without self-interest, and NDA as something that serves common interests (see sections 4.1, 9.4, and 12.1). NDA is perceived to be governed by either 'neutral values' or by universal values that everyone supports or should support (see section 9.5). Through this emphasis the development workers also escape the accusation of taking on an illegitimate role of trusteeship. As their involvement is based on internationally shared values, any accusation of imperialism can (seemingly) be dismissed.

Accordingly, a relatively harmonious understanding of both Norwegian politics and international relations seems to be fundamental in the interviewees' understanding of development aid. This is not to say that they lack awareness of the issue of power and its role in NDA. But the power involved in the asymmetry between the rich and the poor, as well as issues of interest and value conflicts, are downplayed. Thus, again traits of the charity approach are implicitly retained.

16.2.5 Micro and macro

A discourse of development aid criticism is articulated by many of the interviewees (see section 9.6), as well as complaints about the perceived inconsistencies between policy documents on the one hand, and the actual work done on the other (see chapter 7). The lack of results, the way aid money finds it way to wealthy development workers, consultants etc., are issues these interviewees not only are aware of, but also make part of their evaluation of the aid industry they are part of. On the other hand, there is also a discourse that stresses how results are actually achieved. In this discourse, emphasis seems to be on individual cases and the micro level, where results can be more easily identified and presented.

Still, several of the interviewees express their limited expectations regarding what kind of results it is possible to achieve through aid efforts. Several of the interviewees seem to perceive NDA as a 'social programme' that aims at making things 'a little better' (see section 6.2 and 9.1). In this, the limited aim and scope of development aid seems to be emphasised, in contrast to the ambitions and convictions regarding results implicit in the policy documents. There are so many other factors that seem to play a much more important role in creating lasting changes in the living conditions of the many poor in developing countries. Accordingly, the results that can be achieved in the long run are very limited if something is not done at the macro level, through changes in the international trade system or at the level of international politics.

Consequently, development aid is widely seen to function as 'band-aid', without addressing the root causes. Development aid does help, and can show results, but in the long run other efforts are necessary. Again, this understanding of development aid seems to have several of the characteristics associated with the charity approach.

16.3 Conclusion

The analysis has shown how the moral discourse of NDA is dominated by a discourse of human rights. This rights discourse highlights the universal right of the poor to receive development aid, as well as a donor responsibility to provide such assistance. The notion of responsibility is, however, distinguished from a notion of having a duty to provide such aid. The concept of responsibility seems to be understood as a concept implying a weaker notion of obligation than that of duty. Accordingly, while the rights discourse stresses the rights of the recipients of development aid, the duties of the donors seem to be downplayed.

Although the human rights discourse is constructed in opposition to discourses of need and compassion, it is primarily in opposition to the charity discourse. Concepts such as compassion and charity are perceived as old fashioned or irrelevant by some of the interviewees and others say such terms are unfamiliar and have lost their meaning. The concept of charity seems to be rejected in the moral discourse due to its perceived disrespectful, patronising implications, as well as its non-binding character. In addition, charity seems to be rejected for its lack of concern for the actual results achieved in development work. Rather than focussing on intentions or motivation, the moral discourse seems to emphasise end results. Rejected as part of the value basis for NDA, the concept of charity seems to be relegated to the personal and private spheres.

Still, dissatisfaction with this situation and a concern that at least elements of the charity terminology should be retained in the development aid discourse is also expressed. Many of the interviewees emphasise the need for the professional development worker to be genuine and empathetic, though there is also a discourse of control and conditionalities. The key critique of the charity approach is, however, retained, and often expressed through an emphasis on respect for the recipients' views, plans, and priorities.

Further, the rights discourse is combined with a discourse of justice. This term seems, however, to be interpreted primarily in terms of distribution rather than rectification. Accordingly, the notion of sharing one's wealth seems to be emphasised, while any causal link between donor wealth and recipient poverty is rejected. An idealistic and harmonious understanding of politics, interests, and values seems to be implied, and although Norwegian development aid is understood as part of a wider macro political context, its results are primarily perceived to be at the micro level.

Thus, although explicitly rejected, several aspects associated with the concept of charity are implicitly retained in the dominant discourse. By downplaying the duty to provide development aid, as well as by emphasising distributive justice rather than rectificatory justice, the moral discourse of Norwegian development aid weakens its practical implications. The discourse provides an understanding of development aid that leaves the donor with a moral justification of development aid, but with little risk of inconvenient consequences or criticism. Although the activities of for example Norwegian oil companies are questioned by some, in the dominant moral discourse of Norwegian development aid Norwegian wealth seems to be neither challenged nor questioned. Thus, while the dominant moral discourse of Norwegian development aid on the one hand emphasises universal human rights, it on the other hand lends legitimacy to Norwegian wealth.

Primary documents

The Ministry of Foreign Affairs

Kamp mot fattigdom! Regjeringens handlingsplan for bekjempelse av fattigdom i sør mot 2015 [Fighting Poverty. The Norwegian Government's Action Plan for Combating Poverty in the South towards 2015] (Ministry of Foreign Affairs 2002a)

Fighting Poverty. Norway's Action Plan 2015 for Combating Poverty in the South. Executive Summary (Ministry of Foreign Affairs 2002b)

Stortingsmelding nr. 35 (2003–2004). Felles kamp mot fattigdom. En helhetlig utviklingspolitikk [Report No. 35 (2003–2004). Fighting Poverty Together. A Comprehensive Development Policy] (Ministry of Foreign Affairs 2004a)

English summary of Report No. 35 (2003–2004). Fighting Poverty Together. A Comprehensive Development Policy (Ministry of Foreign Affairs 2004b)

Norwegian Church Aid

Norwegian Church Aid's Policy Document Together for a Just World (Norwegian Church Aid 2004)

Norwegian Church Aid's Global strategic plan Together for a Just World Working to Uphold Human Dignity 2005–2009 (Norwegian Church Aid 2005a)

Norwegian Church Aid's 10-Point Political Platform 2005–2009 (Norwegian Church Aid 2005b)

Save the Children Norway

Save the Children Norway's Strategy for 2006–2009 (Save the Children Norway 2005a)[1]

Save the Children Norway's Statutes (Save the Children Norway 2005b)

Norwegian People's Aid

Solidarity. Principles and Value Basis for Norwegian People's Aid (Norwegian People's Aid 2003a)

Policy and Strategy for NPA's International Humanitarian and Development Work 2003–2007 (Norwegian People's Aid 2003b)

1 Save the Children Norway regards its strategy as an internal document and does accordingly not publish it in its entirety. I refer here to the presentation of the strategy available on the organisation's internet site (<www.reddbarna.no>).

Bibliography

Alesina, A. and D. Dollar 2000. 'Who Gives Foreign Aid to Whom and Why?' in *Journal of Economic Growth*, Vol. 5. No. 1, p. 33–63.

Alston, P. and M. Robinson 2005. *Human Rights and Development. Towards Mutual Reinforcement*, Oxford, Oxford University Press.

Alvesson, M. and K. Sköldberg 2000. *Reflexive Methodology. New Vistas for Qualitative Research*, London, SAGE Publications.

Amin, S. 1974. *Accumulation on a World Scale. A Critique of the Theory of Underdevelopment*, New York, Monthly Review Press.

Andersen, N. Å. 1994. *Institutionel historie. En introduktion til diskurs- og institutionsanalyse* [Institutional History. An Introduction to Discourse and Institutional Analysis], København, Center for offentlig organisation og styring.

Anderson, M. B. 1999. *Do No Harm. How Aid Can Support Peace – or War*, Boulder, Colo., Lynne Rienner Publishers.

Apthorpe, R. 1997. Writing Development Policy and Policy Analysis Plain and Clear. On Language, Genre and Power, in C. Shore and S. Wright (ed.) 1997: *Anthropology of Policy. Critical Perspectives on Governance and Power*, London, Routledge.

Arce, A. and N. Long (ed.) 2000. *Anthropology, Development and Modernities. Exploring Discourses, Counter-tendencies and Violence*, London, Routledge.

Aristotle 1980. *The Nicomachean Ethics*, Oxford, Oxford University Press.

Baaz, M. E. 2005. *The Paternalism of Partnership. A Postcolonial Reading of Identity in Development Aid*, London, Zed Books.

Baldwin, D. A. 1993. *Neorealism and Neoliberalism. The Contemporary Debate*, New York, Columbia University Press.

Ball, T. 1988. *Transforming Political Discourse. Political Theory and Critical Conceptual History*, Oxford, Basil Blackwell.

Bayles, M. D. 1981. *Professional Ethics*, Belmont, Calif., Wadsworth Publishing Company.

Beauchamp, T. L. 2001. *Principlism and Its Alleged Competitors*, in J. Harris (ed.) 2001: Bioethics, Oxford, Oxford University Press.

Beitz, C. R. 1979. *Political Theory and International Relations*, Princeton, N.J., Princeton University Press.

Berge, B. M. 2005. *Biafra – da Norge våknet. Elias Berge og Kirkens Nødhjelp* [Biafra – When Norway Woke Up. Elias Berge and Norwegian Church Aid], Oslo, Forlaget Press.

Berger, P. L. and T. Luckmann 1967. *The Social Construction of Reality. A Treatise in the Sociology of Knowledge*, Anchor Books. Garden City, N. Y., Doubleday.

Borchgrevink, A. 2004. 'Images of Norwegian Aid', in *Forum for Development Studies*, Vol. 31. No. 1, p. 161–181.

Bourdieu, P. 1990. *The Logic of Practice*, Oxford, Polity Press.

Brehm, V. M., M. Tanner, L. Padrão and E. Harris-Curtis 2004. *Autonomy or Dependence. Case Studies in North-South NGO Partnerships*, Oxford, Intrac.

Breuning, M. 1995. 'Words and Deeds: Foreign Assistance Rhetoric and Policy Behavior in the Netherlands, Belgium, and the United Kingdom', in *International Studies Quarterly*, Vol. 39. No. 2, p. 235–254.

Breuning, M. and J. T. Ishiyama 2003. 'Donor Characteristics and the Dispersion of Foreign Assistance', in *International Politics*, Vol. 40. No. 2, p. 249–268.

Bucher-Johannessen, B. 1999. 'Den norske modellen. Stat og samfunn hånd i hånd til fremme av Norge [The Norwegian Model. State and Society Standing Together to Promote Norway]', in *Internasjonal politikk*, Vol. 57. No. 2, p. 199–220.

Burr, V. 1995. *An Introduction to Social Constructionism*, London, Routledge.

Burrage, M. and R. Torstendahl (ed.) 1990. *Professions in Theory and History. Rethinking the Study of the Professions*, London, SAGE Publications.

Bøås, M. 2002. *Public Attitudes to Aid in Norway and Japan*, Oslo, Centre for Development and the Environment, University of Oslo.

Calderisi, R. 2006. *The Trouble with Africa. Why Foreign Aid Isn't Working*, 1st. New York, Palgrave Macmillan.

Center for Global Development 2006. *Commitment to Development Index Contry Report: Norway.*

Chadwick, R. F. (ed.) 1994. *Ethics and the Professions*, Aldershot, Avebury.

Chambers, R. 1983. *Rural Development. Putting the Last First*, London, Longman.

Chambers, R. 1993. *Challenging the Professions. Frontiers for Rural Development*, London, Intermediate Techonology Publications.

Chambers, R. 1997. *Whose Reality Counts? Putting the First Last*, London, Intermediate Technology Publications.

Christoplos, I. (ed.) 2000. Human Rights and Aid Practice. Workshop on the Practical and Ethical Implications of Rights-Based Perspectives in *Development Co-operation and Humanitarian Assistance*, Uppsala, Uppsala Universitet.

Cohen, G. A. 2000. *If You're an Egalitarian, How Come You're So Rich?*, Cambridge, Mass., Harvard University Press.

Collier, P. and D. Dollar 2001. *An Assessment of the Effect of Norwegian Development Assistance on Poverty Reduction and Conflict Prevention*, Oslo, Norwegian Ministry of Foreign Affairs.

Cowen, M. P. and R. W. Shenton 1996. *Doctrines of Development*, London, Routledge.

Crewe, E. and E. Harrison 1998. *Whose Development? An Ethnography of Aid*, London, Zed Books.

Crocker, D. A. 1991. 'Insiders and Outsiders in International Development', in *Ethics & International Affairs*, Vol. 5. No. 1, p. 149–173.

Crush, J. (ed.) 1995. *Power of Development*, London, Routledge.

Cumming, G. 2001. *Aid to Africa. French and British Policies from the Cold War to the New Millennium*, Aldershot, Ashgate.

Dahl, G. 2001. *Responsibility and Partnership in Swedish Aid Discourse*, Discussion Paper 9, Uppsala, Nordic Africa Institute.

Dahl, T. 2006. *Redd Barna og skolene – med samme mål. Evaluering av Redd Barnas skolesatsing* [Save the Children Norway and the Schools – With the Same Aim. An Evaluation of Save the Children Norway's School Work], Trondheim, SINTEF.

Dean, H. 1992. 'Poverty Discourse and the Disempowerment of the Poor', in *Critical Social Policy*, Vol. 12. No. 35, p. 79–88.

Degnbol-Martinussen, J. and P. Engberg-Pedersen 2003. *Aid. Understanding International Development Cooperation*, London, Zed Books.

Dichter, T. W. 1999. 'Globalization and Its Effects on NGOs: Efflorescence or a Blurring of Roles and Relevance?' in *Nonprofit and Voluntary Sector Quarterly*, Vol. 28. No. 4, p. 38–58.

Dichter, T. W. 2003. *Despite Good Intentions. Why Development Assistance to the Third World Has Failed*, Boston, University of Massachusetts Press.

Dower, N. 1991. World Poverty, in P. Singer (ed.) 1991: *A Companion to Ethics*, Oxford, Blackwell Reference.

Drag, M. 1995. *Byggherren, drømmeren og vokteren. Forholdet til den andre i norsk bistandsdiskurs 1965–1990* [The Contractor, the Dreamer and the Guardian. The Relationship to the Other in Norwegian Development Aid Discourse 1965–1990], Oslo, Universitetet i Oslo.

Dreyer, J. S. 2004. Theological Normativity: Ideology or Utopia? Reflections on the possible contribution of empirical research, in J. van der Veen and M. Scherer-Rath (ed.) 2004: *Normativity and Empirical Research in Theology*, Leiden, Brill.

Dworkin, R. 1977. *Taking Rights Seriously*, London, Duckworth.

Easterly, W. 2002. 'The Cartel of Good Intentions. The Problem of Bureaucracy in Foreign Aid', in *Policy Reform*, Vol. 5. No. 4, p. 223–250.

Easterly, W. 2006. *The White Man's Burden. Why the West's Efforts to Aid the Rest Have Done So Much Ill and So Little Good*, New York, Penguin Press.

Edland, S. O. 2007. *Religionens rolle i bistand. En kvalitativ studie av et utvalg bistandsarbeidere fra Kirkens Nødhjelp og Norsk Folkehjelp* [The Role of Religion in Development Aid – A Qualitative Study of Selected Development Workers in Norwegian Church Aid and Norwegian People's Aid], Oslo, MF Norwegian School of Theology.

Egeland, J. 1988. *Impotent Superpower – Potent Small State. Potentials and Limitations of Human Rights Objectives in the Foreign Policies of the United States and Norway*, Oslo, Norwegian University Press.

Ehrlich, P. R. 1971. *The Population Bomb, London*, Published in association with Pan Books.

Eidhammer, A. 2005. Malawi. *Eit lite land i Afrika* [Malawi. A Small Country in Africa], Høvik, Kolofon.

Elster, J. 1989. *Nuts and Bolts for the Social Sciences*, Cambridge, Cambridge University Press.

Eriksen, T. H. (ed.) 1989. *Hvor mange hvite elefanter? Kulturdimensjonen i bistandsarbeidet* [How Many White Elephants? The Cultural Dimension in Development Aid Work], Oslo, Ad Notam.

Escobar, A. 1995. *Encountering Development. The Making and Unmaking of the Third World*, Princeton, N.J., Princeton University Press.

Esposito, N. 2001. 'From Meaning to Meaning. The Influence of Translation Techniques on Non-English Focus Group Research', in *Qualitative Health Research*, Vol. 11. No. 4, p. 568–579.

Fairclough, N. 1992. *Discourse and Social Change*, Cambridge, Polity Press.

Fairclough, N. 1995. *Critical Discourse Analysis. The Critical Study of Language*, London, Longman.

Fairclough, N. 2003. *Analysing Discourse. Textual Analysis for Social Research*, London, Routledge.

Ferguson, J. 1990. *The Anti-Politics Machine. 'Development,' Depoliticization, and Bureaucratic Power in Lesotho*, Cambridge, Cambridge University Press.

Flem, A. L. 2001. *Barnerettighetsarbeid i Redd Barna* [Children's Rights Work in Save the Children Norway], Trondheim, Tapir Akademisk Forlag.

Fog, J. 1992. 'Den moralske grund i det kvalitative forskningsinterview [Moral Issues in the Qualitative Research Interview]', in *Nordisk Psykologi*, Vol. 44. No. 3, p. 212–229.

Fowler, A. 2000. 'NGO Futures: Beyond Aid: NGDO Values and the Fourth Position', in *Third World Quarterly*, Vol. 21. No. 4, p. 589–603.

Frank, A. G. 1967. *Capitalism and Underdevelopment in Latin America. Historical Studies of Chile and Brazil*, New York, Monthly Review Press.

Frankena, W. K. 1973. *Ethics*, 2nd ed. Englewood Cliffs, N.J., Prentice Hall.

Freire, P. 1970. *Pedagogy of the Oppressed*, New York, The Seabury Press.

Fretheim, K. 2007. Acclaimed and Undefined – Rights and Responsibilities in the Norwegian Development Aid Discourse, in S. Heuser and H. G. Ulrich (ed.) 2007: *Political Practices and International Order. Proceedings of the Annual Conference of the Societas Ethica*, Oxford 2006, Münster, Lit Verlag.

Furre, B. 1992. *Norsk historie 1905–1990. Vårt hundreår* [Norwegian History 1905–1990. Our Century], Oslo, Samlaget.

Garbo, G. 1993. *Makt og bistand. En ambassadørs møte med norsk bistandspolitikk i Afrika* [Power and Aid. An Ambassador's Encounter with Norwegian Development Aid Policy in Africa], Oslo, Spartacus.

Gasper, D. 2004. *The Ethics of Development*, Edinburgh, Edinburgh University Press Ltd.

Geertz, C. 1973. *The Interpretation of Cultures. Selected Essays*, New York, Basic Books.

Giddens, A. 1993. *New Rules of Sociological Method. A Positive Critique of Interpretative Sociologies*, 2nd ed. Cambridge, Polity Press.

Giddens, A. 1996. 'Affluence, Poverty and the Idea of a Post-Scarcity Society', in *Development and Change*, Vol. 27. No. 2, p. 365–377.

Gillham, B. 2000. *The Research Interview*, London, Continuum.

Gillies, D. 1996. *Between Principle and Practice: Human Rights in North-South Relations*, Montreal, McGill-Queens University Press.

Gilligan, C. 1982. *In a Different Voice. Psychological Theory and Women's Development*, London, Harvard University Press.

Glaser, B. G. and A. L. Strauss 1999. *The Discovery of Grounded Theory. Strategies for Qualitative Research*, New York, Aldine de Gruyter.

Goodin, R. E. 1988. 'What Is So Special about Our Fellow Countrymen?' in *Ethics*, Vol. 98. No. 4, p. 663–686.

Grillo, R. D. and R. L. Stirrat (ed.) 1997. *Discourses of Development. Anthropological Perspectives*, Oxford, Berg.

Groth, A. M. 1995. *Frivillige bistandsorganisasjoner som aktører i norsk utenrikspolitikk: en studie av Kirkens Nødhjelp og Norsk Folkehjelps nødhjelpsarbeide i Sudan* [Voluntary Development Aid Organisations as Actors in Norwegian Foreign Policy. A Study on Norwegian Church Aid and Norwegian People's Aid Relief Work in Sudan], Oslo, Universitetet i Oslo.

Hagelund, A. 1998. *Diskurser om bistand, kunnskap og utvikling. En diskursanalytisk tilnærming til NORADs policy* [Discourses on Aid, Knowledge and Development. A Discourse Analytical Approach to NORAD's Policy], Oslo, Universitetet i Oslo.

Hagelund, A. 1999. 'Den vanskelige makten: NORADs diskurs om mottakeransvar [The Difficult Power: NORAD's Discourse on Recipient Responsibility]', in *Internasjonal politikk*, Vol. 57. No. 2, p. 251–269.

Hamelink, C. J. 1997. *Ethics and Development. On Making Moral Choices in Development Co-operation*, Kampen, Uitgeverij Kok.

Hamm, B. I. 2001. 'A Human Rights Approach to Development', in *Human Rights Quarterly*, Vol. 23. No. 4, p. 1005–1031.

Hancock, G. 1991. *Lords of Poverty*, London, Mandarin.

Hansen, H. and F. Tarp 2000. Aid Effectiveness Disputed, in F. Tarp and P. Hjertholm (ed.) 2000: *Foreign Aid and Development. Lessons Learnt and Directions for the Future*, London, Routledge.

Hardin, G. 1968. 'The Tragedy of the Commons', in *Science*, Vol. 162. No. 3859, p. 1243–1248.

Hattori, T. 2001. 'Reconceptualizing Foreign Aid', in *Review of International Political Economy*, Vol. 8. No. 4, p. 633–660.

Hattori, T. 2003. 'The Moral Politics of Foreign Aid', in *Review of International Studies*, Vol. 29. No. 2, p. 229–247.

Hayter, T. 1981. *The Creation of World Poverty*, London, Pluto Press.

Helland, J. and G. Deresse 2004. *Study of the Impact of the Work of Save the Children Norway in Ethiopia. Building Civil Society*, Oslo, NORAD.

Hertz, J. H. 1964. *Political Realism and Political Idealism. A Study in Theories and Realities*, Chicago, University of Chicago Press.

Hilhorst, D. 2003. *The Real World of NGOs. Discourses, Diversity and Development*, London, Zed Books.

Hjertholm, P. and H. White 2000. Foreign Aid in Historical Perspective, in F. Tarp and P. Hjertholm (ed.) 2000: *Foreign Aid and Development. Lessons Learnt and Directions for the Future*, London, Routledge.

Hodder, I. 2000. The Interpretation of Documents and Material Culture, in N. K. Denzin and Y. S. Lincoln (ed.) 2000: *Handbook of Qualitative Research*, 2nd ed. Thousand Oaks, SAGE Publications.

Hoebink, P. 1999. 'The Humanitarianisation of the Foreign Aid Programme in the Netherlands', in *The European Journal of Development Research*, Vol. 11. No. 1, p. 176–202.

Hoebink, P. and O. Stokke (ed.) 2005. *Perspectives on European Development Co-operation. Policy and Performance of Individual Countries and the EU*, London, Routledge.

Hofsvang, E. 2004a. 'Delte reaksjoner på ny melding [Split Reactions to New Report]', in *Bistandsaktuelt* 04/2004.

Hofsvang, E. 2004b. 'Reform-ivrig og utålmodig minister [Reform-Eager and Impatient Minister]', in *Bistandsaktuelt* 4/2004.

Hulme, D. and M. Edwards 1997. *NGOs, States and Donors. Too Close For Comfort?*, New York, Palgrave in association with Save the Children.

Isaksen, J., I. Samset, F. Pacheco and Norsk Folkehjelp 2006. *Mid-Term Review of the Angola Programme of Norwegian People's Aid*, Bergen, Chr. Michelsen Institute.

Jørgensen, M. W. and L. Phillips 2002. *Discourse Analysis as Theory and Method*, London, SAGE Publications.

Klitgaard, R. 1991. *Tropical Gangsters*, London, I.B.Tauris.

Klug, F. 2000. *Values for a Godless Age. The Story of the UK's New Bill of Rights*, London, Penguin Books.

Knorr-Cetina, K. 1981. *The Manufacture of Knowledge. An Essay on the Constructivist and Contextual Nature of Science*, Oxford, Pergamon.

Knudsen, K. K. 2006. *'Sustainable Capacities': Norwegian People's Aid through 13 Years of Humanitarian Mine Action in Mozambique*, Oslo, Universitetet i Oslo.

Knutsen, T. L. 1997. Norsk utenrikspolitikk som forskningsfelt [Norwegian Foreign Policy As a Field of Research], in T. L. Knutsen, G. M. Sørbø and S. Gjerdåker (ed.) 1997: *Norges utenrikspolitikk*

[Norway's Foreign Policy], 2nd ed. Oslo, Cappelen Akademisk Forlag.

Korten, D. C. 1990. *Getting to the 21st Century. Voluntary Action and the Global Agenda*, West Hartford, Conn., Kumarian Press.

Kristiansen, T. 1994. *Mor Afrika* [Mother Africa], Oslo, Cappelen.

Kvale, S. 1996. *InterViews. An Introduction to Qualitative Research Interviewing*, Thousand Oaks, Calif., SAGE Publications.

Laclau, E. and C. Mouffe 1985. *Hegemony & Socialist Strategy. Towards a Radical Democratic Politics*, London, Verso.

Lancaster, C. 2007. *Foreign Aid. Diplomacy, Development, Domestic Politics*, Chicago, The University of Chicago Press.

Liland, F. and K. A. Kjerland 2003. 1989–2002. *På bred front* [1989–2002. On Wide Front], Bergen, Fagbokforlaget.

Lincoln, Y. S. and E. G. Guba 1985. *Naturalistic Inquiry*, Newbury Park, Calif., SAGE Publications.

Linde, E. 1999. *Realistiske idealister. Bistandsarbeidere – virkelighetsutforming og hverdagsforståelse* [Realistic Idealists. Development Workers – Sense of Reality and Everyday Understanding], Oslo, Universitetet i Oslo.

Lindenberg, M. 1999. 'Declining State Capacity, Voluntarism and the Globalization of the Not-for-Profit Sector', in *Nonprofit and Voluntary Sector Quarterly*, Vol. 28. No. 4, p. 147–167.

Liska, G. 1968. *The New Statecraft. Foreign Aid in American Foreign Policy*, Chicago, The University of Chicago Press.

Lister, R. 2004. *Poverty*, Cambridge, Polity.

Lister, S. 2000. 'Power in Partnership? An Analysis of an NGO's Relationship with Its Partners', in *Journal of International Development*, Vol. 12. No. 2, p. 227–239.

Little, D. 2003. *The Paradox of Wealth and Poverty. Mapping the Ethical Dilemmas of Global Development*, Boulder, Colo., Westview Press.

Lofland, J. and L. H. Lofland 1995. *Analyzing Social Settings. A Guide to Qualitative Observation and Analysis*, 3rd. Belmont, Calif., Wadsworth.

Lumsdaine, D. H. 1993. *Moral Vision in International Politics. The Foreign Aid Regime, 1949–1989*, Princeton, N.J., Princeton University Press.

Lundestad, G. 1999. 'Lange linjer i norsk utenrikspolitikk [Trends in Norwegian Foreign Policy]', in *Internasjonal politikk*, Vol. 57. No. 2, p. 271–293.

Lyshagen, G. 1989. *50 år i krig og fred. Norsk Folkehjelp 1939–89* [50 Years in War and Peace. Norwegian People's Aid 1939–89], Oslo, Norsk Folkehjelp.

Marcussen, H. S. 1996. Comparative Advantages of NGOs: Myths and Realities, in O. Stokke (ed.) 1996: *Foreign Aid Towards the Year 2000: Experiences and Challenges*, London, Frank Cass.

Mason, J. 2002. *Qualitative Researching*, London, SAGE Publications.

Mathismoen, O. 2004. 'Gir mer, skjerper kravene til ulandene [Gives More, Intensifies the Conditionalities to Developing Countries]', in *Aftenposten* 30.04.2004.

Matlary, J. H. 2002. *Verdidiplomati – kilde til makt? En strategisk analyse av norsk utenrikspolitikk* [Value Diplomacy – A Source of Power? A Strategic Analysis of Norwegian Foreign Policy], Oslo, Makt- og demokratiutredningen 1998–2003.

Mauss, M. 2002. *The Gift. The Form and Reason for Exchange in Archaic Societies*, London, Routledge.

McNeill, D. 2004. Koherens, fattigdomsbekjempelse og milleniumsmål: overordnet perspektiv på meldingen [Coherence, the Fight Against Poverty and Millennium Development Goals: A General Perspective on the Report], in A. Borchgrevink and K. F. Hansen (ed.) 2004: *Felles kamp mot fattigdom? Kritiske blikk på regjeringens utviklingsmelding* [Fighting Poverty Together? Critical Perspectives on the Government's Development Report], Oslo, Norsk Utenrikspolitisk Institutt, NUPI Rapport nr. 281.

Melandsør, K. G. 2002. *Ny retorikk – ny virkelighet? en analyse av bistandsrelasjonen slik den framstilles i NORADs strategier* [New Rhetoric – New Reality? An Analysis of the Aid Relation as Presented in NORAD's Strategies], Oslo, Universitetet i Oslo.

Miles, M. B. and A. M. Huberman 1994. *Qualitative Data Analysis. An Expanded Sourcebook*, 2nd ed. Thousand Oaks, Calif., SAGE Publications.

Mills, S. 2004. *Discourse*, London, Routledge.

Ministry of Foreign Affairs 2002a. *Kamp mot fattigdom! Regjeringens handlingsplan for bekjempelse av fattigdom i sør mot 2015* [Fighting Poverty. The Government's Action Plan for Combating Poverty in the South Towards 2015].

Ministry of Foreign Affairs 2002b. *Fighting Poverty. Norway's Action Plan 2015 for Combating Poverty in the South. Executive Summary.*

Ministry of Foreign Affairs 2004a. *Stortingsmelding nr. 35 (2003–2004). Felles kamp mot fattigdom. En helhetlig utviklingspolitikk* [Report to the Storting No. 35 (2003–2004). Fighting Poverty Together. A Comprehensive Development Policy].

Ministry of Foreign Affairs 2004b. *Report No. 35 to the Storting (2003–2004) – Summary. Fighting Poverty Together. A Comprehensive Development Policy.*

Mishler, E. G. 1986. *Research Interviewing. Context and Narrative*, Cambridge, Mass., Harvard University Press.

Morgenthau, H. J. and K. W. Thompson 1993. *Politics Among Nations. The Struggle for Power and Peace*, Brief. New York, McGraw-Hill.

National Assembly of France 2001. French Declaration of the Rights of Man and of the Citizen, in P. Hayden (ed.) 2001: *The Philosophy of Human Rights*, St. Paul, Paragon House.

Nederveen Pieterse, J. 2001. *Development Theory. Deconstructions/ Reconstructions*, New Dehli, Vistaar Publications.

Nel, P. 1998. 'Idealism Resurgent (and what realists should do about it): Ideas and Foreign Aid', in *The South African Journal of International Affairs*, Vol. 5. No. 2, p. 96–112.

Neumann, I. B. 1999. 'Norsk sørpolitikk. Den disaggregerte stats diplomati [Norwegian South Policy. The Diplomacy of the Disaggregated State]', in *Internasjonal politikk*, Vol. 57. No. 2, p. 181–197.

Neumann, I. B. 2001. *Mening, materialitet, makt. En innføring i diskursanalyse*, Bergen, Fagbokforlaget.

Norwegian Church Aid 2004. *Together for a Just World. Norwegian Church Aid's Policy Document.*

Norwegian Church Aid 2005a. *Together for a Just World. Working to Uphold Human Dignity 2005–2009.*

Norwegian Church Aid 2005b. *Norwegian Church Aid's 10-Point Political Platform.*

Norwegian People's Aid 2003a. *Solidarity. Principles and Value Basis for Norwegian People's Aid.*

Norwegian People's Aid 2003b. *Policy and Strategy for NPA's International Humanitarian and Development Work 2003–2007.*

Nozick, R. 1974. *Anarchy, State, and Utopia*, Oxford, Blackwell.

Nussbaum, M. C. 2000a. *Women and Human Development. The Capabilities Approach*, Cambridge, Cambridge University Press.

Nussbaum, M. C. 2000b. Why Practice Needs Ethical Theory: Particularism, Principle, and Bad Behaviour, in S. J. Burton (ed.) 2000b: *The Path of Law and Its Influence. The Legacy of Oliver Wendell Holmes, Jr.*, Cambridge, Cambridge University Press.

Nustad, K. G. 2003. *Gavens makt. Norsk utviklingshjelp som formynderskap* [The Power of the Gift. Norwegian Development Aid as Trusteeship], Oslo, Pax Forlag.

O'Neill, O. 1986. *Faces of Hunger. An Essay on Poverty, Justice and Development*, London, Allen & Unwin.

O'Neill, O. 1988. Hunger, Needs, and Rights, in S. Luper-Foy (ed.) 1988: *Problems of International Justice*, Boulder, Westview Press.

O'Neill, O. 2001. 'Agents of Justice', in *Metaphilosophy*, Vol. 32. No. 1–2, p. 180–195.

OECD 2006. *Final ODA Data for 2005.*

Olsen, G. R. 2001. 'European Public Opinion and Aid to Africa: Is There a Link?' in *Journal of Modern African Studies*, Vol. 39. No. 4, p. 645–674.

Omoruyi, L. O. 2001. *Contending Theories on Development Aid. Post-Cold War Evidence from Africa*, Aldershot, Ashgate.

Opeskin, B. R. 1996. 'The Moral Foundations of Foreign Aid', in *World Development*, Vol. 24. No. 1, p. 21–44.

Otter, M. 2003. 'Domestic Public Support for Foreign Aid. Does It Matter?' in *Third World Quarterly*, Vol. 24. No. 1, p. 115–125.

Owens, E. and R. Shaw 1972. *Development Reconsidered. Bridging the Gap between Government and People*, Lexington, Mass., Lexington Books.

Patton, M. Q. 2002. *Qualitative Research & Evaluation Methods*, 3rd. Thousand Oaks, California, SAGE Publications.

Pearce, J. 2000. Development, NGOs, and Civil Society: the Debate and Its Future, in D. Eade (ed.) 2000: *Development, NGOs, and Civil Society*, Oxford, Oxfam GB.

Pharo, H. 2003. 'Altruism, Security and the Impact of Oil: Norway's Foreign Economic Assistance Policy, 1958–1971', in *Contemporary European History*, Vol. 12. No. 4, p. 527–546.

Pogge, T. 1992. 'O'Neill on Rights and Duties', in *Grazer Philosphische Studien*, Vol. 43. No. -, p. 233–247.

Pogge, T. W. 2002. *World Poverty and Human Rights. Cosmopolitan Responsibilities and Reforms*, Cambridge, Polity.

Potter, J. and M. Wetherell 1987. *Discourse and Social Psychology. Beyond Attitudes and Behaviour*, London, SAGE Publications.

Rahnema, M. and V. Bawtree (ed.) 1997. *The Post-Development Reader*, London, Zed Books.

Riddell, R. C. 1987. *Foreign Aid Reconsidered*, London, James Currey.

Riste, O. 2001. *Norway's Foreign Relations – A History*, Oslo, Universitetsforlaget.

Robson, C. 2002. *Real World Research. A Resource for Social Scientists and Practitioner-Researchers*, 2nd ed. Oxford, Blackwell.

Rostow, W. W. 1960. *The Stages of Economic Growth. A Non-Communist Manifesto*, Cambridge, University Press.

Rubin, H. J. and I. Rubin 2005. *Qualitative Interviewing. The Art of Hearing Data*, 2nd ed. Thousand Oaks, Calif., SAGE Publications.

Rugumamu, S. 1997. *Lethal Aid. The Illusion of Socialism and Self-Reliance in Tanzania*, Trenton, N.J., Africa World Press.

Rustad, U. 2005. *På drømmedagen står vi opp klokka fire om morgenen. Stemmer og historier fra Afghanistan* [On the Day of Dreams We Get Up at Four in the Morning. Voices and Stories from Afghanistan], Oslo, Oktober.

Ruud, A. E. and K. A. Kjerland 2003. *1975–1989: vekst, velvilje og utfordringer* [1975–1989: Growth, Benevolence and Challenges], Bergen, Fagbokforlaget.

Ryen, R. 2005. *Mottakerdeltakelse. En studie av to norske bistandsorganisasjoners erfaringer og refleksjoner over dilemmaer knyttet til mottakerdeltakelse* [Recipient Participation. A Study on Two Norwegian Development Aid Organisations' Experiences and Reflections on Dilemmas of Recipient Participation], Oslo, Universitetet i Oslo.

Sachs, J. D. 2005. *The End of Poverty. Economic Possibilities for Our Time*, New York, Penguin Press.

Sachs, W. (ed.) 1992. *The Development Dictionary. A Guide to Knowledge as Power*, London, Zed Books.

Sahlins, M. 2004. *Stone Age Economics*, London, Routledge.

Sano, H.-O. 2000. 'Development and Human Rights: The Necessary, but Partial Integration of Human Rights and Development', in *Human Rights Quarterly*, Vol. 22. No. 3, p. 734–752.

Save the Children Norway 2005a. *Redd Barnas strategi 2006–2009* [Save the Children Norway's Strategy 2006–2009].

Save the Children Norway 2005b. *Statutter* [Statutes].

Schmidt, U. 2006. *Metoder i etikkforskningen – utfordringer og muligheter*, in Å. Slettebø and P. Nortvedt (ed.) 2006: Etikk for helsefagene, Oslo, Gyldendal.

Schraeder, P. J., S. W. Hook and B. Taylor 1998. 'Clarifying the Foreign Aid Puzzle: A Comparison of American, Japanese, French and Swedish Aid Flows', in *World Politics*, Vol. 50. No. 2, p. 294–323.

Schön, D. A. 1983. *The Reflective Practitioner. How Professionals Think In Action*, New York, Basic Books, Inc., Publishers.

Seale, C. 1999. *The Quality of Qualitative Research*, London, SAGE Publications.

Selbervik, H. B. 2003a. *Power of the Purse? Norway as a Donor in the Conditionality Epoch 1980–2000*, Bergen, University of Bergen.

Selbervik, H. B. 2003b. *Mottakeransvar: Et særnorsk, verneverdig prinsipp?* [Recipient Responsibility: A Distinctively Norwegian Principle Worth Preserving?], Bergen, Christian Michelsens Institutt.

Sen, A. 1999. *Development as Freedom*, New York, Knopf.

Sengupta, A. 2000. 'Realizing the Right to Development', in *Development and Change*, Vol. 31. No. 3, p. 553–578.

Shalendra, S. 2005. 'The War Against Poverty. The Encouraging Truth about Foreign Aid', in *Challenge*, Vol. 48. No. 4, p. 11–25.

Shanmugaratnam, N. 2003. *NPA's Southern Sudan Programme. An Assessment with Reference to the Current and Future Institutional Cooperation with Noragric*, Ås, Noragric.

Shue, H. 1980. *Basic Rights: Subsistence, Affluence, and U.S. Foreign Policy*, Princeton, N.J., Princeton University Press.

Silverman, D. 2000. Analyzing Talk and Text, in N. K. Denzin and S. Lindholm (ed.) 2000: *Handbook of Qualitative Research*, 2nd ed. Thousand Oaks, SAGE Publications.

Simensen, J. 2003. *1952–1975: Norge møter den tredje verden* [1952–1975: Norway Meets the Third World], Bergen, Fagbokforlaget.

Singer, P. 1996 [1972]. Famine, Affluence, and Morality, in W. Aiken and H. LaFollette (ed.) 1996 [1972]: *World Hunger and Morality*, 2nd ed. Upper Saddle River, N.J., Prentice Hall.

Slim, H. 2000. 'Dissolving the Difference Between Humanitarianism and Development: The Mixing of a Rights-Based Solution', in *Development in Practice*, Vol. 10. No. 3 & 4, p. 491–494.

Sogge, D. 2002. *Give and Take. What's the Matter with Foreign Aid?*, London, Zed Books.

Stjernø, S. 2005. *Solidarity in Europe. The History of an Idea*, Cambridge, Cambridge University Press.

Stokke, O. 2005. Norwegian Aid Policy: Continuity and Change in the 1990s and Beyond, in P. Hoebink and O. Stokke (ed.) 2005: *Perspectives on European Development Co-operation. Policy and Performance of Individual Donor Countries and the EU*, London, Routledge.

Stout, J. 2001. Ethics After Babel. *The Languages of Morals and Their Discontents*, Princeton, Princeton University Press.

Streeten, P. and S. J. Burki 1981. *First Things First. Meeting Basic Human Needs in the Developing Countries*, Oxford, Oxford University Press.

Sumberg, T. A. 1973. *Foreign Aid as a Moral Obligation*, Beverly Hills, SAGE Publications.

Temple, B. and A. Young 2004. 'Qualitative Research and Translation Dilemmas', in *Qualitative Research*, Vol. 4. No. 2, p. 161–178.

Thérien, J.-P. 2002. 'Debating Foreign Aid: Right Versus Left', in Third World Quarterly, Vol. 23. No. 3, p. 449–466.

Thérien, J.-P. and C. Lloyd 2000. 'Development Assistance on the Brink', in *Third World Quarterly*, Vol. 21. No. 1, p. 21–38.

Thorbecke, E. 2000. The Evolution of the Development Doctrine and the Role of Foreign Aid, 1950–2000, in F. Tarp and P. Hjertholm (ed.) 2000: *Foreign Aid and Development. Lessons Learnt and Directions for the Future*, London, Routledge.

Thrane, T. 1998. *Redd Barna* [Save the Children Norway], Oslo, Libretto forlag.

Tomasevski, K. 1989. *Development Aid and Human Rights. A Study for the Danish Center of Human Rights*, London, Pinter.

Tvedt, T. 1990. Bilder av "de andre". Om utviklingslandene i bistands-epoken [Pictures of 'the Others'. On the Developing Countries in the Aid Era], Oslo, Universitetsforlaget.

Tvedt, T. 1998. *Angels of Mercy, or Development Diplomats? NGOs & Foreign Aid*, Trenton, N.J., Africa World Press.

Tvedt, T. 2003. *Utviklingshjelp, utenrikspolitikk og makt. Den norske modellen* [Development Aid, Foreign Policy and Power. The Norwegian Model], Oslo, Gyldendal.

Tønnessen, A. V. 2001. 'Fra nødhjelpsorganisasjon til bistands-organisasjon. Kirkens Nødhjelp 1947–1974 [From Relief Organisa-tion to Development Organisation. Norwegian Church Aid 1947–1974]', in *Kirke & Kultur*, Vol. 106. No. 5/6, p. 529–543.

Tønnessen, A. V. 2007. *Kirkens Nødhjelp. Bistand, tro og politikk* [Norwegian Church Aid. Aid, Faith, and Politics], Oslo, Gyldendal.

Ulveseth, H. 2005. *Førestellingar om utvikling og utviklingshjelp. Ein diskursanalyse av handsaminga av norsk utviklingshjelp i Stortinget gjennom 50 år* [Ideas about Development and Aid. A Discourse Analysis of the Treatment of Norwegian Development Aid in the Norwegian Parliament over 50 Years], Bergen, Universitetet i Bergen.

Ulveseth, K. 2004. *Fra misjonsmark til markedsplass. En diskursanalyse av Kirkens Nødhjelps fremstillinger av Nigeria og Sudan fra 1960 til 2000* [From Mission Field to Market Place. A Discourse Analysis of Norwegian Church Aid's Depictions of Nigeria and Sudan from 1960 to 2000], Oslo, Universitetet i Oslo.

United Nations Development Programme 2006. *Beyond Scarcity. Power, Poverty and the Global Water Crisis*.

Uvin, P. 2004. *Human Rights and Development*, Bloomfield, Conn., Kumarian Press.

van de Walle, N. 1999. 'Aid's Crisis of Legitimacy. Current Proposals and Future Prospects', in *African Affairs*, Vol. 98. No. 392, p. 337–352.

van der Veen, A. M. 2002. *National Identity and the Origins of Development Assistance, Boston*, MA, paper presented at the Annual Meeting of the American Political Science Association, August 29–Sept. 1, 2002.

van Dijk, T. A. 1993. *Elite Discourse and Racism*, Newbury Park, Calif., SAGE Publications.

van Oorschot, W. and L. Halman 2000. 'Blame or Fate, Individual or Social? An international comparison of popular explanations of poverty', in *European Societies*, Vol. 2. No. 1, p. 1–28.

Vandersluis, S. O. and P. Yeros 2000. Ethics and Poverty in a Global Era, in S. O. Vandersluis and P. Yeros (ed.) 2000: *Poverty in World Politics. Whose Global Era?*, Basingstoke, Macmillan in association with Millenium Journal of International Studies.

Vikinge, L. 1997. *Etik och biståndspolitik. En konstruktion av bedömningsgrund för inriktningen av svensk biståndspolitik* [Ethics and Development Aid Policy. A Construction of a Basis for Assessing the Orientation of Swedish Development Aid Policy], Uppsala, Distributor: Uppsala University Library.

Vilberg, H. 2003. "*Sammen for en rettferdig verden*"? *En analyse av Kirkens nødhjelps rettferdighetstenkning, og dens følger for forståelsen av internasjonal diakoni* ['Together for a Just World'? An Analysis of Norwegian Church Aid's Understanding of Justice and Its Consequences for the Understanding of International Diaconia], Oslo, Universitetet i Oslo.

Visnes, K. 1999. *Suverenitet og stat i norsk bistandsdiskurs. Utvikling i fem tiår* [Sovereignty and State in the Norwegian Development Aid Discourse. Development over Five Decades], Oslo, Universitetet i Oslo.

Weiss, R. S. 1994. *Learning from Strangers. The Art and Method of Qualitative Interview Studies*, New York, Free Press.

Wenar, L. 2006. 'Accountability in International Development Aid', in *Ethics & International Affairs*, Vol. 20. No. 1, p. 1–23.

Wetherell, M. and J. Potter 1988. Discourse Analysis and the Identification of Interpretative Repertoires, in C. Antaki (ed.) 1988: *Analysing Everyday Explanation. A Casebook of Methods*, London, SAGE Publications.

Wetherell, M. and J. Potter 1992. *Mapping the Language of Racism. Discourse and the Legitimation of Exploitation*, New York, Harvester Wheatsheaf.

Williams, R. 1983. *Keywords – A Vocabulary of Culture and Society*, Rev. and exp. London, Fontana Press.

Østerud, Ø. 2006. 'Lite land som humanitær stormakt? [Small Country as Humanitarian Superpower?]', in *Nytt Norsk Tidsskrift*, Vol. 23. No. 4, p. 303–316.

Internet references

BBC: <news.bbc.co.uk>

Center for Global Development: <www.cgdev.org>

Médecins Sans Frontières: <www.msf.org>

Norconsult: <www.norconsult.no>

Norwegian Agency for Development Cooperation: <www.norad.no>

Norwegian Church Aid: <www.nca.no>

The Norwegian Government: <www.regjeringen.no>

Norwegian Missions in Development: <www.bistandsnemnda.no>

Norwegian People's Aid: <www.folkehjelp.no>

Org. for Economic Cooperation and Development: <www.oecd.org>

Plan International: <www.plan-international.org>

Red Cross: <www.redcross.int>

Save the Children Norway: <www.reddbarna.no>

SOS Children's Villages: <www.sos-childrensvillages.org>

South Centre: <www.southcentre.org>

Statistics Norway: <www.ssb.no>

Statoil: <www.statoil.com>

UNICEF: <www.unicef.org>

United Nations Development Programme: <www.undp.org>

UN High Commissioner for Human Rights: <www.ohchr.org>

www.ingramcontent.com/pod-product-compliance
Ingram Content Group UK Ltd.
Pitfield, Milton Keynes, MK11 3LW, UK
UKHW021015120926
8556IPUK00040B/1206

9 783039 116621